An Introduction to Educology

JAMES E. CHRISTENSEN

First published by James E. Christensen
as an Amazon Kindle Edition™ e-Book

An Introduction to Educology

Revised Editon 2023

Printed by Amazon Kindle Direct Publishing

Available from Amazon.com and other retail outlets

DEDICATION

To Henry Denison "Denny" Baylor, Jr (1912-1998),

For being a kind and loving man,

a good and effective teacher,

and wise and inspirational leader in education

CONTENTS

FIGURES

INTRODUCTION

Education has the same relationship to educology as

(1) society has to sociology, or
(2) living organisms have to biology, or
(3) disease has to pathology.

Education is a field of phenomena. Educology is the fund of knowledge about the field.

In the field of phenomena denoted by the term <*education*>, people play the roles of teachers and students. Teachers provide opportunities, guidance and help to students to study intentionally some content (some fund of knowledge and/or some range of knowing) with the purpose in mind that the students extend their range of knowing. Teachers and students always conduct their activities within some span of time and within some physical, social and cultural setting. Members of the wider society and culture take an interest in, have expectations for and make demands on what teachers and students do and achieve. And what teachers and students do and achieve affects the wider society and culture.

Educology is the set of recorded true statements about the structure, function and purpose of education. It is knowledge about the people (teachers and students) who participate in education, the relations among the people, the people's intentions, their activities, the results of their activities and the mutual effects of people participating in education and the wider physical, social and cultural environment in which the education takes place.

A heap of stones does not make a house, and a collection of true statements about education does not make educology. Educology is organized knowledge about education. It has system, and the system has structure, function and purpose. Educology is a system which consists of a structure of mutually implied true statements. The mutually implied true statements provide descriptive, explanatory and normative educological theory. Educological theory connects and organizes educological facts. Descriptive educological theory consists of well-defined terms which clearly denote distinct categories of roles, activities, processes, relations, objects, events, occurrences, happenings and purposes in education. Explanatory educological theory consists of statements which use the well-defined terms from descriptive theory to describe the controlling conditions for resultants in education and to predict resultants from specified controlling conditions. Normative educological theory consists of statements that provide evaluations and prescriptions for states of affairs in education and justifications for the evaluations and prescriptions. The purpose of educology is to provide a fund of knowledge which can be used to develop an understanding of what happens in education, why it happens and what rational action can be taken

(1) to achieve desirable states of affairs in education and desirable outcomes from education and
(2) to eliminate and/or prevent undesirable states of affairs in education and undesirable outcomes from education.

Education is located in the existential, observable world of phenomena. We can observe people at work as teachers and students, and we can observe students as they provide exemplifications of their newly acquired range of knowing.

In contrast to education, educology is located in the realm of recorded true statements about education. The statements are located in any medium suitable for recording and storing sentences – printed books, journals, research reports, audio recordings, audiovisual recordings, computer memory storage, etc.

Educological discipline is the set of rules, procedures and techniques which educological inquirers (investigators, researchers) follow

(1) to form well-defined terms that can be used in discourse about education, and thereby form descriptive

educological theory,

(2) to form unambiguous, descriptive, verifiable statements about education, and thereby form hypotheses which can be tested in an appropriate way for their truth value,

(3) to transform statements about education (through logical operations), and thereby form explanatory educological theory and/or normative educological theory,

(4) to verify statements (determine their truth value) about education (through adducing necessary and sufficient evidence), and thereby establish facts about education and evaluate explanatory and/or normative educological theories.

Educological inquiry (investigation, research) is the set of sequential activities of asking questions about education, answering those questions and verifying the answers by adducing necessary and suffice-ent evidence. The product of successful educological inquiry is educology, or recorded true statements (organized into a system) about education.

Note what educology is not. It is not a study, and it is not a discipline. It is not a study because it is not an activity, and it is not a discipline because it is not a set of rules. The term <*study*> denotes the activity of undertaking to extend one's range of knowing about something and/or to produce true statements about something. The term <*discipline*> denotes the relevant set of rules, logical procedures and techniques which an inquirer (investigator, researcher) must follow in a study if the study is to succeed in verifying any statements. It takes both study and discipline to produce educology, but it is obvious that study and discipline are not educology, just as a blueprint and carpenters are not a house.

Like most funds of knowledge, educology is substantial, extensive and complex. It is too big a job for one person to develop an understanding of the whole of educology. For the purposes of educological research, educological exposition and/or teaching and intentionally studying under guidance some aspect of educology, parts of educology are typically selected and organized into subfunds of educology. A part (or subfund) of educology is an educology of some aspect of education. There are many possibilities for the <***Educology of….***> There is

(1) the educology of good states of affairs in education, or

philosophical educology,

(2) the educology of past states of affairs in education, or historical educology,
(3) the educology of extant states of affairs in education, or scientific educology,
(4) the educology of effective practices and relations in education, or praxiological educology,
(5) the educology of laws, rules and regulations which mandate, prohibit and/or allow practices, arrangements and states of affairs in education, or jurisprudential educology.

Many other aspects of the field of education can be chosen for the arrangement (organization) of educology. They include, for example,

(1) the educology of early childhood education,
(2) the educology of secondary education,
(3) the educology of sports education,
(4) the educology of health education,
(5) the educology of mathematics education,
(6) the educology of women's education,
(7) the educology of adult education,
(8) the educology of art education,
(9) the educology of music education,
(10) the educology of school administration,
(11) the educology of counselors and counseling,
(12) the educology of curriculum,
(13) the educology of inclusive education,
(14) the educology of learning management,
(15) the educology of special needs children, etc.

There is a logic of educology and a logic of education. The set of rules to which we make our activities conform in conducting careful, disciplined inquiry (investigation, research) about education to produce knowledge about education is the logic of educology. The set of rules to which we make our activities conform as we engage in the process of education as teachers and students is the logic of education.

Careful, well-disciplined discourse which consists of true statements about what educological inquirers (investigators, researchers) must do to establish that some statement about education is true (or false) is meta-educology. Careful, well-disciplined discourse which consists of true statements about what has happened, what happens, what will happen, why it happens, what is effective (or ineffective) and what is good (or bad) between teachers and students is educology.

This book is not an exposition of meta-educology. The questions of what constitutes meta-educology and how to use it have been addressed elsewhere (see J. Christensen, 2013, 2016, 2018). This book is an introduction to educology. It is an exposition about the basic elements of education – teacher, student, content, setting – and the relations among those four elements. It is also an exposition about official and unofficial education, the basic activities of education, the basic products of education and the derivative components of education. The questions addressed in this book are as follows.

(1) What is education?
(2) What are the essential elements of education?
(3) What are the primary activities of education?
(4) What are the basic products of education?
(5) What are the derivative components of education?
(6) What relations are there among the basic elements and what are the resultants of those relations?
(7) How does education differ from learning and what variant of learning is possible to achieve with education?
(8) How does unofficial education differ from official education?
(9) How does ineffective education differ from effective education?
(10) How does bad education differ from good education?

1 DESCRIPTIVE EDUCOLOGICAL THEORY

Every fund of knowledge has its descriptive theory. Descriptive theory is the set of well-defined terms which are conceived such that they can be used to give precision and clarity to the discourse of the fund. For example, the fund of knowledge that is physics uses the terms <*mass, force, acceleration, velocity, energy, work*>, etc. in very different ways from ordinary English usage, and the terms are well-defined to give the discourse of physics clarity, precision and system (mutually implied statements). The same is true of any other fund of knowledge, for example, biology, botany, zoology, virology, economics, sociology, psychology, anatomy, chemistry, etc.

Descriptive theory of educology (or descriptive educological theory) is the set of well-defined terms which give clarity, precision and system to the discourse of educology. Key terms which have special, stipulated meanings in educological discourse include <*education, teacher, teaching, student, studying, content, knowledge, knowing, learning, intended learning outcomes, context.*> Stipulated definitions for these terms are required for educological discourse because ordinary English language usage of these terms is ambiguous. Ambiguity leads to confusion and mistakes in observations, analyses and logical argument. Confusion and mistakes in observation, analyses and logical argument are undesirable features to have in careful, disciplined educological inquiry (investigation, research) and discourse which aim to present facts about, valid explanations for, accurate predictions of, justified evaluations of and warranted prescriptions for the elements, relations, activities and purposes of education.

The need to eliminate ambiguity in discourse about education (and the need to dispel the consequent confusion from the ambiguity) can easily be demonstrated with the following scenario.

Suppose that the question is posed to us, "What is education?" We are told that to answer it, we must go out, find some instances of education and write a description of what we observe. Would we know how to do that? If we speak and write the English language, the probability is very high that we would. Where would we go? Some of us might go to a school and describe the activities of the teachers and the students in the classrooms. Others of us might go to a restaurant and watch a trainee be led by a senior employee through the procedures of taking orders from customers and the trainee practicing taking orders. Perhaps others of us would go to the local river and watch a stand-up paddle board instructor explain and demonstrate to a group of adult novices how to stand on the paddle board and handle the paddle and the novices doing some paddle boarding.

Now, suppose we are given a task that is similar to the previous one, but this time the question is, "What is <*tlacahuapahualiztli*>?" We are told that to answer this question, we again must go out, find some instances of <*tlacahuapahualiztli*> and write a description of what we observe. Would we know how to do that? Probably not. Most of us would be stumped by this task, unless we spoke, read and wrote Nahuatl, one of the languages of the ancient Aztecs. What does this demonstrate? If we are given a term, told to find instances of the set of phenomena that the term denotes and to describe the phenomena that we see, then we first must understand the meaning of the term. We need to know what the term denotes.

It is not initially apparent that the question, "What is education?" is ambiguous. But the question calls for us to answer two questions. The first question is, "What does the term <*education*> denote?" The second question is, "When we discern instances of education in the field of phenomena denoted by the term <*education*>, what particular distinguishing characteristics of the instances of education do we see and what essential details can we describe?" The first question is calling for us to state the rule for using the term <*education*>. The second question is calling for us to discern instances of education in the field of phenomena denoted by the term <*education*> and report about what we see. We cannot answer the second question before we have answered the first, as demonstrated with the term <*tlacahuapahualiztli*>.

To answer adequately the question, "What is education?" requires us to understand a few fundamentals about terms, definitions and concepts.

A term is a set of words. A set of words can be a set of one word, two words, three words, etc. The term <*education*> is a set of one word, or a one-word term. The term of <*intentional guided study*> is a set of three words, or a three-word term. Terms can be mentioned, and they can be used. When we say that the term <*forest*> denotes a landscape covered with trees, we are mentioning the term <*forest*>. When we say that the forest has been damaged by fire, we are using the term <*forest*> to denote the existential, observable forest.

A concept is a language habit of using a term. In English, we follow the language habit of using the term <*forest*> to denote a landscape covered with trees. As infants and children experiencing the process of learning our language, we typically form habits of using terms without ever actually stating the rule to which our language habits conform. When we express the rule for using a term, we are giving the definition for a term. A definition is a statement which expresses the rule for using a term. A term can be defined connotatively and/or denotatively, except for some terms which have no denotation, such as <*and, if, but*>.

The connotative definition of a term is the other set of terms which mean the same as the term. The other set of terms are synonyms or equivalent expressions of the term being defined. The denotative definition of a term is the set of phenomena to which a term refers. For example, the term <*forest*> has the connotative definition of the words <*a landscape covered by trees*>. The conative definition of the term <*forest*> is expressed in the statement

> "The term <*forest*> means the same as the set of words <*a landscape covered by trees*>."

The denotative definition of the term <*forest*> is the existential, observable forest. The set of phenomena to which a term refers is the denotation of the term. A landscape covered by trees is the denotation of the term <*forest*>. The denotative definition of the term <*forest*> is expressed in the statement

> "The term <*forest*> denotes a landscape covered by trees."

Five Conceptions of the Term <*Education*>

Now let's turn our attention to the question, "What set of phenomena does the term <*education*> denote? We will answer this question by identifying the language rule (or rules) which English speakers follow in their use of the term <*education*>. An efficient way to do this is to think of sentences in which the term <*education*> is used. Consider the following sentences.

(1) My profession is <**education**>.
(2) Travel to a foreign land is always an <**education**>.
(3) Every walk that I take in my neighborhood adds to my <**education**>.
(4) <**Education**> is the responsibility of the schools.
(5) Henry holds a PhD in <**education**>.

What is notable about the term <*education*> in these sentences is that there is a different denotation for it in each sentence. This can be demonstrated by some term substitution.

In the first sentence, substitute the term <*education*> with the term <*teaching*>, and the meaning of the sentence does not change.

(1) My profession is <**teaching**>.

So, one denotation of the term <*education*> is teaching. Let this denotation of the term <*education*> be distinguished by a subscript <1>, <education_1>, and also by the symbol <$\mathbf{E_1}$>.

In the second sentence, substitute the term <*education*> with the term <*learning process*>, and the meaning of the sentence does not change.

(2) Travel to a foreign land is always a <**learning process**>.

So, a second denotation of the term <*education*> is learning process. A learning process is one in which we extend our range of knowing. A learning process (**L**) can be one in which there is conduced learning ($\mathbf{L_1}$), discovery learning ($\mathbf{L_2}$), compelled learning ($\mathbf{L_3}$) or accidental learning ($\mathbf{L_4}$). Let this denotation of the term <*education*> be distinguished by a subscript <2>, <education_2>, and also by the symbol <$\mathbf{E_2}$>.

In the third sentence, substitute the term <*education*> with the term <*range of knowing*>, and the meaning of the sentence does not change.

(3) Every walk that I take in my neighborhood adds to my <**range of knowing**>.

So, a third denotation of the term <*education*> is range of knowing. A range of knowing is a cognitive state of mind which enables the knower to be able to do a host of things, e.g. to discern, recognize, appreciate, anticipate, plan, describe, explain, predict, evaluate, prescribe, justify, to solve problems, to take effective action, etc. Let this denotation of the term <*education*> be distinguished by a subscript <3>, <education$_3$>, and also by the symbol <$\mathbf{E}_3$>.

In the fourth sentence, substitute the term <*education*> with the term <*teaching and intentional guided studying*>, and the meaning of the sentence does not change.

(4) <**Teaching and intentional guided studying**> is the responsibility of the schools.

So, a fourth denotation of the term <*education*> is the field of phenomena that includes teaching and intentional guided studying. Let this denotation of the term <*education*> be distinguished by a subscript <4>, <education$_4$>, and also by the symbol <$\mathbf{E}_4$>.

In the fifth sentence, substitute the term <*education*> with the term <*educology*>, and the meaning of the sentence does not change.

(5) Henry holds a PhD in <**educology**>.

So, a fifth denotation of the term <*education*> is educology, or the fund of knowledge about education. Let this denotation of the term <*education*> be distinguished by a subscript <5>, <education$_5$>, and also by the symbol <$\mathbf{E}_5$>.

From this brief analysis, we have identified five language rules (and hence five definitions) which English speakers use with the term <*education*>. They use the term <*education*> to denote

(1) Education$_1$ ($\mathbf{E}_1$), or teaching,
(2) Education$_2$ ($\mathbf{E}_2$), or learning process,
(3) Education$_3$ ($\mathbf{E}_3$), or range of knowing,
(4) Education$_4$ ($\mathbf{E}_4$), or teaching and intentional guided studying,
(5) Education$_5$ ($\mathbf{E}_5$), or educology.

In educological discourse, it is counterproductive to use the term <*education*> to denote five different categories (four different fields of phenomena and a fund of knowledge about a field of phenomena). The ambiguity can only lead to misunderstanding, confusion and mistakes. Clarity in educological discourse can be achieved by eliminating the ambiguity of the term <*education*>. The ambiguity can be removed by choosing one, and only one, denotation for the term

<*education*> and following one, and only one, language rule for the use of the term <*education*> while engaging in educological discourse.

Which of these language rules is the best to use in educological inquiry, discourse and intentional guided study of educology? The question calls for an evaluation of each of the five conceptions of the term <*education*>. An evaluation requires, first, a selection of criteria (denoted by <**c**>, second, a scrutiny of the evaluatum (denoted by <**e**>), the thing being evaluated, in relation to the criteria (**c**), and third, a decision about which evaluatum (**e**) among the evaluata (**e**) conforms most closely with the set of criteria. The evaluata (**e**), in this case, of course, are the five conceptions of the term <*education*>, and the question being posed in the evaluation is which of the five is the most suitable for the purposes of conducting educological inquiry, producing educological knowledge and developing, intentionally and under guidance, an educological range of knowing. The relevant and appropriate criteria (**c**), to use in the evaluation are

(1) inclusiveness,
(2) exclusiveness,
(3) internal consistency,
(4) exhaustiveness,
(5) external relatedness,
(6) fruitfulness.

The criterion of inclusiveness is a standard for determining the degree to which a conception of the term <*education*> is sufficiently broad to denote all cases and instances which are members of the field of educational phenomena and which are related to each other in essential ways.

The criterion of exclusiveness is a standard for determining the degree to which a conception of the term <*education*> is sufficiently exclusive to reject all cases or instances which are not members of the field of educational phenomena.

The criterion of internal consistency is a standard for determining the degree to which a conception of the term <*education*> denotes cases or instances of phenomena which are consistent and clearly related to each other in essential ways.

The criterion of exhaustiveness is a standard for determining the degree to which a conception of the term <*education*> denotes every instance or case that should be counted as a member of the field of educational phenomena, or whether there are some cases which are mistakenly left out and which should be included.

The criterion of external relatedness is a standard for determining to what degree a conception of the term <*education*> denotes phenomena that are sufficiently related to other phenomena (such as schooling, studying, learning, teaching, coaching, tutoring, mentoring, counseling, curriculum, knowing, understanding and knowledge) such that the conception of <*education*> can be useful in promoting clear and unambiguous discourse about educational phenomena.

The criterion of fruitfulness is a standard for determining the degree to which the conception of the term <*education*> is generally useful in permitting unambiguous and clear discourse about educational phenomena and whether the use of the concept promotes progress in developing and extending descriptions, characterizations, explanations, predictions, evaluations, prescriptions and justifications of educational phenomena.

The conception of <*education*> as <$\mathbf{E}_5$>, or education$_5$, or educology, can be immediately excluded in our evaluation because educology is not a field of phenomena. Rather, it is a set of recorded true statements (organized by descriptive, explanatory and normative theory) about a field. The task before us is to identify the essential properties of the field of phenomena about which we should conduct educological inquiry, produce educological knowledge and develop a range of educological knowing. The use of the terms <$\mathbf{E}_5$>, <*education*$_5$>, or <*educology*> has no relevance in addressing the question of which set of phenomena is denoted by the term <*education*>.

The conception of <*education*> as <$\mathbf{E}_1$>, or education$_1$, or teaching does denote a field of phenomena. The term <*teaching*> denotes someone intentionally acting in ways to provide opportunities, guidance and help to others (students) to study intentionally some content with a view in mind that the students extend their range of knowing. Suppose that in universities in the curriculum of colleges of education (educology), the courses offered only provided opportunities to study teaching, but not study the characteristics of students of different age groups, the unique challenges in teaching particular content (agriculture, music, art, human movement, drama, English literature, mathematics, French, etc.) and the expectations and demands of the social and cultural context upon teaching and studying. That would be a strange curriculum, indeed. An evaluation of the conception of <*education*> as <$\mathbf{E}_1$>, education$_1$, or teaching shows that education as teaching is too narrow, too exclusive. Inclusion of only teaching in the field of phenomena that would count as educational phenomena excludes the

(1) study by students – intentional guided attempts to come to know,
(2) effective study by students – intentional guided and successful attempts to come to know,
(3) the content being taught and studied and
(4) the effects of the expectations and demands made by the social and cultural context upon the teaching, studying and learning and
(5) the effects of teaching, studying and learning upon the expectations and demands made by the social and cultural context.

The conception of <*education*> as <$\mathbf{E}_2$>, education$_2$, or learning process includes all learning processes (**L**). There is conduced learning ($\mathbf{L}_1$), which is achieved from being taught and undertaking intentional guided study. There is discovery learning ($\mathbf{L}_2$), which is achieved by independent, self-directed, unguided inquiry, such as from trial and error or systematic research. There is compelled learning ($\mathbf{L}_3$), which is achieved from undergoing socialization, enculturation or indoctrination. There is accidental learning ($\mathbf{L}_4$), which is achieved from chance occurrences, including misadventure and/or serendipity. The conception of <*education*> as <$\mathbf{E}_2$>, education$_2$, or learning process is too inclusive in that it includes all learning (<**L**> including <$\mathbf{L}_1$>, < $\mathbf{L}_2$>, < $\mathbf{L}_3$>, < $\mathbf{L}_4$>), and it is too exclusive in that it excludes teaching, unsuccessful attempts to learn (ineffective intentional guided study), content which is taught and studied and the social and cultural context which places expectations and demands upon teachers and students.

The conception of <*education*> as <$\mathbf{E}_3$>, education$_3$ or a range of knowing is too exclusive in its conception. Education as a range of knowing excludes

(1) learning$_1$ ($\mathbf{L}_1$) – intentionally coming to know under guidance, or conduced learning,
(2) teaching – intentionally providing opportunities and guidance to study (denoted by <$\mathbf{T}_\mathbf{P}$>),
(3) studying intentionally and under guidance (denoted by <$\mathbf{S}_{\mathbf{P}1}$>).

A conception of <*education*> which excludes learning, teaching and studying from the field of phenomena denoted by the term <*education*> would lead to an extremely limited range of educological inquiry, educological knowledge and educological intentional guided study.

The conception of <*education*> as <$\mathbf{E_4}$>, education$_4$, or teaching and intentional guided studying includes the following as part of the field of phenomena of education:

(1) ineffective intentional guided study (unsuccessful attempts to learn under guidance),
(2) effective intentional guided study (successful attempts to learn under guidance),
(3) ineffective teaching (unsuccessful attempts to provide opportunities, guidance and help to someone to learn under guidance),
(4) effective teaching (successful attempts to provide opportunities, guidance and help to someone to learn under guidance),
(5) intentional guided learning (conduced learning <$\mathbf{L_1}$>), achieved from effective teaching and effective intentional guided studying,
(6) range of knowing ($\mathbf{K_2}$) achieved from intentional guided learning ($\mathbf{L_1}$),
(7) content (denoted by <**C**>), selections of knowledge and/or exemplifications of knowing organized for teaching and studying intentionally and under guidance,
(8) physical, social and cultural context (**X**) in which the teaching and intentional guided studying take place.

Education$_4$ ($\mathbf{E_4}$), or teaching and intentional guided studying excludes the following from the field of phenomena denoted by the term <*education*>:

(1) unguided and intentional learning (discovery learning or learning from self-directed inquiry <$\mathbf{L_2}$>),
(2) guided and unintentional learning (compelled learning <$\mathbf{L_3}$>),
(3) unguided and unintentional learning (induced or accidental learning <$\mathbf{L_4}$>).

The exclusion of the above three variations of learning ($\mathbf{L_2}$, $\mathbf{L_3}$, $\mathbf{L_4}$) from the field of phenomena denoted by the term <*education*> is advantageous from the point of view of being able to distinguish the phenomenon of education from

(1) learning from unguided self-directed research, unguided self-directed inquiry, unguided self-directed trial and error (discovery learning without guidance, but with intention on the part of the learner $<\mathbf{L}_2>$),
(2) learning from conditioning, manipulating, indoctrinating, propagandizing, proselytizing, advertising, socializing and enculturating (processes that cause compelled learning unintentionally on the part of the learner, but with guidance by someone other than the learner $<\mathbf{L}_3>$),
(3) learning from random events and accidents (induced or accidental learning without guidance and without intention on the part of the learner $<\mathbf{L}_4>$).

Although education$_4$ ($\mathbf{E}_4$) is distinct from

(1) the general process of learning (**L**),
(2) the activity of inquiry (**Q**) (investigation, research) and
(3) the product of coming to know (i.e. a range of knowing $<\mathbf{K}_2>$),

it has an external relatedness to them. It also has a close relationship with enculturation, socialization and schooling.

Education$_4$ ($\mathbf{E}_4$) or the synchronous activities of teaching ($\mathbf{T}_P$) and intentional guided studying ($\mathbf{S}_{P1}$), then, provides necessary and sufficient distinguishing characteristics to

(1) include all that belongs to the field of educational phenomena (and thus meets the criterion of appropriate inclusions),
(2) exclude all that does not belong to the field of educational phenomena (and thus meets the criterion of appropriate exclusions),
(3) connect all that belongs to the field of educational phenomena through a system of internal coherency (and thus meeting the criterion of internal consistency),
(4) exhaust the possibilities of instances that could be counted as part of the field of educational phenomena (and thus meeting the criterion of exhaustiveness),
(5) relate the field of educational phenomena to other phenomena outside of the field (e.g. enculturation, socialization, conditioning) and thus meeting the criterion of external relatedness and

(6) establish a fruitful basis for extending careful, disciplined, mindful educological discourse, educological inquiry and educological intentional guided study (and thus meeting the criterion of fruitfulness).

Therefore, in relation to the six criteria for evaluation of a suitable conception of the term <*education*> to use in educological inquiry (**Q**) (investigation, research), education$_4$ (**E$_4$**) or teaching and intentional guided studying with the view in mind that students achieve some range of knowing, is the most appropriate one, and it is the one that ought to be followed in determining the limits of the field of educational phenomena. Education$_4$ (**E$_4$**) is the object of knowledge (denoted by <**O$_{K1}$**>) of educology.

This is the beginning of the development of a set of well-defined terms that can be used in careful, disciplined educological discourse, inquiry and intentional guided study, or to state this in another way, this is the beginning of the development of descriptive educological theory. Another term which means the same as the term <*descriptive educological theory*> is the term <*conceptual educological theory*>. The well-defined terms are also denoted by the term <*constructs*>.

We have presented sufficient justification to stipulate that for educological purposes, the term <*education*> should be reserved to denote only, education$_4$ (**E$_4$**) or teaching and intentional guided studying and that education$_4$ (**E$_4$**) is the object of knowledge (**O$_{K1}$**) of educology.

The relationships among **E$_1$**, **E$_2$**, **E$_3$**, **E$_4$** and **E$_5$** can be expressed as follows.

(1) $\mathbf{E_1 = T_P}$: Education$_1$ (**E$_1$**) is the same as (=) teaching (**T$_P$**).
(2) $\mathbf{E_2 = L = L_1 \cup L_2 \cup L_3 \cup L_4}$: Education$_2$ (**E$_2$**) is the same as (=) learning (**L**), and the essential elements of learning (**L**) are the union of ($\cup$) the essential elements of conduced learning (**L$_1$**), discovery learning (**L$_2$**), compelled learning (**L$_3$**) and accidental learning (**L$_4$**).

To assure clarity in educological discourse, inquiry and intentional guided study of educology, let's further develop descriptive educological theory by adopting the following conventions for the use of terms.

(1) Henceforth, when the term <*education*> is mentioned or used, let it be used to denote, and only to denote education$_4$ (**E$_4$**), or teaching and intentional guided studying, and let the symbol <**E**> denote education$_4$ as well.

(2) When, in our discourse, the phenomenon of teaching is intended, let's use only the term <*teaching*> and the symbol <$\mathbf{T_P}$> to denote teaching. Let's never use the term <*education*> to denote teaching.

(3) When, in our discourse, the phenomenon of intentional guided studying is intended, let's use the term <*intentional guided studying*> and the symbol <$\mathbf{S_{P1}}$> to denote intentional guided studying, and let's never use the terms <*learning*> or <*education*> to denote intentional guided studying.

(4) When, in our discourse, the process of learning as the process of coming to achieve a range of knowing is intended, then let's use the term <*learning*> and the symbol <**L**> to denote learning as the process of coming to achieve a range of knowing. Let's never use the term <*education*> to denote learning as the process of coming to achieve a range of knowing, and let's never use the term <*education*> as a synonym for the term <*learning*>.

(5) When, in our discourse, the process of conduced learning (learning achieved from teaching and intentional guided studying) is intended, then let's use the term <*learning*$_1$> and the symbol <$\mathbf{L_1}$> to denote conduced learning.

(6) When, in our discourse, the process of discovery learning (learning achieved from trial and error and/or systematic inquiry, investigation, research) is intended, then let's use the term <*learning*$_2$> and the symbol <$\mathbf{L_2}$> to denote discovery learning.

(7) When, in our discourse, the process of compelled learning (learning achieved from socialization, enculturation, indoctrination) is intended, then let's use the term <*learning*$_3$> and the symbol <$\mathbf{L_3}$> to denote compelled learning.

(8) When, in our discourse, the phenomenon of accidental learning (learning from happenstance, either misadventure or serendipity) is intended, then let's use the term <*learning*$_4$> and the symbol <$\mathbf{L_4}$> to denote accidental learning.

The conception of the term <*education*> as education$_4$ ($\mathbf{E_4}$), or the phenomena of teaching and intentional guided studying with the view in mind that students achieve some range of knowing, can be further developed by using the techniques of classificatory definition, explication and exemplification.

Logically, a connotative definition takes the sentence form,

"The term <*A*> means the same as the set of terms <*B*>."

In a connotative definition, the term being defined is the <*definiendum*>, and the set of terms doing the defining is the <*definiens*>. The goal in connotative definition is to make the meaning of the definiendum equivalent to the meaning of the definiens. This relationship of equivalency can be expressed as,

Definiendum $=_{Df}$ *Definiens*

where the symbol set <$=_{Df}$> stands for the words <*is defined as*>.

Connotative definition can take several forms, e.g. synonymy, equivalent expression and classificatory forms. A basic form of definition for development of well-defined terms in educological discourse is classificatory form definition. In the definiens of a classificatory definition, the referent of the definiendum is assigned to its logical class, and essential characteristics (denoted by the term <*differentiae*>) are asserted which distinguish the referent from other members of the same logical class.

We have developed a denotative definition of the term <*education*> as education$_4$ (**E**$_4$) or the phenomena of teaching and intentional guided studying. Now let's develop a connotative definition of the term <*education*> in classificatory form.

The term <*education*> is defined as a set of phenomena [a set of phenomena is the logical class]

(1) in which someone playing the role of teacher intentionally provides opportunities, guidance and help to [the first of the differentiae]
(2) someone playing the role of student to study intentionally under guidance [the second of the differentiae]
(3) some content (some fund of knowledge and/or some range of knowing organized for the purposes of teaching and studying intentionally and under guidance) [the third of the differentiae]
(4) in some physical, social and cultural setting [the fourth of the differentiae]
(5) with a common purpose in mind (shared by teacher and student) that the student achieves some range of knowing

[the fifth of the differentiae].

Phenomenon is the logical class of the referent of the term <*education*>. The five distinguishing characteristics of the referent which make the phenomenon discernable from all other phenomena are

(1) education has teachers and teaching,
(2) education has students and intentional guided studying,
(3) education has content (fund of knowledge and/or range of knowing) for teaching and intentional guided studying,
(4) education has context (physical, social and cultural setting),
(5) education has intention (purpose) in the minds of the teachers and students that students achieve some range of knowing.

The distinction between a connotative definition of the term <*education*> and a denotative definition of the term <*education*> is expressed in the following two sentences.

(1) **Connotative definition**: The term <*education*> means the same as the words <*the set of phenomena in which someone playing the role of teacher intentionally provides opportunities, guidance and help to someone playing the role of student to study intentionally under guidance some content (some fund of knowledge and/or some range of knowing) in some physical, social and cultural setting with a common purpose in mind (shared by teacher and student) that the student achieves some range of knowing*>.
(2) **Denotative definition**: The term <*education*> denotes the set of phenomena in which someone playing the role of teacher intentionally provides opportunities, guidance and help to someone playing the role of student to study intentionally under guidance some content (some fund of knowledge and/or some range of knowing) in some physical, social and cultural setting with a common purpose in mind (shared by teacher and student) that the student achieves some range of knowing.

A clear implication from these definitions is that education consists of four essential elements (teacher, student, content and setting), all standing in some relation to each other (sustaining, constructive, re-constructive, destructive). The relationship of education to its four essential elements can be expressed in set theory notation in the following statement.

E = T U S U C U X

In this definition, the definiendum is <**E**>. The definiens is the set of symbols, <**T**>, <**S**>, <**C**>, <**X**> and <U>. This definition reads in ordinary English that

(1) the essential elements of education (**E**)
(2) consist of, or are equivalent to (**=**)
(3) the union of the essential elements of (**U**)
(4) teacher (**T**),
(5) student (**S**),
(6) content (**C**) and
(7) context (**X**) or setting (physical, social and cultural setting).

This definition of the term *<education>* gives us clear guidance about what to look for when we want to discern and describe education. Suppose we are in Australia, and we happen upon a new employee in a grocery store. An experienced employee is showing the new employee how to determine whether a particular item is available and how to find the item in the storeroom. The senior employee shows the new employee how to use the barcode reader to swipe the barcode on the grocery shelf and read the information about the item. The senior employee explains how to interpret the information that is displayed. The information shows the description of the item, its price, the number of items in the storeroom and the location in the storeroom. The senior employee then tells the new employee to go to another item on the shelf, swipe the barcode, read the information on the barcode reader and go to the storeroom to locate the item. The new employee follows the instructions, reads the information and goes to the storeroom and locates the item. From this observation, we can conduct an educological analysis. This is an instance of education because there is a teacher, a student, a content and a context. The senior employee is the teacher. The new employee is the student. The content is how to use a barcode reader to obtain information about an item in the grocery store inventory. The physical setting is a building with shelves. The social setting is a pair of employees in a grocery store. The cultural setting is in Australian culture, and the language being used for communication is English. The teacher uses explanation, demonstration and assigned practice as teaching methods. The student uses attentive listening and appropriate practice as intentional guided study methods. The education is effective because the student successfully achieves the range of knowing required to operate the barcode reader competently. The education is unofficial because the teacher is not a certified teacher, the student is not an enrolled student, there is no certification for achievement of the intended range of knowing, and the social setting is outside of an institution such as a school, institute, academic, college or university.

Now suppose that we observe one of our neighbors. He steps outside of his house, checks the skies for possible rain, goes back in the house and returns with an umbrella. Is this an instance of education? It is not even remotely related to an instance of education. There is no teacher. There is no student. There is no content. There is no context for teaching and intentional guided studying. This is clearly not an instance of the field of phenomena denoted by the term <*education*>.

Now suppose a man walks up to woman on the street and asks where the nearest post office is. The woman gives the first man directions to the post office. She says, "Go to the intersection and turn left. Walk three blocks. Turn right and walk a half block. You'll find the post office on the right side of the street in the middle of the block." The man thanks the woman for the directions and proceeds on his way. Was this education (**E**)? This is an ambiguous case. Maybe it is. Maybe it isn't. It seems more like a case of passing on some information than a case of someone intentionally providing opportunities, guidance and help to someone to study intentionally under guidance some content with a view in mind that the student achieves a new range of knowing. A bit of information about the location of the post office hardly seems substantial enough to qualify as content. It is true that the man succeeded in extending his range of knowing to include knowing where the post office is located and what to do to reach the post office, and it is true that the woman intentionally provided the information. So, the scenario remains ambiguous.

Education (**E** or $\mathbf{E_4}$) is a system. It has the elements of teacher, student, content and context (**T**, **S**, **C**, **X**), all standing in relation to each other. It has structure, function and purpose. It exists within time and space. It exists within a context (an environment <**X**>). It affects its environment (**X**), and its environment (**X**) affects it. When parts of education (**E** or $\mathbf{E_4}$) change, other parts of the system change in response.

Three Conceptions of the Term <*Teaching*>

Explication is the definition of terms in a definition. A useful and productive way to extend the implicative meaning of the definition

$$\mathbf{E = T \cup S \cup C \cup X}$$

is to develop an explication of the key terms in the definition. The key terms are <*teacher*>, <*student*>, <*content*> and <*setting*>. Let's start with an explication of the terms <*teacher*> and <*teaching*>. Consider the following sentences in which the term <*teaching*> is used.

(1) Gary is <**teaching**> his seven-year-old son William how to ride his new bicycle.

(2) Susan has been <**teaching**> her seven-year-old daughter Jessica the multiplication tables up through the number 10, and Jessica can now recite the multiplication tables quickly and correctly up through the number 10.

(3) Jeffrey, a boy of age five, ran across the hot pavement and blistered his feet. The hot pavement was <**teaching**> him the importance of wearing shoes in the summer.

From these three sentences, it is apparent that in the English language the term <*teaching*> can be used to denote at least three categories of phenomena.

In the first sentence, Gary is providing opportunities, guidance and help for William to develop knowing how to ride his new bicycle. Has the teaching been successful? Can William now ride his bicycle? The case is ambiguous. Perhaps William now knows how to ride his bicycle. Perhaps he does not. In this first denotation of the term <*teaching*> the possibility is left open that the teaching may be effective, and it may not be effective. This first denotation of teaching is like hunting and fishing. It is a task, rather than an achievement. In the case of Gary and William, it is also clear that the teaching is performed by a person. Gary is the teacher. Let's distinguish this denotation of teacher with the term <*teacher*$_1$> and the symbol <$\mathbf{T_1}$>. And let's distinguish this denotation of teaching with the term <*teaching*$_1$> and the symbol <$\mathbf{T_{P1}}$>.

In the second sentence, it is clear that Susan has been successful in providing opportunities, guidance and help for Jessica to develop knowing the multiplication tables through the number 10. Susan's teaching has been effective. Let's distinguish this second denotation of teacher (effective teacher) with the term <*teacher*$_2$> and the symbol <$\mathbf{T}_2$>. This second denotation of teaching is not like hunting and fishing. It is like having bagged the game and having caught the fish. It is an achievement, rather than a task. In the case of Susan and Jessica, it is also clear that the teaching is performed by a person. Susan is the teacher. Let's distinguish this second denotation of teaching (effective teaching) with the term <*teaching*$_2$> and the symbol <$\mathbf{T}_{P2}$>.

In the third sentence, it is clear that there has been a misadventure. Jeffrey ran onto the hot pavement barefoot without any anticipation that the pavement would be hot enough to blister his feet. He accidentally learned that the sun is intense enough in the summer to heat the pavement such that it will blister bare feet. This third denotation of the term <*teaching*> is circumstances which cause accidental learning. There is no person who acts intentionally to guide a second person in intentional guided study of some content. There is only misadventure or serendipity. Let's distinguish this third denotation of teacher with the term <*teacher*$_3$> and the symbol <$\mathbf{T}_3$>. And let's distinguish this denotation of teaching with the term <*teaching*$_3$> and <$\mathbf{T}_{P3}$>.

The relationship of these three denotations of the term <*teacher*> can be expressed in set theory notation as follows.

$$\mathbf{T}_1 \supset \mathbf{T}_2$$

$$\mathbf{T}_1 \notin \mathbf{T}_3$$

The first statement <$\mathbf{T}_1 \supset \mathbf{T}_2$> reads in ordinary English that

(1) teacher$_1$ ($\mathbf{T}_1$), someone who provides opportunities, guidance and help (effective and/or ineffective) to some student with the intention that the student develops some range of knowing,

(2) is a superset of ($\supset$), or includes all the elements of, but more elements than,

(3) teacher$_2$ ($\mathbf{T}_2$), or someone who provides opportunities, guidance and help (effective, and only effective) that results in the student developing some range of knowing.

The second statement <$\mathbf{T}_1 \notin \mathbf{T}_3$> reads in ordinary English that

(1) teacher$_1$ ($\mathbf{T}_1$), someone who provides opportunities, guidance and help (effective and/or ineffective) to some student with the intention that the student develops some range of knowing,

(2) shares no elements with ($\notin$), or is completely separate

from, or is of a completely different category from,

(3) teacher$_3$ ($\mathbf{T}_3$), a set of circumstances from which someone accidentally learns something, either by misadventure or serendipity.

The relationship of the three denotations of the term <*teaching*> can be expressed in set theory notation as follows.

$$\mathbf{T}_{P1} \supset \mathbf{T}_{P2}$$

$$\mathbf{T}_{P1} \notin \mathbf{T}_{P3}$$

The first statement <$\mathbf{T}_{P1} \supset \mathbf{T}_{P2}$> reads in ordinary English that

(1) teaching$_1$ ($\mathbf{T}_{P1}$), providing opportunities, guidance and help (effective and/or ineffective) to some student with the intention that the student develops some range of knowing,

(2) is a superset of ($\supset$), or includes the elements of, but more elements than,

(3) teaching$_2$ ($\mathbf{T}_{P2}$), providing opportunities, guidance and help (effective, and only effective) that result in the student developing some range of knowing.

The second statement <$\mathbf{T}_{P1} \notin \mathbf{T}_{P3}$> reads in ordinary English that

(1) teaching$_1$ ($\mathbf{T}_{P1}$), providing opportunities, guidance and help (effective and/or ineffective) to some student with the intention that the student develops some range of knowing,

(2) shares no elements with ($\notin$), or is completely separate from, or is of a completely different category from,

(3) teaching$_3$ ($\mathbf{T}_{P3}$), experiencing circumstances from which the person having the experience accidentally learns something, either by misadventure or serendipity.

Of these three conceptions of <*teacher*> and <*teaching*>, which one is best for use in educological discourse, educological inquiry and intentional guided educological study? Educological discourse, inquiry and intentional guided study require that there be a human agent who is acting in the role of teacher. Thus, the concept of <*teacher*> as teacher$_3$ or happenstance, and the concept of <*teaching*> as teaching$_3$, or experiencing misadventure and/or serendipity, are ruled out. Happenstance and accidents do not have relevance in the task of someone intentionally providing opportunities, guidance and help for someone to develop some range of knowing. The question of whether a task should still be denoted with the term <*teaching*> if the student does not achieve some range of knowing to some specified standard is like the question of whether practicing medicine should still be denoted by the term <*practicing medicine*> if the patient is not cured, or whether practicing law should still be denoted by the term <*practicing law*> if the judgment goes against the client. Suppose that the assertion is made, "If the students have not learned, then the teacher has not been teaching them." This is much like asserting that someone has not been fishing if no fish have been caught, or someone has not been hunting if no game has been bagged.

Again, using the criteria which were used in the evaluation of the different conceptions of the term <*education*>, teaching as teaching$_3$, is completely inappropriate because there is no human agent who is providing opportunities, guidance and help to learn. Teaching as teaching$_2$ is too exclusive in that it does not include unsuccessful attempts to provide opportunities, guidance and help for someone to develop a range of knowing. Teaching as teaching$_1$ satisfies all criteria,

(1) inclusiveness,
(2) exclusiveness,
(3) internal consistency,
(4) exhaustiveness,
(5) external relatedness,
(6) fruitfulness,

for a conception of the term <*teaching*> that is appropriate for educological discourse, inquiry and intentional guided study.

We can now extend descriptive educological theory by adding some well-defined terms to the theory. Let's agree to use the term <*teaching*> and the symbol <$\mathbf{T}_{P}$> to denote <$\mathbf{T}_{P1}$>, or teaching$_1$, or intentionally providing opportunities, guidance and help for students with the intention that the students develop some range of knowing.

Let's use the term <*effective teaching*> and the symbol <$\mathbf{T}_{PE}$> to denote <$\mathbf{T}_{P2}$>, or teaching$_2$, or intentionally providing opportunities, guidance and help (which are effective, and only effective) that result in students developing a range of knowing.

Let's use the term <*ineffective teaching*> and the symbol <$\mathbf{T}_{PI}$> to denote intentionally providing opportunities, guidance and help (which are ineffective, and only ineffective) that do not result in students developing a range of knowing.

Let's use the term <*accidental learning*> and the symbol <$\mathbf{L}_{4}$> to denote <$\mathbf{T}_{P3}$>, or experiencing happenstance which leads to someone unintentionally and without guidance achieving some range of knowing. Let's also agree never to use the term <*teaching*> to denote learning$_4$ ($\mathbf{L_4}$) or teaching$_3$ ($\mathbf{T_{P3}}$).

Let's use the term <*teacher*> and the symbol <**T**> to denote anyone who provides opportunities, guidance and help (whether effective or not) for students with the intention that students develop some range of knowing.

Let's use the term <*effective teacher*> and the symbol <$\mathbf{T_E}$> to denote anyone who provides opportunities, guidance and help (which are effective, and only effective) that result in students achieving some range of knowing.

Let's use the term <*ineffective teacher*> and the symbol <$\mathbf{T_I}$> to denote anyone who provides opportunities, guidance and help which are ineffective (do not result in students achieving some range of knowing).

Given the conception of the term <*teaching*> as someone providing opportunities, guidance and help to students with the intention that students develop some range of knowing, let's consider what teaching includes and does not include. Teaching is always intentional. It is not merely doing something from which someone else learns something. For example, a child may observe his mother smoking a cigarette and, from that set of observations, learn the basics of taking a cigarette, lighting it and pulling in the smoke by sucking on the cigarette. While the mother is occupied elsewhere, the child takes a cigarette from her pack, uses her lighter, lights the cigarette and proceeds to smoke. So, was the mother teaching the child how to smoke? Clearly not. She did not smoke with the intention of providing opportunities, guidance and help for the child to develop a range of knowing about how to smoke. The child learned how to smoke by observing his mother, and that learning was achieved through intentional unguided study. The child's range of knowing how to smoke is the result of discovery learning ($\mathbf{L_2}$).

Teaching is not only done by professional, certified schoolteachers. Anyone can play the role of teacher at any time and in any place. A businessman purchases a new accounting software for his business. He hires a trainer to come to his business premises and show him and his staff how to use the accounting system. The trainer demonstrates the operations and features of the accounting system and assigns some practice tasks for the businessman and his staff. They complete the tasks, and the trainer evaluates their performance. The trainer concludes the training session by giving the participants a website address which they can use to ask for help when they encounter problems which they do not know how to solve. The trainer was teaching ($\mathbf{T_P}$) the staff. A child shows another child how to play Minecraft on the computer, and the second child starts to play Minecraft. The first child was teaching ($\mathbf{T_P}$), and the second child was intentionally studying under guidance. A boy shows his sister strategies to use in solving the Rubik's Cube. His sister uses the strategies to solve the Cube. The boy was teaching ($\mathbf{T_P}$). The sister was intentionally studying under guidance.

The activities which can count as teaching ($\mathbf{T_P}$) are many. A high school teacher arranges several sets of apparatus which can be used to generate carbon dioxide from heating a quantity of copper carbonate. When the students arrive, the teacher provides guidance in how to use the apparatus to extract the carbon dioxide, how to test for carbon dioxide and how to write the report of the experiment. The teacher then observes and supervises the students. The teacher's activities of arranging, directing and supervising are all teaching ($\mathbf{T_P}$) activities. A farmer shows his hired hand how to operate the tractor and scarifier. He is teaching ($\mathbf{T_P}$) by describing explaining and demonstrating. A musician listens to a student saxophonist play. He recommends ways to improve technical and interpretational aspects of the saxophonist's recital. He is teaching ($\mathbf{T_P}$) by observing, listening, evaluating and recommending. A train driver sits alongside a trainee train driver and observes the trainee handling the controls of the locomotive to accelerate, decelerate and brake the train all the while looking out for obstacles, hazards, signals and speed limits. The senior train driver identifies correct procedures and errors, recommends things to anticipate and reminds the trainee driver about the essential checks to make for safe and efficient control of the train. The senior train driver is teaching ($\mathbf{T_P}$) by observing, evaluating, directing, prescribing, recommending and explaining.

Observation may not be enough to determine whether someone is teaching. The observer must also ascertain the intentions of the person being observed to determine whether the person is teaching.

With our analysis of the use of the terms <*teacher*> and <*teaching*>, and with acceptance of the conventions of the use of <**T**> and <$\mathbf{T_P}$>, descriptive educological theory, through explication, has now been extended to include the following set of well-defined terms.

(1) <**E**> is the symbol for education. Education is the set of phenomena with the elements of teacher, student, content and setting.
(2) <**T**> is the symbol for teacher. Teacher is a person who provides opportunities, guidance and help to students to intentionally study under guidance some content with the purpose in mind that the students achieve some range of knowing.
(3) <$\mathbf{T_P}$> is the symbol for teaching. Teaching is the providing of opportunities, guidance and help to students to intentionally study under guidance some content with the purpose in mind that the students achieve some range of knowing.

Four Conceptions of the Term <*Studying*>

A second key term to be explicated in the definition of education as expressed in the statement

$$\mathbf{E = T \cup S \cup C \cup X}$$

is the term <*student*> (**S**) and the related terms <*study*> and <*studying*> (both denoted by <$\mathbf{S_P}$>). A student (**S**) is a person who intentionally undertakes to extend his or her range of knowing, and study or studying ($\mathbf{S_P}$) is what the person does in playing the role of student. Consider the following four sentences in which the term <*studying*> is used.

(1) Marcia is <**studying**> guitar under the tutelage of the noted guitarist Sabastian Vargas.
(2) Gerard is <**studying**> a book about the care of orchids.
(3) The medical research team is <**studying**> ways to prevent dementia.
(4) The cotton farmer is <**studying**> samples of cotton bolls from his crop to detect any sign of boll weevils.

In the first sentence, the term <*studying*> can be substituted with the term <*intentionally undertaking under guidance to develop conventional knowing*>, and the meaning of the sentence does not change.

(1) Marcia is <**intentionally undertaking under guidance to develop conventional knowing**> [of] guitar under the tutelage of the noted guitarist Sabastian Vargas.

So, one denotation of the term <*studying*> is intentionally undertaking under guidance to develop conventional knowing. This denotation of the term <*studying*> can be distinguished with a subscript <1>, studying$_1$, and the symbol ($\mathbf{S_{P1}}$). The person who does the studying$_1$ can be distinguished by a subscript <1>, student$_1$, and by the symbol <$\mathbf{S_1}$>. Studying$_1$ is done with the guidance of a teacher (**T**).

In the second sentence, the term <*studying*> can be substituted with the term <*intentionally undertaking without guidance to develop conventional knowing*>, and the meaning of the sentence does not change.

(2) Gerard is **<intentionally undertaking without guidance to develop conventional knowing**> [from] a book about the care of orchids.

So, a second denotation of the term <*studying*> is intentionally undertaking without guidance to develop conventional knowing. This denotation of the term <*studying*> can be distinguished with a subscript <2>, studying$_2$, and the symbol <$\mathbf{S_{P2}}$>. The person who does studying$_2$ can be distinguished by a subscript <2>, student$_2$, and by the symbol <$\mathbf{S_2}$>. Another term which denotes a student$_2$ ($\mathbf{S_2}$) is the term <*auto-didact*>. Studying$_2$ ($\mathbf{S_2}$)is done without the guidance of a teacher (**T**).

In the third sentence, the term <*studying*> can be substituted with the term <*intentionally undertaking to develop without guidance postconventional knowing*>, and the meaning of the sentence does not change.

(3) The medical research team is **<intentionally undertaking to develop without guidance postconventional knowing**> [about] ways to prevent dementia.

So, a third denotation of the term <*studying*> is intentionally undertaking without guidance to develop postconventional knowing. Knowing is postconventional when it is a neo-knowing. Up to the present, the knowing has not been developed by anyone. This denotation of the term <*studying*> can be distinguished with a subscript <3>, studying$_3$, and the symbol <$\mathbf{S_{P3}}$>. Other terms which denote studying$_3$ are <*neo-search*>, <*original disciplined inquiry*> and <*original research*>. The person who does studying$_3$ can be distinguished by the subscript <3>, student$_3$, and the symbol <$\mathbf{S_3}$>. Studying$_3$ is done without a teacher (**T**).

In the fourth sentence, the term <*studying*> can be substituted with the term <*intentionally undertaking to develop without guidance knowing about a particular state of affairs*> without changing the meaning of the sentence.

(4) The cotton farmer is **<intentionally undertaking to**

> **develop without guidance knowing about a particular state of affairs**> [of] samples of cotton bolls from his crop to detect any sign of boll weevils.

So, a fourth denotation of the term <*studying*> is intentionally undertaking to develop without guidance knowing about a particular state of affairs. This denotation of the term <*studying*> can be distinguished by a subscript <4>, studying$_4$, and the symbol <$\mathbf{S}_{P4}$> The person who does studying$_4$ can be distinguished by the subscript <4>, student$_4$, and the symbol <$\mathbf{S}_4$>.

In relation to education (**E**), teachers (**T**) and teaching ($\mathbf{T}_P$), it is evident that the relevant and appropriate denotation of the term <*student*> is student$_1$ ($\mathbf{S}_1$), and the relevant and appropriate denotation of the term <*studying*> is studying$_1$ ($\mathbf{S}_{P1}$). Let's follow the convention of using the term <*student*> to denote, and only denote, student$_1$ ($\mathbf{S}_1$). And let's follow the convention of using the term <*study*> and <*studying*> to denote, and only denote, study$_1$, studying$_1$ ($\mathbf{S}_{P1}$). Let's also agree that another term which can be used to denote study$_1$ and studying$_1$ ($\mathbf{S}_{P1}$) is the term <*studenting*>. A student (**S**), then, is one who accepts the opportunities, guidance and help provided by a teacher (**T**) and intentionally undertakes to develop under guidance some conventional range of knowing. Thus, a student (**S**) conducts intentional guided studying (studying$_1$ <$\mathbf{S}_{P1}$>) or studenting).

With our analysis and explication of the use of the terms <*student*> and <*studying*>, and with acceptance of the conventions of the use of the terms <**S**> and <$\mathbf{S}_{P1}$>, we can extend descriptive educological theory by adding the following well-defined terms.

(1) <**S**> is the symbol for student$_1$, a person who accepts the opportunities, guidance and help provided by a teacher (**T**) and intentionally undertakes to develop under guidance some conventional range of knowing.

(2) <$\mathbf{S}_{P1}$> is the symbol for studying$_1$ or studenting. Studying$_1$ is accepting the opportunities, guidance and help provided by a teacher (**T**) and intentionally undertaking to develop under guidance some conventional range of knowing.

(3) <$\mathbf{S}_{P2}$> is the symbol for studying$_2$ or intentionally undertaking without guidance to develop a range of conventional level knowing. Studying$_2$ is what an autodidact does, and studying$_2$ is done outside of education (**E**).

(4) <$\mathbf{S_{P3}}$> is the symbol for studying$_3$ or intentionally undertaking without guidance to develop postconventional knowing. Studying$_3$ is what investigators or researchers do in original research or neo-search. Studying$_3$ is done outside of education (**E**).

(5) <$\mathbf{S_{P4}}$> is the symbol for studying$_4$ or intentionally undertaking to develop without guidance knowing about a particular state of affairs. Studying$_4$ is what a veterinarian might do to determine what medication to administer, a ship's captain might do to determine what course to take or an appliance repair technician might do to determine what spare part to replace. Studying$_4$ is done outside of education (**E**).

Two Conceptions of the Term <*Content*>

A third key term to be explicated in the definition of education as expressed in the statement

E = T U S U C U X

is the term <*content*> (**C**). Consider the following sentences.

(1) In this course, the <**content**> that you will be studying is the geography of the Australian continent.

(2) In this course, the <**content**> that you will be studying is the psychology of infants and early childhood.

(3) The <**content**> that you will be studying in this course is the Cha Cha, the Rhumba and the Tango.

(4) The <**content**> that you will be studying in this course is welding butt joints, edge joints, lap joints, corner joints and tee joints.

In the first sentence, we can substitute the term <*content*> with the term <*selection of knowledge organized for the purposes of teaching and intentional guided studying*>, and the meaning of the sentence remains unchanged.

(1) In this course, the <**selection of knowledge organized for the purposes of teaching and intentional guided studying**> that you will be studying is the geography of the Australian continent.

So, in the first sentence, the term <*content*> denotes a selection of knowledge organized for the purposes of teaching ($\mathbf{T_P}$) and intentional guided studying ($\mathbf{S_{P1}}$). Let this denotation of the term <*content*> be distinguished by a subscript <1>, content$_1$, and by the symbol <$\mathbf{C_1}$>. Examples of selections of knowledge include zoology of arachnids (selected from the fund of knowledge that is zoology), chemistry of acids (selected from the fund of knowledge that is chemistry), geometry of solid figures (selected from the fund of knowledge that is mathematics), mechanical physics (selected from the fund of knowledge that is physics), etc. A fund of knowledge is a collection of recorded true statements typically organized into a system of well-defined terms and mutually implied statements.

In the second sentence, the same substitution as the first sentence can be made of the term <*content*> with the term <*selection of knowledge organized for the purposes of teaching and intentional guided studying*>, and the meaning of the sentence is not changed.

> (2) In this course, the <**selection of knowledge organized for the purposes of teaching and intentional guided studying**> that you will be studying is the psychology of infants and early childhood.

So, in the second sentence, the term <*content*> again denotes a selection of knowledge organized for the purposes of teaching and intentional guided studying or content$_1$ (**C_1**).

In the third sentence, we can substitute the term <*content*> with the term <*selection of exemplifications of knowing organized for the purposes of teaching and intentional guided studying*>, and the meaning of the sentence does not change.

> (3) The <**selection of exemplifications of knowing organized for the purposes of teaching and intentional guided studying**> that you will be studying in this course is the Cha Cha, the Rhumba and the Tango.

So, in the third sentence, the term <*content*> denotes a selection of exemplifications of knowing organized for the purposes of teaching and intentional guided studying. We can distinguish this denotation of the term <*content*> with a subscript <2>, content$_2$, and the symbol <**C_2**>. Knowing is a cognitive state of mind which enables the knower to solve problems and achieve desired goals. We can observe knowledge (**K_1**), as a set or recorded true statements, by seeing the words and sentences on a page and conceiving their meaning. We cannot observe knowing (**K_2**), as a cognitive state of mind, but we can observe exemplifications of knowing (**K_2**). Does Nancy know how to dance the Cha Cha? The proof of her knowing is her performing the Cha Cha. We can observe her performing the Cha Cha. When she stops performing, she still knows how to dance the Cha Cha. Her cognitive state of mind remains, but she is not giving any exemplification of her knowing at that moment. If Nancy is teaching (**T_P**) the Cha Cha, she is providing opportunities, guidance and help to students in the expectation that the students will accept the opportunities and practice, intentionally and under guidance, the pattern of movements which constitutes the Cha Cha. Through their intentional guided practice, if they are successful, the students develop the range of knowing requisite for performing the Cha Cha.

In the fourth sentence, the same substitution as the third sentence can be made of the term <*content*> with the term <*selection of exemplifications of knowing organized for the purposes of teaching and intentional guided study*>, and the meaning of the sentence is not changed.

(4) The <**selection of exemplifications of knowing organized for the purposes of teaching and intentional guided study**> that you will be studying in this course is welding butt joints, edge joints, lap joints, corner joints and tee joints.

So, in the fourth sentence, the term <*content*> denotes a selection of exemplifications of knowing organized for the purposes of teaching and intentional guided studying, or content$_2$ (**C_2**).

The relationship of content to knowledge and knowing can be expressed in set theory notation as

$$C_1 = K_{1O}$$
$$C_2 = K_{2O}$$
$$C = C_1 \cup C_2 = K_{1O} \cup K_{2O}$$

In ordinary English these statements read as follows.

(1) The statement <**$C_1 = K_{1O}$**> reads that content$_1$ (**C_1**) is a selection of didactically organized knowledge (**K_{1O}**) (organized for the purposes of teaching <**T_P**> and intentional guided studying <**S_{P1}**>).

(2) The statement <**$C_2 = K_{2O}$**> reads that content$_2$ (**C_2**) is a selection of a range of didactically organized knowing (**K_{2O}**) (organized for the purposes of teaching <**T_P**> and intentional guided studying <**S_{P1}**>).

(3) The statement <**$C = C_1 \cup C_2 = K_{1O} \cup K_{2O}$**> reads that the essential elements of content (**C**) are (=) the union of ($\cup$) the essential elements of content$_1$ (**C_1**) and content$_2$ (**C_2**) and that the union ($\cup$) of content$_1$ and content$_2$ is the same as (=) the union of didactically organized knowledge

($\mathbf{K_{1O}}$) and knowing ($\mathbf{K_{2O}}$) (organized for the purposes of teaching <$\mathbf{T_P}$> and intentional guided studying <$\mathbf{S_{P1}}$>).

With our analysis and explication of the use of the term <*content*>, and with acceptance of the conventions of the use of the terms <$\mathbf{C_1}$> and <$\mathbf{C_2}$>, we can extend descriptive educological theory by adding the following well-defined terms.

(1) <$\mathbf{C_1}$> is the symbol for content$_1$ or a selection of didactically organized knowledge ($\mathbf{K_{1O}}$) (organized for the purposes of teaching <$\mathbf{T_P}$> and intentional guided studying <$\mathbf{S_{P1}}$>).

(2) <$\mathbf{C_2}$> is the symbol for content$_2$ or a selection of didactically organized knowing ($\mathbf{K_2}$) (organized for the purposes of teaching ($\mathbf{T_P}$) and intentional guided studying <$\mathbf{S_{P1}}$>).

(3) <**C**> is the symbol for content, including content$_1$ ($\mathbf{C_1}$) and content$_2$ ($\mathbf{C_2}$). The statement <$\mathbf{C = C_1 \cup C_2 = K_{1O} \cup K_{2O}}$> means that the essential elements of content (**C**) are (=) the union of ($\cup$) the essential elements of content$_1$ ($\mathbf{C_1}$) and content$_2$ ($\mathbf{C_2}$). The union ($\cup$) of content$_1$ ($\mathbf{C_1}$) and content$_2$ ($\mathbf{C_2}$) is the same as (=) the union of a selection of didactically organized knowledge ($\mathbf{K_{1O}}$) and a selection of didactically organized knowing ($\mathbf{K_{2O}}$).

Two Conceptions of the Term <*Knowledge*>

In our analysis and explication of the term <*content*>, the distinction was made between knowledge and knowing. In ordinary English, this distinction is not always clear. Consider the following sentences.

(1) The book, *Goren's Bridge Complete*, by Charles H. Goren (1963), contains extensive and detailed **<knowledge>** about how to bid, rebid and play hands of bridge.

(2) Charles H. Goren proved that he had an extensive **<knowledge>** of how to bid, rebid and play hands of bridge.

In the first sentence, the term <*knowledge*> can be substituted with the term <*recorded true statements*>, and the meaning of the sentence does not change.

(1) The book, *Goren's Bridge Complete*, by Charles H. Goren (1963), contains extensive and detailed <**recorded true statements**> about how to bid, rebid and play hands of

bridge.

So, one denotation of the term <*knowledge*> is recorded true statements. This denotation of the term <*knowledge*> can be distinguished with a subscript <1>, knowledge$_1$, and the symbol <$\mathbf{K}_1$>. Knowledge$_1$ ($\mathbf{K}_1$) is located in any medium where words and sentences can be recorded and stored, such as printed books, journals, articles and electronic media. The author of the book, *Goren's Bridge Complete*, the American bridge player, Charles H. Goren (1901-1991), died some time ago, but the knowledge$_1$ ($\mathbf{K}_1$) in his book has not died. Knowledge$_1$ ($\mathbf{K}_1$), a set of recorded true statements, is not mortal.

In the second sentence, the term <*knowledge*> can be substituted with the term <*range of knowing*>, and the meaning of the sentence does not change.

(2) Charles H. Goren proved that he had an extensive <**range of knowing**> of how to bid, rebid and play hands of bridge.

So, a second denotation of the term <*knowledge*> is a range of knowing. This second denotation of the term <*knowledge*> can be distinguished by a subscript <2>, knowledge$_2$, the symbol <$\mathbf{K}_2$> and the synonyms <*knowing*> and <*range of knowing*>. Knowledge$_2$ ($\mathbf{K}_2$) or knowing, is located in the cognitive function of human beings. When the individual human being who has achieved some range of knowing dies, the range of knowing perishes with the individual. Knowing is mortal.

The relationship of knowledge$_1$ and knowledge$_2$ can be expressed in set theory notation as follows.

$$\mathbf{K}_1 \notin \mathbf{K}_2$$

$$\mathbf{K}_2 \notin \mathbf{K}_1$$

In ordinary English, the statements read as follows.

(1) The statement <$\mathbf{K}_1 \notin \mathbf{K}_2$> reads that knowledge$_1$ ($\mathbf{K}_1$), recorded true statements, contains none of the elements of ($\notin$) knowledge$_2$ ($\mathbf{K}_2$), or knowing.

(2) The statement <$\mathbf{K}_2 \notin \mathbf{K}_1$> reads that knowledge$_2$ ($\mathbf{K}_2$) or knowing, contains none of the elements of ($\notin$) knowledge$_1$ ($\mathbf{K}_1$), recorded true statements.

The implicative meaning of these statements is that knowledge$_1$ ($\mathbf{K}_1$) and knowledge$_2$ ($\mathbf{K}_2$) are two distinct, discrete and mutually exclusive categories of experiential phenomena.

The distinctions of knowledge$_1$ ($\mathbf{K}_1$) and knowledge$_2$ ($\mathbf{K}_2$) can be added to the list of well-defined terms in descriptive educological theory.

(1) $<\mathbf{K}_1>$ is the symbol for knowledge$_1$, or recorded true statements.

(2) $<\mathbf{K}_2>$ is the symbol for knowledge$_2$, or knowing, or a cognitive state of mind.

Knowing and Range of Knowing

Knowing consists of some range of knowing. A range of knowing is some combination of level, form and kind of knowing. Each and every one of us, in our lifetime, achieves a range of knowing which is unique to us as individuals.

Levels of Knowing

Levels of knowing are degrees of extent to which someone has realized the ability to perform in a well-informed, purposeful, adequate and warranted manner in relation to some state of affairs and some aim, goal or intended outcome. Levels of knowing are denoted by $<\mathbf{K}_{2L}>$. At least four levels of knowing can be distinguished (Level 1, 2, 3, 4).

(1) Level 1 knowing is preconventional knowing (denoted by $<\mathbf{K}_{2L1}>$)

(2) Level 2 knowing is conventional intermediate knowing (denoted by $<\mathbf{K}_{2L2}>$)

(3) Level 3 knowing is conventional expert knowing (denoted by $<\mathbf{K}_{2L3}>$)

(4) Level 4 knowing is postconventional knowing (denoted by $<\mathbf{K}_{2L4}>$)

The four levels of knowing are the levels of beginner or novice (Level 1), intermediate (Level 2), expert (Level 3) and expert innovator (Level 4). A person who has Level 1 preconventional knowing is just at the beginning of learning some kind and form of knowing in relation to some state of affairs. The person has not yet achieved the conventions. At the Level 2 conventional intermediate level, the person has learned the conventions and use the conventions efficiently and with little self-consciousness. At the Level 3 conventional expert level, the person has learned the conventions and habitualized them such that there is complete self-confidence, no hesitation and no self-conscious-ness in the manifestation of the conventions. Level 4 postconventional knowing is being manifested when the knower is creating innovations which have not yet become accepted conventions. Innovative expert performers, researchers and inventors who are engaged in neo-search (original inquiry or original research), if successful, are performing at Level 4 postconventional knowing. They are setting new standards or new conventions of knowing about some set of activities, experiential phenomena or some state of affairs.

At Level 1, that of preconventional knowing ($\mathbf{K}_{2L1}$), individuals experience high degrees of disorganization, make many mistakes and have a low degree of control and confidence. It is a level at which there are many trials and errors, and much exertion of self-conscious effort. In the case of a novice sailor of a small one-person sail boat, the novice is just coming to know the difference between the bow and the stern, the port side and the starboard side, the mainsail and the sheet, the boom and the mast, the tiller and the rudder, the keel and the ballast, the transom and the halyards, the sailing zones and the no go zone. The novice is not certain about how to raise and lower the sail, how to handle the tiller for the rudder, how to establish the optimal point of sail, how to react to variations in wind direction and strength, how to tack and jibe and how to recover from a capsized boat. In the case of a trainee pilot just at the beginning of coming to know how to fly a sailplane, Level 1 is the stage of uncertainty, confusion and awkwardness in control of the ailerons, elevators, rudder, flaps, air brakes, and airspeed in take-offs, landings, turns, straight and level flight and recovery from stalls and spins. In the case of a five-year-old child just coming to know how to print Arabic numerals, Level 1 is the stage of producing approximations of the shapes of numerals, but not in the correct sizes and orientations, and with reversals (or mirror images) of the numerals. Level 1 is the level of knowing at which the novice or beginner performs.

At Level 2, that of conventional intermediate knowing ($\mathbf{K}_{2L2}$), the degree of control and confidence becomes extended and refined. Few mistakes are made, and conventions in performance are well on their way to becoming habituated. There are still some self-conscious uses of the conventions. Control is being achieved without any considerable degree of concentration. In the case of the novice sailor, the transition from Level 1 to Level 2 is characterized by less uncertainty, less confusion, less fumbling and an improved awareness of how to handle the sailboat. Control is close to being habitualized and automatic. The intermediate sailor performs competent trim, tacks and jibes, chooses the appropriate sail settings for the different positions of sailing (close hauled, beam reach, broach reach and dead downwind positions). The Level 2 intermediate sailor does not have to put in a great deal of concentration to coordinate the movement of foot, leg, arm and trunk to assure competent handling of the boat. In the case of the intermediate Level 2 trainee sailplane pilot, there is little or no uncertainty, confusion and awkwardness in control of the ailerons, elevators, rudder, flaps, air brakes and airspeed in takes-offs, landings, turns, straight and level flight and recovery from stalls and spins. Coordination and control have become largely habituated. In the case of the five-year-old child and printing the Arabic numerals, the orientation, size and proportions of the numerals are almost always consistently presented.

At Level 3 conventional expert knowing ($\mathbf{K}_{2L3}$), the transition has been made to habituated, confident and competent performance. The conventions of any particular knowing have become completely mastered. Control within the limits of established conventions is manifested without any self-conscious effort exerted in the control. Adequate performance of conventions has become completely routine. In the case of the expert sailor at the expert level of knowing how to sail, the expert has progressed to the stage of conventionally handling the mainsail, sheet and tiller in a smoothly coordinated manner, undertaking safe, smooth well-coordinated port and starboard tacks and jibes, sailing competently at close haul, beam reach, broach reach and dead downwind positions and trimming the sail to optimal positions. In the case of the trainee pilot at the expert Level 3, there is completely confident, habituated and competent control of the ailerons, elevators, rudder, flaps, air brakes, throttle and airspeed in take-offs, landings, turns, straight and level flight and recovery from stalls and spins. In the case of a five-year-old child who is printing the Arabic numerals, the expert child is totally confident, competent and quick in the production of all numerals in correct orientation, size and proportions and in the writing of any number in the Arabic numeral system.

Level 4 postconventional knowing ($\mathbf{K}_{2L4}$) is knowing which has extended beyond established conventions of Levels 1, 2 and 3 knowing. Achievement of Level 4 knowing, or postconventional knowing ($\mathbf{K}_{2L4}$), requires inquiry, innovation and creativity so that the one doing the innovating breaks new ground and forms new standards of performance which extend beyond the conventions of Level 3 knowing. In sailing a boat, postconventional knowing would be the invention of a new way of sailing with a new type of sail such as the inflated wing sail developed by Edouard Kessi and Laurent de Kalbertatten (Matthew Sheahan, 2019). In the flying of a sailplane, it might be the development of new maneuvers with a sailplane that have never been achieved before, for example, the maneuvers performed by the world champion Italian glider pilot, Luca Bertossio, at the Horizon Airmeet at Dönau-worth-Genderkingen Airport in Germany in 2019 (Stefan Langer, 2019). In the use of numerals, it might be the invention of a new positional numeral system with a radix that has never been used before, such as the hexadecimal system created for use in computing. In the use of alphabets, it might be the creation of a new set of symbols for a language such as the syllabary of 86 symbols for the Cherokee language created by the Cherokee innovator and leader, Sequoyah, in 1821. The new standards of performance which might be established at Level 4 of knowing could even contravene or reject the accepted conventions of Level 3 knowing.

The distinctions of levels of knowing (**$\mathbf{K}_{2L1}$, $\mathbf{K}_{2L2}$, $\mathbf{K}_{2L3}$, $\mathbf{K}_{2L4}$**) can be added to the list of well-defined terms in descriptive educological theory.

(1) <$\mathbf{K}_{2L}$> is the symbol for level of knowing, which is the extent or degree to which an individual's cognitive development has been achieved.

(2) <$\mathbf{K}_{2L1}$> is the symbol for Level 1 preconventional knowing, or beginner or novice level of knowing, which is characterized by a low degree of competence, a high degree of disorganization, many mistakes, much hesitancy and uncertainty, a low degree of control and confidence.

(3) <$\mathbf{K}_{2L2}$> is the symbol for Level 2 conventional intermediate knowing, which is characterized by a medium degree of competence within the limit of established conventions, near mastery of conventions, medium degree of organization, few mistakes, little hesitancy or uncertainty, medium degree of control and confidence, almost habituated competent performance.

(4) <$\mathbf{K}_{2L3}$> is the symbol for Level 3 conventional expert knowing, which is characterized by a high degree of competence within the limit of established conventions,

habituated and complete mastery of conventions, high degree of organization, no mistakes, no hesitancy, a high degree of control and confidence.

(5) <**K_{2L4}**> is the symbol for Level 4 postconventional knowing, or the level of the expert innovator, characterized by competency which extends beyond mastery of the limits of established conventions to innovative and creative performances, with no mistakes, no hesitancy, a high degree of control and confidence and habituated highly competent performance.

Forms of Knowing

Forms of knowing are different ways in which knowing can be expressed. Forms of knowing are denoted by <**K_{2F}**>. At least five forms of knowing can be distinguished (linguistic, emotional, imaginal, physiological and physical).

Linguistic knowing (K_{2F1}) is any cognitive performance that signifies meaning with symbols. Linguistic knowing includes speaking, reading, writing, reasoning in sentences with words, reasoning in mathematical propositions with mathematical symbols and performing logical operations such as deduction, reduction, induction, retroduction, abduction, evaluation, prescription and justification. Linguistic performances may be silent, told inwardly, or they may be spoken aloud, or written. They may be signed as in American Sign Language (ASL), or Australian Sign Language (AUSLAN) or Polish Sign Language (PSL). An example of linguistic knowing is a high school chemistry student, Jonathan, describing to his fellow students how to conduct an experiment to measure the number of kilojoules per gram stored in a quantity of refined white sugar. Jonathan is manifesting his knowing linguistically. Another example is that of a blind man, George, who is writing an essay in Braille. A third example is that of a deaf woman, Julie, who is using Australian Sign Language (AUSLAN) to communicate to her friend, Theresa, that she wants to go shopping for groceries.

Emotional knowing (K_{2F2}) is having learned feelings, or emotions, in relation to some state of affairs and some intended set of goals, aims or outcomes. An example is a team of two paramedics transporting a patient to hospital in an ambulance. The patient goes into cardiac arrest. The team remembers their training, and they do not panic. They remain calm and urgently administer adrenaline and CPR to resuscitate the patient. Their suppression of the impulse to panic is an example of emotional knowing. A second example is a professional golf player, Jay, about to play a tournament against a set of formidable opponents for substantial prize money. Jay calms himself and centers his emotional state so that he is motivated to win, but not so excited and nervous as to interfere with playing his best. A third example is a concert pianist, Jason, who is feeling stage fright before going on stage to play a recital, then brings himself to a calm emotional state which enables him to go on with his performance on stage.

Imaginal knowing ($\mathbf{K_{2F3}}$) is any act of forming (or perceiving) images, shapes, imagined sounds and imagined relationships in one's awareness or consciousness. Someone who forms a picture of a pelican in the consciousness (but is not viewing physically a pelican with the eye) is performing imaginally. Likewise, imagining a tune or musical piece by recalling it or creating it (but not audibly singing it or hearing it physically) is an imaginal performance. Imagining where your opponent in a tennis game is going to drive the next shot is an imaginal performance.

Physiological knowing ($\mathbf{K_{2F4}}$) is, for example, through meditation, deliberately slowing one's heart rate, diminishing one's blood pressure, suppressing one's tears, blocking out pain, controlling the timing and duration of sexual orgasm. Like other forms of knowing, physiological knowing is learned, deliberate, organized, coordinated and controlled.

Physical knowing ($\mathbf{K_{2F5}}$) is any performance of deliberate, organized and coordinated movements and gestures, such as swimming, driving a car, bouncing a basketball, operating a crane, flying an aircraft, diving from a high tower into a pool. A dance teacher demonstrating to a set of pupils how to move their feet and arms and how to hold their bodies while dancing the Samba is an example of physical knowing on the part of the teacher.

The distinctions of forms of knowing ($\mathbf{K_{2F1}}$, $\mathbf{K_{2F2}}$, $\mathbf{K_{2F3}}$, $\mathbf{K_{2F4}}$, $\mathbf{K_{2F5}}$) can be added to the list of well-defined terms in descriptive educological theory.

(1) <$\mathbf{K_{2F}}$> is the symbol for form of knowing, which is the way in which knowing can be exemplified or expressed.

(2) <$\mathbf{K}_{2F1}$> is the symbol for linguistic knowing, which is the learned ability to exemplify deliberate, controlled, coordinated and warranted linguistic performances.

(3) <$\mathbf{K}_{2F2}$> is the symbol for emotional knowing, which is the learned ability to exemplify deliberate, controlled, coordinated and warranted emotional performances.

(4) <$\mathbf{K}_{2F3}$> is the symbol for imaginal knowing, which is the learned ability to exemplify deliberate, controlled, coordinated and warranted imaginal performances.

(5) <$\mathbf{K}_{2F4}$> is the symbol for physiological knowing, which is the learned ability to exemplify deliberate, controlled, coordinated and warranted physiological performances.

(6) <$\mathbf{K}_{2F5}$> is the symbol for physical knowing, which is the learned ability to exemplify deliberate, controlled, coordinated and warranted physical performances.

Kinds of Knowing

Kinds of knowing can be distinguished with respect to the state of affairs in relation to which the knowing is performed (the object of knowing <$\mathbf{O}_{K2}$>). Kinds of knowing are denoted by <$\mathbf{K}_{2K}$>). At least four kinds of knowing can be distinguished (adapted from George Maccia, 1973c):

(1) knowing-that-one ($\mathbf{K}_{2K1}$),
(2) knowing-that ($\mathbf{K}_{2K2}$),
(3) knowing-how ($\mathbf{K}_{2K3}$) and
(4) knowing-to ($\mathbf{K}_{2K4}$).

Knowing-that-one ($\mathbf{K}_{2K1}$) is the learned ability to perform deliberately, confidently, competently and justifiably in relation to some unique entity or state of affairs (the unique entity or state of affairs is the object of knowing <$\mathbf{O}_{K2}$>). A person has achieved a state of knowing-that-one ($\mathbf{K}_{2K1}$) when he or she can say (and mean it), "I know that one" (George Maccia, 1973c). An example of knowing-that-one ($\mathbf{K}_{2K1}$) is my knowing my brother Paul. I know Paul, not as a carpenter, or as an American, or as a resident of Oregon, but as Paul, my brother, that one unique human being who is Paul. There are many men named <*Paul*>, but there is only one who is my brother, Paul. I am able to manifest my knowing-that-one ($\mathbf{K}_{2K1}$), the one who is Paul, by picking Paul out from a group of men (a physical knowing <$\mathbf{K}_{2F5}$>), by talking with Paul in ways that Paul understands and appreciates (a linguistic knowing <$\mathbf{K}_{2F1}$>), by anticipating Paul's conduct, moods and choices (an imaginal knowing <$\mathbf{K}_{2F3}$>), by making gestures to Paul which he finds meaningful and appropriate (a physical and a linguistic knowing <$\mathbf{K}_{2F5}$> and <$\mathbf{K}_{2K1}$>). My knowing-that-one ($\mathbf{K}_{2K1}$), the one unique human being who is Paul, my brother, is my cognitive ability to recognize, be acquainted with and have appreciation of Paul in all his uniqueness.

Recognitive knowing-that-one ($\mathbf{K}_{2K1A}$) is achieved when the knower can recognize an entity or state of affairs and discern it from that which is not that entity or state of affairs, and vice versa, viz. discern that which is not that entity or state of affairs from that which is. For example, Mrs James has recognitive knowing-that-one ($\mathbf{K}_{2K1A}$) when

(1) Alden is her 12-year-old son,
(2) she believes that Alden is her 12-year-old son,
(3) she is completely justified in believing that Alden is her 12-year-old son,
(4) no other statement or belief defeats her belief that Alden is her 12-year-old son,
(5) she consistently and unerringly selects Alden from a group of 12-year-old boys and identifies any other 12-year-old boy as not being Alden (George Maccia, 1988).

Acquaintive knowing-that-one ($\mathbf{K}_{2K1B}$) is achieved when the knower, at first hand, experiences a unique entity or state of affairs and becomes familiar with the essential and unique qualities of that given unique entity or state of affairs. The ability to identify the unique qualities of a known unique entity or state of affairs by denotative use of language characterizes acquaintive knowing-that-one ($\mathbf{K}_{2K1B}$). Acquaintive knowing-that-one ($\mathbf{K}_{2K1B}$) includes recognitive knowing-that-one ($\mathbf{K}_{2K1A}$) For example, Mrs James has acquaintive knowing-that-one ($\mathbf{K}_{2K1B}$) when

(1) Alden exists as an actual person,
(2) Alden is her 12-year-old son,
(3) she recognizes Alden as her son,
(4) she selects elements (distinguishing characteristics) and relations (distinguishing relationships) which are determinants of Alden.

Appreciative knowing-that-one ($\mathbf{K}_{2K1C}$) is achieved when the knower recognizes a unique entity or state of affairs, is acquainted with the unique entity or state of affairs, can select elements that are appropriate to the unique entity or state of affairs and can select relations which are appropriate to the unique entity or state of affairs. It is a "discerning judgment ... that appraises the adequacy of part-whole entities and connections" (George Maccia, 1973c, p. 3). For example, Mrs James has appreciative knowing-that-one ($\mathbf{K}_{2K1C}$) when

(1) Alden exists as an actual person,
(2) Alden is her 12-year-old son,
(3) she recognizes Alden as her son,
(4) she is acquainted with Alden as her son,
(5) she selects elements and relations which are appropriate for Alden.

Knowing-that-one ($\mathbf{K}_{2K1}$) consists of recognitive, acquaintive and appreciative knowing ($\mathbf{K}_{2K1A}$, $\mathbf{K}_{2K1B}$, $\mathbf{K}_{2K1C}$). Knowing-that-one ($\mathbf{K}_{2K1}$) can be manifested in all four levels of knowing ($\mathbf{K}_{2L1}$, $\mathbf{K}_{2L2}$, $\mathbf{K}_{2L3}$, $\mathbf{K}_{2L4}$), and it can be manifested in all five forms of knowing ($\mathbf{K}_{2F1}$, $\mathbf{K}_{2F2}$, $\mathbf{K}_{2F3}$, $\mathbf{K}_{2F4}$, $\mathbf{K}_{2F5}$). Appreciative knowing-that-one ($\mathbf{K}_{2K1C}$) includes both acquaintive knowing-that-one ($\mathbf{K}_{2K1B}$) and recognitive knowing-that-one ($\mathbf{K}_{2K1A}$). Acquaintive knowing-that-one ($\mathbf{K}_{2K1B}$) includes recognitive knowing-that-one ($\mathbf{K}_{2K1A}$). Knowing-that-one ($\mathbf{K}_{2K1}$) gives knowers their sensitivity to discern, be acquainted with and appreciate unique entities and states of affairs (unique objects of knowing $<\mathbf{O}_{K2}>$). The relationships of recognitive, acquaintive and appreciative knowing-that-one ($\mathbf{K}_{2K1A}$, $\mathbf{K}_{2K1B}$, $\mathbf{K}_{2K1C}$) can also be expressed as follows.

$$\mathbf{K}_{2K1B} \supset \mathbf{K}_{2K1A}$$
$$\mathbf{K}_{2K1C} \supset \mathbf{K}_{2K1B}$$
$$\mathbf{K}_{2K1} = \mathbf{K}_{2K1A} \cup \mathbf{K}_{2K1B} \cup \mathbf{K}_{2K1C}$$

In ordinary English, the statements read as follows.

(1) The statement $<\mathbf{K}_{2K1B} \supset \mathbf{K}_{2K1A}>$ reads that acquaintive knowing-that-one ($\mathbf{K}_{2K1B}$) has all the elements of, plus more elements than ($\supset$), the elements of recognitive knowing-that-one ($\mathbf{K}_{2K1A}$), or acquaintive knowing-that-one ($\mathbf{K}_{2K1B}$) is a superset of the subset of recognitive knowing-that-one ($\mathbf{K}_{2K1A}$).
(2) The statement $<\mathbf{K}_{2K1C} \supset \mathbf{K}_{2K1B}>$ reads that appreciative knowing-that-one ($\mathbf{K}_{2K1C}$) has all the elements of, plus more elements than ($\supset$) the elements of acquaintive knowing-that-one ($\mathbf{K}_{2K1B}$), or appreciative knowing-that-one ($\mathbf{K}_{2K1C}$) is a superset of the subset of acquaintive

knowing-that-one ($\mathbf{K}_{2K1B}$).

(3) The statement <$\mathbf{K}_{2K1} = \mathbf{K}_{2K1A} \cup \mathbf{K}_{2K1B} \cup \mathbf{K}_{2K1C}$> reads that the essential elements of knowing-that-one ($\mathbf{K}_{2K1}$) consist of, or are (=), the union of ($\cup$) the essential elements of recognitive knowing-that-one ($\mathbf{K}_{2K1A}$), acquaintive knowing-that-one ($\mathbf{K}_{2K1B}$) and appreciative knowing-that-one ($\mathbf{K}_{2K1C}$), or the essential elements of knowing-that-one ($\mathbf{K}_{2K1}$) are the union of ($\cup$) the essential elements of recognitive knowing-that-one ($\mathbf{K}_{2K1A}$), acquaintive knowing-that-one ($\mathbf{K}_{2K1B}$) and appreciative knowing-that-one ($\mathbf{K}_{2K1C}$).

Knowing-that ($\mathbf{K}_{2K2}$) is the learned ability to perform in a purposeful, well-informed, adequate and warranted way in relation to entities or states of affairs as members of categories (George Maccia, 1973c). The categories are the objects of knowing ($\mathbf{O}_{K2}$). People have achieved a state of knowing-that ($\mathbf{K}_{2K2}$) when they say (and mean it), "I now know that is so." An example is that of Mrs Jordan. She is a primary school teacher, and one of her pupils is Andrea. Mrs Jordan can classify Andrea's conduct as typical of 9-year-old girls. She can categorize Andrea's capabilities as characteristic of middle level achievers and relate Andrea's aspirations and motivations to what one might expect of female, middle class pupils of Andrea's age. Mrs Jordan may manifest her knowing-that ($\mathbf{K}_{2K2}$) in

(1) writing an accurate report (linguistic knowing-that <$\mathbf{K}_{2K2F1}$>) which compares Andrea with other girls of her age and background,
(2) having a feeling of familiarity about Andrea's conduct as typical or atypical of girls of her age, social class and cultural heritage (an emotional knowing-that <$\mathbf{K}_{2K2F2}$>),
(3) imagining correctly how Andrea will compare with her peer group in a year's time (imaginal knowing-that <$\mathbf{K}_{2K2F3}$>),
(4) making appropriate gestures towards girls of Andrea's age, social status and cultural background (physical knowing-that <$\mathbf{K}_{2K2F5}$>).

Knowing-that ($\mathbf{K}_{2K2}$) gives the knower adequacy and power with respect to theory, i.e. knowing-that ($\mathbf{K}_{2K2}$) gives theoretical adequacy, or the ability to describe relations among entities and processes. The knower with knowing-that ($\mathbf{K}_{2K2}$) about some entity or state of affairs can describe, characterize, explain and make predictions about some entity or state of affairs in terms of categories and classifications of features or aspects of the entity or state of affairs. Describing, characterizing, explaining and predicting are all essential elements of theorizing. Knowers can theorize with appropriate evidence and sound inferences, if they have knowing-that ($\mathbf{K}_{2K2}$).

At least three categories of knowing-that ($\mathbf{K}_{2K2}$) can be distinguished, viz. instantive, relational and criterial knowing-that ($\mathbf{K}_{2K2A}$, $\mathbf{K}_{2K2B}$, $\mathbf{K}_{2K2C}$) (George Maccia, 1973c). Knowing-that ($\mathbf{K}_{2K2}$) is "non-basic knowing" (following K. Lehrer and T. Paxon, 1968). Whereas a "basic knowing" is relevant to the unique, a "non-basic knowing" is relevant to the general, i.e. to a category or categories. Knowing-that-one ($\mathbf{K}_{2K1}$) is "true belief that is completely justified and which justification does not depend upon any other statement or belief," but knowing-that ($\mathbf{K}_{2K2}$) is "true belief that is completely justified and that justification is not defeated by any other justifying statement or belief" (George Maccia, 1973c, pp. 2, 4). Knowing-that ($\mathbf{K}_{2K2}$) is knowing entities and relations as categories. Having a knowing-that ($\mathbf{K}_{2K2}$) of Alexander Dumas as a notable French author is knowing Dumas as a member of a category. It is knowing that he is an instance of a person who is a member of the category of authors and that he is also a member of the category of French. Having a knowing-that ($\mathbf{K}_{2K2}$) the mass of the Earth's moon is about one sixth the mass of the Earth is knowing the moon as a category. It is knowing that the moon is an instance of a category of objects which has mass, and it is knowing that the moon is an instance of a category of objects which is a satellite of a planet. Having a knowing that ($\mathbf{K}_{2K2}$) telling lies is wrong is knowing that lying is a member of a category of behavior, and it is knowing that lying is a member of the category of wrong.

Instantive knowing-that ($\mathbf{K}_{2K2A}$) is achieved when the knower can make an assertion about an entity or relation as a member of a category. The assertion is warranted by referencing the assertion with adequate authority. Examples of instantive knowing-that ($\mathbf{K}_{2K2A}$) include

(1) saying that the mass of the Earth's moon is approximately 0.012 times that of Earth and citing as evidence what reputable scientists have authoritatively reported (a linguistic form <$\mathbf{K}_{2F1}$> of instantive knowing-that <$\mathbf{K}_{2K2A}$>),

(2) writing that Alexandre Dumas wrote in a wide variety of genres and published a total of 100,000 pages in his lifetime and citing as evidence statements made by authoritative and credible biographers of Dumas (a linguistic form <$\mathbf{K}_{2F1}$> of instantive knowing-that <$\mathbf{K}_{2K2A}$>),

(3) saying (and meaning) that it is wrong to lie and citing as evidence the authoritative scripture from Exodus 20:16, "Thou shalt not bear false witness against thy neighbor" (a linguistic form <$\mathbf{K}_{2F1}$> of instantive knowing-that <$\mathbf{K}_{2K2A}$>).

Relational knowing-that ($\mathbf{K}_{2K2B}$) (George Maccia, 1973c; Maccia used the expression <*theoretical knowing-that*> to denote relational knowing-that <$\mathbf{K}_{2K2B}$>) is achieved when the knower is able to make an assertion about the relations (or mutual effects) among a set of entities or states of affairs and warrant the assertion by appropriate evidence or evidential argument. Examples of relational knowing-that ($\mathbf{K}_{2K2B}$) include

(1) saying that the volume of an irregularly shaped piece of iron is 112 cubic centimeters and citing as evidence the personal observation that when immersed in water in a graduated cylinder, the piece of iron raised the volume of the water by 112 cubic centimeters (a linguistic form <$\mathbf{K}_{2F1}$> of relational knowing-that <$\mathbf{K}_{2K2B}$>),

(2) writing that the mass of an irregularly shaped piece of iron is 879.2 grams and citing as evidence the observation that when placed on a scale, the mass of the iron indicated by the scale is 879.2 grams (a linguistic form <$\mathbf{K}_{2F1}$> of relational knowing-that <$\mathbf{K}_{2K2B}$>),

(3) saying that the mass of insoluble objects with a density greater than liquid water can be measured by the displacement in volume of liquid water when the insoluble object is immersed in liquid water and citing as evidence a number of personal observations of measured displacements of water by insoluble objects with densities greater than water (a linguistic form <$\mathbf{K}_{2F1}$> of relational knowing-that <$\mathbf{K}_{2K2B}$>).

Criterial knowing-that ($\mathbf{K}_{2K2C}$) is achieved when the knower can make an assertion and warrant the assertion by normative argument.

Examples of criterial knowing-that ($\mathbf{K}_{2K2C}$) include

(1) saying that slavery is wrong and presenting normative arguments for the right of human beings to freedom, demonstrating that slavery is a contradiction of the right of human beings to freedom and citing the harmful effects of slavery (a linguistic form <$\mathbf{K}_{2F1}$> of criterial knowing-that <$\mathbf{K}_{2K2C}$>),

(2) writing an editorial in which the position is taken that school yard bullying is wrong and presenting normative arguments about the physical, mental, social and cultural harm caused by bullying (a linguistic form <$\mathbf{K}_{2F1}$> of criterial knowing-that <$\mathbf{K}_{2K2C}$>),

(3) feeling upset at seeing two boys engaged in a physical fight, choosing to intervene to stop the fight and presenting normative arguments for prevention of harm and for resolution of conflict by peaceful means as reasons to justify the intervention (a combination of emotional, physical and linguistic forms <$\mathbf{K}_{2F2}$, $\mathbf{K}_{2F5}$, $\mathbf{K}_{2F1}$> of criterial knowing-that <$\mathbf{K}_{2K2C}$>).

The relationships among knowing-that ($\mathbf{K}_{2K2}$), instantive knowing-that ($\mathbf{K}_{2K2A}$), relational knowing-that ($\mathbf{K}_{2K2B}$) and criterial knowing-that ($\mathbf{K}_{2K2C}$) can also be expressed as the following.

$$\mathbf{K}_{2K2} = \mathbf{K}_{2K2A} \cup \mathbf{K}_{2K2B} \cup \mathbf{K}_{2K2C}$$

The statement <$\mathbf{K}_{2K2} = \mathbf{K}_{2K2A} \cup \mathbf{K}_{2K2B} \cup \mathbf{K}_{2K2C}$> reads that the essential elements of knowing-that ($\mathbf{K}_{2K2}$) consist of, or are (=), the union of ($\cup$) the elements of instantive knowing-that ($\mathbf{K}_{2K2A}$), relational knowing-that ($\mathbf{K}_{2K2B}$) and criterial knowing-that ($\mathbf{K}_{2K2C}$).

Knowing-how ($\mathbf{K}_{2K3}$) is the learned ability to enact a set of performances deliberately, intelligently, competently and with warranted certainty to achieve a desired result. Knowing-how ($\mathbf{K}_{2K3}$) contrasts with knowing-that-one ($\mathbf{K}_{2K1}$) and knowing-that ($\mathbf{K}_{2K2}$). Knowing-how ($\mathbf{K}_{2K3}$) is achieved when the knower can say (and mean it and be justified in saying it), "I can now do that." The object of knowing ($\mathbf{O}_{K2}$) for knowing-how ($\mathbf{K}_{2K3}$) is the competent protocolic, adaptive or creative performance by the knower. Knowing-how ($\mathbf{K}_{2K3}$) can be manifested in all forms of knowing, (linguistic, emotional, imaginal, physiological and physical knowing <$\mathbf{K}_{2F1}$, $\mathbf{K}_{2F2}$, $\mathbf{K}_{2F3}$, $\mathbf{K}_{2F4}$, $\mathbf{K}_{2F5}$>). For example, the performances implied by the statement, "I can do that," include the ability to solve quadratic equations, speak Russian and write essays on existentialism. Knowing-how ($\mathbf{K_{2K3}}$) is the cognitive state of mind which provides the basis for effective action. Knowing-how ($\mathbf{K_{2K3}}$) can be further categorized as protocolic, adaptive and creative knowing-how ($\mathbf{K_{2K3A}}$, $\mathbf{K_{2K3B}}$, $\mathbf{K_{2K3C}}$).

Protocolic knowing-how ($\mathbf{K_{2K3A}}$) is achieved when the knower can execute some performance competently, smoothly, appropriately, repeatedly and with warranted certainty. It is a single-pathed performance characterized by goal attainment through invariant sequences of activity (inclusive of the five forms of knowing). The observable evidence of protocolic knowing-how ($\mathbf{K_{2K3A}}$) is the performance of knowers as they follow a set of single-pathed standard invariant procedures. Examples of protocolic knowing-how ($\mathbf{K_{2K3A}}$) include

(1) consistently, quickly and accurately writing the spelling of the word <*arithmetic*> with the correct shape, orientation and order of the letters (a combination of physical and linguistic forms <$\mathbf{K_{2F5}}$ and $\mathbf{K_{2F1}}$> of protocolic knowing-how <$\mathbf{K_{2K3A}}$>),

(2) responding from the memorized multiplication tables up through the number ten, quickly and correctly, either orally or in writing, to any multiplication problem using numbers from 0 to 10 (a combination of physical and linguistic forms <$\mathbf{K_{2F5}}$ and $\mathbf{K_{2F1}}$> of protocolic knowing-how <$\mathbf{K_{2K3A}}$>),

(3) putting on a sterile plastic glove, handling with the sterile glove only the sliced roast beef in a cold storage case and touching nothing else with the intention of preventing contamination of the roast beef (a physical form <$\mathbf{K_{2F5}}$> of protocolic knowing-how <$\mathbf{K_{2K3A}}$>).

Adaptive knowing-how ($\mathbf{K_{2K3B}}$) (George Maccia, 1973c; Maccia used the expression <*conventional procedural knowing*> to denote adaptive knowing-how <$\mathbf{K_{2K3B}}$>) is achieved when the knower can execute a multi-pathed performance smoothly and attain a goal through adjusted sequences of movement. The observable evidence of adaptive knowing-how ($\mathbf{K_{2K3B}}$) is not the performance of the knower, but rather, the result produced by the knower. Examples of adaptive knowing-how ($\mathbf{K_{2K3B}}$) include

(1) adding a column of ten two-digit numbers without a calculator and without pencil and paper (this is a linguistic form <$\mathbf{K_{2F1}}$> of adaptive knowing-how <$\mathbf{K_{2K3B}}$> and

evidence of the knowing is the product of the knowing, viz. a correct sum),

(2) sailing a yacht as a solo sailor from Sydney, NSW to Honolulu, Hawaii (this is a combination of linguistic, emotional, imaginal, physiological and physical forms <$\mathbf{K}_{2F1}$, $\mathbf{K}_{2F2}$, $\mathbf{K}_{2F3}$, $\mathbf{K}_{2F4}$ and $\mathbf{K}_{2F5}$> of adaptive knowing-how <$\mathbf{K}_{2K3B}$> and the evidence of the knowing is the product of the knowing, viz. a successful voyage),

(3) interpreting a set of blueprints for a driveway and constructing a concrete driveway from the front of a domestic garage to the adjacent street (this is a combination of linguistic, emotional, imaginal, physiological and physical forms <$\mathbf{K}_{2F1}$, $\mathbf{K}_{2F2}$, $\mathbf{K}_{2F3}$, $\mathbf{K}_{2F4}$ and $\mathbf{K}_{2F5}$> of adaptive knowing-how <$\mathbf{K}_{2K3B}$> and the evidence of the knowing is the product of the knowing, viz. a sound and usable driveway built to correct specifications).

Creative knowing-how ($\mathbf{K}_{2K3C}$) is achieved when the knower has the ability to transform elements of a performance into unique forms and to unite disparate ways of realizing goals. The observable evidence of creative knowing-how ($\mathbf{K}_{2K3C}$) is, again, not the performance of the knower, but rather, the result or consequent produced by the knower. Examples of creative knowing-how ($\mathbf{K}_{2K3C}$) include

(1) developing a vaccine which prevents breast cancer (this is a combination of linguistic, emotional, imaginal, physiological and physical forms <$\mathbf{K}_{2F1}$, $\mathbf{K}_{2F2}$, $\mathbf{K}_{2F3}$, $\mathbf{K}_{2F4}$ and $\mathbf{K}_{2F5}$> of creative knowing-how <$\mathbf{K}_{2K3C}$> and the evidence of the knowing is, not the performance of the knower, but the product of the knowing, viz. an effective anti-breast cancer vaccine),

(2) writing an original novel (this is a combination of linguistic, emotional, imaginal and physical forms of knowing <$\mathbf{K}_{2F1}$, $\mathbf{K}_{2F2}$, $\mathbf{K}_{2F3}$ and $\mathbf{K}_{2F5}$> and the evidence of the creative knowing-how <$\mathbf{K}_{2K3C}$> is, not the performance of the knower, but the product of the knowing, viz. the novel),

(3) composing a symphony (this is a combination of linguistic, emotional, imaginal and physical forms of knowing <$\mathbf{K}_{2F1}$, $\mathbf{K}_{2F2}$, $\mathbf{K}_{2F3}$ and $\mathbf{K}_{2F5}$> and the evidence of the creative knowing-how <$\mathbf{K}_{2K3C}$> is, not the performance

of the knower, but the product of the knowing, viz. the symphony).

Adaptive knowing-how ($\mathbf{K}_{2K3B}$) and creative knowing-how ($\mathbf{K}_{2K3C}$) operate only at the postconventional level of knowing ($\mathbf{K}_{2L4}$). Adaptive knowing-how ($\mathbf{K}_{2K3B}$) and creative knowing-how ($\mathbf{K}_{2K3C}$) cannot be taught. They can only be achieved. They are achieved through the activity of inquiry (**Q**) and the process of intentional unguided (discovery) learning ($\mathbf{L}_2$). Knowers inquire (**Q**) (undertake intentionally to extend their knowing without guidance), and if successful, learn ($\mathbf{L}_2$) intentionally and without guidance. The inquiry (**Q**) and the resultant discovery learning ($\mathbf{L}_2$) of some postconventional level knowing ($\mathbf{K}_{2L4}$) take place outside of education (**E**). What can be taught, studied and learned under guidance is the means by which to recognize adaptive knowing-how ($\mathbf{K}_{2K3B}$) and creative knowing-how ($\mathbf{K}_{2K3C}$) (an important knowing for a teacher or an evaluator). And, of course, once adaptive knowing-how ($\mathbf{K}_{2K3B}$) and creative knowing-how ($\mathbf{K}_{2K3C}$) have been achieved by someone, others can follow along, because the new knowing becomes conventional knowing, and the conventional knowing can be selected as content ($\mathbf{C}_2$). Those who follow can learn by intentionally studying under guidance ($\mathbf{S}_{P1}$) the conventional level knowing which has been formed through adaptation and creation by the originator of the knowing. Conventional level knowing ($\mathbf{K}_{2L2}$ and $\mathbf{K}_{2L3}$) (selected as content <$\mathbf{C}_2$>) can always be taught ($\mathbf{T}_P$), studied ($\mathbf{S}_{P1}$) and learned intentionally under guidance ($\mathbf{L}_1$).

The relationships among knowing-how ($\mathbf{K}_{2K3}$), protocolic knowing-how ($\mathbf{K}_{2K3A}$), adaptive knowing-how ($\mathbf{K}_{2K3B}$) and creative knowing-how ($\mathbf{K}_{2K3C}$) can be expressed as follows.

$$\mathbf{K}_{2K3} = \mathbf{K}_{2K3A} \cup \mathbf{K}_{2K3B} \cup \mathbf{K}_{2K3C}$$

In ordinary English, the statement <$\mathbf{K}_{2K3} = \mathbf{K}_{2K3A} \cup \mathbf{K}_{2K3B} \cup \mathbf{K}_{2K3C}$> reads that the essential properties of knowing-how (<$\mathbf{K}_{2K3}$> or the learned ability to perform deliberately, intelligently, competently and with warranted certainty to achieve a desired result) consists of (=) the union of ($\cup$) the essential properties of protocolic ($\mathbf{K}_{2K3A}$), adaptive ($\mathbf{K}_{2K3B}$) and creative knowing-how ($\mathbf{K}_{2K3C}$).

Knowing-to ($\mathbf{K}_{2K4}$) is the learned, realized ability to exercise conscious intention, will and choice in a rational way that is consistent with a set of freely and rationally chosen criteria. The criteria consist of either standards or rules or a combination of both. The object of knowing ($\mathbf{O}_{K2}$) is rational choice consistent with freely and rationally chosen criteria. A synonym for knowing-to ($\mathbf{K_{2K4}}$) is the term <*conative knowing*>. Conative knowing is a psychic state of knowing-to ($\mathbf{K_{2K4}}$), as distinct from knowing-that-one ($\mathbf{K_{2K1}}$), knowing-that ($\mathbf{K_{2K2}}$) or knowing-how ($\mathbf{K_{2K4}}$). Individuals have achieved a state of knowing-to ($\mathbf{K_{2K4}}$) when they can say (and mean and justify it), "I am willing to do that." That state of willingness, or knowing-to ($\mathbf{K_{2K4}}$), is the same as conative knowing (George Maccia, 1973c). Conative knowing ($\mathbf{K_{2K4}}$) is the realized ability to choose rational courses of action which are consistent with standards and rules by which to regulate, control and direct the self. Conative knowing ($\mathbf{K_{2K4}}$) is the basis for living a rational, principled life. Conative knowing ($\mathbf{K_{2K4}}$) gives us the ability to set goals and make plans in relation to criteria and to make choices consistent with chosen plans and goals. Conative knowing, or knowing-to ($\mathbf{K_{2K4}}$), is the realized ability to live consciously, thoughtfully and consistently by a set of standards and rules. Examples of knowing-to ($\mathbf{K_{2K4}}$) include

(1) committing to telling the truth and subsequently choosing to tell the truth rather than to lie,
(2) committing to being a law-abiding driver and subsequently choosing to drive at the road speed limit rather than exceed the limit,
(3) committing to achieving a bachelor's degree and subsequently choosing to do the things necessary to complete the program of study for the BA.

These three examples are instances of saying (and meaning and justifying it), "I am willing to do that." The act of saying, "I am willing to do that," is the committing, the pledging, the assuring, the self obligating. The acting in adherence with the committing is the pragmatic consequence of the committing. The first example is the pragmatic consequence of saying, "I am willing to tell the truth." The second example is the pragmatic consequence of saying, "I am willing to obey the rules of the road." The third example is the pragmatic consequence of saying, "I am willing to do the work for a BA." All three examples are instances of knowing-to ($\mathbf{K_{2K4}}$) because knowing-to ($\mathbf{K_{2K4}}$) is being able to say (and mean and justify it), "I am willing to do that."

Knowing-to ($\mathbf{K_{2K4}}$) is acting thoughtfully. Acting thoughtfully contrasts with acting thoughtlessly. Acting thoughtlessly is acting on urges, desires and impulses without regard for consequences and without anticipation of the results of our uninhibited impulses.

Knowing-to (**K**$_{2K4}$) is a state of mindfulness which enables rational, well-informed, thoughtful choosing. In contrast, willfulness is a state of mindlessness which engages in irrational, uninformed, thoughtless, impulsive choosing. Knowing-to (**K**$_{2K4}$) includes rules-based knowing-to (**K**$_{2K4A}$) and standards-based knowing-to (**K**$_{2K4B}$).

Rules-based knowing-to (K$_{2K4A}$) is obligating one's self to make rational choices according to rules. Rules are of three kinds: injunctions, permissions and prohibitions. Rules which are injunctions are specifications which compel some behavior, entity or state of affairs. Rules which are permissions are specifications which allow some behavior, entity or state of affairs. Rules which are prohibitions are specifications which forbid some behavior, entity or state of affairs.

An example of rules-based knowing-to (**K**$_{2K4A}$) is the following scenario. I check my bank balance and find that the bank has mistakenly deposited $36 million to my account. What should I do? Transfer the money to an offshore account and flee the country? Transfer the money to an interest-bearing account and collect interest until the bank discovers its mistake? Invest the money in the short-term money market and collect the interest until the bank discovers its mistake? Purchase shares with the money and enjoy the capital gains until the bank discovers its mistake? From my rules-based knowing-to (**K**$_{2K4A}$), I know to follow the rules of honesty and truthfulness. My rules-based knowing-to (**K**$_{2K4A}$) guides me to know to choose to contact the bank immediately and alert it to the mistake. In this scenario, the rule being followed is an injunction (vs. a permission or a prohibition). The injunctive rules being followed are honesty and truthfulness.

Standards-based knowing-to (K$_{2K4B}$) is obligating one's self to make rational choices according to standards. Rules are norms to which there is either compliance or not compliance. For example, one either tells the truth or does not tell the truth. There is no degree of truthfulness. Standards are norms to which there are degrees of compliance. We can achieve compliance to a standard to some extent, ranging from nil compliance to complete compliance. Kindness, generosity, persistence and cooperativeness are all norms which are standards. We can choose to comply with them to some degree.

Examples of standards-based knowing-to (**K**$_{2K4B}$) is knowing to be persistent, knowing to be generous, knowing to be cooperative, knowing to be kind. Standards-based knowing-to (**K**$_{2K4B}$) is saying (and meaning it and justifying it), "I am willing to do that," and it is carrying out all the pragmatic consequences of that commitment. "That," of course, refers to the standard to which we commit ourselves.

With knowing-to ($\mathbf{K}_{2K4}$), we have the cognitive ability to live a principled life guided by criteria (rules and/or standards) to which we have committed ourselves. We are empowered to make choices, to have feelings and to conduct our affairs in relation to the set of rules and standards which we have resolved to follow. The relationships among knowing-to ($\mathbf{K}_{2K4}$), rules-based knowing-to ($\mathbf{K}_{2K4A}$) and standards-based knowing-to ($\mathbf{K}_{2K4B}$) can be expressed as follows.

$$\mathbf{K}_{2K4} = \mathbf{K}_{2K4A} \cup \mathbf{K}_{2K4B}$$

The statement <$\mathbf{K}_{2K4} = \mathbf{K}_{2K4A} \cup \mathbf{K}_{2K4B}$> in ordinary English reads that the essential properties of knowing-to ($\mathbf{K}_{2K4}$) consists of (=) the union of ($\cup$) the essential properties of rules-based knowing-to ($\mathbf{K}_{2K4A}$) and standards-based knowing-to ($\mathbf{K}_{2K4B}$).

The distinctions of kinds of knowing ($\mathbf{K}_{2K1}$, $\mathbf{K}_{2K2}$, $\mathbf{K}_{2K3}$, $\mathbf{K}_{2K4}$) can be added to the list of well-defined terms in descriptive educological theory.

(1) <$\mathbf{K}_{2K}$> is the symbol for kind of knowing, which is knowing in relation to some entity or state of affairs (some objective of knowing <$\mathbf{O}_{K2}$>).

(2) <$\mathbf{K}_{2K1}$> is the symbol for knowing-that-one, which is the learned ability to perform deliberately, confidently, competently and justifiably in relation to some unique entity or state of affairs.

(3) <$\mathbf{K}_{2K1A}$> is the symbol for recognitive knowing-that-one, which is the learned ability to recognize a unique entity or state of affairs and discern it from that which is not that entity or state of affairs, and vice versa, viz. discern that which is not that entity or state of affairs from that which is.

(4) <$\mathbf{K}_{2K1B}$> is the symbol for acquaintive knowing-that-one, which is the learned state of mind of being familiar with the essential and unique qualities of a given unique entity or state of affairs.

(5) <$\mathbf{K}_{2K1C}$> is the symbol for appreciative knowing-that-one, which is the learned state of mind of having appreciation for the essential and unique qualities of a given unique entity or state of affairs.

(6) <$\mathbf{K}_{2K2}$> is the symbol for knowing-that, which is the learned ability to perform in a purposeful, well-informed, adequate and warranted way in relation to entities or states of affairs as members of categories.

(7) <$\mathbf{K}_{2K2A}$> is the symbol for instantive knowing-that, which is the learned ability to make an assertion about an entity or relation as a member of a category and to warrant the assertion by referencing the assertion with adequate authority.

(8) <$\mathbf{K}_{2K2B}$> is the symbol for relational knowing-that, which is the learned ability to make an assertion about the relations (or mutual effects) among a set of entities or states of affairs and to warrant the assertion by appropriate evidence or evidential argument.

(9) <$\mathbf{K}_{2K2B}$> is the symbol for criterial knowing-that, which is the learned ability to make an assertion about an entity or relation as a member of a category and to warrant the assertion by normative argument.

(10) <$\mathbf{K}_{2K3}$> is the symbol for knowing-how, which is the learned ability to enact a set of performances deliberately, intelligently, competently, justifiably and with warranted certainty to achieve a desired result.

(11) <$\mathbf{K}_{2K3A}$> is the symbol for protocolic knowing-how, which is the learned ability to execute a single-pathed performance characterized by goal attainment through invariant sequences of activity (inclusive of the five forms of knowing).

(12) <$\mathbf{K}_{2K3B}$> is the symbol for adaptive knowing-how, which is the learned ability to execute a multi-pathed performance smoothly and attain a goal through adjusted sequences of movement.

(13) <$\mathbf{K}_{2K3C}$> is the symbol for creative knowing-how, which is the learned ability to transform elements of a performance into unique forms and to unite disparate ways of realizing goals.

(14) <$\mathbf{K}_{2K4}$> is the symbol for knowing-to, which is the learned ability to exercise conscious intention, will and choice in a rational way that is consistent with a set of freely and rationally chosen and justified criteria.

(15) <$\mathbf{K}_{2K4A}$> is the symbol for rules-based knowing-to, which is the learned ability to exercise conscious intention, will and choice in a rational way that is consistent with a set of freely and rationally chosen and justified rules.

(16) <$\mathbf{K}_{2K4B}$> is the symbol for standards-based knowing-to, which is the learned ability to exercise conscious intention, will and choice in a rational way that is consistent with a set of freely and rationally chosen and justified standards.

Educological Taxonomy of Learning Outcomes

The four kinds of knowing constitute an educological taxonomy of knowing, and the taxonomy provides a structure for intended learning outcomes (George Maccia, 1973b, c). Education (**E**) is defined as teaching and intentional guided studying some content in some setting, and the intended product of education is the achievement by the students of a set of intended learning outcomes. Any intended learning outcome is an educational objective, and all intended learning outcomes are some kind of knowing ($\mathbf{K}_2$).

One of the best known efforts to devise a taxonomy of intended learning outcomes is Bloom's *Taxonomy of Educational Objectives* (Benjamin S. Bloom, 1956). But the attempt was a failure. The categories of educational objectives by B.S. Bloom et al. are a hierarchy, but they are not a taxonomy (even though they are mistakenly named a taxonomy). The categories in the mistakenly named "Bloom's taxonomy" do not constitute a taxonomy because the categories are not well-defined, they are not mutually exclusive of each other when they should be, and they are not complete (or exhaustive).

A hierarchy which qualifies as a taxonomy has a specific structure. Within a taxonomy, a category constitutes a taxon. Taxons are organized in rank from the first rank (the least inclusive category) to some number of rank n (i.e. from 1 to <**n**>), and the largest number of rank <**n**> represents the most inclusive taxon (i.e. the most inclusive category). Every taxon with some rank <**r**>, where <**r**> is less than the total number of ranks <**n**>, is included in a rank of <**r**> plus one (**r** + **1**). Another way to put this is that the taxon in rank <**r**> is a subset of the taxon in rank <**r** + **1**>. Taxons of the same rank are

Figure 1: An Educological Taxonomy of Knowing (K_2)

<table>
<tr><th>Rank</th><th colspan="9">Taxon</th></tr>
<tr><td>5th</td><td colspan="9">Knowing – K_2</td></tr>
<tr><td rowspan="2">4th</td><td>K_{2K1}</td><td colspan="3">K_{2K2}</td><td colspan="3">K_{2K3}</td><td colspan="2">K_{2K4}</td></tr>
<tr><td>Knowing that one</td><td colspan="3">Knowing that</td><td colspan="3">Knowing how</td><td colspan="2">Knowing to</td></tr>
<tr><td rowspan="2">3rd</td><td>K_{2K1A}</td><td>K_{2K2A}</td><td>K_{2K2B}</td><td>K_{2K2C}</td><td>K_{2K3A}</td><td>K_{2K3B}</td><td>K_{2K3C}</td><td>K_{2K4A}</td><td>K_{2K4B}</td></tr>
<tr><td>Appreciative</td><td>Instantive</td><td>Theoretical</td><td>Criterial</td><td>Protocolic</td><td>Adaptive</td><td>Creative</td><td>Rules based</td><td>Standards based</td></tr>
<tr><td rowspan="2">2nd</td><td>K_{2K1B}</td></tr>
<tr><td>Acquaintive</td></tr>
<tr><td rowspan="2">1st</td><td>K_{2K1C}</td></tr>
<tr><td>Recognitive</td></tr>
</table>

mutually exclusive of each other. The number of taxons of rank <**r**> is greater than those of rank <**r**> plus one (**r** + **1**) (Elizabeth Steiner, 1988, p.44).

An example of a well-conceived taxonomy is that of the biologist, Robert Whittaker, who classified living organisms as monera, protista, fungi, plantae and animalia according to the organism's cell type, cell wall, nuclear membrane, body organization and mode of nutrition. A second example is that of the biologist, Carl Woese. He classified living organisms in a three-domain system of bacteria, archaea and eukaryote according to the 16S rRNA gene differences among the three groups of organisms. Both Whittaker's and Woese's classification systems begin with living organisms as the highest rank of taxon. The next highest rank consists of the subcategories of the highest rank of taxon. Whittaker's and Woese's classification systems differ because they use a different set of distinguishing characteristics to establish a taxon.

Let's turn our attention from taxonomies in biology to ones in educology. The taxonomy formed by the categories of kinds of knowing ($\mathbf{K}_{2K}$) begins with the highest rank of taxon, a taxon of rank 5. The most inclusive taxon is that of knowing ($\mathbf{K}_{2}$), which includes all kinds of knowing. The next lower level of the taxonomy, taxons of rank 4, consists of the four kinds of knowing: knowing-that-one ($\mathbf{K}_{2K1}$), knowing-that ($\mathbf{K}_{2K2}$), knowing-how ($\mathbf{K}_{2K3}$) and knowing-to ($\mathbf{K}_{2K4}$). The next lower level of the taxonomy (rank 3) consists of one kind of knowing-that-one (appreciative knowing-that-one < $\mathbf{K}_{2K1C}$>), the three kinds of knowing-that ($\mathbf{K}_{2K2A}$, $\mathbf{K}_{2K2B}$, $\mathbf{K}_{2K2C}$), the three kinds of knowing-how ($\mathbf{K}_{2K3A}$, $\mathbf{K}_{2K3B}$, $\mathbf{K}_{2K3C}$)and the two kinds of knowing-to ($\mathbf{K}_{2K4A}$, $\mathbf{K}_{2K4B}$). The next lower level of the taxonomy (rank 2) consists of one kind of knowing-that-one (acquaintive knowing-that-one <$\mathbf{K}_{2K1B}$>). The lowest level of the taxonomy (rank 1) consists of one kind of knowing-that-one (recognitive knowing-that-one<$\mathbf{K}_{2K1A}$>).

Range of Knowing

No one knows everything. Expertise in designing nuclear power plants does not help much when it comes to knowing how to conduct heart surgery. Expertise as a corporate lawyer doesn't provide much expertise in knowing how to brew beer. Expertise in the history of Great Britain and the British Empire doesn't provide much expertise in how to pilot a freight ship. Within our lifetime, each of us masters a range of knowing, and it is only a very small fraction of the complete range of knowing that is available to learn. A range of knowing is a combination of some selection of kind, level and form of knowing ($\mathbf{K}_{2KLF}$). Any one person's range of knowing is inevitably going to be a small selection from all the possible combinations of kinds, levels and forms of knowing. Every human being is unique, thus every human being's range of knowing is a unique combination of kinds, levels and forms of knowing.

A range of knowing may vary from restricted to extended. It is possible for a person to develop linguistic ($\mathbf{K}_{2F1}$) relational knowing-that ($\mathbf{K}_{2K2B}$) without physical ($\mathbf{K}_{2F5}$) protocolic knowing-how ($\mathbf{K}_{2K3A}$). A person can develop linguistic ($\mathbf{K}_{2F1}$) protocolic knowing-how ($\mathbf{K}_{2K3A}$) without physical ($\mathbf{K}_{2F5}$) adaptive knowing-how ($\mathbf{K}_{2K3B}$). For example, there have been instances of swimming coaches who could not swim themselves, but who were very competent in coaching competitive swimmers. There have been teachers who have taught young people how to play netball, but they have never played the game themselves. There are many people who can identify and describe types of aircraft, but they are not able to fly aircraft. There are people who can describe how an internal combustion engine works, but not have the skills to service or repair an engine. There are people who can service and repair jet engines, but not write manuals about how to repair jet engines.

The range of people's knowing is the same as their degree of understanding. When we say that someone has a good understanding of something, we mean that the person has an extensive range of knowing about that something and can use that range of knowing in making appropriate judgments about some state of affairs relative to some desired outcome. You will hear (and read) in educological discourse that this or that curriculum is intended to develop the student's "deep understanding" of a subject, rather than have only a "surface knowledge" of it. It is a metaphorical way of stating that the intended learning outcome specified by the curriculum is an extensive knowing of some subject matter at the expert conventional level (Level 3 or $\mathbf{K}_{2L3}$), in some specified combination of kinds ($\mathbf{K}_{2K}$) and forms ($\mathbf{K}_{2F}$) of knowing.

An example of an extensive range of knowing (which is also understanding) is that of the medical practitioner, Dr Kennedy, a colorectal surgeon. She can

(1) recognize a fistula in her patient, Susan (exemplifying instantive knowing-that ($\mathbf{K}_{2K2A}$) at Level 3 ($\mathbf{K}_{2L3}$), the expert conventional level of knowing, expressed in the physical form ($\mathbf{K}_{2F5}$) of knowing),

(2) explain to Susan the possible treatments for the fistula (exemplifying relational knowing-that ($\mathbf{K}_{2K2B}$) at the Level 3 ($\mathbf{K}_{2L3}$) expert conventional level of knowing expressed in the linguistic form ($\mathbf{K}_{2F1}$) of knowing),

(3) make plans for conducting surgery to treat the fistula (exemplifying standards-based knowing-to <$\mathbf{K}_{24B}$> and adaptive knowing-how <$\mathbf{K}_{2K3B}$> at the Level 4 <$\mathbf{K}_{2L4}$>

Figure 2A: Range of Knowing as Combinations of Levels, Forms and Kinds of Knowing (K2LFK)

	1	2	3	4	5
a	D-1-a	D-2-a	D-3-a	D-4-a	D-5-a
b	D-1-b	D-2-b	D-3-b	D-4-b	D-5-b
c	D-1-c	D-2-c	D-3-c	D-4-c	D-5-c
d	D-1-d	D-2-d	D-3-d	D-4-d	D-5-d
e	D-1-e	D-2-e	D-3-e	D-4-e	D-5-e
f	D-1-f	D-2-f	D-3-f	D-4-f	D-5-f
g	D-1-g	D-2-g	D-3-g	D-4-g	D-5-g
h	D-1-h	D-2-h	D-3-h	D-4-h	D-5-h
i	D-1-i	D-2-i	D-3-i	D-4-i	D-5-i
j	D-1-j	D-2-j	D-3-j	D-4-j	D-5-j
k	D-1-k	D-2-k	D-3-k	D-4-k	D-5-k
a	C-1-a	C-2-a	C-3-a	C-4-a	C-5-a
b	C-1-b	C-2-b	C-3-b	C-4-b	C-5-b
c	C-1-c	C-2-c	C-3-c	C-4-c	C-5-c
d	C-1-d	C-2-d	C-3-d	C-4-d	C-5-d
e	C-1-e	C-2-e	C-3-e	C-4-e	C-5-e
f	C-1-f	C-2-f	C-3-f	C-4-f	C-5-f
g	C-1-g	C-2-g	C-3-g	C-4-g	C-5-g
h					
i					
j	C-1-j	C-2-j	C-3-j	C-4-j	C-5-j
k	C-1-k	C-2-k	C-3-k	C-4-k	C-5-k

Figure 2B: Range of Knowing as Combinations of Levels, Forms and Kinds of Knowing (K_{2LFK})

	1	2	3	4	5
a	B-1-a	B-2-a	B-3-a	B-4-a	B-5-a
b	B-1-b	B-2-b	B-3-b	B-4-b	B-5-b
c	B-1-c	B-2-c	B-3-c	B-4-c	B-5-c
d	B-1-d	B-2-d	B-3-d	B-4-d	B-5-d
e	B-1-e	B-2-e	B-3-e	B-4-e	B-5-e
f	B-1-f	B-2-f	B-3-f	B-4-f	B-5-f
g	B-1-g	B-2-g	B-3-g	B-4-g	B-5-g
h					
i					
j	B-1-j	B-2-j	B-3-j	B-4-j	B-5-j
k	B-1k	B-2-k	B-3-k	B-4-k	B-5-k
a	A-1-a	A-2-a	A-3-a	A-4-a	A-5-a
b	A-1-b	A-2-b	A-3-b	A-4-b	A-5-b
c	A-1-c	A-2-c	A-3-c	A-4-c	A-5-c
d	A-1-d	A-2-d	A-3-d	A-4-d	A-5-d
e	A-1-e	A-2-e	A-3-e	A-4-e	A-5-e
f	A-1-f	A-2-f	A-3-f	A-4-f	A-5-f
g	A-1-g	A-2-g	A-3-g	A-4-g	A-5-g
h					
i					
j	A-1-j	A-2-j	A-3-j	A-4-j	A-5-j
k	A-1-k	A-2-k	A-3-k	A-4-k	A-5-k

Figure 2C: Range of Knowing as Combinations of Levels, Forms and Kinds of Knowing (K_{2LFK})

Legend

Levels of knowing		
A	=	Level 1 – preconventional level of knowing – K_{2L1}
B	=	Level 2 – conventional intermediate level of knowing – K_{2L2}
C	=	Level 3 – conventional expert level of knowing – K_{2L3}
D	=	Level 4 – postconventional level of knowing – K_{2L4}
Forms of knowing		
1	=	Form of knowing – linguistic – K_{2F1}
2	=	Form of knowing – emotional – K_{2F2}
3	=	Form of knowing – imaginal – K_{2F3}
4	=	Form of knowing – physiological – K_{2F4}
5	=	Form of knowing – physical – K_{2F5}
Kinds of knowing		
a	=	Knowing-that-one – recognitive – K_{2K1A}
b	=	Knowing-that-one – acquaintive – K_{2K1B}
c	=	Knowing-that-one – appreciative – K_{2K1C}
d	=	Knowing-that – instantive – K_{2K2A}
e	=	Knowing-that – relational _ K_{2K2B}
f	=	Knowing-that – criterial – K_{2K2C}
g	=	Knowing-how – protocolic – K_{2K3A}
h	=	Knowing-how – adaptive – K_{2K3B}
i	=	Knowing-how – creative – K_{2K3C}
j	=	Knowing-to – rules-based – K_{2K4A}
k	=	Knowing-to – standards-based – K_{2K4B}

expert postconventional level of knowing expressed in the imaginal <$\mathbf{K}_{2F3}$>, linguistic <$\mathbf{K}_{2F1}$> and physical <$\mathbf{K}_{2F5}$> forms of knowing),

(4) conduct surgery to treat the fistula (exemplifying adaptive knowing-how <$\mathbf{K}_{2K3B}$> at the Level 4 <$\mathbf{K}_{2L4}$> expert postconventional level of knowing expressed in the imaginal <$\mathbf{K}_{2F3}$>, linguistic <$\mathbf{K}_{2F1}$> and physical <$\mathbf{K}_{2F5}$> forms of knowing),

(5) evaluate the results of the surgery on Susan (exemplifying criterial knowing-that <$\mathbf{K}_{2K2C}$> at the Level 3 <$\mathbf{K}_{2L3}$> expert conventional level of knowing expressed in the imaginal <$\mathbf{K}_{2F3}$>, linguistic <$\mathbf{K}_{2F1}$> and K_{2F5} physical <$\mathbf{K}_{2F5}$> forms of knowing).

In addition, Dr Kennedy can teach her skills in colorectal surgery to her resident surgeons (exemplifying adaptive knowing-how <$\mathbf{K}_{2K3B}$>). It would be fair to characterize Dr Kennedy as having an extensive range of knowing about colorectal surgery, and it would also be appropriate to say that Dr Kennedy has an extensive understanding of colorectal surgery. The expressions <*extensive range of knowing*> and <*extensive understanding*> both denote the same cognitive state of mind.

The possible combinations of four levels, five forms and eleven kinds of knowing gives 220 combinations. But adaptive ($\mathbf{K}_{2K3B}$) and creative ($\mathbf{K}_{2K3C}$) knowing-how are only possible at the postconventional level ($\mathbf{K}_{2L4}$) because they can only be achieved through the experience of unguided intentional inquiry and problem solving (**Q**), not through teaching ($\mathbf{T}_{P}$) and intentional guided studying ($\mathbf{S}_{P1}$). Therefore, the actual numbers of combinations are 190 ({3 levels × 5 forms × 9 kinds = 135} + {1 level × 5 forms × 11 kinds = 55}).

Here are some examples of combinations of knowing. John knows how to write the chemical formula for the reactions which result in concrete. This is part of his protocolic knowing-how ($\mathbf{K}_{2K3A}$) at the intermediate conventional level ($\mathbf{K}_{2L2}$) in the linguistic form ($\mathbf{K}_{2F1}$). The table in Figure 2A represents this range of knowing in the cell <**B-1-g**> where <**B**> stands for intermediate conventional level of knowing ($\mathbf{K}_{2L2}$), <**1**> stands for linguistic form of knowing ($\mathbf{K}_{2F1}$) and <**g**> stands for protocolic knowing-how ($\mathbf{K}_{2K3A}$) kind of knowing.

Ethan knows that the formation of concrete is a hydration process in which water combines with the cement material in Portland cements, and he knows that the reaction generates heat, so it is called an exothermic reaction. This is part of his relational knowing-that

($\mathbf{K_{2K2B}}$) at the Level 2 ($\mathbf{K_{2L2}}$) intermediate conventional level of knowing in the linguistic form of knowing ($\mathbf{K_{2F1}}$). The table in Figure 2A represents this range of knowing in the cell <**B-1-e**> where <**B**> stands for Level 2 intermediate conventional knowing ($\mathbf{K_{2L2}}$), <**1**> stands for linguistic form of knowing ($\mathbf{K_{2F1}}$) and <**e**> stands for relational knowing-that ($\mathbf{K_{2K2B}}$) kind of knowing. But Ethan doesn't know how to mix concrete, pour it and finish it. He is not a competent concreter. This gap of protocolic knowing-how ($\mathbf{K_{2K3A}}$) at the Level 2 intermediate conventional level of knowing ($\mathbf{K_{2L2}}$) in the physical form ($\mathbf{K_{2F5}}$) in his range of knowing is represented in the table in Figure 2A by cell <**B-5-g**> where <**B**> stands for Level 2 intermediate conventional knowing ($\mathbf{K_{2L2}}$), <**5**> for physical form of knowing ($\mathbf{K_{2F5}}$) and <**g**> for protocolic knowing-how kind of knowing ($\mathbf{K_{2K3A}}$).

Through a microscope, Stella can recognize a basal cell carcinoma from a skin biopsy, and she can say with confidence, "The cells on this slide contain basal cell carcinoma." This is part of her instantive knowing-that ($\mathbf{K_{2K2A}}$) at the Level 3 expert conventional level of knowing ($\mathbf{K_{2L3}}$) in the linguistic form of knowing ($\mathbf{K_{2F1}}$) and the physical form of knowing ($\mathbf{K_{2F5}}$). The table in Figure 2B represents her range of knowing in the cells <**C-1-d**> and <**C-5-d**>. In <**C-1-d**>, <**C**> stands for Level 3 expert conventional level of knowing ($\mathbf{K_{2L3}}$), <**1**> stands for linguistic form of knowing ($\mathbf{K_{2F1}}$), and <**d**> stands for instantive knowing-that ($\mathbf{K_{2K2A}}$) kind of knowing. In <**C-5-d**>, <**C**> stands for Level 3 expert conventional level of knowing ($\mathbf{K_{2L3}}$), <**5**> stands for physical form of knowing ($\mathbf{K_{2F5}}$), and <**d**> stands for instantive knowing-that ($\mathbf{K_{2K2A}}$) kind of knowing. Stella knows to prepare a report and have it sent to the referring skin specialist who sent in the biopsy for analysis. This is part of her Level 3 expert conventional level of knowing ($\mathbf{K_{2L3}}$), her rules-based knowing-to ($\mathbf{K_{2K4A}}$) and her linguistic form of knowing ($\mathbf{K_{2F1}}$). The table in Figure 2B represents her range of knowing in the cell <**C-1-j**>, where <**C**> stands for Level 3 expert conventional level of knowing ($\mathbf{K_{2L3}}$), <**1**> for linguistic form of knowing ($\mathbf{K_{2F1}}$) and <**j**> for rules-based knowing-to ($\mathbf{K_{2K4A}}$) kind of knowing.

The tables in Figures 2A and 2B, with the legend in Figure 2C, provide a system for classifying and for articulating intended learning outcomes (**ILO**s). An intended learning outcome (**ILO**) can be specified (1) by nominating what kind of knowing is intended to be achieved at what level and in which form and (2) by describing, in detail, exemplifications of the particular range of knowing necessarily included in the intended learning outcome (**ILO**). These specifications of intended learning outcomes (**ILO**s) follow the educological taxonomy of knowing.

The distinction of range of knowing (**K_{2KLF}**) can be added to the list of well-defined terms in descriptive educological theory. <**K_{2KLF}**> is the symbol for a range of knowing, which is a combination of some kind of knowing (**K_{2K}**), some level of knowing (**K_{2L}**) and some form of knowing (**K_{2F}**).

Five Conceptions of the Term <*Learning*>

Because the intention of both teacher (**T**) and student (**S**) in an educational transaction (**E**) is that the student learns intentionally under guidance (**L_1**) some range of knowing (**K_{2KLF}**), it is important to ask, "What is learning?" Consider the following sentences.

(1) Through completing the study activities which her teacher provided for her over the year, Karen was gradually <**learning**> to read.

(2) It was clear that the Supreme Court Justice had achieved an extensive <**learning**> of the law and its implications.

In the first sentence, the term <*learning*> can be substituted with the term <*coming to know*>, and the meaning of the sentence is not changed.

(1) Through completing the study activities which her teacher provided for her over the year, Karen was gradually <**coming to know**> [how] to read.

So, one denotation of the term <*learning*> is the process of coming to know (denoted by <**L**>).

In the second sentence, the term <*learning*> can be substituted with the term <*range of knowing*>, and the meaning of the sentence is not changed.

(2) It was clear that the Supreme Court Justice had achieved an extensive <**range of knowing**> of the law and its implications.

So, a second denotation of the term <*learning*> is the product of coming to know, viz. a range of knowing (**K_{2KLF}**).

The two sentences demonstrate that we English speakers use the term <*learning*> is ambiguously. We use the term to denote both a process and a product. We sometimes use the term <*learning*> to denote the process of coming to know. We sometimes use the term <*learning*> to denote the product that is the outcome of the process, which is some range of knowing. The distinction between learning as a process and learning as a product is the distinction between travelling on a path to a destination and being at the destination itself.

The learning process (**L**) is the resultant of education (**E**), when the teaching ($\mathbf{T_P}$) and intentional guided studying ($\mathbf{S_{P1}}$) are effective. The variant of the learning process (**L**) that is produced from effective education ($\mathbf{E_E}$) is intentional guided (learning$_1$ <$\mathbf{L_1}$>). A boy wants to learn (**L**) how to iron his own clothes. He asks his father to show him how to iron. His father shows him how to fill the steam iron with distilled water, how to turn the power on, how to set the iron to the correct setting for different types of fabrics. The father starts with shirts. He shows his son how to iron the collar, the yoke, the left front panel, the back, the right front panel and the sleeves, then hang the finished shirt on a hanger with the collar buttoned. The father turns off the iron, empties the water from the iron, sets the iron to its coolest setting and tells the boy that it's his turn to iron a shirt. The father watches as the boy proceeds to iron. The boy fills the iron with distilled water. He sets the iron to the "cotton" setting to match the fabric of the shirt. He turns on the power to the iron. He waits for the iron to heat to the optimal temperature. He proceeds to iron the shirt – first the collar, then the yolk, the left panel, back panel, right panel and finally the sleeves. He places the shirt on a hanger and buttons the collar. The father is satisfied with the boy's ironing skills and tells the boy to proceed to iron the six shirts in the basket, put them on hangers and put them in the closet. This scenario is an example of effective teaching ($\mathbf{T_{PE}}$) and effective intentional guided studying ($\mathbf{S_{PIE}}$), producing intentional guided learning (learning$_1$ <$\mathbf{L_1}$>). The learning process in education is always guided intentional learning ($\mathbf{L_1}$). The product of the intentional guided learning ($\mathbf{L_1}$) is the boy's range of knowing ($\mathbf{K_{2KLF}}$) how to iron shirts efficiently. The relationship of education (**E**), learning$_1$ ($\mathbf{L_1}$) and a range of knowing ($\mathbf{K_2}$) as the product of learning$_1$ ($\mathbf{L_1}$) is expressed in set theory notation in the following sentences.

(1) $\mathbf{E = T \cup S \cup C \cup X}$

(2) $\mathbf{E \supset E_I}$

(3) $\mathbf{E} \supset \mathbf{E}_E$
(4) $\mathbf{E}_E \rightarrow \mathbf{L}_1$
(5) $\mathbf{L}_1 \rightarrow \mathbf{K}_2$
(6) $\mathbf{L}_1 \neq \mathbf{K}_2$

The first statement <$\mathbf{E} = \mathbf{T} \cup \mathbf{S} \cup \mathbf{C} \cup \mathbf{X}$> reads in ordinary English that the essential properties of education (**E**) consist of (=) the union of ($\cup$) the essential properties of teacher (**T**), student (**S**), content (**C**) and context (**X**).

The second statement <$\mathbf{E} \supset \mathbf{E}_I$> reads in ordinary English that education (**E**) has all the elements of, but more elements than ($\supset$), the essential elements of ineffective education ($\mathbf{E}_I$).

The third statement <$\mathbf{E} \supset \mathbf{E}_E$> reads in ordinary English that education (**E**) has all the elements of, but more elements than ($\supset$), the essential elements of effective education ($\mathbf{E}_E$).

The fourth statement <$\mathbf{E}_E \rightarrow \mathbf{L}_1$> reads in ordinary English that effective education ($\mathbf{E}_E$) is the set of controlling conditions for ($\rightarrow$) the resultant process of intentional guided (conduced) learning ($\mathbf{L}_1$).

The fifth statement <$\mathbf{L}_1 \rightarrow \mathbf{K}_2$> reads in ordinary English that the process of intentional guided (conduced) learning ($\mathbf{L}_1$) is the set of controlling conditions for the resultant product of a range of knowing ($\mathbf{K}_2$).

The sixth statement <$\mathbf{L}_1 \neq \mathbf{K}_2$> reads in ordinary English that the process of intentional guided (conduced) learning ($\mathbf{L}_1$) is not the same as a range of knowing <$\mathbf{K}_2$>.

In contrast to intentional guided (conduced) learning ($\mathbf{L}_1$), discovery learning (learning$_2$ <$\mathbf{L}_2$>) is intentional and unguided. A boy is curious about what an electric shock feels like. He unscrews a globe from a lamp, puts his finger in the socket and turns on the lamp. He feels the heat, the jolt of muscle contractions and the pain from the electrical current. He intentionally comes to know without guidance the feeling of an electrical current. A team of medical researchers investigates the possibility of preventing cervical cancer with a vaccine, develops a number of vaccines, trials them and finds that one of the vaccines works in 99.9% of cases with minimal harmful side effects. The team intentionally comes to know without guidance how to prevent cervical cancer. A group of structural engineers develops a modular system of steel frames and concrete panels for construction of schools based on a one meter by one meter steel frame module. They test the modular construction system for its soundness and conduct a cost effective analysis to determine its financial feasibility. Their tests demonstrate that the system is structurally sound, flexible in design, fast to construct and economical to build compared to other systems. The team intentionally comes to know without guidance how to use a system to construct buildings quickly and economically. These three scenarios are examples of intentional and unguided (discovery) learning (learning$_2$ <$\mathbf{L}_2$>) achieved from intentional, unguided, self-directed inquiry and problem solving (**Q**).

In addition to conduced learning ($\mathbf{L}_1$) and discovery learning ($\mathbf{L}_2$), there is compelled learning (learning$_3$ <$\mathbf{L}_3$>). It is unintentional and guided. It is the learning which comes from socialization, enculturation and indoctrination. Someone intentionally acts in ways to guide a second party to learn something, and the second party does not undertake any intentional guided study to learn the something. Children watch TV, see the advertisements for a new toy and beg their parents to buy the toy for them. The advertisers are guiding the learning of the children, and they also are motivating the children to behave in ways desired by the advertisers. The children do not undertake any intentional guided study to achieve the advertisers' intended learning outcomes. The mother of a young girl, aged 5, tells her to pick up her toys and get ready for dinner. The girl says that she does not want to pick up her toys. The mother has her daughter go to the punishing stool and sit on it for ten minutes. Then she tells her daughter to gather up her toys and wash her hands. The daughter feels both angry and chastened, but she does as she is told. The daughter learns that there are undesirable consequences for disobeying her mother. A young man grows up in Saudi Arabia and comes to believe that it is the natural order of things that his sisters should do as he tells them to do, that his sisters may not leave the house without his company or that of his father's or uncle's, that he may marry up to four wives, provided that he can afford them. He has learned his beliefs and his attitudes from exposure to his social and cultural environment. These scenarios are all examples of unintentional and guided (compelled) learning (learning$_3$ <$\mathbf{L}_3$>).

A fourth variant of learning, accidental learning (learning$_4$ <$\mathbf{L}_4$>) is unintentional and unguided. It is learning which comes from happenstance and chance occurrences. A 21-year-old woman is driving her car and texting on her phone at the same time. Her inattention to her driving leads her to drift off the road and into a ditch. She survives the crash, although terribly injured. She unintentionally comes to know from this experience that it is very dangerous to drive and text at the same time. A young man dives into a muddy river, and his head strikes a submerged tree trunk. The impact breaks his neck. He survives the injury, but he is left a quadriplegic. He unintentionally comes to know that diving into muddy water without first checking for hazards is very dangerous. Alexander Fleming (1881-1955) went on holiday in August of 1928. When he returned to his laboratory (3 September 1928), he found that one of his cultures of staphylococci had been destroyed by a mold. Thus, by accident, he unintentionally came to know about the bacteria killing properties of Penicillium notatum, from which the antibiotic, penicillin was developed for treatment of infections. These scenarios are all examples of unintentional and unguided learning (learning$_4$ <$\mathbf{L_4}$>).

Learning as product (learning$_5$ <$\mathbf{L_5}$>) is the resultant of the process of learning (**L**). It is knowing ($\mathbf{K_2}$). Examples of learning$_5$ ($\mathbf{L_5}$), is a boy knowing how to multiply any number by any number, a girl knowing how to skip rope, a man knowing how to operate a large piece of machinery such as a front end loader, a woman knowing how to speak, read and write Urdu, a surgeon knowing how to replace a knee. Learning$_5$ ($\mathbf{L_5}$) is any range of knowing ($\mathbf{K_{2KLF}}$).

The relationships of learning as process to the processes of learning$_1$, learning$_2$, learning$_3$ and learning$_4$, and the relationship of learning as process to learning as product, or learning$_5$, is expressed in set theory notation in the following statements.

(1) $\mathbf{L = \{L_1 \cup L_2 \cup L_3 \cup L_4\}}$

(2) $\mathbf{L \rightarrow L_5}$

(3) $\mathbf{L_5 = K_2 = K_{2KLF}}$

The first statement <$\mathbf{L = \{ L_1 \cup L_2 \cup L_3 \cup L_4\}}$> in ordinary English reads that the essential elements of learning as process (**L**) consist of the union of ($\cup$) the essential elements of conduced learning ($\mathbf{L_1}$), discovery learning ($\mathbf{L_2}$), compelled learning ($\mathbf{L_3}$) and accidental learning ($\mathbf{L_4}$).

The second statement <$\mathbf{L \rightarrow L_5}$> in ordinary English reads that the process of learning (**L**) is the set of controlling conditions for ($\rightarrow$) the product of learning ($\mathbf{L_5}$).

The third statement <$\mathbf{L_5 = K_2 = K_{2KLF}}$> in ordinary English reads that the product of learning, or learning as product ($\mathbf{L_5}$), is the same as (=) knowing ($\mathbf{K_2}$), and knowing ($\mathbf{K_2}$) is the same as (=) a range of knowing as some combination of kind, level and form of knowing ($\mathbf{K_{2KLF}}$).

The distinctions of the different denotations of the term <*learning*> ($\mathbf{L}$, $\mathbf{L_1}$, $\mathbf{L_2}$, $\mathbf{L_3}$, $\mathbf{L_4}$, $\mathbf{L_5}$) can be added to the list of well-defined terms in descriptive educological theory.

(1) <**L**> is the symbol for learning as process, which is the process of coming to know by any means.

(2) <$\mathbf{L_1}$> is the symbol for conduced learning (intentional guided learning), which is the process of coming to know from participating as a student (**S**) in education (**E**).

(3) <$\mathbf{L_2}$> is the symbol for discovery learning (intentional unguided learning), which is the process of coming to know from conducting intentional unguided inquiry (**Q**) either as trial and error or systematic research.

(4) <$\mathbf{L_3}$> is the symbol for compelled learning (unintentional guided learning), which is the process of coming to know from socialization, enculturation and indoctrination.

(5) <$\mathbf{L_4}$> is the symbol for accidental learning (unintentional unguided learning), which is the process of coming to know from haphazard circumstances, including misadventure and serendipity.

(6) <$\mathbf{L_5}$> is the symbol for the product of the process of learning, or learning as product, which is the knowing ($\mathbf{K_2}$) that is the consequent of having come to know.

Explication of the Concept of the Term <*Context*>

From our analysis and evaluation of the five conceptions of the term *education*, we determined that the most suitable conception of the term *education* for the purposes of educological discourse, inquiry and intentional guided study is expressed in the definition,

E = T U S U C U X

This definition of the term <*education*> as **E** became the first well-defined term in our development of descriptive educological theory. We have extended descriptive educological theory by having explicated key terms in the definition of education, viz. the terms <*teacher*> (**T**), <*student*> (**S**), <*content*> (**C**) and the related terms <*teaching*> ($\mathbf{T_P}$), <*studying*> ($\mathbf{S_{P1}}$), <*knowledge*> ($\mathbf{K_1}$), <*knowing*> ($\mathbf{K_2}$) and <*learning*> (**L**).

Let's now turn our attention to the phenomena denoted by the term <*context*> (represented by the symbol <**X**> in the definition of education <**E**>). The symbol <**X**> denotes the context in which teaching ($\mathbf{T}_{P}$) and intentional guided studying ($\mathbf{S}_{P1}$) take place. The context (**X**) includes the physical setting ($\mathbf{X}_{P}$), the social setting ($\mathbf{X}_{S}$) and the cultural setting ($\mathbf{X}_{C}$) for education (**E**).

The physical context ($\mathbf{X}_{P}$) is the observable, existential place in which teaching ($\mathbf{T}_{P}$) and intentional guided studying ($\mathbf{S}_{P1}$) take place. The physical context ($\mathbf{X}_{P}$) is at times the family kitchen, the laundry, the garage, the footpath, the playground, the park, a primary school classroom, a middle school classroom, a university lecture hall, a library, a laboratory, a garden, a gymnasium, a swimming pool, a tennis court, etc. It is any physical place in which someone playing the role of teacher (**T**) might provide opportunities, guidance and help to someone else playing the role of student (**S**) to study ($\mathbf{S}_{P1}$) intentionally under guidance some content (**C**) with a view that the student (**S**) learns$_1$ ($\mathbf{L}_1$) some new range of knowing ($\mathbf{K}_{2KLF}$).

The social context ($\mathbf{X}_{S}$) is the society in which the teachers (**T**) teach ($\mathbf{T}_{P}$) and students (**S**) study intentionally under guidance ($\mathbf{S}_{P1}$) some content (**C**) with a view in mind that the students (**S**) intentionally learn under guidance (learn$_1$ <$\mathbf{L}_1$>) some new range of knowing ($\mathbf{K}_{2KLF}$). A society consists of a population of people, the roles that people in the population assume and the groups that people form. Examples of roles are father, mother, brother, sister, preacher, priest, rabbi, mullah, lawyer, teacher, tutor, coach, counselor, professor, medical doctor, judge, policeman or policewoman, chef, waiter, employer, employee, politician, president, governor, prime minister, musician, poet, artist, entertainer, actor, soldier, etc. Example of social groups are nuclear families, extended families, clans, tribes, friendship groups, neighbors, peer groups, tennis clubs, yacht clubs, baseball clubs, soccer clubs, church congregations, upper social class, lower social class, high caste, low caste, legislative assemblies, parliaments, courts, prisons, hamlets, villages, cities, counties, states, provinces, nation-states, militias, armies, etc.

The cultural context ($\mathbf{X}_{C}$) is, for example, Canadian culture, Nigerian culture, French culture, Australian culture, etc. It is the set of norms, traditions, values, customs and the like to which members of a society adhere or conform. It is the way of life (**WoL**) of a set of people. The elements of a cultural context ($\mathbf{X}_{C}$) include the following:

(1) a sense of common identity and a sense of ethnocentrism which leads members of the community to think of their ways as the normal, correct ones, and the ways of other cultures as strange and incorrect,
(2) a communication system including signed and/or spoken (and sometimes, but not always, written language) with characteristic forms of gestures, facial expressions, postures and physical distance between communicators,
(3) a system of kinship with rules that designate paternal and maternal lineage, relationships of grandparents, parents, children, grandchildren, aunts, uncles, cousins, who can, must and must not marry, etc.,
(4) a system of social organization and association in which members receive assignment of and assume different roles, gather together (or avoid gathering together) along the lines of kinship, age, status, wealth, gender, friendship, etc.,
(5) a system of political organization which establishes leadership, rules of accession to leadership, relations of superiors and subordinates, authority to make behaviors and/or states of affairs mandatory, optional or prohibited, and power (i.e. the ways and means) to enforce rules of obligation, permission and prohibition,
(6) a system of production and distribution of goods and services which provides shelter and subsistence (and, but not always, surpluses),
(7) a system of sexual identity, sexual behavior accepted as normal (or abnormal) and roles assigned according to gender,
(8) a system of maintaining spatial distances and territoriality, allocation, tenure and use of land and property, and rules of inheritance of property,
(9) a system of time keeping and temporality, including the passage of time and the prediction of events (e.g. seasons, solstice, equinox, moon phases, tides),
(10) a system of recreation and play, including traditional games, age related games and games related to social groups, and allocation of times and places for play,
(11) a system of defense and protection, including selection,

organization and training, provision of equipment and shelter and tactics and strategies used in the protection of people, property and resources,

(12) a system of worship and religion, including allocation of sacred sights and places for worship, beliefs, rituals and ceremonies of gratitude, forgiveness, redemption, placation, celebration, sacrifice, rebirth, divine intervention, etc.,

(13) a system of tools and techniques including ways and means of utilization of energy from animals, wind, water, sunlight, gravity and minerals,

(14) a system of caring for and nurturing of children, including providing for their teaching, studying and learning,

(15) a system of rules, customs and conventions (usually unwritten and not explicitly stated nor justified) for moral, right and correct (and immoral, wrong and incorrect) conduct, behavior, emotions and desires,

(16) a system of rituals and ceremonies to mark important occasions in life such as birth, sexual maturity, marriage and death,

(17) a system of laws, regulations, resolution of conflicts, judgments of right and wrong behavior, punishments for wrong doing, enforcement of laws and regulations,

(18) a system of art and artistic expression, including instrumental music, vocalized music, dance, stories, plays, costumes, sculptures, paintings, etc.,

(19) a system for accumulating, recording, organizing and accessing funds of knowledge important to the culture,

(20) a system of travel and transport,

(21) a system for the exchange of goods and services, sometimes based on mutual favors and obligations, sometimes based on a barter system and sometimes based on some medium of exchange,

(22) a system for diagnosing, explaining and dealing with illnesses, injuries and childbirth,

(23) a range of knowing which individuals typically develop (and must develop) to function competently within their culture.

The possible relationships between context (**X**) and the other elements of education (teacher, student, content <**T**, **S**, **C**>) are ones of mutual effect. The context (**X**) in which education (**E**) functions can have constructive, sustaining, reconstructive and destructive effects on teachers, students and content (**T**, **S**, **C**). And teachers, students and content (**T**, **S**, **C**) can have constructive, sustaining, reconstructive and destructive effects on the physical, social and cultural setting, or context <**X**>). These relationships are expressed in the following sentences.

(1) **X → {T, S, C}**

(2) **{T, S, C} → X**

The first statement <**X → {T, S, C}**> in ordinary English reads that the context (**X**) for education (**E**) is the set of controlling conditions for (→) the resultant three other elements of teachers, students and content (**T**, **S**, **C**) in education (**E**).

The second statement <**{T, S, C} → X**> in ordinary English reads that the three elements of teachers, students and content (**T**, **S**, **C**) in education (**E**) is the set of controlling conditions for the resultant of the context (**X**) for education (**E**).

An example of a relationship of construction between context (**X**) and teachers, students and content (**T**, **S**, **C**), in which

X → {T, S, C}

is that of the introduction of computer studies and the use of personal computers in schools. As personal computers were developed and released onto the market in the mid-1970s, schools in the USA and elsewhere began to acquire them. With the introduction of personal computers into schools, a new curriculum was developed which included programming skills, use of word processing, spread sheets and database applications. With the innovation of the Transmission Control Protocol and Internet Protocol (TCP/IP) in the early 1980's and the creation of the World Wide Web in 1990, students were introduced to ways of conducting inquiry by searching for information on the Web. So, as a gradual process over a period of 10 to 15 years, students were introduced to procedures for writing basic programs, then to using applications (word processing, spread sheets, databases, computer assisted design, graphics production & editing, photos & photo editing, videos & video editing, audio recording, editing & production), then to using TCP/IP as a means of transmitting data, then to using the Web as a source of information and a tool for inquiry. As innovators, such as the computer scientists and engineers, Robert

Kahn, Vinton Cerf and Tim Bernes-Lee, among many others, and entrepreneurs extended the capabilities and availability of personal computers, schools bought personal computers and bought connectivity services with the World Wide Web (www). In response to innovations in personal computers and worldwide connectivity (the physical, social and cultural context <**X**>), a whole new curriculum for education (**E**) in schools was constructed (a relationship of <**X** → **{T, S, C}**>.

An example of a relationship of construction between context (**X**) and the elements of teachers, students and content (**T**, **S**, **C**) of education (**E**) in which

{T, S, C} → X

is that of the establishment of missionary schools in British East Africa (what is now Kenya, Uganda and Tanzania) during the late 1800s and early 1900s. The schools introduced written language to societies and cultures which previously had not had written language. With the introduction of written language through teachers, students and content (**T**, **S**, **C**) and the development of reading and writing by the students, the traditional societies and cultures of East Africa (the context, **X**) were dramatically transformed by way of this new means of communication.

An example of a relationship of maintenance between context (**X**) and the elements of teachers, students and content (**T**, **S**, **C**) of education (**E**) in which

X → {T, S, C}

is that of the requirements for compulsory schooling. Virtually every country in the world has laws and regulations which require children of a specified age range to attend school. The number of school days per year is legally prescribed. For example, in the state of Queensland in Australia, children are required to attend school from ages 6 years and 6 months to 16 years, and the number of prescribed school days in the year is 193 days. In California in the USA, the compulsory school age is 6 to 18 years, and there is an average of 180 prescribed school days in the year. In France, 98% of children start school at age 3, but the compulsory school age is from 6 to 16 years. The average prescribed days of school in France in a year is 162. Societies supporting their lawmakers to provide the resources and the regulations to sustain provision of school education (**E**) for children of the prescribed age for the specified number of days in the year is clearly an example of a maintenance relationship in which context (**X**) is the set of controlling conditions for the resultant of the elements of teachers, students and content (**T**, **S**, **C**) of education (**E**).

An example of a relationship of maintenance between the elements of teachers, students and content (**T**, **S**, **C**) of education (**E**) and the element of context (**X**) of education (**E**) in which

$$\{\mathbf{T}, \mathbf{S}, \mathbf{C}\} \rightarrow \mathbf{X}$$

is that of the lessons about citizenship and government provided in primary, middle and high schools in the USA. These lessons function to develop and maintain in each generation of students the same range of knowing, set of values and conceptual perspectives about the principles, structures and functions of American government and the rights and responsibilities of citizens of the USA. The lessons are provided with the intention that students achieve an understanding, acceptance and appreciation of the American system of representative democracy, the levels of government (municipal, county, state, federal), the division of responsibilities and powers between states and the federal government, the separation of powers in the three branches of government (legislative, judiciary, executive) and the rights guaranteed to citizens in the Bill of Rights (right of assembly, right of free speech, freedom to worship, etc.) The lessons perpetuate myths about the foresight of the Founding Fathers, the virtue of George Washington, the intelligence of Thomas Jefferson, the wisdom of Benjamin Franklin and the honesty of Abraham Lincoln. By means of these lessons, the elements of teachers, students and content (**T**, **S**, **C**) maintain and perpetuate a common set of values, attitudes and beliefs in the wider community (the physical, social and cultural context<**X**>).

An example of a relationship of reconstruction between the element of context (**X**) and the elements of teachers, students and content (**T**, **S**, **C**) in education (**E**) in which

$$\mathbf{X} \rightarrow \{\mathbf{T}, \mathbf{S}, \mathbf{C}\}$$

is that of the replacement of the phlogiston theory of combustion with the oxidation theory of combustion in the curriculum of schools and universities. The German alchemist, Johann Joachim Becher (1635-1682), proposed the idea that all things which burn contain a substance (phlogiston) which is released when something burns (the substance dephlogisticates). Becher's proposition was further explicated by the German chemist, Georg Erst Stahl (1659-1734). The phlogiston theory of combustion was generally accepted among chemists until it was challenged by the work of the French nobleman and chemist, Antoine-Laurent de Lavoisier (1743-1794). He conducted experiments (1772-74) with the burning of various substances (phosphorus, sulfur) and the slow heating of mercury, tin and lead in closed systems which allowed no entry or escape of additional air. He found that in all cases, the total mass of air and burnt substances remained the same, even though the burnt and/or heated substances changed in mass and the volume of air was reduced. He proposed that, instead of phlogiston being released from burning substances, a portion of the air was combining with the burning substances, and he gave the name <*oxygen*> to the relevant portion of air. Lavoisier's experiments were replicated and extended by other chemists, and eventually the oxidation theory of combustion replaced the phlogiston theory. The oxidation theory of combustion became a standard explanation of combustion in chemical treatises and textbooks. The context (**X**) created by Lavoisier and his fellow chemists reconstructed the content of chemistry taught in school and university education (**T**, **S**, **C**).

An example of a relationship of reconstruction between the elements of teachers, students and content (**T**, **S**, **C**) in education (**E**) and the element of context (**X**) in which

$$\{T, S, C\} \rightarrow X$$

is that of the reconstruction of West Germany's society and culture under Allied occupation after the Second World War through a reconstruction of the school system and curriculum. By the end of the war, many German schools had been destroyed or had ceased to function because of disruptions from bombings, combat and economic collapse. The Nazi curriculum had featured development of physical fitness, devotion to the Führer, commitment to National Socialism, beliefs in racial superiority and purification, service to the state and denunciation of criticism of the Nazi party and/or the Führer as treason. The British and American occupation forces undertook to achieve denazification of German society and culture through a reconstruction of German schools and curriculum. The curriculum was extended to include a broad range of subjects. Prohibitions and bans were placed on Nazi symbols (the swastika, flags, monuments), photographs, posters and gestures (especially, the <*Hitlergruß*>, translated into English as <the Hitler greeting> and also called by the Nazi Party <*deutscher Gruß*>, translated into English as <the German greeting>). Free and open speech, political criticism and critical thinking were taught, studied and practiced. The principles, structures and functions of representative liberal democracy, free and contested elections and open political debate were taught, studied and practiced. The doctrines of racial superiority and purity were debunked and replaced with the doctrines of equality, liberty and justice for all regardless of race, religion, ethnic origins and mental and physical capabilities (the policy of racial improvement under the Nazis included extermination, not only of Jews, but also of all dark-skinned people, dwarves, gypsies and those born with physical and mental disabilities). Through the work of the schools and other agencies, postwar West Germany developed into a liberal democratic society and culture, thus exemplifying the relationship of <**{T, S, C} → X**>.

An example of a destructive relationship between the element of context (**X**) and the elements of teachers, students and content (**T**, **S**, **C**) in which

X → {T, S, C}

is that of the Taliban's policy regarding the education of women in Afghanistan. The Taliban held power over perhaps three-fourths of Afghanistan from 1996 to 2001. During that time, they applied their interpretation of Sharia Law, and they placed an array of requirements and prohibitions upon women. One of the prohibitions was that females be permitted to study only the Qur'an, and only to the age of 8. Whatever school education was provided for women before the ascendency of the Taliban was banned. The physical, social and cultural context (**X**) established by the Taliban, and especially their interpretation of Sharia Law, destroyed school education (**E**) for Afghani girls and women.

An example of a destructive relationship between the elements of teachers, students and content (**T**, **S**, **C**) and the element of context (**X**) in which

{T, S, C} → X

is that of the Bureau of Indian Affairs (BIA) schools in the USA. In the late 1800s and early 1900s, the BIA established several boarding schools for first nation students. The stated intention of the educational programs in these schools was to erase any vestiges of first nation culture among the students, to provide the students with skills in manual trades and to achieve assimilation of the students into white American culture as household servants and manual laborers. Children were forcibly removed from their homes and placed in distant boarding schools. The schools required the students to adopt English Christian names, to use only the English language, to dress in white American fashion, to wear their hair in the length and fashion of white American haircuts and to learn and practice the Christian religion as understood and practiced by white Americans.

The explication of context (**X**, **X_P**, **X_S** and **X_C**) as an element of education (**E**) can be added to the list of well-defined terms in descriptive educological theory.

(1) <**X**> is the symbol for the context in which teachers and students transact with content; the context includes the physical, social and cultural context.
(2) <**X_P**> is the symbol for the physical context in which teachers and students transact with content, for example, homes, street corners, playing fields, classrooms, lecture halls, libraries, laboratories, gymnasiums, etc.
(3) <**X_S**> is the symbol for the social context in which teachers and students transact with content, for example, families, peer groups, church groups, work mates, schools, academies, institutes, universities, the wider community, the wider society.
(4) <**X_C**> is the symbol for the cultural context in which teachers and students transact with content, for example, French culture, German culture, Spanish culture, Indonesian culture, etc.

Explication of the Concept of the Term <*Mind*>

We have previously characterized knowing (**K_2**) as a cognitive state of mind. There are obviously some mutual effects between education (**E**) and mind (**M**). Any extension of one's range of knowing (**K_2**) is an extension of one's mind (**M**). This leads to the question of "What is mind?" Let's rephrase the question so that it reads, "When we use the term <*mind*>, what are we denoting with the term?" Consider the following sentences in which the term <*mind*> is used.

(1) Keep in <**mind**> the possibility of mudslides, washed out bridges and fallen trees during tropical cyclones.
(2) I have changed my <**mind**> about going to Germany.
(3) You need to use your <**mind**> to solve this puzzle.

(4) Mr Rose was gradually losing his <**mind**> because of the effects of an inoperable brain tumor.
(5) Travel improves the <**mind**>.
(6) What Mary said about George has been troubling my <**mind**>.
(7) Put that thought right out of your <**mind**>.
(8) That story calls to <**mind**> my grandmother's 80th birthday.
(9) Keep in <**mind**> that a trip to Darwin, Australia during January is in the cyclone season.

Now let's ask and answer, "What terms can we substitute for the term <*mind*> in the sentence, and not change the meaning of the sentence?"

In the first sentence, the term <*mind*> can be substituted by the term <*anticipation*>, and the sentence reads,

(1) Keep in <**anticipation**> the possibility of mudslides, washed out bridges and fallen trees during tropical cyclones.

The substitution of the term <*anticipation*> for the term <*mind*> does not change the meaning of the sentence. In this sentence, the term <*mind*> is denoting a psychic state of alertness, caution, expectation.

In the second sentence, the term <*mind*> can be substituted by the term <*decision*>, and the sentence reads,

(2) I have changed my <**decision**> about going to Germany.

The substitution of the term <*decision*> for the term <*mind*> does not change the meaning of the sentence. In this second sentence, the term <*mind*> is denoting choice, resolution, commitment, determination, will.

In the third sentence, the term <*mind*> can be substituted by the term <*reasoning*>, and the sentence reads,

(3) You need to use your <**reasoning**> to solve this puzzle.

The substitution of the term <*reasoning*> for the term <*mind*> does not change the meaning of the sentence. In this third sentence, the term <*mind*> is denoting problem solving, hypothesis testing, investigative skills, rational inquiry.

In the fourth sentence, the term <*mind*> can be substituted by the set of terms <*memory, cognitive function* and *rationality*>, and the sentence reads,

(4) Mr. Rose was gradually losing his <**memory, cognitive function and rationality**> because of the effects of an

inoperable brain tumor.

The substitution of the set of terms <*memory, cognitive function* and *rationality*> does not change the meaning of the sentence. In this third sentence, the term <*mind*> is denoting a complex of functions (remembering, knowing, reasoning).

In the fifth sentence, the term <*mind*> can be substituted by the set of terms <*range of knowing and understanding*>, and the sentence reads,

(5) Travel improves the <**range of knowing and understanding**>.

The substitution of the set of terms <*range of knowing and understanding*> for the term <*mind*> does not change the meaning of the sentence. In this fifth sentence, the term <*mind*> is denoting cognitive function, enlightenment, knowledgeability, competence, expertise.

In the sixth sentence, the term <*mind*> can be substituted by the term <*emotional equilibrium*>, and the sentence reads,

(6) What Mary said about George has been troubling my <**emotional equilibrium**>.

The substitution of the term <*emotional equilibrium*> for the term <*mind*> does not change the meaning of the sentence. In this sixth sentence, the term <*mind*> is denoting an emotional state of being upset, puzzled, ill at ease, anxious, fraught, confused, concerned, worried.

In the seventh sentence, the term <*mind*> can be substituted by the set of terms <*memory and reasoning*> and the sentence reads,

(7) Put that thought right out of your <**memory and reasoning**>.

The substitution of the set of terms <*memory and reasoning*> for the term <*mind*> does not change the meaning of the sentence. In this seventh sentence, the term <*mind*> is denoting remembering and inferring conclusions from a set of premises.

In the eighth sentence, the term <*mind*> can be substituted by the term <*memory*>, and the sentence reads,

(8) That story calls to <**memory**> my grandmother's 80th birthday.

The substitution of the term <*memory*> for the term <*mind*> does not change the meaning of the sentence. In this eighth sentence, the term <*mind*> is denoting remembering events, sounds, sights, people, personalities.

In the ninth sentence, the term <*mind*> can be substituted by the term <*awareness*>, and the sentence reads,

(9) Keep in <**awareness**> that a trip to Darwin, Australia during January is in the cyclone season.

The substitution of the term <*awareness*> for the term <*mind*> does not change the meaning of the sentence. In this ninth sentence, the term <*mind*> is denoting consciousness, alertness, attention, discernment.

As term substitutions for the term <*mind*>, we've used the words, <*anticipation, alertness, caution, expectation, decision, choice, resolution, commitment, determination, will, reasoning, problem solving, hypothesis testing, investigative skills, rational inquiry, memory, cognitive function, rationality, range of knowing, understanding, enlightenment, knowledgeability, competence, expertise, emotional equilibrium, upset, puzzled, ill at ease, anxious, fraught, confused, remembering, awareness, consciousness, alertness, attention, discernment*>.

So, an initial answer to the question, "What is mind?" is that the connotative meaning of the term <*mind*> is the set of words which have been used as substitutions for the term <*mind*>. The denotative meaning of the term <*mind*> is the set of phenomena to which this set of words refers.

Clearly the term <*mind*> refers to a function. Let's think of familiar functions. There's photosynthesis in green plants. That's a function. There's water falling from a cliff to the valley below. That's a function. There's the turning of a windmill. That's a function. There's the formation of tropical cyclones. That's a function. How does the function of mind differ from those functions? None of those functions has consciousness. None of them has choice, or perception or cognition. Choice, perception and cognition are distinguishing characteristics of mind. Mind is a function which has consciousness. The consciousness includes the functions of choice, perception and cognition. So, we can say confidently that when we use the term <*mind*> that we are denoting consciousness, and when we use the term <*consciousness*> we are denoting choice, perception and cognition.

Consciousness is a continuous flow of experiencing. We experience choice. We experience perception. We experience cognition. And we experience all of them simultaneously in a system of experiencing from birth to death. Every waking moment, we are choosing. We choose to get up or stay in bed. We choose to shower or not to shower. We choose to eat eggs and bacon for breakfast or porridge or noodles or pea and ham soup. We choose to wear a blue shirt or a green shirt.

We choose to watch TV or read or surf the internet. We choose to study history or mathematics or dance or gymnastics. We choose to live near our parents or to move away. We choose to obey the traffic rules and the speed limits or not. We choose to spend our money on milk or wine or bread. We choose to exercise regularly or to sit and rest. We choose to befriend someone or not. We choose to speak kindly about someone or not. We choose to show respect or not.

Many things we do automatically without thinking about them. Is that choosing? Consider how water falls from a cliff into a valley. The water clearly does not choose to fall. The sun rises in the east and sets in the west. The sun clearly is not choosing to rise and fall in this way. The stars shine at night. They clearly do not choose to shine. Now think of the things that we do automatically. They are very different from water falling from a cliff, the sun rising and setting and stars shining. But in what way? Obviously, the difference is choice. We can choose to stop an automatic behavior. Aren't automatically chosen actions clearly the habits that we have chosen to develop at some time or another? We don't set aside time to consider the benefits of brushing our teeth because long ago our parents directed us to brush our teeth after each meal. We may have asked why, and they told us that it was to prevent cavities, to give us a good taste in our mouth, to give us a good breath, or some other benefit. We accepted their explanations and their directives, and we developed the habit of brushing our teeth. Even though it is a habit, we still have the option of saying, "Wait a minute. Is this a habit that we want to continue? Are there benefits from not brushing which outweigh the benefits of brushing?" And we can make a choice. Choices can be made without much consideration or with no consideration at all because they have become habits, but they remain choices that can be changed if we decide to change them. Other terms which denote the act of choosing are <*volition*> and <*conation*>. Experiencing volition (conation) is experiencing choosing, whether considered or not considered, deliberated or undeliberated, rational or irrational.

Experiencing volition (conation) is one part of experiencing human consciousness. A second part is perception. We can perceive emotions. Some examples of emotions which we commonly experience are happiness, joy, anxiety, fear, hate, depression, despair, hopelessness, helplessness, elation. So, clearly, one category of perception is experiencing emotions. There are other categories which can be distinguished, so to keep track of them all, let's use the terms <*perception*$_1$> and <$\mathbf{P}_1$> to denote this first category of perception.

Now let's consider another category of perception. It is experiencing imagined objects, such as imagined sights, sounds, emotions. Suppose we are consulting with our architect, and he or she wants to get an idea of our vision for our house. He or she says, "Imagine in your mind's eye what you want your new house to look like." The use of the expression <*mind's eye*> is a metaphor for denoting the experiencing of imagined objects. The German composer, Ludwig van Beethoven (1770-1827), went deaf, but continued to write musical scores. In doing so, he clearly was experiencing his music by imagining its sounds. Let's denote this second category of perceptions with the terms, <*perception*$_2$> and <$\mathbf{P}_2$>.

A third category of perception is the experiencing of thirst, hunger, pain, itching, sexual orgasm, the urge to urinate and defecate, the feeling of light headedness, headaches, muscle aches, joint aches and the like. These are physiological objects, and the experiencing of physiological objects is another kind of perception. Let's denote this category of perception with the terms <*perception*$_3$> and <$\mathbf{P}_3$>.

A fourth category of perception is experiencing urges, desires and whims. Examples include the experiencing of wanting very much to have sexual intercourse, feeling the urge to run away, having the impulse to scream, wanting to hit someone in the face, feeling the strong desire to have a glass of wine, having a strong craving for a piece of chocolate, etc. Let's denote this category of perception with the terms <*perception*$_4$> and <$\mathbf{P}_4$>. Perception$_4$ ($\mathbf{P}_4$) is experiencing a kind of motivational state of mind. It's experiencing, for example, the urge to have pleasure or the desire to avoid pain. A motivational state of mind is a motivational psychical state. This psychical state can arise spontaneously, on its own, or it can arise as a response to some set of events, to some set of relations or to some state of affairs. The psychical state can be constructive, destructive or neutral in its effect on the person experiencing the urges and desires. When the experiencing of urges and desires becomes persistent, long term and extremely difficult, if not impossible to resist, the experiencing is that of experiencing obsessions and addictions. Experiencing urges and desires is innate and unlearned. Experiencing urges and desires is an introspective perceiving, i.e. a psychical connecting with objects inside the psyche.

All four categories of perceiving ($\mathbf{P_1}$, $\mathbf{P_2}$, $\mathbf{P_3}$, $\mathbf{P_4}$) are introspective perceptions. The differences among the categories are the objects which are perceived. Perception$_1$ ($\mathbf{P_1}$) is perceiving emotional objects. Perception$_2$ ($\mathbf{P_2}$) is perceiving imaginal objects. Perception$_3$ ($\mathbf{P_3}$) is perceiving physiological objects. Perception$_4$ ($\mathbf{P_4}$) is perceiving motivational objects.

Now, let's look at experiencing memories. We remember so many categories of things. We remember people, what they looked like, what they said, what their personalities were like, how they influenced us. We remember events, like the assassination of John F. Kennedy, the birth of our first child, our wedding day, our first job, our first day at school. We remember emotions, such as how frightened we felt as the plane we were in fell in a dive for 20 seconds before it recovered and safely landed. We remember an enormous number of words and how to put them together. The experience of remembering can be distinguished from other kinds of perception with the terms <*perception$_5$*> or ($\mathbf{P_5}$). Experiencing memories is another introspective perceiving, i.e. a psychical connecting with objects, and in this case, remembered objects, inside the psyche.

We can denote the experiencing of phenomena through the five senses with the terms <*perception$_6$*> and <$\mathbf{P_6}$>. We perceive physical objects by experiencing the physical objects with our five senses – taste, smell, touch, seeing and hearing. We smell the fragrance of frangipani. We feel the cold wind blowing against our face. We taste the sweetness of a fresh ripe peach. We see the waves crashing on the beach. We hear the thunder of an approaching storm. Perception$_6$ ($\mathbf{P_6}$) is an extrospective perceiving. It's a psychical connecting with objects, in this case, physical objects, outside the psyche, objects that are existent in the experiential natural world of air, rocks, soil, animals, flowers, water and snow.

The relationship of mind to conation, perception and cognition can also be expressed with set theory notation as

(1) $\mathbf{M = V \cup P \cup N}$

(2) $\mathbf{P = P_1 \cup P_2 \cup P_3 \cup P_4 \cup P_5 \cup P_6}$

The first statement<$\mathbf{M = V \cup P \cup N}$> in ordinary English reads that the essential elements of mind ($\mathbf{M}$) consist of (=) the union ($\cup$) of the essential elements of conation ($\mathbf{V}$), perception ($\mathbf{P}$) and cognition ($\mathbf{N}$).

The second statement <$\mathbf{P = P_1 \cup P_2 \cup P_3 \cup P_4 \cup P_5 \cup P_6}$> in

Figure 3: Volition and Perception as Elements of Mind

The term *mind* $=_{Df}$ (is defined as) human psyche $=_{Df}$ (is defined as) consciousness		
The term *consciousness* $=_{Df}$ volition, perception & cognition		
Volition $=_{Df}$ *V*	*Perception* $=_{Df}$ *P*	Cognition $=_{Df}$ *N*
V = experiencing • choice • will • deliberation	*P* = experiencing • emotional objects. e.g. joy, happiness, anxiety, fear, hate, depression, hopelessness, etc (P_1) • imagined objects, e.g. imagined sights, sounds, emotions, etc (P_2) • physiological objects, e.g. pain, thirst, hunger, sexual orgasm, itching, etc (P_3) • motivational objects, i.e. urges and desires (P_4) • remembered objects, e.g. memories of entities, people, events, relations, emotions, states of affairs, etc (P_5) • physical objects (P_6)	

ordinary English reads that the essential elements of perception (**P**) consist of, or are (=), the union (U) of the essential elements of perception$_1$ (<**P**$_1$> perceiving emotion-al objects), perception$_2$ (<**P**$_2$> perceiving imagined objects), perception$_3$ (<**P**$_3$> perceiving physio-logical objects), perception$_4$ (<**P**$_4$> perceiving motivational objects), perception$_5$ (<**P**$_5$> perceiving remembered objects) and perception$_6$ (<**P**$_6$> perceiving physical objects).

Cognition (**N**) is experiencing a variety of things. One part of cognition is conception (**O**). Experiencing conception is creating meaning with logical objects. A logical object is a symbol. A symbol is anything (a sound, a gesture, a written mark, a hole in a piece of paper, etc.) which is made to stand for something. A symbol can be used to connote another set of symbols or it can be used to denote some set of phenomena. Experiencing conception is experiencing language, and experiencing language is experiencing a symbol system which has grammatical, syntactical, semantic and pragmatic properties. The grammatical properties of a symbol system are the rules for maintaining correct forms and inflexions of the different parts of a symbol system. An example of grammar in English is the use of <*she*> as a subject pronoun and <*her*> as an object pronoun. An English speaker says, "She gave the book to her," but never, "Her gave the book to she." The syntactical properties are the rules for the order of terms to form sentences in a symbol system. An example of syntax in English is the order of subject, verb, adverb, adjective and object in a sentence. An English speaker says, "She sang the song beautifully," never "Song the sang beautifully she." The semantic properties of a symbol system are the relations between symbols and the set of phenomena to which the symbols refer. An example of semantics in English is the relation between the sentence, "There are six chairs in the room," and the actual objects of six chairs located in the room to which the sentence refers. Not all symbol systems have semantic properties, e.g. in mathematics, the symbols <*1*, *2*, *3*>, etc. do not refer to any set of phenomena. Pragmatic properties of a symbol system are the functions which the symbol system is made to perform, e.g. describe, question, request, command, exclaim, persuade, characterize, prescribe, predict, evaluate, instruct, resolve, justify, etc. For example, an English speaker says to another speaker, "Would you please close the door?" intending that the second speaker take the action of closing the door. The pragmatic property of uttering the sentence is that of a request for an action to be performed.

Another part of cognition is experiencing knowing ($\mathbf{K_2}$) in its different kinds, levels and forms. We have already provided a detailed explication of knowing and combinations of kinds ($\mathbf{K_{2K}}$), levels ($\mathbf{K_{2L}}$) and forms ($\mathbf{K_{2F}}$) of knowing as ranges of knowing ($\mathbf{K_{2KLF}}$), so we will not add anything thing to the explication and exemplification of knowing and ranges of knowing.

A third part of cognition is understanding (**U**), and as we have already argued, the term <*understanding*> denotes the same cognitive state as the term <*range of knowing*> ($\mathbf{K}_{2KLF}$). Degrees of understanding correspond with the four levels of knowing, viz. preconventional, intermediate conventional, expert conventional and postconventional understanding. Preconventional understanding is the lowest level of understanding, and postconventional level understanding is the highest level. Understanding restricted to one kind of knowing and one form of knowing is narrow understanding. Understanding which includes all four kinds of knowing and five forms of knowing is extensive understanding. Thus, understanding can range from low level and narrow to high level and extensive.

A fourth part of cognition is inquiry (**Q**). Experiencing inquiry is experiencing problem solving, and experiencing problem solving is having the experience of

(1) encountering a state of affairs which is curious, puzzling, perplexing, bewildering or confusing,
(2) engaging in a line of reasoning which includes asking questions about the problematic state of affairs, answering questions about it, finding necessary and sufficient evidence to deem that the answers are warranted assertions,
(3) testing in a fair, reasonable and appropriate way the practical consequences of the answers deemed to be warranted,
(4) determining whether acting in accordance with the warranted assertions leads to achieving one's goals,
(5) adjudicating whether the effectiveness and efficiency of the actions are satisfactory and that the outcomes are acceptable and
(6) repeating the process when one encounters another problematic state of affairs.

The American educologist, John Dewey (1859-1952), described the act of inquiry as

> "... the controlled or directed transformation of an indeterminate situation into one that is so determinate in its constituent distinctions and relations as to convert the elements of the original situation into a unified whole" (John Dewey, 1938, pp. 104-105).

The transformation achieved by inquiring, to which Dewey refers, is a three-fold one of

(1) conception (**O**) (i.e. making meaning with words and sentences),
(2) volition (**V**) (a deliberately and well considered choice) and
(3) action in some form (i.e. a sequence of activities guided by conception) within the experiential world.

The transformation of conception through inquiry consists of converting unverified statements to verified statements about the problematic state of affairs. The verified, warranted, true statements may be made to function in various ways, e.g. to discern, characterize, describe, diagnose, explain, predict, prescribe, evaluate, justify, etc.

The situation is a relationship of the problem solver (or inquirer) with his or her environment, i.e. his or her experiential world. The problem solver encounters an environment with which he or she does not know how to deal. This is the initial indeterminate situation. The problem solver can't determine, and has no certainty about, what to do to achieve his or her goals, intended outcomes or desired state of affairs. Through problem solving, the problem solver learns (learns$_2$ <$\mathbf{L}_2$>) how to deal with the environment. He or she thus transforms the situation from one in which he or she does not know how to deal with the environment to one in which he or she does know how to deal with it. The indeterminate situation is one in which the problem solver does not have an adequate range of knowing ($\mathbf{K}_{2KLF}$). The determinate situation is one in which the problem solver does have an adequate range of knowing. An adequate range of knowing is one which enables the problem solver, or knower, to discern, describe, explain and predict some state of affairs, and also to evaluate the state of affairs and prescribe courses of action which are most likely to achieve the outcome that the problem solver wants to attain. The transformation of action through inquiry comes from achieving a state of knowing. The state of knowing consists of some appropriate, adequate combination of kinds of knowing, viz.,

(1) knowing-that-one ($\mathbf{K}_{2K1}$),
(2) knowing-that ($\mathbf{K}_{2K2}$),
(3) knowing-how ($\mathbf{K}_{2K3}$) and
(4) knowing-to ($\mathbf{K}_{2K4}$).

The range of knowing achieved from inquiry (**Q**) is a combination of some or all of the kinds of knowing and one or all of the forms of knowing (linguistic, emotional, imaginal, physiological and physical

$<\mathbf{K}_{2F1}, \mathbf{K}_{2F2}, \mathbf{K}_{2F3}, \mathbf{K}_{2F4}, \mathbf{K}_{2F5}>$), and the knowing is at the Level 4 (postconventional level $<\mathbf{K}_{2L4}>$) of knowing. The range of knowing achieved from inquiry transforms choice of action from ineffective, uninformed, uncertain action to effective, well-informed, intelligent, justifiably confident action which obtains desired outcomes. The "unified whole" to which Dewey refers is the connection between a range of knowing held by a problem solver and the state of affairs which the problem solver can control to the extent that, through use of the relevant range of knowing to guide effective action, he or she can obtain desired outcomes or states of affairs.

Inquiry (**Q**) is a task rather than an achievement. It's like teaching, fishing, hunting and searching. It can be either successful or unsuccessful. Inquiry, when successful, moves us from a state of not knowing to a state of knowing. The state of knowing consists of some combination of the kinds, levels and forms of knowing, and the state of knowing places us in a position of being able to cope with our immediate and future situations more adequately and more competently. States of affairs with which we don't know how to deal are indeterminate situations. States of affairs with which we do know how to deal are determinate situations.

We can have the experience of conducting inquiry and fail to achieve the range of knowing that we wanted to achieve. But we can still learn from our failures. Any information is valuable. Knowing what doesn't work to achieve what we want is often times as important as, or even more important than, knowing what does work. What's more, success is always contextual, so our range of knowing may be inadequate in one context, but it may be adequate in another.

Inquiring is always experienced within some existential context (i.e. within some physical, social and cultural setting). Dewey noted

> "An organism does not live in an environment; it lives by means of an environment" (John Dewey, 1938, p. 25).

We human beings are, of course, organisms, and we indeed live by means of our physical, social and cultural environment. It is largely through inquiry that we human beings improve our ability to live by means of our environment. Our continuous inquiry results in continuous extension of our range of knowing, individually and collectively. The extension of our range of knowing empowers us to transact with and use our environment to achieve our nominated goals and desired outcomes.

Inquiry can be (and is) conducted at all ages and stages of life and in all physical, social and cultural settings. Consider how infants are touching and tasting everything that they can reach. And think of the myriad of questions that small children ask. They are obviously engaging in inquiry. Inquiry is conducted in every-day life to solve common-place problems, such as how to roast a turkey, how to improve one's health and fitness, how to achieve a feeling of well being, happiness and fulfillment, how to maintain harmonious family relations, etc.

Inquiry is also conducted in special circumstances to solve special problems. Examples of special inquiries which address special problems include the questions which are addressed in physical scientific inquiry, social scientific inquiry and historical inquiry. In physical scientific inquiry, a question that is currently being addressed is whether there is dark matter and how can it be observed and measured. A question in social scientific inquiry that is currently being addressed is what contributes to urban decay and what are the social effects of urban decay. A current question in historical inquiry is the question of what were the different modes of slavery in the past and how have the legacies of the different modes manifested themselves in current societies. Other examples of special problems include the questions addressed in jurisprudential inquiry, criminological investigations, medical re-search, engineering research and automotive research & development.

Inquiring and knowing have mutual effects. Our range of knowing guides our inquiring, and our inquiring extends our range of knowing. Experiencing inquiry or problem-solving is a major means by which we as human beings extend our range of knowing, and our range of knowing is a major means by which we hone our skills of inquiry and problem-solving. Experiencing inquiry is a very important part of extending our cognition. Experiencing inquiry is a very important part of extending our cognition. The mutual effects of inquiry (**Q**), discovery learning ($\mathbf{L_2}$) and discovered knowing ($\mathbf{K_{2D}}$) can be expressed as follows.

(1) $\mathbf{Q \rightarrow L_2 \rightarrow K_{2D}}$

(2) $\mathbf{K_{2D} \subset K_2}$

(3) $\mathbf{K_2 \rightleftarrows Q}$

The first statement <$\mathbf{Q \rightarrow L_2 \rightarrow K_{2D}}$> in ordinary English reads that inquiry (**Q**) is the set of controlling conditions for ($\rightarrow$) the process of discovery learning ($\mathbf{L_2}$), and discovery learning ($\mathbf{L_2}$) is the set of controlling conditions for a discovered range of knowing ($\mathbf{K}_{\mathbf{2D}}$).

The second statement <$\mathbf{K}_{\mathbf{2D}} \subset \mathbf{K}_{\mathbf{2}}$> in ordinary English reads that a discovered range of knowing ($\mathbf{K}_{\mathbf{2D}}$) has some, but not all the elements of ($\subset$), a range of knowing ($\mathbf{K}_{\mathbf{2}}$), or a discovered range of knowing ($\mathbf{K}_{\mathbf{2D}}$) is a subset of ($\subset$) a range of knowing ($\mathbf{K}_{\mathbf{2}}$).

The third statement <$\mathbf{K}_{\mathbf{2}} \rightleftarrows \mathbf{Q}$> in ordinary English reads that a range of knowing ($\mathbf{K}_{\mathbf{2}}$) is the set of controlling conditions for ($\rightarrow$) inquiry (**Q**), and inquiry (**Q**) is the set of controlling conditions for ($\rightarrow$) a range of knowing ($\mathbf{K}_{\mathbf{2}}$), or a range of knowing ($\mathbf{K}_{\mathbf{2}}$) and inquiry (**Q**) have mutual effects ($\rightleftarrows$).

Another essential element of cognition (**N**) is reasoning (**R**). Just as language first developed over the millennia through usage, then people started analyzing the moves in language to identify the rules that they used in language moves, so it has been with reasoning. We as human beings over the millennia have used reasoning in problem solving, then later we have analyzed moves that we make in reasoning to identify the rules that we follow in reasoning. Our understanding of the rules of reasoning (**R**) have evolved from our use of reasoning in problem solving (**Q**).

An easily understandable way to talk about reasoning is to say,

> "Here is a statement. If the statement is true or false, what other statements are also true or false?"

Experiencing reasoning is making an inference about the implication of a set of propositions.

In any exposition of reasoning, three terms that are essential to clarify are <*inference, implication* and *proposition*>.

The term <*proposition*> denotes the meaning of a statement. A statement is a declarative sentence, as opposed to an interrogative, explanatory or imperative sentence. As it is with terms, so it is with declarative sentences. Declarative sentences can have denotative meaning and connotative meaning. The denotative meaning of a declarative sentence is the experiential state of affairs to which the declarative sentence refers. The connotative meaning of a declarative sentence is the other declarative sentences which are equivalent in meaning to the original declarative sentence. Again, as it is with terms, so it is with declarative sentences. Not all declarative sentences have denotative meaning. Some have only connotative meaning.

The declarative sentence,

> <Three plus two forms the sum of five>,

has the same connotative meaning as the following sentences.

(1) <3 + 2 = 5> in the base ten Arabic numeral system.

(2) <III + II = V> in the Roman numeral system.

(3) 11 + 10 = 101> in the base two Arabic numeral system.

All four declarative sentences form the same proposition. None of the statements refers to any experiential state of affairs or observable existential phenomena. The statements have connotative meaning, but no denotative meaning. They are intensionally equivalent, and they have no extensional meaning.

The declarative sentence,

<Education consists of the elements of teacher, student, content and setting>,

denotes an experiential state of affairs or a set of existential phenomena. We can use our perception (perception$_6$ <$\mathbf{P_6}$>) to observe, through extrospection with our senses (to perceive$_6$), the physical objects of teachers, students, content and setting. The declarative sentence,

<Teachers, students, content and setting are essential elements of education>,

has the same connotative meaning as the original sentence. A third way to state the sentence is with set theory notation:

$$\mathbf{E = T \cup S \cup C \cup X}$$

All three statements express the same proposition, so they are intensionally equivalent. They also denote the same set of phenomena, and thus they are extensionally equivalent. So, this set of statements has both equivalent connotative and denotative meaning.

Declarative sentences form statements. Declarative sentences contrast with interrogative sentences, which form questions, exclamatory sentences, which form exclamations, and imperative sentences, which form commands. Only declarative sentences form statements. Propositions are the meanings of statements. Statements with the same connotative meaning are intensionally equivalent. Statements with the same denotative meaning are extensionally equivalent. Not all statements have denotative meaning because not all statements refer to a set of phenomena.

The term <*implication*> denotes the properties of a proposition. Implication is an attribute or characteristic of a proposition such that the attribute or characteristic determines whether other connected propositions are true or false. Thus, the property of the proposition determines the truth value of other, as yet unstated, propositions. The truth or falsity of the other, as yet unstated, propositions are the logical consequence of the initial proposition. We do not have to do any observation of the experiential world to find evidence to support affirmation or disaffirmation of the, as yet unstated, propositions. It is the property of the initial proposition that determines the truth value of the, as yet unstated, consequent propositions.

Unstated propositions become stated by performing some logical operation on the original proposition, and we thereby transform the implied, unstated proposition into an explicit, stated proposition. Operations on an initial proposition produce new propositions, and the truth value of the new propositions is determined by the properties of the initial proposition. The first proposition is the antecedent. The second, necessarily implied proposition is the consequent.

The term <*inference*> denotes one of the functions of the human mind. Inference is drawing a conclusion about the implicative meaning of a set of propositions and judging the truth value of the conclusion.

As an example of implication and inference, let's use the technical definition of the term <*education*> that we have already established.

> **E** = Education is a system with the basic elements of teacher, student, content and setting.

Let this statement be denoted by the letter <**E**>, and let teacher be denoted by the letter <**T**>. The statement <**E ⊃ T**> expresses an implication. It reads in ordinary language that education (**E**) includes the essential properties, and more than the essential properties of (**⊃**) teacher (**T**).

The set of statements

(1) **E ⊃ T**
(2) **E**
(3) ∴
(4) **T**

expresses an inference. The set of statements reads in ordinary language that

(1) education (denoted by <**E**>)
(2) includes the essential properties, and more than the essential properties of (denoted by <**⊃**>),
(3) teacher (denoted by <**T**>).
(4) It is the case that there is education (denoted by <**E**>),
(5) therefore by inference (connoted by <∴>)

(6) it is the case that there is a (i.e. at least one) teacher (denoted by <**T**>).

If there is education, then there necessarily must be a teacher. And suppose that there is no teacher, then what conclusion can we infer by implication? There is no education. Without a teacher, one of the necessary elements of education is missing.

It is true that there are those who contend that more education takes place without teachers than with teachers. They are shifting the meaning of the term <*education*> ($\mathbf{E = T \cup S \cup C \cup X}$) to denote learning (**L**), and only learning (**L**). They are contending that there is more learning (**L**) that takes place without teachers than there is with teachers. And it is reasonable to agree with that statement, if we are talking about the lifelong process of discovery learning ($\mathbf{L_2}$), coerced learning ($\mathbf{L_3}$) and accidental learning ($\mathbf{L_4}$). All of those processes take place outside of intentional guided learning (<$\mathbf{L_1}$> conduced learning, achieved through education <**E**>).

Now, back to the point that without a teacher, there is no education. It is also true that without at least one student, or without content, or without some physical, social and cultural setting, there also is no education. They are all essential elements of education. And what we have just presented is a set of additional examples of inferences made from the implication of the statement,

> Education is a system consisting of the essential elements of teacher, student, content and setting.

It is patent that we engage in reasoning (**R**) as part of our conduct of inquiring (**Q**). And it is also patent that in our inquiring, at one time or another, depending on the stage to which we have progressed our inquiring, we use all forms of reasoning. Reasoning is an essential element of inquiring, and inquiring exemplifies the use of all the forms of reasoning. All human beings have the capability to reason to some extent. It is a genetically determined human attribute to be able to reason, just as it is a genetically determined human attribute to be bipedal and to have binocular vision and opposable thumbs. Thus, reasoning is a constituent element of the human psyche.

The basic elements of reasoning are statements. Statements used in reasoning consist of premises, axioms, postulates, empirical facts and conclusions. Premises are statements which precede, and form the basis for, conclusions. A premise may be an axiom, a postulate or an empirical fact.

Axioms are statements which form definitions, thus axioms are rules for using terms. Postulates are statements which are deemed to be true, for the sake of advancing an argument, until otherwise proven to be false. Empirical facts are statements which are found to be true by observation (including introspection – in all its variations – $\mathbf{P_1}$, $\mathbf{P_2}$, $\mathbf{P_3}$, $\mathbf{P_4}$, $\mathbf{P_5}$ – and extrospection – $\mathbf{P_6}$). Conclusions are statements which are inferred to be true (or false) because of the implicative meaning of the premises (i.e. the implicative meaning of axioms, postulates and/or empirical facts) which precede the conclusion. Premises are antecedents. Conclusions are consequences.

In reasoning, we follow a set of rules in arranging the order of a set of statements. Three of the basic rules are the rule of identity, the rule of non-contradiction and the rule of the excluded middle. We know and follow these basic rules from a very young age. It is a set of genetically determined talents.

Consider the rule of identity. A child knows that one person is its mother, and that all other persons are not its mother. A child knows that a particular teddy bear is its teddy bear and that other teddy bears may resemble it, but they are not it. The rule of identity has been elegantly stated by the British philosopher Bertrand Russell (1872-1970): "Whatever is, is" (Bertrand Russell, 1912, 1997 edition, p. 72), or stated in logical notation,

for all **<a: a = a, or ∀a: a = a>**

We have just used this rule in our discourse about education and teachers. The statement,

> There is no education without a teacher,

and the statement,

> There is more education without teachers than there is with teachers,

cannot both be true. The rule of identity requires that the term *<education>* either denotes (1) the process of learning (**L**) or denotes (2) the elements of teacher (**T**), student (**S**), content (**C**) and setting (**X**), all standing in relation to each other, but not both (1) and (2). The relationship of education (**E**) to the learning process (**L**) can be expressed in logical notation as follows.

(1) The statement **<∀E: E = T ∪ S ∪ C ∪ X>** reads that for all instances (**∀**) of the phenomenon of education (**E**), the phenomenon of education (**E**) is (=) the union (**∪**) of the essential properties of the elements of teacher (**T**),

student (**S**), content (**C**) and setting (**X**) standing in relation to each other.

(2) The statement <**∀E: E ≠ L**> reads that for all instances (∀) of education (**E**), education (**E**) is not (≠) the learning process (**L**).

The rule of non-contradiction can be stated simply as, "Nothing can both be and not be," (Bertrand Russell, 1912, 1997 edition, p. 72) or stated in logical notation,

$$\neg(\mathbf{A} \land \neg\mathbf{A})$$

The statement <**¬(A ∧ ¬A)**> reads that nothing (¬) can both be (**A**) and (∧) not be (¬**A**). Some examples which violate the rule of non-contradiction include the following statements.

(1) The students understand, and they don't understand.
(2) The students were taught, and they weren't taught.
(3) The teachers prepared their lessons, and they didn't prepare their lessons.

For discourse to make any sense, self-contradictory statements must be avoided.

A third rule for sound reasoning is the rule of the excluded middle. It can be simply stated as, "Everything must either be or not be" (Bertrand Russell, 1912, 1997 edition, p. 72), or stated in logical notation

$$\mathbf{A} \lor \neg\mathbf{A}$$

The statement <**A ∨ ¬A**> in ordinary English reads that either everything must be (**A**) or (∨) everything must not be (¬**A**). This rule requires that there be no middle ground between true or false. Either a statement is true, or it is false. It cannot be neither true nor false. Here are some statements from discourse about education which exemplify compliance with the rule of the excluded middle.

(1) Either it is true that teaching is intentional, or it is false that teaching is intentional, but it cannot be true that teaching is neither intentional nor unintentional.
(2) Either it is true that the learning process achieved through education is intentional, or it is false that the learning process achieved through education is intentional, but it cannot be true that the learning process achieved through education is neither intentional nor unintentional.
(3) Either it is true that unguided unintentional learning is accidental, or it is false that unguided unintentional

learning is accidental, but it cannot be true that unguided unintentional learning is neither accidental nor nonaccidental.

There are other rules of sound reasoning, and they may be found by consulting any basic reference in propositional logic or sentential calculus.

Experiencing reasoning (**R**) can take different forms. The forms include

(1) intuiting
(2) deducing
(3) reducing
(4) retroducing
(5) inducing
(6) abducing
(7) evaluating
(8) prescribing
(9) justifying

Intuiting is having the experience of drawing a conclusion about the implicative meaning of a single premise and judging the truth value of the conclusion without making explicit the implicative meaning of any premises other than the first premise. In logical notation, intuiting can be expressed as follows.

$$\mathbf{A \supset B}$$

which reads in ordinary language that the second statement (**B**), the conclusion, is necessarily implied by the first statement (**A**), the premise. An alternative reading is that if that statement (**A**) is true, then the statement (**B**) is true.

The American savant, Kim Peek (1951-2009) could identify the day of the week, given any date. For example, given the date of July 17, 1852, he could immediately and correctly say that it was a Saturday. He could do it very quickly, without mistake and with no apparent calculation (B. Weber, 2009). The pattern of his reasoning exemplified intuiting because it proceeded from (1) premise to (2) inference to (3) conclusion. There was the initial premise that <*There is a date in the calendar of July 17, 1852*>. There is the inference which Peek made, and there is the conclusion that <*It was a Saturday*>.

Daniel Tammet, a British mathematician born in 1979, intuits answers to complex mathematical problems without any apparent calculation. For example, he can say that the number 37 to the power of 4 is 1,874,161 within a few seconds. He says that he perceives ($\mathbf{P}_2$) images of the numbers in his imagination. For him, each number has a special size, shape and color, and the images form patterns. The images of the numbers appear in his imaginal perception ($\mathbf{P}_2$). The patterns appear, and the solutions to the mathematical problems appear, all in his visual imagination (Richard Johnson, 2005).

Deducing is having the experience of drawing a conclusion about the implicative meaning of a set of premises and judging the truth value of the conclusion such that the conclusion is deemed necessarily true (or necessarily false) without exception. Experiencing deducing can be (and is) done by conceiving with ordinary language & symbol systems and with special languages & symbol systems. In logical notation, deducing can be expressed in the same way as intuiting is expressed,

A ⊃ B

which reads that if the first statement (**A**), the premise, is true, then (if-then is denoted by <⊃>) the second statement (**B**), the conclusion, is necessarily true. That which distinguishes deducing from intuiting is the intermediate steps in reasoning which are usually taken in deducing. An example of a set of intermediate steps of reasoning leading to a conclusion is exemplified in the following statements.

(1) **A ⊃ B**
(2) **B ⊃ C**
(3) ∴
(4) **A ⊃ C**

The statements read in ordinary English as follows.

(1) The statement <**A ⊃ B**> reads that if the statement <**A**> is true, then (if-then is denoted by <⊃>) the statement <**B**> is true.
(2) The statement <**B ⊃ C**> reads that if the statement <**B**> is true, then (if-then is denoted by <⊃>) the statement <**C**> is true.
(3) Therefore (∴)
(4) the conclusion <**A ⊃ C**> is that if the statement <**A**> is true, then (if-then is denoted by <⊃>) the statement <**C**> is true.

The common property among all exemplifications of experiencing deducing is the necessary connection between the premises and the conclusion. With deduction, the conclusion is necessarily implied by the premises, and if the premises are true, the conclusion is necessarily true, not probably true.

Reducing is having the experience of restating a proposition (or set of propositions) in the most simple, economical way, without changing the meaning of the original proposition (or the set of propositions). Almost all of us have had the experience of reducing fractions in mathematics, say, expressing <*12/24*> as <*1/2*>. That is an example of reductive reasoning. Here is another example. Suppose there is a boy, Robert, who is a student in year 6 or 6th grade. He is given a question, "Is a mouse a reptile?" He is further instructed to give his reasons for his answer. Robert thinks back to his lessons about classification of animals, and he has also been studying logical notation. He decides that the most economical way to present his answer is with the following statement.

$$\forall m(Mm)\rightarrow\neg(Rm)$$

In ordinary English, his statement <$\forall m(Mm)\rightarrow\neg(Rm)$> reads that for all mice (denoted by <$\forall m$>), if (denoted by <$\rightarrow$>) mice are mammals (denoted by <**Mm**>), then (denoted by <$\rightarrow$>) mice are not reptiles (denoted by <$\neg(Rm)$>).

The statement <$\forall m(Mm)\rightarrow\neg(Rm)$> is an example of a reductive statement expressed with special symbols, and it answers the question of whether mice are reptiles and provides the argument for why mice are not reptiles.

Retroducing is having the experience of starting with a true statement about an existential situation (i.e. an experiential material state of affairs) and seeking to answer the question why (or how) did this result (or state of affairs) come about. Another way to pose this question is to ask what are the determinants which control the resultant (or set of resultants). In retroducing, we start with a fact which is known to be true, and we think of reasons which explain why it is true. The logic of retroduction is expressed in the following sentences.

(1) Statement <**S**> is true about the set of phenomena <**P**>.
(2) What axioms or postulates imply statement <**S**>?
(3) Statement <**S**> is necessarily implied by axioms <$a_1, a_2 ... a_n$> or postulates <$p_1, p_2 ... p_n$>.
(4) The axioms <$a_1, a_2 ... a_n$> or postulates <$p_1, p_2 ... p_n$> constitute the explanatory theory for statement <**S**>.

The conception of the set of the axioms <$a_1, a_2 ... a_n$> or postulates <$p_1, p_2 ... p_n$> constitutes the creation of the explanatory theory for the true statement <**S**> (i.e. the empirical fact). Thus, retroduction is the means by which explanation (or explanatory theory) is devised.

An example of experiencing retroducing is that of Graham, a medical practitioner in general practice. One of his patients, Dean, presents with a fever, a rash and swollen glands in the neck, armpits and groin. Graham's challenge is to diagnose Dean's condition and prescribe a therapy. Graham thinks that there are three possible causes, viz. some bacterial infection, some viral infection or some toxin causing a reaction. Graham judges that the worst scenario is a meningococcal infection, so he decides to hospitalize Dean immediately and treat him with intravenous antibiotics. Meanwhile Graham, to confirm his conjectures, consults with another MD for a second opinion and orders blood tests for bacterial infection, viral infection and presence of toxic substances.

Graham, is working with three competing explanations for Dean's condition. He has conceived of three postulates, or three competing explanations, or three explanatory theories. His retroductive reasoning can be expressed symbolically as

(1) $\mathbf{R}$

(2) $\therefore$

(3) $(\mathbf{D}_1 \rightarrow \mathbf{R}) \oplus (\mathbf{D}_2 \rightarrow \mathbf{R}) \oplus (\mathbf{D}_3 \rightarrow \mathbf{R})$

which reads in ordinary language as follows.

(1) Given the resultant condition of fever, rash and swollen glands (denoted by <**R**>),

(2) therefore (symbolized by <$\therefore$>)

(3) either (symbolized by <$\oplus$>) bacterial infection (denoted by <$\mathbf{D}_1$>) is the set of controlling conditions (symbolized by <$\rightarrow$>) for the resultant <**R**>,

(4) or (symbolized by <$\oplus$>) viral infection (denoted by <$\mathbf{D}_2$>) is the set of controlling conditions (symbolized by <$\rightarrow$>) for the resultant <**R**>,

(5) or (symbolized by <$\oplus$>) a toxic substance (denoted by <$\mathbf{D}_3$>) is the set of controlling conditions (symbolized by <$\rightarrow$>) for the resultant <**R**>.

Each of the postulated determinates constitutes a hypothesis to be tested by perception$_6$ (<$\mathbf{P}_6$> or observation by extrospection). Blood tests will provide the conditions for observing the presence of a bacterial infection, a viral infection or a toxic substance.

Inducing is having the experience of inferring from a set of premises that their implicative meaning makes the conclusion probably true (but not necessarily true). Experiencing inducing is the means by which postulates or hypotheses are tested. By extension, experiencing inducing is forming an inferential statistical argument. It is a form of reasoning which we use to infer that a true statement about a sample of a population is true about the entire population. The logic of induction is expressed in the following sentence.

> If members $<\mathbf{m_1}, \mathbf{m_2} \ldots \mathbf{m_n}>$ of a category <**M**> have properties <**P**> in some amount $<\mathbf{A_1}, \mathbf{A_2} \ldots \mathbf{A_n}>$, then, to some degree of probability <**p**>, all members of category <**M**> have properties <**P**> in some amount $<\mathbf{A_1}, \mathbf{A_2} \ldots \mathbf{A_n}>$.

An explanation is an explanatory theory. An explanatory theory is formed from a retroductive argument in which the conclusion of the argument is used to conceive postulates which necessarily imply the conclusion of the argument. The postulates of an explanatory theory can be used to form a deductive argument which implies some new necessarily true conclusion in addition to the original conclusion used in the retroductive argument. The premises and the new implied conclusion constitute a material theorem of the explanatory theory. It is called <*material*> because it denotes some experiential state of affairs. Through deduction, the theorem is proved using the principle of necessity reasoning. But there is, as yet, no evidence from the experiential world that the implied conclusion denotes an actual experiential set of phenomena. Thus, the conclusion is an empirical hypothesis. It is an empirical statement awaiting verification from necessary and sufficient evidence. Evidence for the material hypothesis must be adduced by observation (extrospection – perception$_6$ – $<\mathbf{P_6}>$) of phenomena extant in the experiential world. Verification of the material hypotheses to a high degree of probability (using inductive reasoning) indicates confirmation of the explanatory theory. The explanatory theory is apparently sound. Nullification of the hypotheses indicates that the explanatory theory may not be sound. It probably needs to be corrected in some way. Thus, conducting observation of phenomena in the experiential world to test an empirical hypothesis, generated deductively from an explanation, gives an indication of how sound the explanatory theory is. An evaluation of a theory is the judgment about how sound a theory is. A sound explanatory theory accounts for all the relevant facts and accurately predicts what will happen, given a specified set of circumstances.

An example of induction is that of the work of Robin Warren and

Barry Marshall. For years it was taught in medical schools that bacteria could not live in the human stomach because of the acidity. Then, in 1982, an Australian medical scientist, Robin Warren, observed a colony of bacterium (Helicobacter pylori) living in the lower part of a human stomach (BBC News, 3 October 2005). His colleague, the gastroenterologist, Barry Marshall, took an interest in Warren's findings. Marshall personally ingested some of the bacterium to test the proposition that the bacterium H. pylori causes ulcers. He developed signs and symptoms consistent with stomach ulcers, and he cured himself with a course of antibiotics. So, there was the existing explanatory theory that lifestyle and stress caused ulcers. The postulate, "Lifestyle and stress cause ulcers," implied the material hypothesis, "No ulcer-causing bacteria live in the stomach." Observation adduced evidence of colonies of the bacterium H. pylori living in the lower part of the stomach. Observation also adduced that ingestion of the bacterium H. pylori resulted in the symptoms produced by stomach ulcers. And a course of antibiotics eliminated the bacterium, the symptoms and the ulcers. The material hypothesis, "No ulcer-producing bacteria live in the stomach," was disaffirmed, and the explanatory theory, "Lifestyle and stress cause stomach ulcers," was evaluated as being inadequate. It was revised to the explanatory theory, "The bacterium H. pylori causes stomach ulcers."

Abducing is having the experience of using a concept from one domain of discourse to describe, characterize and/or explain states of affairs referred to by another domain of discourse. Abduction is a means by which an explanation (i.e. an explanatory theory) can be extended or expanded to a greater degree of functionality and generality. The line of reasoning when we are abducing is expressed in the following sentences.

(1) Theory <**T**> includes the concept (or construct) <**C**>.

(2) The concept <**C**> from theory <**T**> can be used in axioms <$\mathbf{a}_1, \mathbf{a}_2 \ldots \mathbf{a}_n$> or postulates <$\mathbf{p}_1, \mathbf{p}_2 \ldots \mathbf{p}_n$> in a second theory <$\mathbf{T}_2$>.

An example of extending one domain of discourse by using the concepts from a second domain of discourse is that of using concepts from hydrology to extend concepts in the physics of electricity. The concepts of <*volume*, *pressure* and *flow*> from disciplined discourse about water can be (and have been) used to extend the disciplined discourse about electricity. The concept of <*volume*> of water is analogous to <*Wattage*> as a measure of an amount of electrical energy. The concept of <*pressure*> of water is analogous to <*Voltage*> as a measure of the intensity of electricity in a circuit. And the concept of <*flow*> of water is analogous to <*Amperage*> as a measure of the amount of electricity moving through a circuit.

An example of abducing in discourse about education is the SIGGS theory developed by Elizabeth [Steiner] Maccia and George S. Maccia (1966). They developed an educological theory using concepts which they abduced from set theory, information theory, graph theory and general systems theory. Their published work was *Development of Educational Theory Derived from Three Theory Models.* They used concepts from set theory and systems theory to define education as a system made of the elements of teacher, student, content and context. They used concepts from information theory to develop a description of how information is communicated from teacher to student, and vice versa. They used concepts from graph theory to develop a map of the information flow. And they called their theory *the SIGGS Theory Model*, from **S**et theory, **I**nformation theory, **G**raph theory and **G**eneral **S**ystems theory. Steiner and Maccia abduced concepts from four domains of discourse and used those concepts in a fifth domain of discourse (educological discourse) to develop a theory to describe and explain education and to make predictions about education.

Evaluating, another part of reasoning, is making a judgment about the worth of something. Experiencing evaluating is having the experience of engaging in normative reasoning. Normative reasoning for evaluation is

(1) conceiving of and adopting a set of criteria,
(2) using the set to make a judgment about the worth of something and
(3) reporting the judgment.

The criteria can be either rules or standards. The something being evaluated is the evaluatum (the plural of the term <*evaluatum*> is the term <*evaluata*>). The report of the judgment about the worth of something is either a rating or a ranking (Paul W. Taylor, 1961, pp. 9-10).

The steps in evaluative reasoning, using rules for the criteria, are language moves in which the evaluator

(1) selects an evaluatum (or set of evaluata) to rate (the evaluatum may be an object, an action, a state of affairs, etc.),

(2) conceives and adopts a set of rules (i.e. stipulations for what is required, what is allowed and/or what is prohibited) for judging the worth of the evaluatum,
(3) clarifies the rule (or set of rules) in unambiguous and explicit detail such that the rule can clearly and easily be used to determine whether the evaluatum (or set of evaluata) does or does not comply with the rule (or set of rules),
(4) makes a judgment about (deduces) whether the evaluatum (or set of evaluata) complies (or does not) comply with the rules.

The evaluator reports the judgment with a statement in the form of

- <**e**> (the evaluatum or set of evaluata) is good (or bad), or
- <**e**> is compliant (or noncompliant), or
- <**e**> is correct (or incorrect), or
- <**e**> is right (or wrong), or
- <**e**> is acceptable (or not acceptable), or
- <**e**> is adequate (or not adequate), or
- <**e**> is satisfactory (or not satisfactory), or
- <**e**> is competent (or not competent), or
- <**e**> has achieved (or has not achieved) the intended outcomes.

Reporting a judgment about whether an evaluatum (or set of evaluata) complies with a rule is expressed as a rating. The rating consists of two, and only two, categories, viz. complies with the rule or does not comply with the rule. Evaluating with a set of rules as the criteria does not allow for degrees of goodness or badness. Either the evaluatum is compliant with the rule, or it is not.

In contrast with evaluating with rules, evaluating with a set of standards as the criteria does allow for judgments about the degrees of goodness or badness of the evaluatum. The evaluatum can be judged to comply with (or fulfil) the standards of goodness (or badness) to some extent. The report of the value judgment is in the form of either a rating or a ranking. The steps in evaluative reasoning, using standards for the criteria, are language moves in which the evaluator

(1) selects an evaluatum (or set of evaluata) to rate or rank,
(2) conceives and adopts a set of standards (i.e. stipulations of the characteristics that constitute a good evaluatum)

for judging the worth of the evaluatum,
(3) clarifies the standard (or set of standards) in unambiguous and explicit detail such that the standard (or set of standards) can clearly and easily be used to determine that the evaluatum (or set of evaluata) fulfils the standard (or set of standards) to some degree, ranging from not at all to somewhat to almost entirely to entirely,
(4) specifies a set of objects (i.e. other members of the category to which the evaluatum belongs) against which the evaluatum (or set of evaluata) is to be compared (i.e. specifies a field of comparison),
(5) makes a judgment about the degree to which the evaluatum (or set of evaluata) fulfils the standard (or set of standards),
(6) reports the value judgment as either a rating with gradations of categories of excellence or a ranking with ordinal placement among a set of evaluata.

The reporting of the judgment about the worth of the evaluatum (or evaluata) as a rating, with gradations of categories of excellence, is expressed, for example, in the sentence forms,

(1) <**e**> has a rating of A (or B or C or D or F) – a rating system with five categories, or
(2) <**e**> has a rating of 4 (or 3 or 2 or 1) – a rating system with four categories, or
(3) <**e**> has a rating of 10 (or 9 or 7 or 6 or 5 or 4 or 3 or 2 or 1) – a rating system with 10 categories, or
(4) <**e**> has a rating of excellent (or good, or satisfactory, or poor, or unsatisfactory) – a rating system with five categories, etc.

An alternative way to report the judgment about the worth of an evaluatum in relation to a set of standards is by ranking. Ranking is an ordinal placement of an evaluatum among a set of evaluata. Reporting as ranking is expressed, for example, in the sentence forms,

(1) <$\mathbf{e}_1$> is better than (or worse than) <$\mathbf{e}_2$>,
(2) <$\mathbf{e}_1$> has a rank of 1st, <$\mathbf{e}_2$> has a rank of 2nd ... <$\mathbf{e}_n$> has a rank of <$\mathbf{n}^{th}$>,
(3) <$\mathbf{e}_1$> has a rank of 99th percentile, <$\mathbf{e}_2$> has a rank of 98th percentile..., <$\mathbf{e}_n$> has a rank of <$\mathbf{n}^{th}$> percentile,
(4) <$\mathbf{e}_1$> has a rank expressed as a Z score of +2.00, <$\mathbf{e}_2$>

has a rank expressed as a Z score of + 1.99 ..., $<\mathbf{e}_n>$ has a rank expressed as a Z score of <**n**>, etc.

An example of experiencing evaluating is that of Gordon. Gordon is a nine-year-old boy who is asked, "Which game does he think is the best, Minecraft or Mandala?" He responds that Minecraft is the best. When asked, "Why?" he responds that Minecraft is much more exciting and has much more variation. Mandala, he remarks, is just moving stones from one cup to another, and it is the same thing again and again. In this example, how did Gordon report his evaluation? He reported it as a ranking. Minecraft ranks above Mandala. Minecraft, 1st. Mandala, 2nd. Gordon's evaluative reasoning can be expressed in the following set of sentences.

(1) The evaluatum $<\mathbf{e}_1>$ (the game of Minecraft) meets the set of criteria <**c**> (the two standards of $<\mathbf{s}_1>$ exciting and $<\mathbf{s}_2>$ variation) to a higher degree <**d**> than does $<\mathbf{e}_2>$ (the game Mandala).

(2) $<\mathbf{e}_1>$ (the evaluatum Minecraft) is better than $<\mathbf{e}_2>$ (the evaluatum Mandala).

Prescribing, another part of reasoning, is telling a person what ought to be done in some given set of circumstances. Experiencing prescribing is having the experience of engaging in normative reasoning with a view to making a judgment about the worth of a course of action and reporting that judgment as a recommendation. The criteria can be either rules or standards.

Prescribing parallels evaluating. There is prescribing according to rules and prescribing according to standards. A rule, for example, is "Always tell the truth." A standard, for example, is the standard of fairness. Prescriptive reasoning which uses rules as the criteria produces prescriptions which are universal. Prescriptive reasoning which uses standards as the criteria produces prescriptions which are particular to a given context or set of circumstances. In either case, universal or particular, the prescription is expressed in the sentence form,

You ought to do <**x**>.

A universal prescription is a recommendation produced from using a rule to make and express a judgment about the worth of a course of action. The language moves in making a judgment about the worth of a course of action can be expressed in the following sentence forms (Paul W. Taylor, 1961, p. 215).

(1) The rule <**r**> requires acts of the kind <**k**>.
(2) Act <**x**> is of the kind <**k**>.
(3) You ought to do <**x**>.

An example of experiencing prescribing which results from using a rule to make a judgment about the worth of a course of action is that of David. David is a 16-year-old schoolboy. His friend, Tom, finds someone's mobile phone lying on the floor in a shopping mall. Tom asks David, "What should we do with it?" David says, "You ought to give it to the people at the information counter. They can give it to lost and found, and maybe the owner will ask for it there." David's prescriptive reasoning is expressed in the following sentences.

(1) The rule <**r**> (viz. always practice honesty) requires acts of the kind <**k**> (viz. return lost property to its rightful owner).
(2) The act <**x**> (viz. give the recovered mobile phone to the information desk in the mall) is of the kind <**k**> (return lost property to its rightful owner).
(3) You ought to do <**x**> (give the recovered mobile phone to the information desk in the mall).

The rule that is being applied is the rule of honesty. There is no degree of honesty. Either one adheres to the rule of honesty, or one does not.

Universal prescriptions contrast with particular prescriptions. A particular prescription is a recommendation produced from using a standard to make and express a judgment about the worth of a course of action. Prescriptive reasoning which produces particular recommendations is expressed in the following sentence forms.

(1) The standard <**s**> is the relevant one for selecting the most appropriate act <**x**>.
(2) The act <**x**> meets the standard <**s**> to a higher degree than alternative acts <$\mathbf{x_1}, \mathbf{x_2} \ldots \mathbf{x_n}$>.
(3) You ought to do <**x**>.

An example of making a prescription in relation to a set of standards is the case of Sarah. Sarah is a 14-year-old high school student. She sees some older students selling marijuana to other students on the school campus, and some of her friends are among those buying the marijuana. She wonders whether she should report the students who are selling the marijuana, but she knows that they may assault her if she does. She also does not want to get her friends into trouble. She is not sure what to do, so she goes to her father and asks him what should she do? Report the students who are selling the marijuana, risk losing her friends and risk being assaulted, as well? Turn a blind eye to it all and say nothing? Or is there some other alternative? Sarah's father responds that obviously the school authorities should be informed of what has been happening, and he also reminds her that the possession and sale of marijuana are criminal offenses. He says that obviously Sarah needs to be protected from any victimization, physical and emotional. He recommends that Sarah let him go to the school, seek reassurances from the school that measures be taken to assure Sarah's anonymity and safety and inform the administration about the marijuana trade.

The prescriptive reasoning in which Sarah's father engages and the recommendations which he makes and reports is expressed in the following sentences.

(1) "You ought to do <**x**>," i.e. Sarah ought to consent to her father making the report to the school authorities and seeking reassurances from the school that Sarah's identity as the source of the information be protected.

(2) "The set of standards <**s**> is the relevant one for selecting the most appropriate act <**x**>," i.e. the set of standards <**s**> relevant to this case is the set of lawfulness, responsibility and self-preservation.

(3) "The act <**x**> meets the set of standards <**s**> to a higher degree than alternative acts <$\mathbf{x}_1, \mathbf{x}_2 \ldots \mathbf{x}_n$>," i.e. the act <**x**> of consenting to the father reporting to the school meets the standards <**s**> of lawfulness, responsibility and self-preservation to a higher degree than the alternative acts of <$\mathbf{x}_1$>, Sarah going directly to the school authorities, and <$\mathbf{x}_2$>, Sarah turning a blind eye and remaining silent about the marijuana trade.

Prescriptive reasoning in relation to standards requires the weighing up of the pros and cons of one course of action as compared to other courses of action. And the prescription from standards is a particular prescription because it is appropriate to a singular set of circum-stances, rather than being appropriate to all circumstances.

Particular prescriptions are made in relation to standards. Universal prescriptions are made in relation to rules. All human beings have the capability to prescribe to some extent. It is common to the experience of all human beings, and it is experientially a constituent element of the human psyche.

Justifying, another part of reasoning, is connected to both evaluating and prescribing. Both evaluating and prescribing imply reasons to justify evaluations and recommendations. If it is asserted that "<**e**> is good," or "<$\mathbf{e}_1$> is better than <$\mathbf{e}_2$>," or that "You ought to do <**x**>," then it is always a legitimate question to ask, "Why?" Experiencing justifying is making language moves which form an argument in support of an evaluation and/or a prescription. Justifying is developing a normative argument that an evaluation or a prescription is verified, validated, vindicated and based on rational choice (Paul W. Taylor, 1961).

The steps in justification are

(1) value verification,
(2) value validation,
(3) value vindication and
(4) rational choice.

Justification of an evaluation follows the report of a value judgment. The value judgment is expressed in sentence form as either

(1) <$\mathbf{e}_n$> is good, better or best, or
(2) <$\mathbf{e}_1$> is 1st, <$\mathbf{e}_2$> is 2nd …, <$\mathbf{e}_n$>is <$\mathbf{n}^{th}$>.

In justification of an evaluation, we start with the report of the evaluation. The report is expressed either as a rating or a ranking. Following the report of the value judgment comes the four steps in the normative justificatory argument in support of the evaluation.

(1) Value verification is expressed in the sentence, "<**e**> is good because <**e**> meets a set of criteria (rules and/or standards) <**c**> to some degree <**d**>."
(2) Value validation is expressed in the sentence, "The set of criteria c constitutes a set of norms <**n**>, and the set of norms <**n**> is good because it is implied by a higher set of norms <$\mathbf{n}_h$>."
(3) Value vindication is expressed in the sentence, "The set of higher norms <$\mathbf{n}_h$> is good because the set is part of a particular way of life <**WoL**>."
(4) Rational choice is expressed in the sentence, "The particular way of life <**WoL**> is good because it is the way of life any well-informed, widely experienced, intelligent, unbiased, free, liberated person would

rationally choose, given a choice among an infinite number of alternative ways of life."

This is the conclusion of the justificatory argument. It cannot be taken any further. Are there actually people who are so well-informed, so widely experienced, so intelligent, so unbiased, so free, so liberated that they can make a rational choice among an infinite number of alternative ways of life? Probably not. It is an ideal to which we, as human beings, can aspire, but probably can never attain. So, the question of which way of life is best is always a question open to further inquiry. We can only operate on our current experience and strive to know and understand more to provide a basis for making perhaps wiser decisions in the future. What we do know, of course, is that the justification, "We live this way because we have always lived this way," is no justification at all. It is a blind, mindless acceptance of what is because it has been. The rational alternative is to conduct inquiry about relative merits of different ways of life.

Justification of prescriptions is similar to, but not exactly the same as, justification of evaluations. Again, there are four steps,

(1) value verification,
(2) value validation,
(3) value vindication and
(4) rational choice.

In the case of universal prescriptions, those based on using a rule or set of rules for making a recommendation for a course of action, the prescription is expressed in the sentence form,

"You ought to do <**x**>."

A prescription always denotes an action rather than an entity or state of affairs, and prescriptions based on rules are always universal prescriptions. Value verification for justification of a universal prescription is expressed in the following sentence forms.

(1) "The rule <**r**> requires acts of the kind <**k**>."
(2) "Act <**x**> is of the kind <**k**>" (Paul W. Taylor, 1961, p. 215).

Value verification for justification of a particular prescription (vs. a universal prescription) is expressed in the following sentence forms.

(1) "The standard <**s**> is the relevant one for selecting the most appropriate act <**x**>."
(2) "The act <**x**> meets the standard <**s**> to a higher degree than alternative acts <$\mathbf{x}_1$, $\mathbf{x}_2$, … $\mathbf{x}_n$>."

Figure 4: Volition, Perception and Cognition as Elements of Mind

The term *mind* $=_{Df}$ (is defined as) human psyche $=_{Df}$ (is defined as) consciousness		
The term *consciousness* $=_{Df}$ volition, perception & cognition		
Volition $=_{Df}$ *V*	*Perception* $=_{Df}$ *P*	Cognition $=_{Df}$ *N*
V = experiencing • choice • will • deliberation	*P* = experiencing • emotional objects. e.g. joy, happiness, anxiety, fear, hate, depression, hopelessness, etc (P_1) • imagined objects, e.g. imagined sights, sounds, emotions, etc (P_2) • physiological objects, e.g. pain, thirst, hunger, sexual orgasm, itching, etc (P_3) • motivational objects, i.e. urges and desires (P_4) • remembered objects, e.g. memories of entities, people, events, relations, emotions, states of affairs, etc (P_5) • physical objects (P_6)	*N* = experiencing • conceiving (*O*), i.e. creating meaning with logical objects – symbols for language, logic, mathematics, music, etc • knowing (K_2) ○ kinds ○ forms ○ levels • understanding (*U*) ○ level 1 ○ level 2 ○ level 3 ○ level 4 • inquiring (*Q*) • reasoning (*R*) ○ intuiting ○ deducing ○ reducing ○ retroducing ○ inducing ○ abducing ○ evaluating ○ prescribing ○ justifying

After the first step of verification, the steps for completion of justification of both cases of prescription, universal and particular, are the same as the steps for justification of evaluations.

(2) Value validation is expressed in the sentence, "The set of criteria <c> constitutes a set of norms <n>, and the set

of norms <**n**> is good because it is implied by a higher set of norms <$\mathbf{n}_h$>."

(3) Value vindication is expressed in the sentence, "The set of higher norms <$\mathbf{n}_h$> is good because the set is part of a particular way of life <**WoL**>."

(4) Rational choice is expressed in the sentence, "The particular way of life <**WoL**> is good because it is the way of life any well-informed, widely experienced, intelligent, unbiased, free, liberated person would rationally choose, given a choice among an infinite number of alternative ways of life."

The justificatory argument ends with the step of rational choice. No further justification is available for the argument.

Focus is a crucial function of mind. Focus (**F**) is coordinating the different elements of mind (**V**, **P**, **N**) such they are attending to the same object, task, concern or state of affairs. We all have had the experience of our mind wandering. We sit down, start to watch a TV program, then think of something other than the program and lose track of what is being presented in the program. As students, we sit down, start to read a book, then think of other things and realize that we have not comprehended what we were reading. We are driving along, listening to a news item on the radio and miss the turn that we wanted because we had stopped paying attention to the road. Sometimes, we can be so focused on something that we do not hear what someone else in the same room has said to us.

The distinctions of mind and elements of mind (**M**, **V**, **P**, **N**, **F**) can be added to the list of well-defined terms in descriptive educological theory.

(1) <**M**> is the symbol for mind, which is defined as human psyche, which in turn is defined as human consciousness.

(2) <$\mathbf{H}_C$> is the symbol for human consciousness, which is defined as experiencing volition, perception and cognition.

(3) <**V**> is the symbol for volition, which is defined as experiencing choice, will, determination, conation.

(4) <**P**> is the symbol for perception, which is defined as experiencing objects through introspection and/or extrospection.

(5) <$\mathbf{P}_1$> is the symbol for perception$_1$, which is experiencing

emotional objects (joy, fear, depression) through introspection.

(6) <$\mathbf{P}_2$> is the symbol for perception$_2$, which is experiencing imagined objects (imagined sights, imagined sounds, imagined emotions) through introspection.

(7) <$\mathbf{P}_3$> is the symbol for perception$_3$, which is experiencing physiological objects (pain, thirst, hunger, orgasm) through introspection.

(8) <$\mathbf{P}_4$> is the symbol for perception$_4$, which is experiencing motivational objects (urges, desires) through introspection.

(9) <$\mathbf{P}_5$> is the symbol for perception$_5$, which is experiencing remembered objects (remembered sounds, sights, events, people) through introspection.

(10) <$\mathbf{P}_6$> is the symbol for perception$_6$, which experiencing physical objects (chairs, grass, trees, people) through extrospection.

(11) <**N**> is the symbol for cognition, which is experiencing conceiving, knowing, understanding, inquiring and reasoning.

(12) <**O**> is the symbol for conceiving, which is experiencing creating meaning with logical objects (ordinary language symbols, special mathematical symbols, special music symbols, special Braille symbols, special sign language symbols).

(13) <**U**> is the symbol for understanding, which is some range of knowing ($\mathbf{K}_{2KLF}$), which varies from low to high level (preconventional to postconventional level) and from narrow (a single kind and form of knowing) to extensive (all kinds and forms of knowing).

(14) <**Q**> is the symbol for inquiring, which is experiencing the undertaking, intentionally and without guidance, to ask questions, answers questions and adduce necessary and sufficient evidence to warrant that the answers to the questions are true or false.

(15) <**R**> is the symbol for reasoning, which is experiencing making inferences and drawing conclusions about the implicative meanings of statements; reasoning includes intuiting, deducing, reducing, retroducing, inducing,

abducing, evaluating, prescribing and justifying.

(16) <**F**> is the symbol for focus, which is the coordinating of the different elements of mind (**V**, **P**, **N**) such they are attending to the same object, task, concern or state of affairs.

Well-Defined Terms for Descriptive Educological Theory

The conduct of careful, disciplined, unambiguous discourse about any set of phenomena requires a set of well-defined terms. The well-defined terms constitute the descriptive theory (also denoted by the terms <*conceptual theory*> and <*constructs*>) of the discourse about the phenomena. The purpose of having a descriptive theory is to have the linguistic objects (terms and concepts) to talk and write sensibly and productively about some nominated set of phenomena. To talk and write clearly and fruitfully about something, we need to know what set of phenomena we are denoting with the words and sentences that we use in our talking and writing. Well-defined terms provide us with the appropriate words and concepts to make our talking and writing important, significant valuable.

Every fund of knowledge (astronomy, botany, virology, etc.) has its descriptive theory (its set of well-defined terms). Descriptive theory of educology, or descriptive educological theory, consists of the set of well-defined terms which can be used to progress discourse and inquiry about education. A summary of descriptive educological theory which we have developed thus far in this first chapter, through our use of definition, explication and exemplification, is as follows. The terms are arranged in alphabetical order by the symbol which denotes the relevant phenomenon, activity, process or state of affairs in education (or related to education).

(1) <**C**> the symbol for content, including content$_1$ and content$_2$. The statement <$\mathbf{C} = \mathbf{C}_1 \cup \mathbf{C}_2 = \mathbf{K}_{1O} \cup \mathbf{K}_{2O}$> means that the essential elements of content (**C**) are the union of ($\cup$) the essential elements of content$_1$ ($\mathbf{C}_1$) and content$_2$ ($\mathbf{C}_2$). The union ($\cup$) of content$_1$ and content$_2$ is the same as the union of knowledge ($\mathbf{K}_{1O}$) (<$_O$ > standards for organized) and knowing ($\mathbf{K}_{2O}$) which are organized for the purposes of teaching ($\mathbf{T}_P$) and

intentional guided studying ($\mathbf{S}_{P1}$).

(2) <$\mathbf{C}_1$> is the symbol for $content_1$ or a selection of knowledge ($\mathbf{K}_{1O}$) organized for the purposes of teaching ($\mathbf{T}_P$) and intentional guided studying ($\mathbf{S}_{P1}$).

(3) <$\mathbf{C}_2$> is the symbol for $content_2$ or a selection of a range of knowing ($\mathbf{K}_{2O}$) organized for the purposes of teaching ($\mathbf{T}_P$) and intentional guided studying ($\mathbf{S}_{P1}$).

(4) <**E**> is the symbol for education ($education_4$). Education is the set of phenomena with the elements of teacher, student, content and setting ($\mathbf{E} = \mathbf{T} \cup \mathbf{S} \cup \mathbf{C} \cup \mathbf{X}$).

(5) <**F**> is the symbol for focus, which is the coordinating of the different elements of mind (**V**, **P**, **N**) such that they are attending to the same object, task, concern or state of affairs.

(6) <$\mathbf{H}_C$>is the symbol for human consciousness, which is defined as experiencing volition, perception and cognition.

(7) <$\mathbf{K}_1$> is the symbol for $knowledge_1$, or recorded true statements.

(8) <$\mathbf{K}_2$> is the symbol for $knowledge_2$, or knowing, or a cognitive state of mind.

(9) K_{2F}: K_{2F} is the symbol for form of knowing, which is the way in which knowing is exemplified.

(10) <$\mathbf{K}_{2F1}$> is the symbol for linguistic knowing, which is the learned ability to exemplify deliberate, controlled, coordinated and warranted linguistic performances.

(11) <$\mathbf{K}_{2F2}$> is the symbol for emotional knowing, which is the learned ability to exemplify deliberate, controlled, coordinated and warranted emotional performances.

(12) <$\mathbf{K}_{2F3}$> is the symbol for imaginal knowing, which is the learned ability to exemplify deliberate, controlled, coordinated and imaginal performances.

(13) <$\mathbf{K}_{2F4}$> is the symbol for physiological knowing, which is the learned ability to exemplify deliberate, controlled, coordinated and warranted physiological performances.

(14) <$\mathbf{K}_{2F5}$> is the symbol for physical knowing, which is the learned ability to exemplify deliberate, controlled, coordinated and warranted physical performances.

(15) <$\mathbf{K}_{2K}$> is the symbol for kind of knowing, which is knowing in relation to some entity or state of affairs (some object of knowing <$\mathbf{O}_{K2}$>).

(16) <$\mathbf{K}_{2K1}$> is the symbol for knowing-that-one, which is the learned ability to perform deliberately, confidently, competently and justifiably in relation to some unique entity or state of affairs.

(17) <$\mathbf{K}_{2K1A}$> is the symbol for recognitive knowing-that-one, which is the learned ability to recognize a unique entity or state of affairs and discern it from that which is not that entity or state of affairs, and vice versa, viz. discern that which is not that unique entity or state of affairs from that which is.

(18) <$\mathbf{K}_{2K1B}$> is the symbol for acquaintive knowing-that-one, which is the learned state of mind of being familiar with the essential and unique qualities of a given unique entity or state of affairs.

(19) <$\mathbf{K}_{2K1C}$> is the symbol for appreciative knowing-that-one, which is the learned state of mind of having appreciation for the essential and unique qualities of a given unique entity or state of affairs.

(20) <$\mathbf{K}_{2K2}$> is the symbol for knowing-that, which is the learned ability to perform in a purposeful, well-informed, adequate and justifiable way in relation to entities or states of affairs as members of categories.

(21) <$\mathbf{K}_{2K2A}$> is the symbol for instantive knowing-that, which is the learned ability to perform in a purposeful, well-informed, adequate and justifiable way in relation to an entity or relation as a member of a category and to warrant the performance by referencing the assertion with adequate authority.

(22) <$\mathbf{K}_{2K2B}$> is the symbol for relational knowing-that, which is the learned ability to perform in a purposeful, well-informed, adequate and justifiable way in relation to the mutual effects (e.g. dependent, independent, co-dependent, etc.) between entities, processes and/or states of affairs and to warrant the performance by appropriate evidence or evidential argument.

(23) <$\mathbf{K}_{2K2C}$> is the symbol for criterial knowing-that, which is the learned ability to perform in a purposeful, well-informed, adequate and justifiable way in relation to the relations between (1) norms and (2) entities, processes and/or states of affairs and to warrant the performance by justificatory argument.

(24) <$\mathbf{K}_{2K3}$> is the symbol for knowing-how, which is the learned ability to enact a set of performances deliberately, intelligently, justifiably and with warranted certainty to achieve a desired result.

(25) <$\mathbf{K}_{2K3A}$> is the symbol for protocolic knowing-how, which is the learned ability to execute a single-pathed performance characterized by goal attainment through invariant sequences of activity (inclusive of the five forms of knowing).

(26) <$\mathbf{K}_{2K3B}$> is the symbol for adaptive knowing-how, which is the learned ability to execute a multi-pathed performance smoothly and attain a goal through adjusted sequences of movement.

(27) <$\mathbf{K}_{2K3C}$> is the symbol for creative knowing-how, which is the learned ability to transform elements of a performance into unique forms and to unite disparate ways of realizing goals (planned for and/or serendipitous goals).

(28) <$\mathbf{K}_{2K4}$> is the symbol for knowing-to, which is the learned ability to exercise conscious intention, will and choice in a rational way that is consistent with a set of freely and rationally chosen and justified criteria (rules and/or standards).

(29) <$\mathbf{K}_{2K4A}$> is the symbol for rules-based knowing-to, which is the learned ability to exercise conscious intention, will and choice in a rational way that is consistent with a set of freely and rationally chosen and justified rules.

(30) <$\mathbf{K}_{2K4B}$> is the symbol for standards-based knowing-to, which is the learned ability to exercise conscious intention, will and choice in a rational way that is consistent with a set of freely and rationally chosen and justified standards.

(31) <$\mathbf{K}_{2KLF}$>is the symbol for a range of knowing, which is a

combination of some kind of knowing ($\mathbf{K}_{2K}$), some level of knowing ($\mathbf{K}_{2L}$) and some form of knowing ($\mathbf{K}_{2F}$).

(32) <$\mathbf{K}_{2L}$>is the symbol for level of knowing, which is the extent or degree to which an individual's cognitive development has been achieved.

(33) <$\mathbf{K}_{2L1}$>is the symbol for Level 1 preconventional knowing, or beginner or novice level of knowing, which is characterized by a low degree of competence, a high degree of disorganization, many mistakes, much hesitancy and uncertainty, a low degree of control and confidence.

(34) <$\mathbf{K}_{2L2}$>is the symbol for Level 2 conventional intermediate knowing, which is characterized by a medium degree of competence within the limit of established conventions, near mastery of conventions, medium degree of organization, few mistakes, little hesitancy or uncertainty, medium degree of control and confidence, almost habituated competent performance.

(35) <$\mathbf{K}_{2L3}$>is the symbol for Level 3 conventional expert knowing, which is characterized by a high degree of competence within the limit of established conventions, habituated and complete mastery of conventions, high degree of organization, no mistakes, no hesitancy, a high degree of control and confidence.

(36) <$\mathbf{K}_{2L4}$> is the symbol for Level 4 postconventional knowing, or the level of the expert innovator, characterized by competency which extends beyond mastery of the limits of established conventions to innovative and creative performances, with no mistakes, no hesitancy, a high degree of control and confidence and habituated highly competent performance.

(37) <**L**> is the symbol for the process of learning (coming to know) by any means and in any circumstance.

(38) <$\mathbf{L}_1$> is the symbol for the process of conduced learning (intentional guided learning), which is the process of coming to know a prescribed range of knowing ($\mathbf{K}_{2P}$) from participating as a student (**S**) in education (**E**).

(39) <$\mathbf{L}_2$> is the symbol for the process of discovery learning (intentional unguided learning), which is the process of coming to know a discovered range of knowing ($\mathbf{K}_{2D}$)

from conducting intentional unguided inquiry (**Q**) either as trial and error or systematic research.

(40) <$\mathbf{L}_3$> is the symbol for the process of compelled learning (unintentional guided learning), which is the process of coming to know a coerced range of knowing ($\mathbf{K}_{2C}$) from socialization, enculturation and indoctrination.

(41) <$\mathbf{L}_4$> is the symbol for the process of accidental learning (unintentional unguided learning), which is the process of coming to know an accidental range of knowing ($\mathbf{K}_{2A}$) from haphazard, random circumstances, including misadventure and serendipity.

(42) <$\mathbf{L}_5$> is the symbol for learning as product, which is the range of knowing ($\mathbf{K}_2$) that is the consequent of having come to know. <$\mathbf{L}_5$> is equivalent in meaning to <$\mathbf{K}_2$>.

(43) <**M**>is the symbol for mind, which is defined as human psyche, which in turn is defined as human consciousness ($\mathbf{H}_C$), which in turn is defined as experiencing of volition (**V**), perception (**P**) and cognition (**N**).

(44) <**N**> is the symbol for cognition, which is experiencing conceiving (**O**), knowing ($\mathbf{K}_2$), understanding (**U**), inquiring (**Q**) and reasoning (**R**).

(45) <**O**> is the symbol for conceiving, which is experiencing creating meaning with logical objects (ordinary language symbols, special mathematical symbols, special music symbols, special Braille symbols, special sign language symbols).

(46) <**P**> is the symbol for perception, which is defined as experiencing objects through introspection and/or extrospection.

(47) <$\mathbf{P}_1$> is the symbol for perception$_1$, which is experiencing, through introspection, emotional objects (joy, fear, depression).

(48) <$\mathbf{P}_2$> is the symbol for perception$_2$, which is experiencing, through introspection, imagined objects (imagined sights, imagined sounds, imagined emotions).

(49) <$\mathbf{P}_3$> is the symbol for perception$_3$, which is experiencing, through introspection, physiological objects (pain, thirst, hunger, orgasm).

(50) <$\mathbf{P}_4$> is the symbol for perception$_4$, which is

experiencing, through introspection, motivational objects (urges, desires).

(51) <$\mathbf{P}_5$> is the symbol for perception$_5$, which is experiencing, through introspection, remembered objects (remembered sounds, sights, events, people).

(52) <$\mathbf{P}_6$> is the symbol for perception$_6$, which experiencing, through extrospection, physical objects (chairs, grass, trees, people).

(53) <**Q**> is the symbol for inquiring, which is experiencing the undertaking, intentionally and without guidance, to ask questions, answer questions and adduce necessary and sufficient evidence to warrant that the answers to the questions are true or false.

(54) <**R**> is the symbol for reasoning, which is experiencing making inferences and drawing conclusions about the implicative meanings of statements; reasoning includes intuiting, deducing, reducing, retroducing, inducing, abducing, evaluating, prescribing and justifying.

(55) <**S**> is the symbol for student, who is a person who accepts the opportunities, guidance and help provided by a teacher (**T**) and intentionally undertakes to develop under guidance some conventional level prescribed range of knowing ($\mathbf{K}_{2P}$).

(56) <$\mathbf{S}_{P1}$> is the symbol for studying$_1$. A synonym for studying$_1$ is the term <*studenting*>. Studying$_1$ is accepting the opportunities, guidance and help provided by a teacher (**T**) and intentionally undertaking to develop under guidance some conventional level prescribed range of knowing ($\mathbf{K}_{2P}$).

(57) <$\mathbf{S}_{P2}$> is the symbol for studying$_2$ or intentionally undertaking without guidance to develop some conventional level range of knowing ($\mathbf{K}_2$). Studying$_2$ ($\mathbf{S}_{P2}$) is what an autodidact does, and studying$_2$ ($\mathbf{S}_{P2}$) is done outside of education (**E**). A synonym for studying$_2$ ($\mathbf{S}_{P2}$) is <*autodidactism*>.

(58) <$\mathbf{S}_{P3}$> is the symbol for studying$_3$ or intentionally undertaking without guidance to develop postconventional knowing. Studying$_3$ ($\mathbf{S}_{P3}$) is what investigators or researchers do in original research or neo-

search. Studying$_3$ ($\mathbf{S}_{P3}$) is done outside of education (**E**).

(59) <$\mathbf{S}_{P4}$> is the symbol for studying$_4$ or intentionally undertaking to develop without guidance knowing about a particular state of affairs. Studying$_4$ ($\mathbf{S}_{P4}$) is what a veterinarian might do to determine what medication to administer to an ailing dog, a ship's captain might do to determine what course to take achieve optimal fuel consumption or an appliance repair technician might do to determine what spare part to replace. Studying$_4$ ($\mathbf{S}_{P4}$) is done outside of education (**E**).

(60) <**T**> is the symbol for teacher (teacher$_1$). A teacher (**T**) is a person who provides opportunities, guidance and help to students to intentionally study under guidance some content with the purpose in mind that the students achieve some prescribed range of knowing ($\mathbf{K}_{2P}$).

(61) <$\mathbf{T}_P$> is the symbol for teaching (teaching$_1$ <$\mathbf{T}_{P1}$>). Teaching is the providing of opportunities, guidance and help to students to study intentionally under guidance some content with the purpose in mind that the students achieve some prescribed range of knowing ($\mathbf{K}_{2P}$).

(62) <**U**> is the symbol for understanding, which is a synchronous combination of awareness (**W**), judgment (**J**) and some range of knowing ($\mathbf{K}_{2KLF}$), which varies from low to high level (preconventional to postconventional level) and from small (a single kind and form of knowing) to extensive (all kinds and forms of knowing).

(63) <**V**> is the symbol for volition, which is defined as experiencing conation, choice, will, deliberation about what choice to make or what action to take.

(64) <**X**> is the symbol for the context in which teachers and students transact with content; the context (**X**) includes the physical ($\mathbf{X}_P$), social ($\mathbf{X}_S$) and cultural context ($\mathbf{X}_C$).

(65) <$\mathbf{X}_P$> is the symbol for the physical context in which teachers and students transact with content, for example, houses, apartments, street corners, playing fields, classrooms, lecture halls, libraries, laboratories, gymnasiums, etc.

(66) <$\mathbf{X}_S$> is the symbol for the social context in which teachers and students transact with content, for example,

families, peer groups, church groups, work mates, schools, academies, institutes, universities, the wider community, the wider society.

(67) <$\mathbf{X}_C$> is the symbol for the cultural context in which teachers and students transact with content, for example, French culture, German culture, Spanish culture, Indonesian culture, etc.

2 EXPLANATORY EDUCOLOGICAL THEORY

Descriptive educological theory provides the terms and concepts to discern, describe and analyze education. Explanatory educological theory uses descriptive educological theory to discern phenomena, activities, processes and states of affairs in education, to describe what happens in education, to explain why it happens and to predict what will happen, given a particular set of controlling conditions.

Explanatory educological theory includes scientific educological theory and praxiological educological theory. Scientific educological theory describes relations among the elements of education. It describes, explains and predicts what happens in education. Praxiological educological theory describes effective relations and activities in education. It describes, explains, predicts and prescribes what will work (and what will not work) in education to achieve some desired state of affairs in education and/or to achieve some desired set of intended learning outcomes.

Scientific Educological Theory

Education (**E**) is a system consisting of the elements of teacher (**T**), student (**S**), content (**C**) and context (**X**), all standing in some relation to each other. Education (**E**) is not learning (**L**), but it is one of the means to learning (**L**). Learning (**L**) is the process by which some range of knowing ($\mathbf{K}_{2KLF}$) is achieved. Education (**E**) is one of the sets (among other sets) of controlling conditions for the resultant process of learning (**L**) some range of knowing ($\mathbf{K}_2$), but it is not the only means by which we, as human beings, learn (**L**) a range of knowing ($\mathbf{K}_2$).

Learning (**L**) some range of knowing ($\mathbf{K}_2$) contributes to the extension of the human mind. The human mind (**M**) consists of human consciousness ($\mathbf{H}_C$), and human consciousness ($\mathbf{H}_C$) consists of a system of relations among three major categories of experience, viz. volition, perception and cognition. Volition (**V**) is experiencing conation, choice, will, deliberation. Perception (**P**) is experiencing the introspection of emotional objects (perception$_1$ or $\mathbf{P}_1$), the introspection of imagined objects (perception$_2$ or $\mathbf{P}_2$), the introspection of physiological objects (perception$_3$ or $\mathbf{P}_3$), the introspection of urges and desires (perception$_4$ or $\mathbf{P}_4$), the introspection of memories (perception$_5$ or $\mathbf{P}_5$), and the extrospection of physical objects (perception$_6$ or $\mathbf{P}_6$). Cognition (**N**) is the experiencing of conceiving (**O**), the experiencing of knowing ($\mathbf{K}_2$), the experiencing of understanding (**U**), the experiencing of inquiring (**Q**) and the experiencing of reasoning (**R**).

All the categories of experiencing stand in a complex set of relations in which each category of experiencing influences, and is influenced by, each other category of experiencing. The mutual effects of <**V**>, <**P**> and <**N**> can be expressed as follows.

V ↔ P
P ↔ N
N ↔ V

The first statement <**V ↔ P**> reads in ordinary English that volition (**V**) and perception (P) have mutual effects (↔). Volition (**V**) is the set of controlling conditions for (→) perception (**P**), and perception (**P**) is the set of controlling conditions for (→) volition (**V**).

The second statement <**P ↔ N**> reads in ordinary English that perception (**P**) and cognition (**N**) have mutual effects (↔). Perception (**P**) is the set of controlling conditions for (→) cognition (**N**), and cognition (**N**) is the set of controlling conditions for (→) perception (**P**).

The third statement <**N ↔ V**> reads in ordinary English that cognition (**N**) and volition (**V**) have mutual effects (↔). Cognition (**N**) is the set of controlling conditions for (→) volition (**V**), and volition (**V**) is the set of controlling conditions for (→) cognition (**N**).

In addition to the relationships of <**V ↔ P**>, <**P ↔ N**> and <**N**

↔ **V**>, there is focus of attention (**F**). Our focus of attention has the properties of object of attention, duration of attention and intermittency of attention. We focus on some entity, process, relation or state of affairs. That is our object of attention ($\mathbf{F_O}$). We focus on some object for some period of time (a few seconds, a few minutes, rarely more than an hour). That is our duration of attention ($\mathbf{F_D}$). Our focus flits from one object to another and another and sometimes back again to the first. Our focus of attention is intermittent, and it changes continually. That is our change in focus ($\mathbf{F_C}$). Focus can be expressed as follows.

$$\mathbf{F = F_O \cup F_D \cup F_C}$$

The statement <$\mathbf{F = F_O \cup F_D \cup F_C}$> reads in ordinary English that the essential properties of focus of attention (**F**) consist of (**=**) the union of ($\cup$) the essential properties of the object of focus ($\mathbf{F_O}$), the duration of focus ($\mathbf{F_D}$) and the change in focus ($\mathbf{F_C}$).

Focus of attention (**F**) is not a category of volition (**V**), perception (**P**) or cognition (**N**), but rather, it is a function of them. Focus of attention (**F**) is the direction which we give our consciousness. Focus of attention (**F**) is the function of mind (**M**) which coordinates volition (**V**), perception (**P**) and cognition (**N**). Focus of attention (**F**) has mutual effects with volition (**V**), perception (**P**) and cognition (**N**). Focus of attention (**F**) can be the set of controlling conditions for the resultants of volition (**V**), perception (**P**) and cognition (**N**), and volition (**V**), perception (**P**) and cognition (**N**) can be the set of controlling conditions for the resultant of focus (**F**). The relationship of mutual effects can be expressed as follows.

$$\mathbf{F \leftrightarrow V \cup P \cup N}$$

The statement <$\mathbf{F \leftrightarrow V \cup P \cup N}$> reads in ordinary English that focus of attention (**F**) has mutual effects (↔) with the union ($\cup$) of the essential elements of volition (**V**), perception (**P**) and cognition (**N**). Focus of attention (**F**) is the set of controlling conditions (→) for the union of the essential elements of volition (**V**), perception (**P**) and cognition (**N**), and the union ($\cup$) of the essential elements of volition (**V**), perception (**P**) and cognition (**N**) is the set of controlling conditions (→) for focus of attention (**F**).

We as human beings extend our minds by a variety of means. We extend our minds (**M**) through unguided problem solving or inquiry (**Q**). The resultant of successful inquiry is intentional unguided (discovery) learning ($\mathbf{L_2}$), a process which results in some discovered range of knowing ($\mathbf{K}_{2D}$). We extend our minds through socialization, enculturation and indoctrination. The resultant of socialization, enculturation and indoctrination is unintentional guided (coerced) learning ($\mathbf{L}_3$), a process which results in some compelled range of knowing ($\mathbf{K}_{2C}$). We extend our minds through happenstance, including accidents and serendipity. The resultant of happenstance is unintentional unguided (accidental) learning ($\mathbf{L}_4$), a process which results in some accidental range of knowing ($\mathbf{K}_{2A}$). These three processes of learning (**L**) a range of knowing ($\mathbf{K}_2$) occur outside education (**E**).

Intentional guided learning (conduced) learning ($\mathbf{L}_1$) is the resultant process of effective teaching ($\mathbf{T}_{PE}$) and effective studying$_1$ under guidance ($\mathbf{S}_{P1E}$) some content (<**C**> including content$_1$ <$\mathbf{C}_1$>, some selection of didactically organized knowledge <$\mathbf{K}_{1O}$> and/or content$_2$ <$\mathbf{C}_2$>, some selection of didactically organized knowing <$\mathbf{K}_{2O}$>) in some physical, social and cultural context (**X**). When education (**E**) is effective ($\mathbf{E}_E$), the resultant is the process of conduced learning (learning$_1$ <$\mathbf{L}_1$>), and the process of conduced learning (learning$_1$ <$\mathbf{L}_1$>) is the set of controlling conditions for the resultant of some prescribed range of knowing ($\mathbf{K}_{2P}$) at the conventional intermediate ($\mathbf{K}_{2L2}$) and/or conventional expert level ($\mathbf{K}_{2L3}$) of knowing.

Functional Education

For education (**E**) to function properly, the relations among the elements must be optimal. The teachers (**T**) must have the necessary range of knowing ($\mathbf{K}_{2KLF}$) and the willingness (**V**) to teach the content (**C**) to the students (**S**). The students (**S**) must be willing (**V**) to study ($\mathbf{S}_{P1}$) under the guidance of the teacher, have a desire ($\mathbf{P}_4$) to achieve the prescribed range of knowing ($\mathbf{K}_{2P}$) and have the capability to learn ($\mathbf{L}_1$) the intended learning outcomes (**ILO**s, i.e. some prescribed range of knowing <$\mathbf{K}_{2P}$>). The content (**C**) must be at an optimal level of difficulty for the students (not too easy, but not too difficult) and must be accepted by the teachers and students as worthwhile to teach and study. The physical setting ($\mathbf{X}_P$) must be favorable to the teaching and studying activities. The social ($\mathbf{X}_S$) and cultural ($\mathbf{X}_C$) context must be supportive of the activities of the teachers and students, it must be appreciative of the content (**C**) and it must attribute value to the intended learning outcomes (**ILO**s).

Consider the student, George, in a compulsory 10th grade high school English class. The teacher, Mr Hanson, is conducting a unit of study on Shakespeare's play, *Julius Caesar*. The teacher assigns the students the task of writing an essay which analyzes the struggle that the character Brutus has with the conflicting demands of friendship, honor and patriotism and what Brutus does to resolve the conflict. George has an intense interest in the works of Shakespeare, and he especially likes the play, *Julius Caesar*. He reads the play carefully, maps out how Brutus feels torn among his conflicting values of friendship for Caesar, patriotism for the Republic of Rome and the demands of acting honorably as a member of the Roman aristocracy. George writes a well-researched, thoughtful and carefully reasoned draft essay. He consults with his teacher, Mr Hanson, about how he might improve his essay, and he heeds the advice of his teacher. In this scenario, George is **in the experience** and **of the experience** of intentionally studying ($\mathbf{S_{P1}}$) under guidance. George acts in good faith as a student. He wants to achieve an understanding of the complexities of the dilemma in which Brutus finds himself. He is willing to accept the advice and guidance of his teacher. He is willing to complete the assigned task of writing the essay to the best of his ability. The majority of members of the wider community in which George's school exists thinks that it is appropriate for students in the 10th grade to be reading and studying Shakespeare's *Julius Caesar*. This is a clear case of functional education.

Dysfunctional Education

Dysfunctional education is a state of affairs in which one or more of the elements stands in an unsupportive, oppositional and/or disruptive relation to the other elements. Any one of the following conditions will make education dysfunctional. The teachers (**T**) do not have the necessary range of knowing ($\mathbf{K_{2KLF}}$) and/or are not willing (**V**) to teach the content (**C**) to the students (**S**). The students (**S**) are not willing (**V**) to study ($\mathbf{S_{P1}}$) under the guidance of the teacher, or have little or no desire ($\mathbf{P_4}$) to achieve the prescribed range of knowing ($\mathbf{K_{2P}}$), or lack the capability to learn ($\mathbf{L_1}$) the intended learning outcomes (**ILO**s). The content (**C**) is not at an optimal level of difficulty for the students (too easy or too difficult), and/or the content is not accepted by the teachers and/or students to be worthwhile to teach and study. The physical setting ($\mathbf{X_P}$) is not favorable to the teaching and studying activities. The social ($\mathbf{X_S}$) and cultural ($\mathbf{X_C}$) contexts are not supportive of (or stand in opposition to) the activities of the teachers and students, and the community is not appreciative of (or is opposed to) the content (**C**) and the intended learning outcomes (**ILO**s).

Consider the student, Gary, one of George's classmates in the same compulsory 10th grade high school English class. The teacher, Mr Hanson, is conducting a unit of study on Shakespeare's play, *Julius Caesar*. The teacher assigns the students the task of writing an essay which analyzes the struggle which the character Brutus has with the conflicting demands of friendship, honor and patriotism and what Brutus does to resolve the conflict. Gary, in contrast to George, has no love for English literature. He daydreams in class, pays little or no attention to his teacher's guidance, makes no attempt to complete the in-class study activities and tries to distract his fellow students with pranks. At home, he makes a cursory attempt to read the play, but he finds the language obtuse and incomprehensible. He decides that it is much more interesting to play games on his Xbox than to read *Julius Caesar*. For completion of his assignment, he does a Google search and finds a copy of *CliffsNotes* on Julius Caesar, reads the one-page summary of the play and writes a superficial essay without references and without addressing the main issue of the conflicts among friendship, honor and patriotism with which Brutus struggles. In this scenario, Gary is **in the experience** of intentional guided study ($\mathbf{S_{P1}}$), but he is not **of the experience**. He acts in bad faith as a student. He is not willing to complete the assigned study activities ($\mathbf{S_{P1}}$), and he attempts to distract his fellow students. He does a cursory job of writing the assigned essay, and he has no genuine care about the quality of his work as a student, nor the extension of his range of knowing ($\mathbf{K_{2KLF}}$) about the play *Julius Caesar*. Gary's parents think that studying the plays of Shakespeare is a complete waste of Gary's time. In this scenario, it is clear that Gary participated only marginally as a student in education (**E**), and for him, the education is dysfunctional.

In the case of Gary, education is dysfunctional because the student (**S**), Gary, does not value the content (**C**), nor does he value the intended learning outcomes (**ILO**s). Because he does not value the content and the intended learning outcomes, he does not play the role of student (**S**) competently. He does not focus (**F**) his attention on the opportunities, guidance and help which his teacher provides. He does not complete the recommended study activities ($\mathbf{S_{P1}}$). Education (**E**) does not function properly, and there is little in the way of consequential intentional guided learning ($\mathbf{L_1}$) by Gary of the intended learning outcomes (**ILO**s).

Dysfunctional education can be caused by any of the four elements (**T**, **S**, **C**, **X**) being in an unsupportive, oppositional, disruptive and/or destructive relation with the other elements. The American schoolteacher, lecturer and diversity trainer, Jane Elliot (b. 1933) first used her "Blue eyes – Brown eyes" exercise with her primary school class on 5 April 1968, the day after the assassination of Martin Luther King, Jr (1926-1968). She divided the students according to eye color, blue eyes and brown eyes. One group received preferentially favorable treatment. The other group received harsh, unfair, oppressive treatment. She reversed the treatment for the two groups. Afterwards, she had the students write descriptions of their feelings about being a member of the socially superior privileged group and the socially inferior oppressed group. As word spread in her small community (Riceville, Iowa) of her lessons about racial discrimination, many residents of Riceville condemned her for subjecting small children to the harsh treatment accorded to the socially inferior group in her Blue eyes – Brown eyes exercise. Her fellow teachers condemned her and ostracized her. The case of Jane Elliot is one in which dysfunctional education is caused by the social and cultural context (**X**) being in an oppositional relation to the content (**C**), the intended learning outcomes (**ILO**s) and the teaching ($\mathbf{T}_{P}$) and studying ($\mathbf{S}_{P1}$) activities. The education (**E**) was functional and effective to the extent that the students were willing to study the content and achieve the intended learning outcomes. They accepted the study activities, the content and the intended learning outcomes as worthwhile, and they achieved the intended learning outcomes (knowing the consequences of unfair oppressive treatment on the basis of physical appearance). The education (**E**) was dysfunctional to the extent that many community members (**X**) did not value the teaching and studying activities. They regarded the intended learning outcomes (**ILO**s) as emotionally harmful, and they opposed the teacher (**T**), her teaching activities ($\mathbf{T}_{P}$), the students' studying activities ($\mathbf{S}_{P1}$) and the content (**C**).

Unofficial Education

Education (**E**) can be unofficial or official. In unofficial education ($\mathbf{E}_{U}$), the four essential elements of the system are teacher (**T**), student (**S**), content (**C**) and physical, social and cultural setting (**X**). In unofficial education ($\mathbf{E}_{U}$), episodes of teaching ($\mathbf{T}_{P}$) and intentional guided studying ($\mathbf{S}_{P1}$) are spontaneous and sporadic.

Consider the example of Evan. Evan is a 9-year-old boy. He is visiting his cousin, Gary. Evan sees a Mandala board. He says, "What's this?" Gary says that it's a Mandala board. "What's Mandala?" asks Evan. Gary says, "It's a game." "How do you play it?" asks Evan. Gary says, "Here, let's play a game. I'll show you how." Gary tells Evan about the basic rules of the game and the general strategy to follow to win. Evan follows Gary's instructions. Evan likes the game, and they continue to play for the next two hours. In this episode of unofficial education ($\mathbf{E}_U$), Gary was teaching ($\mathbf{T}_P$). Evan was studying intentionally under guidance ($\mathbf{S}_{P1}$). The content (**C**) was the rules, strategies and the playing of the game Mandala. The setting (**X**) was, physically, a cousin's house, socially, part of an extended family, and culturally, Australian culture. The outcome of the unofficial education ($\mathbf{E}_U$) was the extension of Evan's range of knowing-how ($\mathbf{K}_{2K3}$) to play Mandala.

This example illustrates the basic elements, activities and products of unofficial education ($\mathbf{E}_U$). The basic elements are teacher (**T**), student (**S**), content (**C**) and setting (**X**). The basic activities are teaching ($\mathbf{T}_P$) and intentional guided studying ($\mathbf{S}_{P1}$). When the education is effective ($\mathbf{E}_E$), intentional learning under guidance (learning$_1$ <$\mathbf{L}_1$>) is the resultant process of the teaching ($\mathbf{T}_P$) and intentional guided studying ($\mathbf{S}_{P1}$), and the product of the process of intentional guided learning ($\mathbf{L}_1$) is a prescribed range of knowing ($\mathbf{K}_{2P}$). The product of education (**E**), when education is effective ($\mathbf{E}_E$), is students experiencing the process of conduced learning (learning$_1$ <$\mathbf{L}_1$>) of a prescribed range of knowing ($\mathbf{K}_{2P}$) and consequentially an extension of the minds (**M**) of the students.

Unofficial education ($\mathbf{E}_U$) takes place as sporadic episodes in the course of daily life, and we swiftly and frequently alternate between the roles of teacher and student. A grandchild (the teacher <**T**>) shows his grandmother (the student <**S**>) how to send an email, and the grandmother (the teacher <**T**>) shows the grandson (the student <**S**>) how to crochet. A farmer (the teacher <**T**>) shows his daughter (the student <**S**>) how to operate the power train on a tractor, and the daughter (the teacher <**T**>) shows her father (the student <**S**>) how to use an accounting application to keep track of his expenditures and revenues. A car salesman (the teacher <**T**>) shows his client (the student <**S**>) how to operate the controls on a newly purchased car, and the client (the teacher <**T**>), whose hobby is flying drones, shows the car salesman (the student <**S**>) how to fly a drone. In unofficial education (**E**$_U$), the persons playing the role of teacher (**T**) have no requirement to be certified. They have no need nor any obligation to write intended learning outcomes (**ILO**s), prepare lesson plans, organize resources, conduct testing, provide evaluations or certify learning achievements or keep attendance records. In unofficial education (**E**$_U$), the persons playing the role of student (**S**) have no requirements to enrol in courses, attend classes regularly, complete assignments, do homework or sit tests.

Official Education

In official education (**E**$_O$), the basic elements, activities, processes and products are the same as unofficial education (**E**$_U$). The basic elements are teacher, student, content and context (**T**, **S**, **C**, **X**). The basic activities are teaching (**T**$_P$) and intentionally studying under guidance (**S**$_{P1}$). The basic process that proceeds from the teaching (**T**$_P$) and intentional guided studying (**S**$_{P1}$), when the education (**E**) is effective (**E**$_E$), is intentional guided (conduced) learning (**L**$_1$). The basic product of the process of conduced learning (**L**$_1$) is a prescribed range of knowing (**K**$_{2P}$) achieved by the students. In addition, official education (**E**$_O$) has a number of distinguishing characteristics or properties (denoted by <**P**$_{EO}$>, which stands for <*properties of official education*>). They include

(1) enrolled students who are typically required to attend classes on a regular basis,
(2) licensed, certified or approved teachers who are paid for their services,
(3) licensed, certified or approved administrators who are paid for their services, e.g. principals, superintendents, directors, headmasters, head teachers, department heads, inspectors, etc.,
(4) written lesson plans, written unit plans or other written instructional programs,
(5) published syllabi and curricula documents,
(6) regularly scheduled class meetings,
(7) specially designated buildings and rooms to provide places for class meetings, e.g. classrooms, lecture halls,

libraries, laboratories, playing fields, studios, gymnasia, etc.,
(8) systematic assessments, evaluations and certifications of student achievement, and documentation of student achievement with presentation (often as a public event) of certificates, diplomas, degrees, etc. to students.
(9) records of student attendance and achievement,
(10) bureaucratic units of governance, e.g. boards of trustees, boards of governors, directors of education, boards of education, municipal departments of education, county departments of education, state departments of education, national or federal departments of education, etc.,
(11) funding arrangements, e.g. taxes, private fees, endowments, donations, etc., to finance the buildings, resources and activities of teachers, students, administrators, and ancillary staff,
(12) laws, regulations, rules and policies which require, allow and/or prohibit activities and states of affairs in teaching and intentional guided studying.

The social and cultural setting (**X**) for official education ($\mathbf{E_O}$) places expectations upon the institution (i.e. the academy, institute, school, college, university, etc.) that it

(1) provides appropriate and fair opportunities to students to develop an explicitly prescribed range of knowing ($\mathbf{K_{2P}}$) and
(2) fairly, honestly and correctly certifies the students' attainment of the prescribed range of knowing ($\mathbf{K_{2P}}$) with documents of achievement, e.g. transcripts, diplomas, certificates, degrees (BA, MA, PhD, MD, etc.).

If official education ($\mathbf{E_O}$) fails to perform these two functions, then it fails its two major definite purposes.

Levels of Education

It is obvious, and well documented, that there is a progression in human development which corresponds with age. Physically, the progression is characterized by increase in size, strength and stamina. It is also characterized by improvement in capability and ability in coordination, mobility and movement. The progression in the development of mind (**M**) is characterized by changes of capability and

Figure 5: Elements and Age Levels of Unofficial and Official Education

E: Education	E_L: Age levels	E_{BE}: Basic elements
E_O: **Official education**	E_{OL1}: Early childhood or preschool E_{OL2}: Primary or elementary school E_{OL3}: Middle school or junior high school E_{OL4}: Secondary school E_{OL5}: Tertiary institutions, universities, colleges, institutes, etc.	**T**: Teacher **S**: Student **C**: Content **X**: Setting
E_U: **Unofficial education**	E_{UL1}: Early childhood E_{UL2}: Middle childhood E_{UL3}: Adolescence E_{UL4}: Early adulthood E_{UL5}: Middle adulthood E_{UL6}: Senescence	**T**: Teacher **S**: Student **C**: Content **X**: Setting

ability in volition (**V**), perception (**P**), cognition (**N**) and focus of attention (**F**). Both unofficial ($\mathbf{E_U}$) and official education ($\mathbf{E_O}$) make provisions to accommodate the different stages of development in body and mind which correspond with age.

In unofficial education ($\mathbf{E_U}$), the different age levels relevant to the way in which education (**E**) functions are early childhood (including infancy, ages 0 to 6), middle childhood (ages 7 to 12), adolescence (ages 13 to 18), early adulthood (ages 18 to early 30s), middle adulthood (early 30s to mid-60s) and senescence (mid-60s and onwards).

In official education ($\mathbf{E_O}$), specific institutions are established and maintained to accommodate the capabilities and abilities of different age levels. The institutions, found in almost every society and culture worldwide, are schools for early childhood or preschool (in different places denoted by various terms, e.g. *<preschool, preparation, kindergarten, transition>*, etc. for ages 3 to 5), primary (or elementary) schools for ages 6 to 11, middle schools (or junior high schools) for ages 12 to 13, secondary schools (or high schools) for ages 14 to 18 and tertiary institutions (academies, institutes, colleges, universities, technical and further education colleges, polytechnical institutes, adult education institutes, etc.) for ages 18 and onwards. In official education (**E_O**), most countries have laws which require compulsory school attendance for children from ages 5 or 6 to ages 16 or 18 for a specified number of days in the year (somewhere between 140 to 180 days depending on the state, province, region and/or country).

Effective and Ineffective Education

Education (**E**) can be effective (**E_E**) and ineffective (**E_I**). Teaching (**T_P**) and intentional guided studying (**S_{P1}**) are tasks, not achievements. It is not a desirable state of affairs, but it is entirely possible for teachers (**T**) to teach (**T_P**) (provide opportunities, guidance and help) some content (**C**) to students (**S**), who in turn, study intentionally under guidance (**S_{P1}**) (accept the opportunities and follow the guidance and help), and the students (**S**) do not achieve the intended learning outcomes (**ILO**s) to the desired standard of achievement. We, as students (**S**) can study intentionally under guidance (**S_{P1}**) some content (**C**) and fail to achieve the prescribed range of knowing (**K_{2P}**) to the standard to which we aspire. We can try to succeed, but not succeed. When teachers (**T**) and students (**S**) work cooperatively, and the students (**S**) achieve the intended learning outcomes (**ILO**s), the education (**E**) has been effective (**E_E**). When the students (**S**) do not achieve the intended learning outcomes (**ILO**s), the education (**E**) has been ineffective (**E_I**).

Something which educational institutions (schools, colleges, institutes, academies, universities, etc.) and professional teachers (**T**) cannot do in good faith, no matter how competent, accountable and responsible they are, is to guarantee that students (**S**) will achieve some set of intended learning outcomes (**ILO**s). Nor is it reasonable to expect and/or demand guaranteed achievement of a prescribed range of knowing (**K_{2P}**) by students from teaching (**T_P**). Lawyers cannot responsibly and in good faith guarantee that they will win their clients' cases, but to attract clients, they sometimes offer a no-win no-payment service. Medical practitioners cannot responsibly and in good faith guarantee that their patients will be cured of their illnesses, and unlike solicitors, they do not offer a no-cure no-fee service. In any case, practicing law, practicing medicine and practicing teaching are transactive activities, not reactive activities. Push a rock off a cliff, and it falls, every time, without exception. Add sodium to water, and the results are heat, sodium hydroxide and hydrogen gas, every time, without exception. Place a bowl of water in sunlight on a warm summer's day, and the water evaporates, every time, without exception. These are invariant, mindless reactions. Transactions between human beings are mindful, and the outcomes are variable. The parties involved in the transactions of law, medicine and education have volition, perception and cognition, and, for their own reasons and motivations, they choose to go in one direction or another. Like lawyers and medical practitioners, teachers and educational institutions can offer what is currently understood as best practice in the provision of opportunities to study (**S**$_{P1}$) and learn (**L**$_1$) intentionally under guidance. It is the choice of those playing the role of student (**S**) to accept the opportunities, to complete the intentional guided study activities (study$_1$ <**S**$_{P1}$>) and to endeavor to learn (learn$_1$ <**L**$_1$>) the prescribed range of knowing (**K**$_{2P}$) which is specified by the intended learning outcomes (**ILO**s). Just as some people can run faster than others, so too can some people learn (**L**) faster than others, and the pace and extent of the range of knowing (**K**$_2$) that is achieved differs with the content (**C**) and the intended learning outcomes (**ILO**s). We differ in our talents, and our differences are manifested in our different kinds, levels and forms of cognitive achievement. And just as some people choose to run, and some choose not to run, so it is with studying and learning. Some people choose to accept guidance, to study (study$_1$ <**S**$_{P1}$>) and to endeavor to learn intentionally with guidance (learn$_1$ <**L**$_1$>) some prescribed range of knowing (**K**$_{2P}$) in relation to some content (**C**) (history, geography, chemistry, welding, carpentry, plumbing, sculpting, singing, playing hockey, etc.), and some do not, for whatever reason and motivation. We all have our own reasons and motivations when choosing to study intentionally under guidance some content (**C**) or not to study (**S**$_{P1}$) some particular content (**C**). Teachers (**T**) provide opportunities to study intentionally under guidance (**S**$_{P1}$) some content (**C**), but it is not possible, in education (**E**), to coerce students to learn intentionally under guidance ($\mathbf{L_1}$) a prescribed range of knowing ($\mathbf{K_{2P}}$) about some content (**C**). Coerced learning ($\mathbf{L_3}$) of a compelled range of knowing ($\mathbf{K_{2C}}$) is possible, and it does take place as a result of the processes of socialization, enculturation and indoctrination. But it is not the variant of learning (conduced learning $<\mathbf{L_1}>$) of a prescribed range of knowing ($\mathbf{K_{2P}}$) which are the process and products of effective education ($\mathbf{E_E}$), whether official ($\mathbf{E_O}$) or unofficial ($\mathbf{E_U}$). These relationships can be expressed as follows.

$$\mathbf{E_E \rightarrow L_1 \rightarrow K_{2P}}$$
$$\mathbf{X \rightarrow L_3 \rightarrow K_{2C}}$$
$$\mathbf{(E_E \rightarrow L_1 \rightarrow K_{2P}) \neq (X \rightarrow L_3 \rightarrow K_{2C})}$$
$$\mathbf{(E_E \rightarrow L_1 \rightarrow K_{2P}) \subset E}$$
$$\mathbf{(X \rightarrow L_3 \rightarrow K_{2C}) \not\subset E}$$

The first statement $<\mathbf{E_E \rightarrow L_1 \rightarrow K_{2P}}>$ reads that the effective education ($\mathbf{E_E}$) is the set of controlling conditions for ($\rightarrow$) for the resultant process of intentional guided (conduced) learning ($\mathbf{L_1}$), and the process of intentional guided (conduced) learning ($\mathbf{L_1}$) is the set of controlling conditions for ($\rightarrow$) the resultant cognitive state of a prescribed range of knowing ($\mathbf{K_{2P}}$).

The second statement $<\mathbf{X \rightarrow L_3 \rightarrow K_{2C}}>$ reads that the context (the social and cultural environment) (**X**) is the set of controlling conditions for ($\rightarrow$) for the resultant process of unintentional guided (coerced) learning ($\mathbf{L_3}$), and the process of unintentional guided (coerced) learning ($\mathbf{L_3}$) is the set of controlling conditions for ($\rightarrow$) the resultant cognitive state of a compelled range of knowing ($\mathbf{K_{2C}}$).

The third statement $<\mathbf{(E_E \rightarrow L_1 \rightarrow K_{2P}) \neq (X \rightarrow L_3 \rightarrow K_{2C})}>$ reads that the relationships among effective education ($\mathbf{E_E}$), conduced learning ($\mathbf{L_1}$) and a prescribed range of knowing ($\mathbf{K_{2P}}$) are not the same as, or are not equivalent to ($\neq$), the relationships among the social and cultural context (**X**), coerced learning ($\mathbf{L_3}$) and a compelled range of knowing ($\mathbf{K_{2C}}$).

The fourth statement $<\mathbf{(E_E \rightarrow L_1 \rightarrow K_{2P}) \subset E}>$ reads that the relationships among effective education ($\mathbf{E_E}$), conduced learning ($\mathbf{L_1}$) and a prescribed range of knowing ($\mathbf{K_{2P}}$) are a subset of, or are a part of, or are a set of relations which occur in ($\subset$), education (**E**).

The fifth statement $<\mathbf{(X \rightarrow L_3 \rightarrow K_{2C}) \not\subset E}>$ reads that the relationships among the social and cultural context (**X**), coerced learning ($\mathbf{L_3}$) and a compelled range of knowing ($\mathbf{K_{2C}}$) are not a subset of, or are not a part of, or are not a set of relations which occur in ($\not\subset$), education (**E**).

Good and Bad Education

Education (**E**) can be extrinsically good (or bad) and intrinsically good (or bad). The extrinsic worth of education (**E**) is determined by the degree to which it contributes (or does not contribute) to achieving some desired (or desirable) state of affairs. The intrinsic worth of education (**E**) is determined by the degree to which education is worthwhile (or not worthwhile) in and of itself.

Education (**E**) is extrinsically good, for example, to the extent that it prepares young people for adult life as responsible, caring, well-informed, law-abiding citizens, or as young adults with employable skills, or as young adults with a range of knowing about how to budget finances and spend wisely, or how to invest in property, shares and business wisely, or how to achieve optimal health through eating wisely, exercising regularly and abstaining from use of harmful substances. Education (**E**) is extrinsically bad, for example, when it results in young people learning how to steal cars, how to prepare heroin for intravenous injection, how to break into business premises and steal money and goods, how to circumvent alarm systems to avoid detection while committing crimes or how to drug young women so that they can be easily raped.

Education (**E**) is intrinsically good, for example, when students and teachers treat each other ethically and morally, or treat each other fairly and justly, or treat each other with kindness and respect. Education (**E**) is intrinsically bad, for example, when teachers and/or students are victimized, abused physically and emotionally, oppressed, terrorized, bullied. Education (**E**) is intrinsically bad, for example, when teachers victimize, abuse physically and emotionally, oppress, terrorize and/or bully students, and vice versa, when students victimize, abuse physically and emotionally, oppress, terrorize and/or bully teachers. Education (**E**) is intrinsically bad, for example, when university administrators accept bribes for admission to their institutions, or when examination invigilators collude with students so that students can cheat on examinations, or when teachers clandestinely offer grades for sale, or when schools and/or universities deny admission to applicants on the basis of gender, race, skin color, ethnic origins, religious convictions or political views.

There can be bad education (**E_B**) which is also effective education

($\mathbf{E_E}$). There can be good education ($\mathbf{E_G}$) which is also effective education ($\mathbf{E_E}$). There can be bad education ($\mathbf{E_B}$) which is also ineffective education ($\mathbf{E_I}$). And there can be good education ($\mathbf{E_G}$) which is also ineffective education (E_I). The four combinations can be expressed as follows.

(1) $\mathbf{E_{BE} = E_B \cup E_E}$
(2) $\mathbf{E_{GE} = E_G \cup E_E}$
(3) $\mathbf{E_{BI} = E_B \cup E_I}$
(4) $\mathbf{E_{GI} = E_G \cup E_I}$

The statement $<\mathbf{E_{BE} = E_B \cup E_E}>$ reads in ordinary English that the essential properties of bad and effective education ($\mathbf{E_{BE}}$) consist of (=) the union of ($\cup$) the properties of bad education ($\mathbf{E_B}$) and the properties of effective education ($\mathbf{E_E}$). A classic example of bad effective education ($\mathbf{E_{BE}}$) is that of the character Fagin in the novel *Oliver Twist* (1838) by the English author Charles Dickens (1812-1870). Fagin is consummately effective in what he does, which is to recruit waifs, strays and street urchins and teach them how (and they learn how) to be skillful pickpockets and thieves.

The statement $<\mathbf{E_{GE} = E_G \cup E_E}>$ reads in ordinary English that the essential properties of good and effective education ($\mathbf{E_{GE}}$) consist of (=) the union of ($\cup$) the properties of good education ($\mathbf{E_G}$) and the properties of effective education ($\mathbf{E_E}$). An example of good effective education ($\mathbf{E_{GE}}$) is that of agricultural education in secondary schools in Uasin Gishu County, Kenya. In a study conducted by E.K. Saina et al. (2012), it was found that

> farmers with secondary school agriculture knowledge [range of knowing] perform significantly better in all farming aspects as compared to farmers without. The secondary school agriculture knowledge [range of knowing] not only broadens farmers' capacity, but also makes them more effective, self reliant, resourceful and capable of solving farming problems and as a result, significantly improves their crop productivity and hence guarantee food security for the family.

The statement $<\mathbf{E_{BI} = E_B \cup E_I}>$ reads in ordinary English that the essential properties of bad and ineffective education ($\mathbf{E_{BI}}$) consist of (=) the union of ($\cup$) the properties of bad education ($\mathbf{E_B}$) and the properties of ineffective education ($\mathbf{E_I}$). An example of bad ineffective education ($\mathbf{E_{BI}}$) is that of a convicted criminal in prison advising another convicted criminal how to bypass an electronic alarm system, but is mistaken about the procedure for bypassing the system. The criminal playing the role of student thus studies (**S_{P1}**) and learns$_1$ (**L_1**) the incorrect procedure for bypassing the system.

The statement <**$E_{GI} = E_G \cup E_I$**> reads in ordinary English that the essential properties of good and ineffective education (**E_{GI}**) consist of (**=**) the union of (**$\cup$**) the properties of good education (**E_G**) and the properties of ineffective education (**E_I**). An example of good ineffective education (**E_{GI}**) is that of Bill, an 18-year-old who decides that he would like to learn to play the guitar. He buys an inexpensive guitar. He finds a professional guitar teacher, and he enrolls with the teacher for private lessons for a 6-month period. He takes a lesson with his teacher once a week, and he practices his guitar 30 minutes a day. After the sixth-month period, he has not achieved the standard of playing to which he aspired. He decides that his interest and commitment to developing his knowing-how (**K_{2K3}**) to play the guitar are not sufficient to work at getting any better at playing. He decides to discontinue his lessons, and he sells his guitar.

Derivative Components of Education

In addition to the basic elements of teachers (**T**), students (**S**), content (**C**) and setting (**X**), there are derivative components (**E_{DC}**) of education (**E**), in both official (**E_O**) and unofficial education (**E_U**). Derivative components (**E_{DC}**) are not essential elements of education (**E**), which means that they are not determinants of education (E). Without them, there still can be education (**E**). Derivative components (**E_{DC}**) of education are often found in association with education (**E**). The components are as follows.

(1) Language (**E_{DC1}**)
(2) Resources (**E_{DC2}**)
(3) Methods (**E_{DC3}**)
(4) Styles (**E_{DC4}**)
(5) Focus (**E_{DC5}**)
(6) Organization (**E_{DC6}**)
(7) Pace (**E_{DC7}**)
(8) Sequence (**E_{DC8}**)
(9) Initiation (**E_{DC9}**)
(10) Intentions (**E_{DC10}**)
(11) Goal structures (**E_{DC11}**)

(12) Assessment ($\mathbf{E}_{DC12}$)
(13) Evaluation ($\mathbf{E}_{DC13}$)
(14) Certification ($\mathbf{E}_{DC14}$)
(15) Curriculum ($\mathbf{E}_{DC15}$)
(16) Syllabus ($\mathbf{E}_{DC16}$)
(17) Unit plans ($\mathbf{E}_{DC17}$)
(18) Lesson plans ($\mathbf{E}_{DC18}$)
(19) Instructional design ($\mathbf{E}_{DC19}$)
(20) Strategies ($\mathbf{E}_{DC20}$)

Language

Language ($\mathbf{E}_{DC1}$) is a derivative component of education (**E**), both official ($\mathbf{E}_{O}$) and unofficial ($\mathbf{E}_{U}$). Language derives from the teachers (**T**), students (**S**), content (**C**) and setting (**X**). It is patent that it would be impossible to engage in education (**E**) without having some language. Language is a necessity for communication among teachers (**T**), students (**S**) and interested third parties (from the social and cultural setting <**X**> of education <**E**>). But teachers (**T**) and students (**S**) do not use just any language. They use a particular language from a particular culture (either mandated by law, rule, regulation and/or policy, or out of cultural habit and custom). They make their language function in characteristic ways in the course of performing their roles as teachers and students. And they use both ordinary and specialized language in discourse while teaching ($\mathbf{T}_{P}$) and intentionally studying under guidance ($\mathbf{S}_{P1}$). The specialized language is the language of the content (**C**). The content that is mathematics has its own special set of terms (its descriptive theory) and special discourse (its facts and its explanatory theory), as does the content that is physics, history, art, music, computer sciences, metal working, dance, French, German, Japanese, etc.

The language which teachers and students use to communicate with each other must be some language chosen from some cultural group, for example, English, French, German, Swahili, American Sign Language (ASL), Australian Sign Language (AUSLAN), Polish Sign Language, etc. In multilingual societies, where two or more languages are spoken, the question of which language is to be used as the medium of instruction becomes an important, and sometimes politically contentious, issue. In past times, language groups have been forbidden to use their first language in schools, and severe penalties were imposed for breaches of the rule. For example, the English forbade the Scots to use Scottish Gaelic (after the Battle of Culloden in 1746 and during the Highland Clearances). American First Nation students (Hopi, Navajo, Cherokee, etc.), in the late 19th to the mid-20th century, were forbidden to use their first language in US Bureau of Indian Affairs boarding schools. Australian First Nation children (Palyku, Wawula, Yulparitja, etc.) were forbidden to use their first language in missionary schools in the late 19th to mid-20th century. After the defeat of France in the Franco-Prussian War (1870-71), the medium of instruction in schools in the newly acquired German imperial territory of Alsace-Lorraine became the German language, and the French language was removed from the curriculum. In some contemporary ESL (English as Second Language) institutions, for the purposes of accelerating the students' learning (**L_1**), there is the policy which forbids students to speak any language but English. The same is true of some French as second language institutions, German as second language institutions, etc.

The language that is used as the medium of instruction in official education (**E_O**) is almost invariably determined by the group which holds the dominant political and economic power within an institution, community, state or nation. Sometimes a second language is chosen as the medium of instruction because there are so many first languages competing for dominance. For example, in India, English became a preferred language in schools because it was regarded as being a neutral, universal, nationally unifying language, which was not in competition with, nor showed political favor to, other languages such as Gujarati, Hindi, Kannada, Kashmiri, Konkani, Urdu, etc. There is the example of Canada, which has an official policy of giving equal status to English and French in all government institutions, which of course includes schools. In Kenya, it was common practice in the 1960s and 70s for primary teachers to use the local community language (e.g. Kamba, Kikuyu, Nandi, etc.) as the medium of instruction in the first few years, then use Swahili as the medium of instruction in middle to upper primary, then use English as the medium of instruction in high schools, technical colleges and universities. This was done to cater for the diversity of languages used throughout the country. In Switzerland, language policies vary with the Canton. Generally, children start with their first language (either Swiss German, Swiss French, Swiss Italian or Rhaeto-Romanic), then receive instruction in a second, a third and sometimes a fourth language, depending on the policy of the Canton. There is contemporary discussion in Switzerland about using English as the second language to be taught, beginning in primary schools.

Another issue with language is the necessity to provide to children (whose first language is not the one used for the medium of instruction in schools) opportunities to study intentionally under guidance (**S_{P1}**) and learn intentionally under guidance (**L_1**) the language which is used as the medium of instruction. In Australia, for example, a country with a large immigrant population, it is common for students to arrive from overseas to study in schools and universities, but lack the level of English usage to participate in classrooms. It is commonplace to provide instruction in English as a second language to help students achieve a sufficient level of English to participate in classrooms in which English is used as the medium of instruction.

In addition to using the language of one or more cultural groups within a specific social and cultural setting as a medium of instruction, teachers and students typically make their language perform a variety of functions which are characteristic of their transactions with each other. Those functions include the following.

- analyzing
- characterizing
- comparing
- contrasting
- describing
- defining
- demonstrating
- directing
- emphasizing
- evaluating
- exemplifying
- explaining
- explicating
- guiding
- illustrating
- justifying
- predicting
- prompting
- questioning
- recommending
- relating
- stating
- suggesting
- summarizing

This is not an exhaustive list of language moves, but it gives an indication of what teachers and students do with their language in their transactions with each other.

Resources

Resources and materials (**E_{DC2}**) are the physical objects that are used in teaching and intentional guided studying. Examples include pens, paper, films, books, desks, balls, engines, tools, shoes, cameras, computers, e-book readers, puzzles, workbooks, work sheets, video players, photographs, diagrams, gymnasiums, playing fields, play equipment, laboratory equipment, machinery, hand tools, TVs, etc. In official education (**E_O**), one of the major tasks of professional teachers and of schools is to locate and/or create resources, evaluate them, organize them, allocate them to students and/or distribute them to students and build a fund, collection and/or library of resources which can be used over many terms, semesters and/or years. Resources and materials ($\mathbf{E}_{DC2}$) are also used in unofficial education ($\mathbf{E}_{U}$). A father who teaches his daughter how to handle a rod and reel for fishing is using the rod and reel as resources. A sister who shows her brother how to play the cat's cradle string game is using string as a resource.

Methods

Methods ($\mathbf{E}_{DC3}$) are procedures. Procedures are activities which are ordered into sequential patterns. In education ($\mathbf{E}$), there are both methods of teaching ($\mathbf{E}_{DC3T}$) and methods of studying ($\mathbf{E}_{DC3S}$). Some examples of teaching methods ($\mathbf{E}_{DC3T}$) include the following.

- answering questions
- arranging resources
- asking questions
- assigning activities
- assigning appropriate practice
- assigning projects
- defining terms
- demonstrating procedures
- evaluating performances
- evaluating products of performances
- explicating concepts
- giving directions
- giving examples
- leading discussions
- listening attentively
- modeling procedures
- observing carefully
- organizing activities
- playing games
- playing roles
- posing problems
- providing advice
- providing explanations
- providing resources

Some examples of methods of intentional guided studying ($\mathbf{E}_{DC3S}$) include the following.

- answering questions
- asking questions
- completing tasks
- conducting experiments
- conducting appropriate practice
- conducting research
- creating models
- defining terms
- demonstrating procedures
- drawing diagrams
- drawing pictures
- observing carefully
- organizing activities
- paraphrasing texts
- participating in discussions
- playing games
- playing roles
- posing problems
- preparing reports
- providing examples
- reading resources
- rehearsing procedures

- evaluating performances
- explicating concepts
- finding resources
- following directions
- following guidance
- giving directions
- leading discussions
- listening attentively
- making charts
- making presentations
- modeling procedures
- rehearsing roles
- selecting activities
- selecting resources
- solving problems
- summarizing texts
- undertaking appropriate practice
- undertaking projects
- watching demonstrations
- writing texts (notes, essays, speeches, etc.)

These examples are not intended as exhaustive lists, and the lists that anyone produces is going to depend on how one goes about classifying teaching methods ($\mathbf{E}_{DC3T}$) and methods of intentional guided studying ($\mathbf{E}_{DC3S}$). But these two lists give a start for something to consider, analyze and develop.

Styles

Styles ($\mathbf{E}_{DC4}$) of teaching and intentional guided studying are the manner in which a method is used or executed. Terms which characterize style include <*supportive, unsupportive, friendly, unfriendly, personable, aloof, kind, sarcastic, patient, impatient, abrupt, jaded, enthusiastic, concerned, disinterested, anxious, calm, confident, hesitant, fun loving, humorless, stern, mocking, cruel*>, etc. Styles may be a reflection of an individual's personality, and both student and teacher manifest styles (teacher styles <$\mathbf{E}_{DC4T}$> and student styles <$\mathbf{E}_{DC4S}$>) with their methods. An identical method can be executed in different styles. The method of asking questions, for example, can be employed using a warm, supportive style, or an aloof, abrupt style. Teachers and students usually start with no awareness of their styles because they are not self-conscious of their habits of social interaction. But once teachers and students become self-conscious of their styles, they can choose a style to suit the circumstances. With knowing about their own styles and the styles of others, teachers and students can make a rational choice about which style is the most appropriate for an educational situation.

Focus

Focus of attention ($\mathbf{E}_{DC5}$) is the direction which we give our volition (**V**), perception (**P**) and cognition (**N**). As human beings, we typically focus on one or a few aspects of our environment and experience at

Figure 6: Student Focus of Attention

▪ **Teacher focused activities**	**Students are intended to pay attention to a teacher** ▪ defining the concept of nationalism, ▪ demonstrating how to factor quadratic equations, ▪ modeling the fingering of a chord on the guitar
▪ **Student focused activities**	**Students are intended to watch & listen to a student** ▪ delivering a report, ▪ playing the violin, ▪ reciting a poem, ▪ integrating a function, ▪ demonstrating an electric motor the student has made
▪ **Self focused activities**	**A student is intended to focus on her or his own performance as she or he** ▪ practices touch typing, ▪ fingers notes on the flute, ▪ practices bead welding, ▪ writes an original short play
▪ **Resource focused activities**	**A set of students is intended to** ▪ watch a video about tropical cyclones, ▪ add an acid to a base and watch for a change in the indicator color, ▪ read a text and write answers to comprehension questions
▪ **Situation focused activities**	**A set of students is intended to** ▪ visit a pig farm and note steps in pig breeding & husbandry, ▪ visit a water purification plant & note the steps in water purification ▪ visit a ginger processing factory & note the steps in ginger processing ▪ visit a bee farm & note the steps in bee husbandry ▪ visit the beach, collect plastic and measure the amount of plastic per square meter in the sand on the beach

any one moment, and our attention typically moves from one thing to another rapidly. This is especially so of children, but it is generally true of anyone at any age. It is through selective attention that we focus and discern those aspects of our experience that matter to us at the moment. Daydreaming is natural, and we drift in and out of focus on the people, activities, things and states of affairs which are immediately before us.

Both teachers and students have focus. The students' focus of attention is a major concern for teachers (in both unofficial and official education), and teachers typically endeavor (sometimes with more success than at others) to manage the classroom such that students will be focused on the relevant study task. At least five centers (or objects) of focus are possible. Students may focus their attention on (1) teachers, (2) other students, (3) themselves, (4) resources or (5) situations. Or they may become completely distracted and focus on matters outside of what is happening immediately in the educational process.

Teacher-focused activities are those in which the teacher intends that the attention of the student or students be upon the teacher's performance. Student-focused activities are those in which the teacher intends that the attention of the students be upon the performances of another student or other students. Self-focused activities are those in which the teacher intends that the attention of the student be upon his or her performance (e.g. his or her pronunciation, golf swing, tennis serve, etc.). Resource-focused activities are those in which the teacher intends that the attention of the student or students be upon the resources. Examples of resource-focused activities include those in which the students are intended to be focused on pictures, diagrams, photographs, computer programs, books, question sets, videos, etc. Situation-focused activities are ones in which the teacher intends the student or students to be focused upon a set of circumstances, phenomena, events or states of affairs. For example, their focus of attention might be intended to be on the things that may be observed on a field trip to a factory, a farm, a beach, a forest, a court room, a museum, an art gallery, an observatory, a planetarium or a market.

Organization

Organization ($\mathbf{E_{DC6}}$) in education (**E**) is the arrangement of both teachers and students as individuals, small groups or whole groups as they conduct their teaching and intentional guided study activities. In unofficial education ($\mathbf{E_U}$), the organization is typically a one-on-one arrangement, with one person playing the role of teacher and one person playing the role of student. For example, a father shows his daughter how to adjust the tension on the chain of her bicycle, and she makes adjusts the chain while her father watches and advises her.

In official education ($\mathbf{E_O}$), professional teachers may choose to organize themselves as individuals, operating independently of each other, or as groups or teams of teachers working in connection with each other to some greater or lesser degree of cooperation and consultation. Professional teachers typically organize their students in one of three ways, viz. as

(1) individuals studying (**S_{P1}**) independently or
(2) small groups studying (**S_{P1}**) with each other or
(3) one large whole group studying (**S_{P1}**) with each other.

There are pros and cons for each of these organizations.

Organization of students as individuals gives the flexibility for each student to be engaged in some unique study (**S_{P1}**) activity (using a set of resources different from all other students) of some unique content (**C**) with a view to learning (**L_1**) some unique range of knowing (**K_2**) and achieving some unique intended learning outcome (**ILO**).

Figure 7: Organization of Students and Study Activities

▪ **Students organized as individuals**	**Study task or activity can be** ▪ **the same for all students** ▪ **the same for some students and different for others** ▪ **unique to the individual** ▪ **initiated by teacher, student or both parties**
▪ **Students organized as small groups**	**Study task or activity can be** ▪ **the same for all students in other groups** ▪ **the same for students in the same group but different from other groups** ▪ **unique to the individual** ▪ **initiated by teacher, student or both parties**
▪ **Students organized as one large group**	**Study task or activity can be** ▪ **the same for all students** ▪ **the same for some students and different for others** ▪ **unique to the individual** ▪ **initiated by teacher, student or both parties**

Organization of students in small groups, as opposed to being organized as independent individuals, gives the flexibility for different groups of students to be using different sets of resources and to be undertaking different study activities ($\mathbf{S}_{P1}$) and tasks at the same time.

Organization of students into a whole group provides the opportunity for all students to be focused on the same study resources and study activities at the same time.

Organization of students into a whole group provides the opportunity for all students to be focused on the same study resources and study activities at the same time.

Students may be organized at various times to suit various circumstances. They may be organized according to various criteria, for example, age, ability, gender, previous experiences, interests, achievement, availability of resources, etc.

Regardless of how students might be organized, they may be engaged in

(1) the same intentional guided study activity simultaneously,
(2) various intentional guided study activities simultaneously,
(3) an intentional guided study activity unique to the individual student.

The nature of the study task or activity is not necessarily tied to the grouping of the students. For example, teachers may organize students as individuals and direct them to be engaged in the same study activity. The students can be organized in small groups and be engaged in the same study activity. They can be organized as a whole class, and each student can be engaged in an activity that is unique to each individual student.

Pace

The pace ($\mathbf{E}_{DC7}$) of teaching ($\mathbf{T}_{P}$) and intentional guided studying ($\mathbf{S}_{P1}$) is the time frame in which students are expected and/or required to achieve a set of intended learning outcomes (**ILO**s). Some intended learning outcomes (**ILO**s) can be achieved within a few minutes. Others take a few days. Others take a few months, or even a year or several years.

It may be the case that teachers specify the pace at which some content is taught and studied. Students might specify the pace. The pace might be mutually established by teachers and students in cooperation with each other. Or the pace might be established by interested third parties, for example the administration of a school district, state departments of education, administrators of universities, publishers of educational materials, funding bodies, etc. In institutions such as the US Air Force, there is a specified time in which candidates are required to master the range of knowing (**K_2**) required to pilot and navigate an aircraft, engage in combat maneuvers and conduct formation flying. If they don't achieve mastery of the required range of knowing within the specified time, they are excluded from the training program.

Pace can be determined by a wide range of factors – available resources, ability of students, the extant range of knowing (**K_2**) of students, difficulty of the intended learning outcome (**ILO**), expectations of the teachers, demands of the funding organizations, etc.

In official education (**E_O**), professional teachers must either set the pace of intentional guided studying (**S_{P1}**) and intentional guided learning (**L_1**), negotiate with students to agree upon the pace of intentional guided studying (**S_{P1}**), allow the students to set their own pace, either individually or as a group, or professional teachers must work at the pace prescribed by the setting (**X**), (third parties – school administrators, boards of governors, state departments of education, national departments of education, funding authorities, etc.).

In unofficial education (**E_U**), pace is established as a natural rhythm between the person playing the role of teacher (father, mother, uncle, aunt, brother, sister, cousin, friend, etc.) and the person playing the role of student (father, mother, uncle, aunt, brother, sister, cousin, friend, etc.). For example, a cousin asks another cousin to show him how to play the card game of Hearts. The two cousins invite two other cousins to join in the game, and the first cousin listens to the explanation given about how to play Hearts. The four cousins proceed to play Hearts, and the novice extends his range of knowing (**K_2**) about how to play by playing and paying attention to the guidance and explanations given by the other three cousins. In this scenario, there are three people who play the role of teacher (**T**) and one who plays the role of student (**S**). The pace of the teaching (**T_P**) and intentional guided studying (**S_{P1}**) are set through a mutual, unspoken agreement to play the game at a pace that the novice can follow and from which he can learn intentionally with guidance (**L_1**).

Sequence

Sequence is the order in which events occur or actions are undertaken. Within the education (**E**), sequence (**E_{DC8}**) is the order in which acts of teaching (**T_P**) and intentional guided studying (**S_{P1}**) take place within a given time frame.

The sequence can be determined by the teacher (**T**), by the students (**S**), by mutual agreement between teacher and students or by interested third parties who are part of the setting (**X**).

An example of a sequence determined by a teacher (**T**) in official education (**E_O**) is the scenario in which a teacher has pupils in year 1 (or grade 1) (average age of 6 years)

(1) first, trace over simple three-letter words,
(2) second, join the dots for the same set of words presented in line-dot form,
(3) third, write one missing letter in the same set of words with a single missing letter,
(4) fourth, write the last two missing letters in the same set of words,
(5) fifth, write the three letters of each of the words after hearing them spoken.

An example of a sequence determined by a student (**S**) in official education (**E_O**) is the scenario in which a 10-year-old boy, Graham, goes to his first piano lesson, shows the piano teacher a piece of sheet music that he wants to learn to play, and the teacher shows him where to place his fingers for his left hand and his right hand on the piano for the notes on the sheet music, gives him guidance and practice in wrist position, finger placement, rhythm and tempo and helps him until he can play the piece to his satisfaction.

An example of a sequence established by a third party (**X**) in official education (**E_O**) is the administration of a school district prescribing that secondary school mathematics be studied in this order:

(1) year or grade 9 – introductory algebra,
(2) year or grade 10 – geometry,
(3) year or grade 11 – advanced algebra and trigonometry,
(4) year or grade 12 – calculus.

An example of a sequence determined by a teacher (**T**) in unofficial education (**E_U**) is a scenario in which a mother announces to her husband and three children that she is tired of preparing meals for the five of them. She wants each family member to learn to cook and to prepare a dinner once a week. The father and children agree that it would be a fair arrangement, and the mother (playing the role of teacher <**T**>) gives each of the family members (playing the role of students <**S**>) instructions on how to prepare a variety of meals, starting with salads and progressing to pastas and sauces, stews, casseroles, roasts, poached fish, steamed vegetables, etc. Each family member practices meal preparation (the prescribed range of knowing <$\mathbf{K}_{2P}$>) following a recipe (the content <**C**>). The family agrees upon a roster, and each, in turn, prepares one of the dinners for the weekdays in accordance with a menu that the family writes for each week.

Initiation

Initiation ($\mathbf{E}_{DC9}$) of intentional guided studying ($\mathbf{S}_{P1}$) is the choice to begin some set of intentional guided study activities. Intentional guided study activities ($\mathbf{S}_{P1}$) are any activities that students undertake under guidance with the intention of extending their prescribed range of knowing ($\mathbf{K}_{2P}$). Study activities or tasks can be initiated by

(1) the teacher or teachers,
(2) the student or students,
(3) some third party, or
(4) a combination of initiatives from teachers, students and/or some third party.

An example in official education ($\mathbf{E}_{O}$) of a teacher-initiated study task ($\mathbf{S}_{P1}$) is the case of a year 11 (11th grade) secondary school teacher telling the class that they will be reading, analyzing and interpreting the novel *Moby-Dick* by Herman Melville. In unofficial education ($\mathbf{E}_{U}$), an example of a teacher-initiated study activity ($\mathbf{S}_{P1}$) is a situation in which a father tells his son that he wants to show him how to clean the filter on the clothes washer.

An example of a student-initiated study task ($\mathbf{S}_{P1}$) in official education ($\mathbf{E}_{O}$) is the case of a student (a girl) bringing in some tadpoles in a jar and saying that she would like to make a study of the life cycle of frogs. Other students agree that it is a great idea, and the class proceeds to conduct a study of frogs. In unofficial education ($\mathbf{E}_{U}$), an example of a student-initiated study task ($\mathbf{S}_{P1}$) is the situation in which a child asks another child to show him how to skip rope. The other child says okay and shows the first child how to do it.

An example of a third-party initiated study activity ($\mathbf{S}_{P1}$) in official education ($\mathbf{E}_{O}$) is that of a legislative requirement to allocate 20 hours of study in year 10 (10th grade) about the dangers of alcohol abuse and abuse of substances such as tobacco, cannabis, cocaine, methamphetamine and heroin. Every student in schools under the jurisdiction of the legislative body is given a set of intentional guided study activities (to be completed over a 20 hour period) which focuses on the dangers of alcohol consumption and the use of other dangerous substances.

An example in official education (**E_O**) of a mutually-initiated (i.e. initiated by teacher and student) study task (**S_{P1}**) is the case in which a teacher assigns a research project to the students, but does not specify what is to be researched. Each student decides upon what it is that she or he wishes to research and consults with the teacher about how to conduct the research and report the results of the research.

Intention

Within the education (**E**), there is always intention (**E_{DC10}**). Teachers, students and interested third parties (e.g. parents, administrators, funding bodies, law makers, philanthropists, etc.) all have the general intention that students will extend their prescribed range of knowing (**K_{2P}**). Intention is an essential distinguishing characteristic of aims, goals and objectives. An educational aim, goal or objective is an intended learning outcome (**ILO**) that someone wants students to achieve by means of using the activities of teaching (**T_P**) and intentional guided studying (**S_{P1}**).

Possible intended learning outcomes (**ILO**s) might include achieving a knowing-how (**K_{2K3}**) to

(1) drive a car safely and responsibly, or
(2) distinguish poisonous mushrooms from harmless ones, or
(3) resolve conflicts through negotiation and finding mutually agreeable solutions.

We can conceive of a seemingly infinite number of learning outcomes (**ILO**s). The outcomes will always be a selection from the possible kinds, levels and forms of knowing (**K_{2KLF}**). A statement of an intended learning outcome will always be a specification of some prescribed range of knowing (**K_{2P}**) that a student aspires to, or is expected to, achieve.

There are intentions (**E_{DC10}**) in unofficial education (**E_U**) and intentions (**E_{DC10}**) in official education (**E_O**). In unofficial education (**E_U**), people rarely articulate, either in spoken or written language, their intended learning outcomes (**ILO**s), but they, at times, do. A child will say that she or he wants to know how to tie shoelaces, snap fingers, play the piano, ride a bicycle, skip rope or bake a cake. Parents rarely say that they want their children to master speaking, reading and writing their native language, but their conduct in helping their children achieve these ranges of knowing provides sufficient evidence to infer confidently that they do. Also, it is clear that parents want their children to develop attitudes and values that are consistent with the familial group. They rarely articulate these intentions, most probably because they take them to be self-evident and totally unnecessary to specify explicitly.

There is a clear contrast between unofficial ($\mathbf{E_U}$) and official education ($\mathbf{E_O}$). In official education, teachers, students, curriculum developers, administrators, funding bodies and regulatory agencies insist upon an articulation of explicitly stated and recorded intended learning outcomes (**ILO**s). Those who fund official education generally want an accounting of how their money is spent and what results are achieved. For accountability to be achieved, for decisions to be made about the rational allocation of funds and for choices to be made about relevant resources for educational programs, clear written statements of intended learning outcomes (**ILO**s) become imperative.

Goal Structures

Within education (**E**), both official and unofficial, it is possible to structure educational goals ($\mathbf{E_{DC11}}$) for the students. That is, we can establish rules that govern how the goals can be achieved. Goal structures are distinguishable by the degree of dependence that one student has on other students in being able to achieve an intended learning outcome. There are at least three possible structures: individualized, competitive and cooperative (David W. Johnson and Robert T. Johnson, 1975).

An individualized goal structure is a set of rules which stipulates that an individual student may achieve an intended learning outcome without transactions with other students. The student does not depend on other students in achieving the intended learning outcome. The educational goal is unique to the individual, and the individual may achieve the intended learning outcome regardless of what other students are studying or aiming to achieve.

An example of an individualized goal structure is that of a six-year-old girl who wants to learn to play flute. Her parents tell her that her aspirations are wonderful. They arrange a music teacher for her. She takes flute lessons over a period of six years, and she develops an advanced level of proficiency in flute playing. She does this on her own, without having to depend on any other students. The educational goal structure for her is an individualized one, and her education is official (**E_O**) because it is conducted as a set of regularly scheduled private tutorials by a qualified flute instructor who follows a system of graded music examinations and who receives payment for teaching.

A competitive goal structure is a set of rules which stipulates that only one individual student can achieve an intended learning outcome to the exclusion of other students. All students are engaged in activities to achieve the same goal, but the first one to achieve the intended learning outcome at the specified criteria of excellence blocks all others from achieving the goal. An example of a competitive goal structure in education (**E**) is that of a youth tennis club. At the end of the year, only one of the male club members will be selected to play in the state finals in the tournament for under 16-year-old boys. There are 24 boys in the under 16 group. All 24 boys are engaged in the educational process with a view to developing their knowing-how to play the game of tennis. They receive coaching. They practice their serves, strokes and ball placement. They watch videos of themselves to improve their game. They do cross training to improve their strength and endurance. They receive, accept and follow guidance and counseling in sports psychology. They eat in accordance with the instructions from their nutritionist. They play games against each other and compete until one of the 24 players consistently defeats the other players. That one boy consistently demonstrates his superior range of knowing-how (**K_{2K3}**) to play tennis. He is selected to play in the state tournament.

A cooperative goal structure is a set of rules which stipulates that an intended learning outcome can be achieved if, and only if, all students linked in the same group or team, achieve the goal simultaneously and together. An example of a cooperative goal structure is the following scenario. A group of four students in year 9 (9th grade, age 14) are given the task of producing a six-minute video which illustrates the origin and development of the light bulb. The purpose of the task is for them to demonstrate their knowing-that (**K_{2K2}**) and knowing-how (**K_{2K3}**) in relation to the invention of the incandescent light bulb and subsequent improvements in the 20th and 21st centuries. They conduct research together. They write a script for the video. They construct a story board. They draw figures and pictures to be used as animation in the video. They select some music for background. They put all the elements together and produce a video which narrates and illustrates the origin of the light bulb. Together, as a team, they achieve the intended learning outcomes of knowing-that ($\mathbf{K}_{2K2}$) in relation to the origins of the light bulb and of knowing-how ($\mathbf{K}_{2K3}$) to produce a video which narrates and illustrates the origin and development of the light bulb.

Assessment and Evaluation

Assessment ($\mathbf{E}_{DC12}$) and evaluation ($\mathbf{E}_{DC13}$) are derivative components ($\mathbf{E}_{DC}$) of education (**E**). In official education ($\mathbf{E}_{O}$), a central concern of teachers, students and interested third parties is that students demonstrate their prescribed range of knowing ($\mathbf{K}_{2P}$) such that they can be certified as having achieved a specified range of knowing ($\mathbf{K}_{2P}$). In this context of expectations, assessment ($\mathbf{E}_{DC12}$) consists of the activity of collecting evidence of students having achieved some prescribed range of knowing ($\mathbf{K}_{2P}$). Evaluation ($\mathbf{E}_{DC13}$) consists of the activity of comparing the evidence with criteria (standards, rules or both) to make judgments about the degree to which cognitive achievement ($\mathbf{K}_{2}$) matches the criteria for excellence. The comparison of the evidence of achievement of a range of knowing ($\mathbf{K}_{2}$) with the criteria for achievement provides the basis for making a judgment about the degree to which students have achieved their intended learning outcomes (**ILO**s). The achievement is usually reported as a rating (e.g. *A, B, C, D, F*) or a ranking (e.g. *1st, 2nd, 3rd*, etc.). The term <*evaluation*> denotes both the procedure of coming to a value judgment and the report of the value judgment.

The assessor is the person who collects the evidence (the evaluatum <**e**>) for the evaluator, who is the person who makes and reports the value judgment about the value (the merit, significance, worth) of the evaluatum (**e**). In the USA, the SAT scores are used by universities as one of the criteria for university admission. The SAT is created, administered and controlled by the College Board. At various dates during the year and at various locations across the USA invigilators supervise students as they complete the SAT. The invigilators are the assessors. The completed SAT examination answer sheet is the evaluatum (**e**). Each answer sheet is scored and evaluated by personnel of the College Board. Those personnel are the evaluators.

The evaluators report their evaluation as a ranking (a percentile score). Each test score is ranked in relation to all those who have completed the test or against a representative sample of those who typically complete the SAT examinations.

In both unofficial ($\mathbf{E}_U$) and official education ($\mathbf{E}_O$), the assessor and the evaluator are often the same person. That person conducts the assessment, makes the evaluation and reports the evaluation results. The evaluatum (**e**), the thing that is assessed and evaluated, varies with the situation and the purposes of the evaluation. In unofficial education ($\mathbf{E}_U$), the assessor and evaluator are almost always the same person (the person playing the role of teacher <**T**>). In official education ($\mathbf{E}_O$), at times, the assessor is a third party, and the evaluator is another third party. In such cases, the teacher who has provided the instruction is neither the assessor nor the evaluator. At other times, the assessor and the evaluator are the same person (the teacher who has provided the instruction). Sometimes, the assessor and the evaluator may be a group (a teacher or set of teachers, a student or set of students or a third party or a set of third parties or some combination of the three). Likewise, the thing being evaluated, the evaluatum (<**e**>, the plural is <*evaluata*>) is at times, the performance of the teacher or teachers, the product of the performance of the teachers, the performance of the student or students, the product of the performance of the student or students, the appropriateness of the content, the adequacy of the resources and setting, etc. Any aspect or feature of official education ($\mathbf{E}_O$) can be an evaluatum (**e**).

In official education ($\mathbf{E}_O$), there are basically three uses of an evaluation report. One use of the information is to prepare something (prepare a syllabus, prepare a unit plan, prepare a lesson plan, prepare some educational resources, etc.). The term <*preparative*> is used to denote this first use of an evaluation report. A second use of an evaluation report is to monitor the progress of something with a view to making any necessary and/or desirable adjustments (the progress of students in achieving some set of intended learning outcomes, the extent to which teachers' plans match their instructional programs, the degree to which some strategy to effect change and/or reform is achieving desired outcomes, etc.). The term <*formative*> is used to denote this second use of an evaluation report. A third use of an evaluation report is to establish that something has been accomplished (the learning outcomes have been achieved, the admission requirements have been met, the necessary conditions for certification have been satisfied, etc.). The term <*summative*> is used to denote this third use of an evaluation report (Michael Scriven, 1967, 1991).

Both unofficial and official education have assessment and evaluation as derivative components. In unofficial education, a friend, for example, might show a boy how to play chess and ask, "Do you remember what move the knight is allowed to make?" "Two squares forward or back and one sideways, or two squares sideways and one square forward or back," says the boy. "That's right!" says his friend. The statement, "That's right," is the report of the friend's evaluation. In official education, a student will receive a written report or a grade on a paper, or a certificate, diploma, degree, etc.

Certification, Curriculum, Syllabus, Unit Plans and Lesson Plans

Certification ($\mathbf{E}_{DC14}$), curriculum ($\mathbf{E}_{DC15}$), syllabus ($\mathbf{E}_{DC16}$), unit plans ($\mathbf{E}_{DC17}$) and lesson plans ($\mathbf{E}_{DC18}$) are derivative components of official education ($\mathbf{E}_{O}$), but not of unofficial education ($\mathbf{E}_{U}$). The reason may seem fairly obvious. A father does not give his six-year-old daughter a certificate for riding her bicycle. He helps her get started riding her bicycle, encourages her and praises her when she masters her balance and control on her bicycle. Likewise, he does not write a curriculum, a syllabus, a unit plan or a lesson plan when he decides to help his daughter learn to ride her bicycle. He just proceeds with helping her get started and tells her what she is doing right and doing wrong.

Those engaged in unofficial education ($\mathbf{E}_{U}$) are not in the business of issuing certifications of competence and achievement, but those engaged in official education ($\mathbf{E}_{O}$) are. The participants in official education ($\mathbf{E}_{O}$) have the obligation to document their activities and accomplishments. They are obliged to be accountable. Accountability requires written curriculum documents, syllabi, unit plans and lesson plans, attendance records, records of assessments and evaluation, progress reports and certification of achievements (certificates, diplomas, degrees, etc.).

Instructional Designs

Teachers (**T**) in unofficial education ($\mathbf{E}_{U}$) do not, but professional teachers in official education ($\mathbf{E}_{O}$) do, give a great deal of consideration to the design ($\mathbf{E}_{DC19}$) of educational episodes. Educational episodes in unofficial education ($\mathbf{E}_{U}$) are, for the most part, unplanned and spontaneous. Those in official education ($\mathbf{E}_{O}$) are typically planned and carefully deliberated to suit the purpose of the educational episodes, the available resources and the available time allocated for achievement of the intended learning outcomes (**ILO**s). Design ($\mathbf{E}_{DC19}$) of a planned educational episode is the set of decisions about the arrangement and sequencing of activities, events and resources to be included before, during and after the provision of a set of opportunities to undertake intentional guided study ($\mathbf{S}_{P1}$) of some content (**C**) to learn intentionally under guidance ($\mathbf{L}_{1}$) some prescribed range of knowing ($\mathbf{K}_{2P}$) that is specified by some set of intended learning outcomes (**ILO**s). Many designs are possible. One of the simplest and most common design is one in which there is no pre-assessment nor pre-evaluation, one set of opportunities to study intentionally under guidance ($\mathbf{S}_{P1}$) and one post-assessment and post-evaluation. Let's denote this design with the term <*Design 1*> ($\mathbf{D}_{1}$). Design 1 has the following structure.

(1) One, and only one, set of opportunities to study$_1$ ($\mathbf{S}_{P1}$)
(2) Post-assessment (an assessment at the conclusion of the set of opportunities to study$_1$ <$\mathbf{S}_{P1}$>)
(3) Post-evaluation (an evaluation of the results from the assessment at the conclusion of the set of opportunities to study$_1$ <$\mathbf{S}_{P1}$>)
(4) Report of the evaluation results as a rating or a ranking, or both
(5) Summative use of the evaluation report

An example of Design 1 ($\mathbf{D}_{1}$) is the case of a year 9 (grade 9) geography class. The teacher, Mr Georgeadis, gives the class the task of learning how to find locations using longitude and latitude and how to specify locations using longitude and latitude. The teacher's two intended learning outcomes of the unit are that students (1) given any set of co-ordinates, will find and correctly mark the given location on a map, and (2) given any location on a map, will provide the correct co-ordinates of the location. Mr Georgeadis gives no pre-assessment task to the students. He provides an exposition of what longitude and latitude are and how they are expressed by co-ordinates as degrees, minutes and seconds. He provides the students with a video which shows how co-ordinates are used to find a point on a map and how a point on a map can be specified by co-ordinates. He provides several worksheets for students to practice finding points on a map, given co-ordinates, and to practice specifying co-ordinates, given a point on a map. After all students have been provided with the same amount of time to complete all opportunities to study how to use co-ordinates, Mr Georgeadis has the students complete a timed assessment task (30 minutes) which requires them to find locations, given a set of co-ordinates, and to specify co-ordinates, given a set of points on a map. He requires each student to work alone on the assessment task without assistance. He marks the assessment task with a numerical score (number of correct answers on the assessment task, expressed as a percentage). He evaluates the numerical score in relation to a rating scale (*A* = 90% plus, *B* = 80% plus, *C* = 70% plus, *D* =60% plus and *F* = below 60%) and reports the evaluation as one of five categories of rating: *A*, *B*, *C*, *D*, *F*. Mr Georgeadis uses the results of the evaluation summatively to indicate the degree to which each student has satisfied the criteria of the two intended learning outcomes, and then he moves the students on to another unit of instruction. The essential elements of Design 1 (**D_1**) are represented in Figure 8.

Figure 8: Design of Planned Educational Episodes – Design 1

Design Variant	Stage 1: Before S_{P1}	Stage 2: During S_{P1}	Stage 3: After S_{P1}
D_1		1. One, and only one, set of opportunities to study$_1$ (S_{P1})	1. Post-assessment 2. Post-evaluation of the assessment results 3. Post-evaluation report as a ranking or a rating or both 4. Summative use of the evaluation report

A second design is Design 2 (**D_2**). Design 2 has a similar structure to Design 1 (**D_1**), but with the addition of provision to students of a written statement of intended learning outcomes (**ILO**s), assessment tasks and criteria to be used in evaluation of the assessment tasks. The structure of Design 2 is as follows.

(1) Provision to students of a written statement of intended learning outcomes (**ILO**s)
(2) Provision to students of a written statement of assessment tasks
(3) Provision to students of a written statement of criteria to be used in evaluation of assessment tasks
(4) One, and only one, set of opportunities to study$_1$ ($\mathbf{S_{P1}}$)
(5) Post-assessment
(6) Post-evaluation of the assessment results
(7) Report of the post-evaluation results as a ranking or a rating or both
(8) Summative use of the evaluation report

An example which illustrates the essential properties of Design 2 ($\mathbf{D_2}$) is the following scenario. Richard is a first-year university student, and he enrolls in an introductory class in calculus. It is a one-semester course consisting of 16 weeks of classes which meet 3 times a week for one hour. The schedule consists of a lecture each week plus two tutorials. At enrolment, Richard receives a syllabus for the course. The syllabus provides a statement of the intended learning outcomes (**ILO**s) and the topics which will be studied$_1$ ($\mathbf{S_{P1}}$) in the course. In addition, the syllabus provides information about the required textbook and optional reading resources. Richard reads in the syllabus that there is an optional mathematics laboratory where he can seek additional help and guidance, if and when he chooses. Richard also reads that there is an online computer-based course which he can use to supplement his study$_1$ ($\mathbf{S_{P1}}$), if he so chooses. The syllabus provides information about the assessment tasks, which include submission of weekly problem sets with solutions and proofs, a mid-term examination and an end-of-semester final examination. Richard notes that the evaluation procedure consists of a rating system in which his problem sets count as one-third of his final grade, his mid-term examination counts as one-third and his final examination counts as one-third. The grading system is a rating system in which at least a score of 90% correct solutions and proofs is rated as <*A*>, at least 80% correct solutions and proofs is rated as <*B*>, at least 70% correct solutions and proofs is rated as <*C*>, at least 60% correct solutions and proofs is rated as <*D*>, and less than 60% correct solutions and proofs is rated as <*F*>.

Richard is among 400 students who have enrolled in the course.

Figure 9: Design of Planned Educational Episodes – Design 2

Design Variant	Stage 1: Before S_{P1}	Stage 2: During S_{P1}	Stage 3: After S_{P1}
D_2	1. Provision to students of a written statement of intended learning outcomes (ILO) 2. Provision to students of a written statement of assessments tasks 3. Provision to students of a written statement of criteria to be used in evaluation of assessment tasks	1. One, and only one, set of opportunities to $study_1$ (S_{P1})	1. Post-assessment 2. Post-evaluation of the assessment results 3. Post-evaluation report as a ranking or a rating or both 4. Summative use of the evaluation report

One-hour lectures are given by the mathematics professor each Monday. The lectures are video recorded, and they are made available online the day after the lecture. One-hour tutorials for students are held on Wednesdays and Fridays. The tutorials average 14 to 16 students, and they are led by graduate student teaching assistants. Weekly problem sets are due for submission every Tuesday. The teaching assistants mark the problem sets, assign a score as a percentage and keep a record of the scores for each student. At the end of week 8 in the semester, the students are given a mid-semester examination. No opportunity is provided to re-sit the mid-semester examination. The students' examinations are marked and scored, and the scores are recorded on the enrolment records. At the end of the semester, the students complete a final examination. Again, no opportunity is provided to re-sit the final examination. The students' examinations are marked and assigned a score, and the scores are recorded. The final grade for each student is assigned by averaging the scores for each student's problem sets and recording it as a percentage. The three percentages of average problem set score, mid-semester examination score and final examination score are averaged as a course score. The course score is compared with the rating system, and each student is assigned a grade from the range of <*A*, *B*, *C*, *D* or *F*>. The mathematics professor submits the grades to the registrar for recording on the students' transcripts. In addition, the mathematics professor posts online the grades for all students and the rank of scores for students from 1st to 400th, with a graph which shows the distribution, standard deviation, median, mode and mean of scores. The essential properties of Design 2 ($\mathbf{D}_2$) are represented in Figure 9.

A third design is Design 3 ($\mathbf{D}_3$). Design 3 has a similar structure to Design 1 ($\mathbf{D}_1$), but with the addition of a pre-assessment, a pre-evaluation and preparative & formative uses of the pre-evaluation, plus some alternative sets of opportunities to study$_1$ ($\mathbf{S}_{P1}$). Design 3 consists of the following structure.

(1) Pre-assessment prior to the provision of a set of opportunities to study$_1$ ($\mathbf{S}_{P1}$)
(2) Pre-evaluation of the pre-assessment results prior to the provision of a set of opportunities to study$_1$ ($\mathbf{S}_{P1}$)
(3) Pre-evaluation report as a rating or a ranking
(4) Preparative use of the pre-evaluation results
(5) Multiple sets of opportunities to study$_1$ ($\mathbf{S}_{P1}$) sequenced by required prior knowing, level of difficulty and complexity of the intended learning outcome
(6) Provision for students to pace themselves in their study$_1$ ($\mathbf{S}_{P1}$) activities
(7) Multiple opportunities to repeat the completion of a set of opportunities to study$_1$ ($\mathbf{S}_{P1}$) sequenced by required prior knowing, level of difficulty and complexity of the intended learning outcome
(8) Assessment at the conclusion of the set of opportunities to study$_1$ ($\mathbf{S}_{P1}$)
(9) Evaluation of the assessment results
(10) Report of the evaluation results as a rating or a ranking or both
(11) Formative and/or summative use of the evaluation report

An example which illustrates Design 3 ($\mathbf{D}_3$) is that of a year 3 (3rd grade – ages 8 to 9 years) teacher, Mr Brown, who provides a graded reading program for his students. He uses a set of reading resources which are sequenced for difficulty of reading, including vocabulary, complexity of sentence structure and complexity of concepts and

Figure 10: Design of Planned Educational Episodes – Design 3

Design Variant	Stage 1: Before S_{P1}	Stage 2: During S_{P1}	Stage 3: After S_{P1}
D_3	1. Pre-assessment prior to provision of a set of opportunities to study$_1$ (S_{P1}) 2. Pre-evaluation of the pre-assessment results 3. Pre-evaluation report as a rating or a ranking 4. Preparative use of pre-evaluation results	1. Multiple sets of opportunities to study$_1$ (S_{P1}) sequenced by required prior knowing, level of difficulty and complexity of the intended learning outcome 2. Provision for students to pace themselves in their study$_1$ (S_{P1}) activities 3. Multiple opportunities to repeat the completion of a set of opportunities to study$_1$ (S_{P1}) sequenced by required prior knowing, level of difficulty and complexity of the intended learning outcome	1. Post-assessment 2. Post-evaluation of the assessment results 3. Post-evaluation report as a ranking or a rating or both 4. Formative and/or summative use of the evaluation report

propositions. He has each of his pupils complete a reading test (the pre-assessment). He evaluates the results of the reading tests, and from the results, he assigns the appropriate level of reading materials for each pupil to study$_1$ <**S_{P1}**> (a preparative use of the evaluation report). He provides instructions to his pupils on how to use the reading materials, and each day, he allocates time for his pupils to use the reading materials. Each pupil works at his or her own pace with the materials. When a pupil completes reading a set of reading materials, the pupil then completes a reading test (a post-assessment) relevant to the completed set. The pupil's score is evaluated, and provided that the evaluation results meet the minimum requirements to progress, the pupil moves to the next level of reading materials (a summative use of the post-evaluation report). If the evaluation results do not satisfy the minimum requirements, the pupil is directed to an alternate set of reading materials which are at the same level of difficulty as the one the pupil has just completed (a formative use of the post-evaluation report). The pupil completes reading the alternative set of reading materials and completes a second reading test (multiple sets of opportunities to study$_1$ <$\mathbf{S_{P1}}$>). If the pupil's test results meet the minimum requirements, the pupil progresses to the next level of reading materials (a summative use of the post-evaluation report). The essential properties of Design 3 ($\mathbf{D_3}$) are represented in Figure 10.

A fourth design is Design 4 ($\mathbf{D_4}$). Design 4 has the structure of Design 3 ($\mathbf{D_3}$) with the addition of multiple opportunities to engage in opportunities to study$_1$ ($\mathbf{S_{P1}}$) and multiple opportunities to complete the final assessment with a view in mind to achieve a minimum acceptable score and rating. The structure of Design 4 ($\mathbf{D_4}$) is as follows.

(1) Pre-assessment prior to the provision of a set of opportunities to study$_1$ ($\mathbf{S_{P1}}$)
(2) Pre-evaluation of the assessment results
(3) Report of the pre-evaluation results as a ranking
(4) Summative use of the pre-evaluation results for selection of applicants as students
(5) Provision to the students of a written statement of the intended learning outcomes (**ILO**s)
(6) Provision to the students of the assessment tasks to be completed and the criteria by which the assessment tasks will be evaluated
(7) One repeatable set of opportunities to study$_1$ ($\mathbf{S_{P1}}$) sequenced by required prior knowing, level of difficulty and complexity of the intended learning outcomes
(8) Provision for students to pace themselves in their study$_1$ ($\mathbf{S_{P1}}$)
(9) Multiple opportunities to repeat the completion of a set of opportunities to study$_1$ ($\mathbf{S_{P1}}$) sequenced by required prior knowing, level of difficulty and complexity of the intended learning outcomes (**ILO**s)
(10) Post-assessment with repeatable opportunities to complete assessment
(11) Post-evaluation of the assessment result

(12) Report of post-evaluation results as a rating of satisfactory or unsatisfactory
(13) Formative use of the evaluation report if the rating is unsatisfactory
(14) Summative use of the evaluation report if the rating is satisfactory

Design 4 (**D_4**) is well suited for mastery learning (B.S. Bloom, 1968, 1974). In mastery learning, students are provided multiple opportunities to study intentionally under guidance (study$_1$ <**S_{P1}**>) and multiple opportunities to achieve the intended learning outcomes at a specified minimum acceptable level. An example of Design 4 (**D_4**) is the following scenario. A casino advertises for dealers for its roulette game. There are 6 vacancies. The casino human resources manager receives 50 applications. The human resources manager does a cull of the applicants and selects 12 applicants. The casino's education manager has the 12 applicants complete an aptitude test, evaluates the results and reports the evaluation results as a ranking from 1st to 12th. The 6 applicants with the highest ranking are selected for immediate roulette dealer education. The remaining 6 are designated as reserves, to be called upon in the event that any candidates withdraw or are excluded from the roulette dealer education program. The casino education manager describes the roulette dealer education program to the 6 top-ranking candidates, presents the candidates with a list of intended learning outcomes and provides the candidates with a list of assessment tasks which they must complete with a score of 100% to be deemed satisfactory. The education manager demonstrates to the candidates how to navigate the online computer-based roulette dealer course and explains that the candidates are allowed to pace themselves. Also, the manager explains that candidates are permitted to make the judgment that their range of knowing about roulette dealing is sufficient to satisfy all the assessment tasks. If the candidates so judge, they may go directly to the post-assessment tasks, which are all completed online. If unsuccessful, candidates may return to the online roulette dealer course and conduct further study$_1$ (**S_{P1}**), then repeat the post-assessment tasks. When the candidates are successful in the post-assessment tasks, they will be moved on to having actual experience in playing roulette games with other casino personnel. The candidates have a maximum of three weeks to master all variations of bets and odds in roulette – single number bets, group number bets, color (red or black) bets, odd or even number bets, high (19-36) or low number (1-18) bets. If they have not mastered the betting and odds system, and the rules of the game, after three weeks, they will be excluded from the dealership selection and education process, and a reserve applicant will be invited to undertake the roulette dealer course as a candidate. The essential properties of Design 4 (**D_4**) are represented in Figure 11.

A fifth design (Design 5 <**D_5**>) of a planned educational episode is

Figure 11: Design of Planned Educational Episodes – Design 4

Design Variant	Stage 1: Before S_{P1}	Stage 2: During S_{P1}	Stage 3: After S_{P1}
D_4	1. Pre-assessment prior to provision of a set of opportunities to study$_1$ (S_{P1}) 2. Pre-evaluation of the pre-assessment results 3. Report of the pre-evaluation results as a ranking 4. Summative use of pre-evaluation results for selection of applicants as students 5. Provision to students of a written statement of intended learning outcomes 6. Provision to students of the assessment tasks to be completed and the criteria by which the assessment tasks will be evaluated	1. One repeatable set of opportunities to study$_1$ (S_{P1}) sequenced by required prior knowing, level of difficulty and complexity of the intended learning outcomes 2. Provision for students to pace themselves in their study$_1$ (S_{P1}) activities 3. Multiple opportunities to repeat the completion of a set of opportunities to study$_1$ (S_{P1}) sequenced by required prior knowing, level of difficulty and complexity of the intended learning outcomes (ILOs)	1. Post-assessment with repeatable opportunities to complete 2. Post-evaluation of the assessment results 3. Report of post-evaluation results as a rating of satisfactory or unsatisfactory 4. Formative use of the evaluation report if the rating is unsatisfactory 5. Summative use of the evaluation report if the rating is satisfactory

one which requires students to make a contract with a teacher about which set of intended learning outcomes the students wish to achieve. Different sets of intended learning outcomes are grouped in relation to the difficulty of the intended learning outcome, the amount of study$_1$ (**S**$_{P1}$) required to achieve the different sets of intended learning outcomes and the assessment tasks relevant to the intended learning outcomes (**ILO**s). The structure of Design 5 (**D**$_5$) is as follows.

(1) Provision for students to choose one from multiple sets of intended learning outcomes of different levels of difficulty
(2) Commitment from each student in a written contract to undertake to achieve a student-selected set of intended learning outcomes, to engage in the relevant opportunities to study$_1$ (**S**$_{P1}$) and to complete the relevant assessment tasks to a specified minimum set of criteria (rules and/or standards) to demonstrate achievement of the intended learning outcomes
(3) Provision of multiple sets of opportunities to study$_1$ (**S**$_{P1}$) which are sequenced by required prior knowing, level of difficulty and complexity of intended learning outcomes and which are relevant to achievement of the student-chosen set of intended learning outcomes and to successful completion of assessment tasks
(4) Post-assessment tasks
(5) Post-evaluation of results of post-assessment tasks
(6) Report of post-evaluation results
(7) Summative use of post-evaluation report

An example which illustrates the essential properties of Design 5 (**D**$_5$) is the following scenario. Mr Farmer is teaching geography to year 9 (9th grade) students in a large high school. He is about to teach a unit on climate, which includes topics about what is climate, what climates occur in which latitudes, what factors influence climate, how does climate affect human activities and how do human activities affect climate. He has a mixed ability class, and the students differ widely in their motivations to study$_1$ (**S**$_{P1}$). He decides to offer his students a number of options. The <*C*> option is a package consisting of a set of intended learning outcomes (**ILO**s), a set of relevant study$_1$ (**S**$_{P1}$) activities, some homework exercises and a final test with multiple choice, fill in and short answer items. Students must achieve at least a

Figure 12: Design of Planned Educational Episodes – Design 5

Design Variant	Stage 1: Before S_{P1}	Stage 2: During S_{P1}	Stage 3: After S_{P1}
D_5	1. Provision for students to choose one from multiple sets of intended learning outcomes of different levels of difficulty 2. Commitment from each student in a written contract to undertake to achieve a student-selected set of intended learning outcomes, to engage in the relevant opportunities to study$_1$ (S_{P1}) and to complete the relevant assessment tasks to a specified minimum set of criteria (rules and/or standards) to demonstrate achievement of the intended learning outcomes (ILO) 3. Provision to students of a written statement of criteria to be used in evaluation of assessment tasks	1. Provision of multiple sets of opportunities to study$_1$ (S_{P1}) which are sequenced by required prior knowing, level of difficulty and complexity of intended learning outcomes and which are relevant to achievement of the student-chosen set of intended learning outcomes and to successful completion of assessment tasks	1. Post-assessment 2. Post-evaluation of the assessment results 3. Post-evaluation report as a ranking or a rating or both 4. Summative use of the evaluation report

70% score on all assessment items (homework and final test) to receive a grade (a rating) of <*C*>. The <*B*> option is a package consisting of a set of intended learning outcomes (**ILO**s), a set of relevant study$_1$ (**S_{P1}**) activities, some homework exercises, a final test with multiple choice, fill in and short answer items and a final test which requires a short essay. Students must achieve at least an 80% score on all assessment items to receive a grade of <*B*>. The <*A*> option is a package consisting of a set of intended learning outcomes (**ILO**s), a set of relevant study$_1$ ($\mathbf{S_{P1}}$) activities, some homework exercises, a final test with multiple choice, fill in and short answer items, a final test which requires a short essay and completion of a research report. Students must achieve at least a 90% score on all assessment items to receive a grade of <*A*>. Each student makes a choice and signs an <*A*>, <*B*> or <*C*> contract. The students proceed with their studies$_1$ ($\mathbf{S_{P1}}$) and the completion of their contracted assessment tasks. Mr Farmer marks the assessments, assigns them scores, evaluates the scores in relation to his nominated criteria and reports the scores as a rating of <*A*, *B*, *C*, *D* or *F*>. He records the grades on his enrolment list, and he reports the grade results to each student. After completion of the unit on climate, he moves the class on to the next unit of study$_1$ ($\mathbf{S_{P1}}$). The essential properties of Design 5 ($\mathbf{D_5}$) are represented in Figure 12.

A sixth design (Design 6 <$\mathbf{D_6}$>) of a planned educational episode is one which requires students to choose and complete a project. The structure of Design 6 ($\mathbf{D_6}$) is as follows.

(1) Provision to students of one or more topics and/or problems about which to conduct research and produce a report in some medium (written, oral, video, recorded audio, drama, etc.)

(2) Provision to students of guidance and direction on how to conduct research by asking questions, answering questions, finding evidence which supports answers to questions and organizing the answers into a coherent narrative for describing results of the research project

(3) Provision to students of due date for completion of research report and a written statement of criteria for evaluation of the project report

(4) Provision to students of examples of well-produced project reports in some medium (written, oral, video, recorded audio, drama, etc.)

(5) Provision to students of time allocation, resources or resource locations and opportunities to conduct research to establish important and significant facts relevant to the research problem

(6) Supervision, guidance and management of students in the

conduct of their research

(7) Periodic submission by students of progress reports on the state of their conduct of their research and the development of their research report
(8) Provision to students of guidance in developing their research report, including effective ways of organizing and synthesizing the facts found from the research into a coherent narrative and a well-developed report
(9) Post-evaluation of the research report
(10) Report of the evaluation results as a rating or ranking or both
(11) Summative use of the evaluation report

An example which illustrates the essential properties of Design 6 (**D**$_6$) is the following scenario. Mrs Evans is a year 9 (9th grade) science teacher. She assigns her students the task of choosing some aspect of electricity, posing a problem about it, conducting research to resolve the problem and producing a research report in some medium (written, oral, video, audio recording, dramatization, etc.). Mrs Evans provides some examples of research projects which students have produced in the past, and she also gives each student a set of written directions on how to proceed with the research project and the criteria by which the research report will be evaluated. One of Mrs Evans students, Suzanne, decides that she would like to conduct some research about the development of the electric motor. The questions she poses are: (1) Why was the electric motor invented? (2) Who invented the electric motor, where and when? (3) How have electric motors been improved over the years to the present time? She checks with Mrs Evans about whether she is on the right track with her research questions and asks whether she might develop a short video (5 or 6 minutes) which presents the findings from her research. Mrs Evans tells Suzanne that she is right on track with her research project ideas and that she should proceed with her research. Suzanne searches for information to answer her key questions, and she finds a number of facts from a variety of sources. She develops a set of notes which summarizes and/or quotes from her sources. She also develops a bibliography which documents her sources. During her research, she periodically reports to Mrs Evans about her progress, and Mrs Evans advises her on how to make improvements to her research. After completing her research, Suzanne decides to present her report as a short video of 5 to 6 minutes. She

Figure 13: Design of Planned Educational Episodes – Design 6

Design Variant	Stage 1: Before S_{P1}	Stage 2: During S_{P1}	Stage 3: After S_{P1}
D_6	1. Provision to students of one or more topics and/or problems about which to conduct research and produce a report in some medium (written, oral, video, recorded audio, drama, etc.) 2. Provision to students of guidance and direction on how to conduct research by asking questions, answering questions, finding evidence which supports answers to questions and organizing the answers into a coherent narrative for describing results of the research project 3. Provision to students of due date for completion of research report and a written statement of criteria for evaluation of the project report 4. Provision to students of examples of well-produced project reports in some medium (written, oral, video, recorded audio, drama, etc.)	1. Provision to students of time allocation, resources or resource locations and opportunities to conduct research to establish important and significant facts relevant to the research problem 2. Supervision, guidance and management of students in the conduct of their research 3. Periodic submission by students of progress reports on the state of their conduct of their research and the development of their research report 4. Provision to students of guidance in developing their research report, including effective ways of organizing and synthesizing the facts found from the research into a coherent narrative and a well-developed report	1. Post-evaluation of the research report 2. Report of the evaluation results as a rating or a ranking or both 3. Summative use of the evaluation report

writes the script for the video, and she plans a story board for the video. She assembles some photographs and diagrams to be included in the video. She also draws a sequence of figures which she intends to incorporate as animation in the video. She reads her script to establish the length of the video which she wishes to produce. She records her video and records her narrative on the video. In addition, she provides a written report which includes her references, notes, narrative, photographs, diagrams and drawings for the video animation. Finally, she is satisfied with her video about the origins and development of the electric motor, and she submits her written and video report to Mrs Evans for evaluation. Mrs Evans conducts an evaluation of the written report and video report in relation to the nominated criteria, assigns a rating (<*A*> out of a range of ratings from <*A*, *B*, *C*, *D*, *F*>). Mrs Evans records the grade on the student enrolment list. All students do as Suzanne has done – chosen topics, stated questions to be answered, conducted research of several sources to find relevant facts, organized the facts into a research report and submitted the report to Mrs Evans for evaluation. The essential properties of Design 6 ($\mathbf{D}_6$) are represented in Figure 13.

Many other designs are possible. The six presented here are intended as an introduction to what might go into a design. Designs of planned educational episodes are like designs of vehicle. The value of the design is determined by the degree to which it suits the nominated purpose. A car designed for racing is useless for hauling 45 metric tonnes of ore in one trip from the bottom of an open pit mine to the top. In the education of a nurse who is learning how to insert a canula and attach a drip, it's not satisfactory for the nurse to do it right 70% or 80% of the time. It needs to be done correctly 100% of the time. Mistakes in the procedure have lethal consequences. Thus, the educational design should be one which requires the student nurse to practice repeatedly until the nurse can demonstrate performance of the procedure smoothly, confidently and competently 100% of the time. In contrast, a long-haul truck driver may have some vague memories of the causes and consequences of the American Civil War which the driver studied in a high school US history class some years ago. But the hazy recollection in no way impedes the functions of the driver as a safe, competent driver. And should the driver choose, he or she knows how to improve his or her range of knowing by doing further reading about the American Civil War. The design for the high school US history unit about the American Civil War (one, and only one set of opportunities to study$_1$ <$\mathbf{S}_{\mathbf{P1}}$> with a post-assessment, post-evaluation and summative use of the evaluation report) which the truck driver experienced 25 years ago was fit for purpose and matched the available allocation of time and resources. In the selection and development of design for planned educational episodes, it is truly a case of different horses for different courses. The purpose of the planned educational episode needs to be established first. Then an appropriate design needs to be developed to fit the purpose within the constraints of allocated time and available resources.

Strategies

All people who engage in education (**E**) can, and do, devise strategies ($\mathbf{E}_{DC20}$) for participating in education. Students devise strategies for studying ($\mathbf{E}_{DC20S}$). And teachers devise strategies for teaching ($\mathbf{E}_{DC20T}$).

A strategy is a deliberate combination of the derivative components ($\mathbf{E}_{DC}$) of education (**E**) – language, resources, methods, styles, focus, organization, pace, sequence, initiation, intentions, goal structures, assessment, evaluation and design. Hilda Taba (1966) is attributed with being one of the first to promote the term <*teaching strategy*>. However, teaching strategies are only one-half of the picture. The other half is the set of strategies that students use in undertaking to learn something under guidance. Strategies ($\mathbf{E}_{DC20}$) in the educational process include both teaching strategies and studying strategies. See Figure 14.

The relationship of strategy ($\mathbf{E}_{DC20}$) to the other derivative components ($\mathbf{E}_{DC}$) of education (**E**) can be expressed as follows.

(1) $\mathbf{E}_{DC20} = \{\mathbf{E}_{DC1}, \mathbf{E}_{DC2}, \ldots \mathbf{E}_{DC13}, \mathbf{E}_{DC19}\}$

(2) $\mathbf{E}_{DC20} = \mathbf{E}_{DC20T} \cup \mathbf{E}_{DC20S}$

The first statement < $\mathbf{E}_{DC20} = \{\mathbf{E}_{DC1}, \mathbf{E}_{DC2}, \ldots \mathbf{E}_{DC13}, \mathbf{E}_{DC19}\}$> reads in ordinary English that strategies of teaching and studying (denoted by <$\mathbf{E}_{DC20}$>) consist of (=) the derivative components of education (**E**) denoted by <$\{\mathbf{E}_{DC1}, \mathbf{E}_{DC2}, \ldots \mathbf{E}_{DC13}, \mathbf{E}_{DC19}\}$>.

The second statement <$\mathbf{E}_{DC20} = \mathbf{E}_{DC20T} \cup \mathbf{E}_{DC20S}$> reads in ordinary English that strategies of teaching and studying ($\mathbf{E}_{DC20}$) consist of (=) the union of ($\cup$) teaching strategies ($\mathbf{E}_{DC20T}$) and intentional guided studying strategies ($\mathbf{E}_{DC20S}$).

One example of a teaching and studying strategy ($\mathbf{E}_{DC20}$) is student centered learning. The terms <*student centered*>, <*pupil centered*> and <*child centered education*> are names that have been given to this teaching and studying strategy. Other names given to it include <*discovery learning*>, <*inquiry based learning*> and <*project based learning*>. Although the strategy is denoted by several names, the distinguishing characteristics of the strategy remain much the same. It is a strategy in which the teacher establishes a situation that allows, encourages, leads

Figure 14: Strategies of Teaching (E_{DC20T}) and Intentional Guided Studying (E_{DC20S}) in Unofficial and Official Education

E_{DC}: *Derivative components of education*		E_{DC20T}: *Teaching strategies*	E_{DC20S}: *Studying strategies*
E_{DC1}:	Language	Combinations of derivative components of education for teaching	Combinations of derivative components of education for studying
E_{DC2}:	Resources		
E_{DC3}:	Methods		
E_{DC4}:	Styles		
E_{DC5}:	Focus		
E_{DC6}:	Organization		
E_{DC7}:	Pace		
E_{DC8}:	Sequence		
E_{DC9}:	Initiation		
E_{DC10}:	Intentions		
E_{DC11}:	Goal Structures		
E_{DC12}:	Assessment		
E_{DC13}:	Evaluation		
E_{DC19}:	Design		

to and/or compels students in their studies to choose and direct the teaching (**T_P**) and studying$_1$ (**S_{P1}**) of some content (**C**) to learn intentionally under guidance (**L_1**) some prescribed range of knowing (**K_{2P}**). Let this strategy be denoted by the terms <*Strategy 1*> and <**E_{DC20-1}**>. With Strategy 1 (**E_{DC20-1}**), students have the obligation and responsibility to undertake the following.

(1) Initiate study (**S_{P1}**) activities based on their own interests

and curiosities ($\mathbf{E}_{DC9}$)

(2) Specify their own intended learning outcomes ($\mathbf{E}_{DC10}$)
(3) Choose their own goal structures – competitive, cooperative or individualized ($\mathbf{E}_{DC11}$)
(4) Decide upon their own instructional design ($\mathbf{E}_{DC19}$)
(5) Select their own study methods ($\mathbf{E}_{DC3}$)
(6) Focus on problems, states of affairs and matters that interest them ($\mathbf{E}_{DC5}$)
(7) Organize themselves as and when they please, into one large group, or small groups, or as individuals ($\mathbf{E}_{DC6}$)
(8) Set their own pace for their studies and achievement of intended learning outcomes ($\mathbf{E}_{DC7}$)
(9) Decide the sequence of their studies ($\mathbf{E}_{DC8}$)
(10) Locate, choose or make their own resources for study ($\mathbf{E}_{DC2}$)
(11) Formulate their own assessment procedures ($\mathbf{E}_{DC12}$)
(12) Devise their own evaluation procedure and evaluation reports and choose to use their evaluation reports preparatively, formatively and/or summatively ($\mathbf{E}_{DC13}$)

In official education ($\mathbf{E}_{O}$), professional teachers who utilize this teaching and intentional guided studying ($\mathbf{S}_{P1}$) strategy (Strategy 1 <$\mathbf{E}_{DC20\text{-}1}$>) support the students in their choices and provide guidance intended to assist the students to execute their intentional guided study ($\mathbf{S}_{P1}$) plans and achieve their intended learning outcomes. Teachers, for example, provide advice, make recommendations, ask questions for clarification, evaluate activities, organize resources, monitor progress, keep records, etc. In Strategy 1, ($\mathbf{E}_{DC20\text{-}1}$) the teacher is still, of course, teaching and therefore using a combination of derivative components of the educational process. Proponents of Strategy 1 ($E_{DC20\text{-}1}$) have included John Dewey (1916), William Heard Kilpatrick (1918), Carl Rogers (1969), Jean Piaget (1926, 1948, 1953, 1971), Lev Vygotsky (1934), Jerome Bruner (1960, 1971), Idit Harel and Seymour Papert (1991) and Maria Montessori (1947a, b, 1949).

In contrast to Strategy 1 ($\mathbf{E}_{DC20\text{-}1}$), there is direct instruction. The terms <*direct instruction*>, <*systematic teaching*> and <*explicit teaching*> are names that have been given to this second strategy. It is a strategy in which the teacher (or third parties who provide systematic guidance to teachers) chooses and directs the teaching ($\mathbf{T}_{P}$) and intentional guided studying ($\mathbf{S}_{P1}$). Let this strategy be denoted by the terms <*Strategy 2*>

and $<\mathbf{E}_{DC20-2}>$. With Strategy 2 ($\mathbf{E}_{DC20-2}$), the teachers (or the third parties who provide systematic guidance to teachers) have the obligation and responsibility to implement the following.

(1) Initiate study activities based on some analysis and judgments about what is appropriate for students to study and learn intentionally with guidance ($\mathbf{E}_{DC9}$)

(2) Specify intended learning outcomes (**ILO**s) for the students ($\mathbf{E}_{DC10}$)

(3) Choose goal structures (competitive, cooperative or individualized) which they (the teachers) deem appropriate for the students ($\mathbf{E}_{DC11}$)

(4) Decide upon their own instructional design ($\mathbf{E}_{DC19}$)

(5) Select intentional guided study ($\mathbf{S}_{P1}$) methods which they believe to be appropriate for the students ($\mathbf{E}_{DC3}$)

(6) Arrange for students to focus on problems, states of affairs and matters that the teachers deem to be appropriate for achieving the nominated intended learning outcomes ($\mathbf{E}_{DC5}$)

(7) Organize students in ways which they (the teachers) believe to be appropriate for achieving the nominated intended learning outcomes, for example, into one large group, or small groups, or as individuals ($\mathbf{E}_{DC6}$)

(8) Set the pace which they believe to be appropriate for students to achieve the nominated intended learning outcomes ($\mathbf{E}_{DC7}$)

(9) Decide the sequence of studies ($\mathbf{S}_{P1}$) for students ($\mathbf{E}_{DC8}$)

(10) Locate, choose and/or make resources which they believe to be appropriate for assisting students to achieve the nominated learning outcomes ($\mathbf{E}_{DC2}$)

(11) Formulate assessment procedures for students to adduce necessary and sufficient evidence to establish that students have achieved the nominated intended learning outcomes to some required degree ($\mathbf{E}_{DC12}$)

(12) Devise an evaluation procedure and an evaluation report system that fairly expresses conclusions which can be drawn from the evidence gathered from the assessment procedures and use the evaluation report preparatively, formatively and/or summatively ($\mathbf{E}_{DC13}$)

Proponents, developers and/or researchers of Strategy 2 ($\mathbf{E}_{DC20-2}$)

Figure 15: Derivative Components of Education

E	E_L	E_{BE}	E_{DC}: Derivative components
E_o:	E_{OL1} E_{OL2} E_{OL3} E_{OL4} E_{OL5}	T S C X	1. E_{DC1}: Language of teaching & guided studying 2. E_{DC2}: Resources & materials 3. E_{DC3}: Methods of teaching & guided studying 4. E_{DC4}: Styles of social interaction 5. E_{DC5}: Focus of teacher & student attention 6. E_{DC6}: Organization of teachers & students 7. E_{DC7}: Pace of teaching & guided studying 8. E_{DC8}: Sequence of teaching & guided studying 9. E_{DC9}: Initiation of guided studying 10. E_{DC10}: Intentions of teachers & students 11. E_{DC11}: Goal structures 12. E_{DC12}: Assessment 13. E_{DC13}: Evaluation 14. E_{DC14}: Certification 15. E_{DC15}: Curriculum 16. E_{DC16}: Syllabus 17. E_{DC17}: Unit plans 18. E_{DC18}: Lesson plans 19. E_{DC19}: Instructional design 20. E_{DC20}: Strategies of teaching & guided studying
E_u:	E_{UL1} E_{UL2} E_{UL3} E_{UL4} E_{UL5}	T S C X	1. E_{DC1}: Language of teaching & guided studying 2. E_{DC2}: Resources & materials 3. E_{DC3}: Methods of teaching & guided studying 4. E_{DC4}: Styles of social interaction 5. E_{DC5}: Focus of teacher & student attention 6. E_{DC6}: Organization of teachers & students 7. E_{DC7}: Pace of teaching & guided studying 8. E_{DC8}: Sequence of teaching & guided studying 9. E_{DC9}: Initiation of guided studying 10. E_{DC10}: Intentions of teachers & students 11. E_{DC11}: Goal structures 12. E_{DC12}: Assessment 13. E_{DC13}: Evaluation

have included Wesley Becker and Seigfried Engelmann (1995-96), Robert Slavin et al. (1996), Barak Rosenshine and Robert Stevens (1986), Douglas W. Carnine et al. (2009), Madeline Creek Hunter (1967, 1969, 1982, 1994), Robert Marzano et al. (1997, 2001), Dean B. Ceri et al. (2012), Robert Marzano (2007, 2017) and John Hattie (2009).

Other examples of teaching and intentional guided studying strategies ($\mathbf{E_{DC20}}$) can be found in G. Fenstermacher & J. Soltis (2009) and B. Joyce & M. Weil (2011). Fenstermacher and Soltis describe three teaching and intentional guided studying strategies ($\mathbf{E_{DC20}}$), which they name "the executive, the facilitator and the liberationist approaches to teaching." They provide examples of each teaching and intentional guided studying strategy and invite readers to identify the distinguishing characteristics of each strategy and the values implied by each strategy.

Joyce and Weil give the name of <*models of teaching*> to teaching and intentional guided studying strategies ($\mathbf{E_{DC20}}$). They assign similar teaching and intentional guided studying strategies to categories, which they name "families," for example, "the information processing family," "the personal family," etc. They provide detailed characterizations, descriptions and examples of each member of a family (i.e. of a category) of teaching and intentional guided studying strategies.

A teaching and intentional guided studying strategy ($\mathbf{E_{DC20}}$) is any combination of the derivative components ($\mathbf{E_{DC}}$) of education (**E**). There are many combinations that we can make with a dozen or more components ($\mathbf{E_{DC}}$). Thus, there is a huge variety of possible teaching and intentional guided studying strategies ($\mathbf{E_{DC20}}$).

Figure 15 represents official education ($\mathbf{E_{O}}$) and unofficial education ($\mathbf{E_{U}}$), their levels (<$\mathbf{E_{OL}}$> and <$\mathbf{E_{UL}}$>), their basic elements ($\mathbf{E_{BE}}$) and their derivative components ($\mathbf{E_{DC}}$). Official education ($\mathbf{E_{O}}$) has 20 derivative components ($\mathbf{E_{DC}}$). Unofficial education ($\mathbf{E_{U}}$) has 13 derivative components ($\mathbf{E_{DC}}$). The derivative components, <$\mathbf{E_{DC14}}$> through <$\mathbf{E_{DC18}}$> are not extant in unofficial education ($\mathbf{E_{U}}$), and derivative components <$\mathbf{E_{DC19}}$> and <$\mathbf{E_{DC20}}$> are rarely deliberate considerations in unofficial education ($\mathbf{E_{U}}$).

Basic Activities of Education

In addition to official and unofficial education (<$\mathbf{E_{O}}$> and <$\mathbf{E_{U}}$>), the levels of education (<$\mathbf{E_{OL}}$> and <$\mathbf{E_{UL}}$>), the four basic elements of education ($\mathbf{E_{BE}}$) and the derivative components of education ($\mathbf{E_{DC}}$), there are the basic activities in education ($\mathbf{E_{BA}}$). The two basic activities are teaching ($\mathbf{T_{P}}$) and intentional guided studying ($\mathbf{S_{P1}}$).

Teaching ($\mathbf{T_{P}}$) is providing opportunities, guidance and help to someone (playing the role of student <**S**>) to study intentionally under guidance ($\mathbf{S_{P1}}$) some content (**C**) and learn intentionally under guidance

Figure 16: Basic Activities in Education

E	E_L	E_{BE}	E_{DC}	E_{BA}
E_O:	E_{OL1} E_{OL2} E_{OL3} E_{OL4} E_{OL5}	T S C X	1. E_{DC1} 2. E_{DC2} 3. E_{DC3} 4. E_{DC4} 5. E_{DC5} 6. E_{DC6} 7. E_{DC7} 8. E_{DC8} 9. E_{DC9} 10. E_{DC10} 11. E_{DC11} 12. E_{DC12} 13. E_{DC13} 14. E_{DC14} 15. E_{DC15} 16. E_{DC16} 17. E_{DC17} 18. E_{DC18} 19. E_{DC19} 20. E_{DC20}	T_P: Teaching S_{P1}: Intentional guided studying
E_U:	E_{UL1} E_{UL2} E_{UL3} E_{UL4} E_{UL5}	T S C X	1. E_{DC1} 2. E_{DC2} 3. E_{DC3} 4. E_{DC4} 5. E_{DC5} 6. E_{DC6} 7. E_{DC7} 8. E_{DC8} 9. E_{DC9} 10. E_{DC10} 11. E_{DC11} 12. E_{DC12} 13. E_{DC13}	T_P: Teaching S_{P1}: Intentional guided studying

(**L_1**) some prescribed range of knowing (**K_{2P}**) of some kind (**K_{2K}**), at some level (**K_{2L}**) in some form (**K_{2F}**).

An example of teaching (**T_P**) in unofficial education (**E_U**) is that of Gary. Gary shows his workmate, Steve, how to operate the espresso machine in the office to make a cappuccino and how to clean the machine after using it. Gary also explains the importance of cleaning the machine immediately after use to prevent blockages in the steam wand and coffee filter. Then Gary watches Steve practice making a cappuccino and cleaning the machine afterward with a view to making sure that Steve understands the ins and outs of making an espresso coffee and cleaning the espresso machine.

Studying intentionally under guidance (studying$_1$ $<\mathbf{S}_{P1}>$) is undertaking activities in relation to some content (**C**) to learn intentionally under guidance (learn$_1$ $<\mathbf{L}_1>$) a prescribed range of knowing ($\mathbf{K}_{2P}$). Studying intentionally under guidance (studying$_1$ $<\mathbf{S}_{P1}>$) implies acceptance, engagement, endeavor and purpose. The persons playing the role of student (**S**) accept the opportunity to undertake to extend their prescribed range of knowing ($\mathbf{K}_{2P}$). They engage with both the teacher (**T**) and the content (**C**) by focusing their attention both. They endeavor to achieve the prescribed range of knowing ($\mathbf{K}_{2P}$) by completing the activities provided and/or recommended by the teacher (**T**), by heeding the advice and help of the teacher (**T**) and by undertaking appropriate practice which is relevant to the intended learning outcomes (**ILO**s). Students have the purpose in mind (**M**) of achieving the prescribed range of knowing ($\mathbf{K}_{2P}$) as specified by the intended learning outcomes (**ILO**s).

An example of intentional guided studying (studying$_1$ $<S_{P1}>$) in official education ($\mathbf{E}_O$) is the case of Henry. Henry wants to know how to use Microsoft® Word efficiently. He goes to the local community college and enrolls in a short course which offers instruction on how to use all the commands available in Microsoft® Word. Henry accepts the guidance from his teacher (**T**), and he undertakes all the activities which the teacher (**T**) provides in guiding him to extend his range of knowing-how ($\mathbf{K}_{2K3}$) to use the commands and features of Microsoft® Word competently, confidently and justifiably.

Product of Effective Teaching and Intentional Guided Studying

The term <*phenomenon*> denotes an observable (perceivable$_6$ $<\mathbf{P}_6>$) entity, action and/or event. A phenomenon is a set, not a sequence. Teaching ($\mathbf{T}_P$) and intentional guided studying (studying$_1$ $<\mathbf{S}_{P1}>$) are phenomena. They are sets of activities. The term <*process*> denotes a change (sometimes sudden, sometimes gradual) of some entity and/or state of affairs over time. A process is a sequence, not a set. Learning ($\mathbf{L}$), conduced learning ($\mathbf{L}_1$), discovery learning ($\mathbf{L}_2$), coerced learning ($\mathbf{L}_3$) and accidental learning ($\mathbf{L}_4$) are processes. They are sequential changes in some state of affairs over time. The term <*state of affairs*> denotes some circumstance of being. A state of affairs is a condition. Ignorance (not knowing <$\neg\mathbf{K}_2$>) and knowing ($\mathbf{K}_2$) are conditions.

Intentional guided learning (learning$_1$ <$\mathbf{L}_1$>) is the process of extending one's prescribed range of knowing ($\mathbf{K}_{2P}$) by means of education ($\mathbf{E}$). Intentional guided learning (learning$_1$ <$\mathbf{L}_1$>) is the process that happens when the activities of intentional guided studying (studying$_1$ <$\mathbf{S}_{P1}$>) and teaching ($\mathbf{T}_P$) are effective. It is the resultant of the phenomena (activities) of effective teaching ($\mathbf{T}_{PE}$) and effective intentional guided studying (effective studying$_1$ <$\mathbf{S}_{P1E}$>). The relationship of effective teaching ($\mathbf{T}_{PE}$) and effective intentional guided studying (effective studying$_1$ <$\mathbf{S}_{P1E}$>) to intentional guided learning ($\mathbf{L}_1$) and a prescribed range of knowing ($\mathbf{K}_{2P}$) can be expressed as follows.

(1) $\mathbf{T}_{PE} \cup \mathbf{S}_{P1E} \to \mathbf{L}_1$

(2) $\mathbf{L}_1 \to \mathbf{K}_{2P}$

The first statement <$\mathbf{T}_{PE} \cup \mathbf{S}_{P1E} \to \mathbf{L}_1$> reads in ordinary English that the union ($\cup$) of the essential properties of the phenomenon (set of activities) of effective teaching ($\mathbf{T}_{PE}$) and the essential properties of the phenomenon (set of activities) of effective intentional guided studying ($\mathbf{S}_{P1E}$) are the controlling conditions for ($\to$) the resultant of the process (the sequential change) of intentional guided learning ($\mathbf{L}_1$).

The second statement <$\mathbf{L}_1 \to \mathbf{K}_{2P}$> reads in ordinary English that the process (the sequential change) of intentional guided learning ($\mathbf{L}_1$) is the set of controlling conditions for ($\to$) the resultant (the condition of mind) of a prescribed range of knowing ($\mathbf{K}_{2P}$).

An example of intentional guided learning ($\mathbf{L}_1$) produced from official education ($\mathbf{E}_O$) is the case of Karen. Karen wants to qualify for a commercial bus driver's license. She enrolls in a driving school which specializes in instruction in the operation of large vehicles – buses, prime movers, heavy equipment. Her driving instructor provides her with a variety of opportunities to study intentionally under guidance (study$_1$ <$\mathbf{S}_{P1}$>) the ins and outs of driving a large bus on busy urban streets, highways and freeways. Karen undertakes all the study$_1$ ($\mathbf{S}_{P1}$) activities which her instructor provides for her. She studies$_1$ ($\mathbf{S}_{P1}$) the state and federal motor vehicle codes which regulate the operation of buses. She studies ($\mathbf{S}_{P1}$) how to operate all the controls and how to read and interpret all the data provided by the dials and gauges on the bus. Under supervision, she practices driving a large bus, first on an obstacle course, then on suburban streets, then on highways and freeways. At the conclusion of her course, she sits an exam which tests her range of knowing of the state and federal regulations which govern the operation of buses. She also completes an examination in which she operates a large bus in a variety of traffic conditions. Her examiners evaluate her performances, and they certify her as competent to operate a large commercial bus. She submits her documentation to the licensing authority, and the authority grants her a driver's license for the operation of commercial buses. Through the activities of effective teaching ($\mathbf{T}_{PE}$) and effective studying$_1$ ($\mathbf{S}_{P1E}$), Karen learns intentionally and under guidance ($\mathbf{L}_1$) the range of prescribed knowing ($\mathbf{K}_{2P}$) requisite for driving a commercial bus and for qualifying for a commercial bus driver's license.

The relationships of the process of intentional guided (conduced) learning (learning$_1$ $<\mathbf{L}_1>$) as a basic product of education ($\mathbf{E}_{BP}$) and of the cognitive state of mind of a prescribe range of knowing ($\mathbf{K}_{2P}$) as a product of the process of intentional guided (conduced) learning (learning$_1$ $<\mathbf{L}_1>$) are represented in Figure 17.

The product of effective education ($\mathbf{E}_E$) is the process of intentional guided (conduced) learning ($\mathbf{L}_1$), and the product of the process of conduced learning ($\mathbf{L}_1$) is some prescribed range of knowing ($\mathbf{K}_{2P}$) which students have achieved. A prescribed range of knowing ($\mathbf{K}_{2P}$) consists of some combination of

(1) the four kinds of knowing ($\mathbf{K}_{2K1}$, $\mathbf{K}_{2K2}$, $\mathbf{K}_{2K3}$, $\mathbf{K}_{2K4}$),
(2) the five forms of knowng ($\mathbf{K}_{2F1}$, $\mathbf{K}_{2F2}$, $\mathbf{K}_{2F3}$, $\mathbf{K}_{2F4}$, $\mathbf{K}_{2K5}$) and
(3) three of the four levels of knowing ($\mathbf{K}_{2L1}$, $\mathbf{K}_{2L2}$, $\mathbf{K}_{2L3}$ but not $\mathbf{K}_{2L4}$).

Postconventional level ($\mathbf{K}_{2L4}$) is achievable by means of inquiry ($\mathbf{Q}$), not by means of education ($\mathbf{E}$).

Education ($\mathbf{E}$), the activities of teaching ($\mathbf{T}_P$) and intentional guided studying ($\mathbf{S}_{P1}$), can be effective or ineffective. Effective education ($\mathbf{E}_E$) consists of only effective teaching ($\mathbf{T}_{PE}$) and effective intentional guided studying ($\mathbf{S}_{P1E}$), and the process of intentional guided learning ($\mathbf{L}_1$) is the product of, and only the product of, effective education ($\mathbf{E}_E$). Unlike education ($\mathbf{E}$), intentional guided learning ($\mathbf{L}_1$) can never be ineffective. The attributes of effective and ineffective do

Figure 17: Learning$_1$ (L_1) as a Basic Product of Education (E_{BP}) and Prescribed Knowing (K_{2P}) as a Product of Learning$_1$ (L_1)

E	E_L	E_{BE}	E_{DC}	E_{BA}	E_{BP}	Product of L_1: K_{2P}
E_o:	E_{OL1} E_{OL2} E_{OL3} E_{OL4} E_{OL5}	T S C X	1. E_{DC1} 2. E_{DC2} 3. E_{DC3} 4. E_{DC4} 5. E_{DC5} 6. E_{DC6} 7. E_{DC7} 8. E_{DC8} 9. E_{DC9} 10. E_{DC10} 11. E_{DC11} 12. E_{DC12} 13. E_{DC13} 14. E_{DC14} 15. E_{DC15} 16. E_{DC16} 17. E_{DC17} 18. E_{DC18} 19. E_{DC19} 20. E_{DC20}	T_P S_{P1}	L_1	**$K_2 \supset K_{2P}$** **K_{2P} = range of knowing in some combination of** **4 kinds of knowing** (1) knowing-that-one (2) knowing-that (3) knowing-how (4) knowing-to **5 forms of knowing** (1) linguistic knowing (2) emotional knowing (3) imaginal knowing (4) physiological knowing (5) physical knowing **3 of 4 levels of knowing** (1) preconventional (2) conventional intermediate (3) conventional expert (4) <u>NOT</u> postconventional
E_u:	E_{OL1} E_{OL2} E_{OL3} E_{OL4} E_{OL5}	T S C X	1. E_{DC1} 2. E_{DC2} 3. E_{DC3} 4. E_{DC4} 5. E_{DC5} 6. E_{DC6} 7. E_{DC7} 8. E_{DC8} 9. E_{DC9} 10. E_{DC10} 11. E_{DC11} 12. E_{DC12} 13. E_{DC13}	T_P S_{P1}	L_1	**$K_2 \supset K_{2P}$** **K_{2P} = range of knowing In some combination of** **4 kinds of knowing,** (1) knowing-that-one (2) knowing-that (3) knowing-how (4) knowing-to **5 forms of knowing** (1) linguistic knowing (2) emotional knowing (3) imaginal knowing (4) physiological knowing (5) physical knowing **3 of 4 levels of knowing** (1) preconventional (2) conventional intermediate (3) conventional expert (4) <u>NOT</u> postconventional

not apply to the process of learning ($\mathbf{L}$). Learning ($\mathbf{L}$) is always a process of achieving. It is never an attempt at achieving. The product of the process of intentional guided learning ($\mathbf{L}_1$) is always a cognitive state of mind of some prescribed range of knowing ($\mathbf{K}_{2P}$) which someone (the student <**S**>) has developed from effective intentional guided study ($\mathbf{S}_{P1}$).

Intentional guided learning ($\mathbf{L}_1$) of some prescribed range of knowing ($\mathbf{K}_{2P}$) results exclusively from effective education ($\mathbf{E}_E$), but knowing ($\mathbf{K}_2$) does not result exclusively from intentional guided learning ($\mathbf{L}_1$). Prescribed knowing ($\mathbf{K}_{2P}$) is a subset of knowing ($\mathbf{K}_2$). Knowing ($\mathbf{K}_2$) is the resultant of all variations of the process of learning ($\mathbf{L}$), including discovery learning ($\mathbf{L}_2$) of a discovered range of knowing ($\mathbf{K}_{2D}$), compelled learning ($\mathbf{L}_3$) of a coerced range of knowing ($\mathbf{K}_{2C}$) and accidental learning ($\mathbf{L}_4$) of an accidental range of knowing ($\mathbf{K}_{2A}$). These relationships can be expressed in set theory notation as follows.

(1) The statement <$\mathbf{L} = \mathbf{L}_1 \cup \mathbf{L}_2 \cup \mathbf{L}_3 \cup \mathbf{L}_4$> reads that the essential elements of the process of learning ($\mathbf{L}$) consist of (=) the union of ($\cup$) the essential elements of conduced learning ($\mathbf{L}_1$), discovery learning ($\mathbf{L}_2$), compelled learning ($\mathbf{L}_3$) and accidental learning ($\mathbf{L}_4$).

(2) The statement <$\mathbf{L} \rightarrow \mathbf{K}_2$> reads that the process of learning ($\mathbf{L}$) is the set of controlling conditions ($\rightarrow$) for the resultant of the cognitive state of mind of knowing ($\mathbf{K}_2$).

(3) The statement <$\mathbf{E}_E \rightarrow \mathbf{L}_1 \rightarrow \mathbf{K}_{2P}$> reads that effective education ($\mathbf{E}_E$) is the set of controlling conditions ($\rightarrow$) for the resultant of the process of intentional guided learning ($\mathbf{L}_1$), and the process of intentional guided learning ($\mathbf{L}_1$) is the set of controlling conditions ($\rightarrow$) for the resultant of prescribed knowing ($\mathbf{K}_{2P}$).

(4) The statement <$\mathbf{Q} \rightarrow \mathbf{L}_2 \rightarrow \mathbf{K}_{2D}$> reads that inquiry ($\mathbf{Q}$) is the set of controlling conditions ($\rightarrow$) for the resultant of the process of intentional unguided learning ($\mathbf{L}_2$), which is discovery learning, and discovery learning ($\mathbf{L}_2$) is the set of controlling conditions ($\rightarrow$) for the resultant of discovery knowing ($\mathbf{K}_{2D}$).

(5) The statement <$\mathbf{X} \rightarrow \mathbf{L}_3 \rightarrow \mathbf{K}_{2C}$> reads that the social and cultural setting ($\mathbf{X}$) is the set of controlling conditions ($\rightarrow$) for the resultant of the process of unintentional guided learning ($\mathbf{L}_3$), which is compelled learning, and compelled

learning ($\mathbf{L_3}$) is the set of controlling conditions ($\rightarrow$) for the resultant of coerced knowing ($\mathbf{K_{2C}}$).

(6) The statement $<\mathbf{H} \rightarrow \mathbf{L_4} \rightarrow \mathbf{K_{2A}}>$ reads that happenstance ($\mathbf{H}$) is the set of controlling conditions ($\rightarrow$) for the resultant of unintentional unguided learning ($\mathbf{L_4}$), which is accidental learning, and accidental learning ($\mathbf{L_4}$) is the set of controlling conditions ($\rightarrow$) for the resultant of accidental knowing ($\mathbf{K_{2A}}$).

(7) The statement $<\mathbf{K_2} = \mathbf{K_{2P}} \cup \mathbf{K_{2D}} \cup \mathbf{K_{2C}} \cup \mathbf{K_{2A}}>$ reads that the essential properties of knowing ($\mathbf{K_2}$) is, or consists of ($=$), the union of ($\cup$) the essential properties of prescribed knowing ($\mathbf{K_{2P}}$), discovered knowing ($\mathbf{K_{2D}}$), coerced knowing ($\mathbf{K_{2C}}$) and accidental knowing ($\mathbf{K_{2A}}$).

Home Education

Home education is education ($\mathbf{E}$) in which the physical setting ($\mathbf{X_P}$) is the home and the social setting ($\mathbf{X_S}$) is the family. Home education has a much longer history than education in schools, academies, institutes, colleges, universities and the like. Home education can be unofficial education ($\mathbf{E_U}$), but it can also be official education ($\mathbf{E_O}$).

An example of unofficial home education ($\mathbf{E_U}$) is a scenario in which a mother shows her daughter how to operate the clothes washing machine. She shows her how to set the temperature and the type of wash. She shows her the amount of washing powder to put into the machine. She shows her how to sort the colored clothes from the whites. She shows her how to sort the clothes between the hand washables and the machine washables. She shows her how many clothes make a load for the machine. Then she tells her daughter to run a load through the machine, and she watches her daughter to make sure that her daughter remembers all the things to do in preparing for a washing cycle. The daughter does everything correctly. This scenario is clearly unofficial education ($\mathbf{E_U}$) because there is no certification, no written curriculum, no syllabus, no unit plans, no lesson plans (no properties of official education $<\neg\mathbf{P_{EO}}>$).

Here is an example of official home education ($\mathbf{E_O}$). Some parents, Paul and Margaret, decide that they do not want their children to attend the local government funded and administered school. They contact the state department of education to learn what they must do to satisfy the legal requirement for compulsory education. The department informs them that there must be a minimum of 6 hours of instruction per day for 5 days per week in a period of 40 weeks in the year. The department also informs them of the number of hours which must be allocated to various subjects such as English, mathematics, social studies, natural sciences, art, music, etc. The department also informs them they must keep and submit a record of their instructional program, their hours of instruction and the progress of their children in achieving intended learning outcomes (**ILO**). Paul and Margaret conduct an instructional program with their children. They make sure that their program conforms with the requirements of the state department of education, and they submit the required reports about hours of instruction, subject matter taught and studied intentionally under guidance, assessments and evaluations conducted and progress of students towards achievement of the intended learning outcomes. This scenario is clearly official education ($\mathbf{E}_{O}$) because it has enrolment of students, written curriculum, written syllabus, written unit plans, written lesson plans, attendance records, written assessments and evaluations, written certifications, regular instructional times, etc. (properties of official education $<\mathbf{P}_{EO}>$).

Praxiological Educological Theory

Scientific educological theory describes the extant relationships among the elements of education, provides explanations for what happens in education and makes predictions about what will happen, given any set of circumstances.

In contrast, praxiological educological theory describes constructive attitudes, supportive relationships and productive practices in education, provides explanations for why the constructive attitudes, supportive relationships and productive practices are the controlling conditions for effective education and prescribes attitudes, relationships and practices to be established and/or eliminated to achieve desired states of affairs in education and to achieve desired resultants from education.

In effective education ($\mathbf{E}_{E}$), there is a means-end relationship between a set of controlling conditions and a desired resultant. The controlling conditions are the basic elements (**T**, **S**, **C**, **X**) of education (**E**) and the relations among the elements. The desired resultant is the achievement by the students (**S**) of the prescribed range of knowing ($\mathbf{K}_{2P}$) as specified by the set of intended learning outcomes (**ILO**s). The set of intended learning outcomes (**ILO**s) is the set of written statements which specifies the prescribed range of knowing ($\mathbf{K}_{2P}$) that is desired and/or deemed worthwhile (by teachers, students and/or third parties) for students to learn intentionally under guidance ($\mathbf{L}_1$). The means-end relationship can be expressed as follows.

$$\mathbf{E}_E \rightarrow \mathbf{L}_1 \rightarrow \mathbf{K}_{2P}$$

In ordinary English, the statement <$\mathbf{E}_E \rightarrow \mathbf{L}_1 \rightarrow \mathbf{K}_{2P}$> reads that effective education ($\mathbf{E}_E$) is the set of controlling conditions for ($\rightarrow$) the resultant process of learning intentionally under guidance ($\mathbf{L}_1$), and intentionally learning under guidance ($\mathbf{L}_1$) is the set of controlling conditions for ($\rightarrow$) the desired resultant of a prescribed range of knowing ($\mathbf{K}_{2P}$).

The determinants of effective education ($\mathbf{E}_E$) include constructive attitudes of the participants (**T**, **S**, **X**), supportive relationships among the participants (**T**, **S**, **X**) and productive activities of the participants (**T**, **S**, **X**). Effective education ($\mathbf{E}_E$) is the resultant of establishing and maintaining constructive attitudes, supportive relationships and productive activities which enhance the probabilities that students (**S**) achieve the prescribed range of knowing ($\mathbf{K}_{2P}$) that is specified by the intended learning outcomes (**ILO**s). Effective education ($\mathbf{E}_E$) is also the resultant of avoiding and/or eliminating obstructive attitudes, oppositional relationships and counterproductive activities which reduce the probabilities and/or impede the achievement by the students (**S**) of the prescribed range of knowing ($\mathbf{K}_{2P}$) that is specified by the intended learning outcomes (**ILO**s).

When the states of mind are obstructive, relations are oppositional and practices are counterproductive among the participants (**T**, **S**, **X**) in education (**E**), then the resultant is ineffective education ($\mathbf{E}_I$). Ineffective education ($\mathbf{E}_I$) results in little or no process of intentional guided learning (learning$_1$ or $\mathbf{L}_1$) by the students (**S**). Without learning$_1$ ($\mathbf{L}_1$), there is no achievement of a prescribed range of knowing ($\mathbf{K}_{2P}$). The relationship can be expressed as follows.

$$\mathbf{E}_I \rightarrow \neg\mathbf{L}_1 \rightarrow \neg\mathbf{K}_{2P}$$

In ordinary English, the statement <$\mathbf{E}_I \rightarrow \neg\mathbf{L}_1 \rightarrow \neg\mathbf{K}_{2P}$> reads that ineffective education ($\mathbf{E}_I$) is the set of controlling conditions for the resultant of no intentional guided learning ($\neg\mathbf{L}_1$), and no intentional guided learning ($\neg\mathbf{L}_1$) is the set of controlling conditions for the resultant of no prescribed knowing ($\neg\mathbf{K}_{2P}$).

It is the major definite the purpose of praxiological educology to provide knowledge (a fund of recorded true statements <$\mathbf{K_1}$>) about what does not work, as well as what does work, to make education effective ($\mathbf{E_E}$) because it is vital to know (have the range of knowing <$\mathbf{K_2}$> about) what to avoid and/or eliminate as well as what to establish and/or maintain in the attitudes, relationships and practices of the participants (**T**, **S**, **X**) in education (**E**), and especially in official education ($\mathbf{E_O}$).

Constructive Attitudes for Effective Education

An attitude is the linguistic and/or physical expression of a state of mind (**M**). A state of mind (**M**) is an experiencing of volition (**V**), perception (**P**) and cognition (**N**), all coordinated and directed to some degree by focus of attention (**F**). All participants in education (**E**) – teachers (**T**), students (**S**) and members of the social and cultural setting (**X**) – have states of mind (**M**) and express those states of mind (**M**) in linguistic and/or physical form. There are constructive attitudes (the linguistic and/or physical expressions of constructive states of mind <**M**>) of teachers (**T**), students (**S**) and the immediate community (**X**) which enhance the probabilities that those who participate as students (**S**) in education (**E**) will learn (learn$_1$ <$\mathbf{L_1}$>) the prescribed range of knowing ($\mathbf{K_{2P}}$) that is specified by a set of intended learning outcomes (**ILO**s). And there are obstructive attitudes (the linguistic and/or physical expressions of obstructive states of mind <**M**>) which reduce the probabilities, impede or even block the conduced learning ($\mathbf{L_1}$) by students (**S**) of some prescribed range of knowing ($\mathbf{K_{2P}}$) specified by a set of intended learning outcomes (**ILO**s).

Constructive Attitudes for Students

It enhances the effectiveness of the persons playing the role of student (**S**) (and it increases the probabilities that education will be effective <$\mathbf{E_E}$> for them) for students (**S**) to have a constructive state of mind (**M**) (and a resultant attitude) which includes the following.

(1) **Desire to learn**. Students (**S**) enhance their effectiveness in their intentional guided study ($\mathbf{S_{P1}}$) when they have a desire to learn$_1$ ($\mathbf{L_1}$) the prescribed range of knowing ($\mathbf{K_{2P}}$) that is specified by a set of intended learning outcomes (**ILO**s).

(2) **Belief in capability**. Students (**S**) enhance their

effectiveness in their intentional guided study (**S_{P1}**) when they believe that they have the capability (psychical and physical) of achieving the prescribed range of knowing (**K_{2P}**) that is specified by a set of intended learning outcomes (**ILO**s).

(3) **Trust in the teachers**. Students (**S**) enhance their effectiveness in their intentional guided study (**S_{P1}**) when they have trust in their teacher's guidance, help and judgment.

(4) **Respect for teachers**. Students (**S**) enhance their effectiveness in their intentional guided study (**S_{P1}**) when they have and communicate respect for their teacher's abilities, qualities, achievements and rights in the role of teacher.

(5) **Accept study (S_{P1}) opportunities**. Students (**S**) enhance their effectiveness in their intentional guided study (**S_{P1}**) when they are willing to accept the opportunities to study intentionally under guidance (**S_{P1}**) provided by the teacher (**T**).

(6) **Willing to complete study (S_{P1}) tasks**. Students (**S**) enhance their effectiveness in their intentional guided study (**S_{P1}**) when they are willing to complete the intentional guided study (**S_{P1}**) activities provided by their teacher (**T**).

(7) **Willing to conduct appropriate practice**. Students (**S**) enhance their effectiveness in their intentional guided study (**S_{P1}**) when they are willing to conduct appropriate practice with a newly acquired prescribed range of knowing (**K_{2P}**).

(8) **Willing to use a prescribed range of knowing**. Students (**S**) enhance their effectiveness in their intentional guided study (**S_{P1}**) when they are willing to use a newly acquired prescribed range of knowing (**K_{2P}**) to solve a range of problems, some familiar and some novel, some simple and some complex.

(9) **Willing to extend a prescribed range of knowing**. Students (**S**) enhance their effectiveness in their intentional guided study (**S_{P1}**) when they are willing to extend a newly acquired prescribed range of knowing (**K_{2P}**) through additional inquiry (**Q**).

(10) **Willing to emend a range of knowing.** Students (**S**) enhance their effectiveness in their intentional guided study (**S_{P1}**) when they are willing to emend an extant range of knowing (**K_{2KLF}**) to accommodate a newly acquired prescribed range of knowing (**K_{2P}**).

(11) **Willing to integrate a range of knowing.** Students (**S**) enhance their effectiveness in their intentional guided study (**S_{P1}**) when they are willing to integrate a newly acquired prescribed range of knowing (**K_{2P}**) with the extant range of knowing (**K_{2KLF}**).

Desire to Learn Intentionally Under Guidance

It enhances the effectiveness of the persons playing the role of student (**S**) (and it increases the probabilities that their education will be effective <**E_E**>) for them to have a constructive state of mind (and a resultant attitude) which desires to learn intentionally under guidance (**L_1**) a prescribed range of knowing (**K_{2P}**) that is specified by a set of intended learning outcomes (**ILO**s).

For example, a boy, George, age 6, says he is looking forward to starting first grade in school because he wants to learn intentionally under guidance (**L_1**) to read. He has a conative and perceptual state of mind (**M**) that enhances his chances of learning to read, and he expresses his state of mind in his words and physical actions. In contrast, Cathy, a girl of age 15, hates mathematics and has no desire to learn intentionally under guidance (**L_1**) what is on offer in her 10th grade mathematics classes in her high school. Her volition (**V**) and perception (**P**) are obstructions to her achievement of the prescribed range of knowing (**K_{2P}**) specified by the set of intended learning outcomes (**ILO**s) of her mathematics class, and she expresses her state of mind (**M**) in her words about hating mathematics and in her actions of refusing to study intentionally under guidance (**S_{P1}**) mathematics.

It is a natural state of mind (**M**) for human beings (and especially children) to have curiosity, to want to know (**K_2**), to want to solve problems (**Q**) and to want to learn (**L**) some range of knowing (**K_{2KLF}**). As human beings, from birth, we are genetically disposed to be philomaths – beings who love to study (**S_P**) and learn (**L**) – and philosophs – beings who love to know (**K_2**). Outside of education (**E**), we can satisfy a great deal of our curiosity and desire to know (**K_2**) through play, inquiry and problem solving (**Q**). But some ranges of knowing ($\mathbf{K}_{2KLF}$) are difficult to achieve without the help of teachers (**T**), and thus it becomes a necessity to participate in education (**E**) as a student (**S**) to achieve our desired range of knowing ($\mathbf{K}_{2KLF}$).

While it is a natural state of mind (**M**) for individual human beings to have curiosity, to want to know ($\mathbf{K}_{2}$), to want to solve problems (**Q**) and to want to learn (**L**) some range of knowing ($\mathbf{K}_{2KLF}$), individual humans typically do not want to learn (**L**) all ranges of knowing ($\mathbf{K}_{2KLF}$). Curiosity has its limits. Some of us want to develop our range of knowing ($\mathbf{K}_{2KLF}$) of music. Some of us want to develop our range of knowing ($\mathbf{K}_{2KLF}$) of sport. Some of us want to develop our range of knowing of ($\mathbf{K}_{2KLF}$) literature. Some of us want to develop our range of knowing of ($\mathbf{K}_{2KLF}$) cooking and food preparation. Some of us want to develop our range of knowing of ($\mathbf{K}_{2KLF}$) animal husbandry. Some of us want to develop our range of knowing of ($\mathbf{K}_{2KLF}$) horticulture. Some of us want to develop our range of knowing of ($\mathbf{K}_{2KLF}$) French, or German, or Urdu, or Swahili. And the list goes on. Variation in interests, curiosities and desires are characteristic of us as human beings. Thus, the opportunity to learn intentionally under guidance ($\mathbf{L}_{1}$) a prescribed range of knowing ($\mathbf{K}_{2P}$) about some particular phenomenon (some object of knowing $<\mathbf{O}_{K2}>$) will appeal to some of us and not to others. None of us wants to learn (**L**) the range of knowing ($\mathbf{K}_{2KLF}$) about everything, whether by intentional guided learning ($\mathbf{L}_{1}$) or by some other variant of the learning process (**L**). Our desire to learn (**L**) a range of knowing ($\mathbf{K}_{2KLF}$) always has limitations.

The context for education (<**X**> – the community, society, the nation-state) typically wants all its members to have a common core range of knowing ($\mathbf{K}_{2KLF}$), and the context (**X**) mandates official education ($\mathbf{E}_{O}$) to function with a prescribed content (**C**) and a prescribed ranged of knowing ($\mathbf{K}_{2P}$) that is specified by a set of what is deemed to be socially and culturally essential intended learning outcomes (**ILO**s). Conflict arises when the curiosity and desire by the student (**S**) does not match the content (**C**), intentional guided study activities ($\mathbf{S}_{P1}$) and intended learning outcomes (**ILO**s) mandated by the social and cultural context (<**X**> – the community, society and/or nation-state).

Effective education ($\mathbf{E}_{E}$) is structured such that the intended learning outcomes (**ILO**s), the opportunities to study intentionally under guidance ($\mathbf{S}_{P1}$) and the proposed intentional guided study activities ($\mathbf{S}_{P1}$) match the desire of the students (**S**) to achieve the intended learning outcomes (**ILO**s) and/or are structured such that they appeal in some way to the students (**S**) sufficiently for the students (**S**) to choose to engage with the prescribed intentional guided study activities (**S_{P1}**) and endeavor to achieve the intended learning outcomes (**ILO**s).

Belief in Capability to Learn

Belief in our capability to learn intentionally under guidance (**L_1**) a prescribed range of knowing (**K_{2P}**) is a crucial attitude for effective intentional guided studying (**S_{P1E}**). To play the role of student (**S**) effectively, persons playing the role must have, not only the psychical and physical capability to learn intentionally under guidance (**L_1**) the prescribed range of knowing (**K_{2P}**) that is implied by the intended learning outcomes (**ILO**s), but also the belief in their psychical and physical capability to learn$_1$ (**L_1**).

It is of course crucial that teachers (**T**) and curriculum developers design educational episodes and formulate intended learning outcomes (**ILO**s) which match the psychical and physical learning capabilities of the students (**S**). It is patently inappropriate to have 6-year-olds study differentiation and integration of quadratic equations. It is absurd to have 10-year-olds study quantum physics. It is ridiculous to have 8-year-olds study logarithms. For education (**E**) to be effective (**E_E**), the students (**S**), of course, must have the psychical and physical capability to achieve the specified intended learning outcomes (**ILO**s). In addition, it is crucial that the students (**S**) believe that they have the psychical and physical capability.

Over the past century, a great deal of inquiry (**Q**) has been focused on the question of the relationship of ages of children, stages of psychical and physical development and capabilities of children to study intentionally under guidance (**S_{P1}**) particular content (**C**) and learn intentionally under guidance (**L_1**) particular prescribed ranges of knowing (**K_{2P}**). Among the many psychologists and educologists who have addressed this question, some of the most notable include David Ausubel (1918-2008), Albert Bandura (b. 1925), John Bowlby (1907-1990), Jerome Bruner (1915-2016), John Dewey (1859-1952), Erik Erikson (1902-1994), Sigmund Freud (1856-1939), Robert M. Gagné (1916-2002), Maria Montessori (1870-1952), Jean Piaget (1896-1980), Benjamin F. Skinner (1904-1990), James W. Vander Zanden (b. 1930), Lev Vygotsky (1896-1934) and John B. Watson (1878-1958).

Trust in the Teacher

It enhances the effectiveness of the persons playing the role of student (**S**) (and it increases the probabilities that their education will be effective $<\mathbf{E}_{E}>$) to have a constructive state of mind (**M**) (and a resultant attitude) which places trust in the teacher (**T**). This trust includes confidence in the competency of the teacher (**T**) to provide appropriate opportunities to study intentionally under guidance ($\mathbf{S}_{P1}$) some content (**C**), and it includes belief that the teacher (**T**) will act fairly, justly and ethically. When students (**S**) regard their teachers (**T**) as incompetent, unfair, unjust and/or unethical, they are likely to cease to follow the guidance of those teachers (**T**) and to reject the advice and help offered by them. Trust by students (**S**) in the competence, fairness and ethicality of their teachers (**T**) facilitates the learning intentionally under guidance ($\mathbf{L}_{1}$) by students (**S**) of a prescribed range of knowing ($\mathbf{K}_{2P}$) specified by a set of intended learning outcomes (**ILO**s). Lack of trust by students (**S**) obstructs their achievement of the intended learning outcomes (**ILO**s).

Respect for the Teacher

It enhances the effectiveness of the persons playing the role of student (**S**) (and it increases the probabilities that their education will be effective $<\mathbf{E}_{E}>$) to have a constructive state of mind (and a resultant attitude) which accords respect for their teachers (**T**). Students (**S**) who respect their teachers (**T**) have an appreciation and/or admiration for the range of knowing ($\mathbf{K}_{2KLF}$), the personal qualities and the achievements of their teachers (**T**), and the students (**S**) have due regard for the feelings, wishes, standing, authority and rights of their teachers (**T**). Students who do not have respect for their teachers greatly diminish the chances that they will achieve any intended learning outcomes (**ILO**s).

Consider the example of Mrs Faraday. She is a high school teacher, and she is teaching US history to a class of 10th grade students. The students have no respect for Mrs Faraday. In fact, they hold her in absolute contempt. They express their contempt for her in a number of ways. They talk continuously during her lessons. They never pay attention to her instructions. They play pranks on her, do not complete in-class study activities and do no homework. They are especially gleeful if they can do things which make her tearful. Their obstructive state of mind (their lack of respect for Mrs Faraday), and their expression of their state of mind through what they say and otherwise do, places a huge psychical obstacle in the way of their achieving any intended learning outcomes (**ILO**) in Mrs Faraday's class.

An essential element for playing the role of an effective student (**S**) is to have a constructive state of mind (**M**) and a resultant attitude which perceives (perceives$_1$ <$\mathbf{P_1}$>) respect for teachers (**T**), which knows-to ($\mathbf{K_{2K4}}$) practice respectful behavior in relation to teachers (**T**) and which expresses respect and knowing-to ($\mathbf{K_{2K4}}$) in words and physical actions.

Acceptance of Opportunities

It enhances the effectiveness of the persons playing the role of student (**S**) (and it increases the probabilities that their education will be effective <$\mathbf{E_E}$>) to have a constructive state of mind (**M**) (and a resultant attitude) which accepts the opportunities to study intentionally under guidance ($\mathbf{S_{P1}}$). The opportunities may be initiated by the teachers (**T**), the students (**S**), the teachers and students in consultation with each other, or the opportunities may be prescribed by third parties in the context (**X**) of education (boards of governors, school boards, local education authorities, state departments of education, legislative bodies, administrative organizations, funding organizations, standards and certification authorities, etc.) Non-acceptance poses a serious obstacle to the students' achievement of their intended learning outcomes (**ILO**s).

For example, Jack, a 10-year-old boy wants to play trumpet, and he especially wants to play "Flight of the Bumblebee" (by Nikolai Rimsky-Korsakov, 1844-1908). He has never played a musical instrument, and he is a complete novice with the trumpet. He takes his father's trumpet to his cousin, who plays trumpet, and tells his cousin that he wants to play "Flight of the Bumblebee" on the trumpet. His cousin tells him that the first thing he needs to work on is how to hold the trumpet, and then he needs to work on his embouchure for making desired sounds with the trumpet. The second thing he needs to work on is to learn the fingering for each of the notes that can be played on the trumpet. The third thing he needs to work on is to play different scales on the trumpet. The fourth thing he needs to work on is to learn to play some simple tunes on the trumpet. Jack replies that he is not interested in any of that. He wants to learn how to play "Flight of the

Bumblebee." His cousin tells him that learning to play the trumpet is like learning to run. You first learn to crawl, to stand up, to walk and then run. Jack refuses to accept his cousin's advice and insists on learning how to play "Flight of the Bumblebee" as a first step. What are Jack's chances of achieving the range of knowing to which he aspires without engaging in the sequence of study activities which his cousin recommends? It is possible. There are historical examples of autodidacts who have achieved virtuosity with musical instruments without tuition from teachers. But such an achievement is outside of education (**E**). It is a certainty that a student's refusal to accept the study activities offered by a teacher invariably acts as a serious impediment to the student's achievement of any intended learning outcomes through education (**E**).

Willingness to Complete Study Activities

It enhances the effectiveness of the persons playing the role of student (**S**) (and it increases the probabilities that their education will be effective $<\mathbf{E}_{\mathbf{E}}>$ to have a constructive state of mind (**M**) (and a resultant attitude) which is willing, once the opportunities to study$_1$ ($\mathbf{S}_{\mathbf{P1}}$) have been accepted, to complete the study$_1$ activities (S_{P1}) which are chosen, recommended and/or prescribed. The study$_1$ activities ($\mathbf{S}_{\mathbf{P1}}$) may be ones which the teachers choose, the students choose, the teachers and students choose together after consultation, or ones which third parties in the context (**X**) of education (**E**) recommend and/or prescribe. Whatever the case may be, if the persons playing the role of student (**S**) are not willing to undertake and complete the study$_1$ activities ($\mathbf{S}_{\mathbf{P1}}$), the students are not likely to achieve their nominated intended learning outcomes (**ILO**s).

Willingness to Conduct Appropriate Practice

It enhances the effectiveness of the persons playing the role of student (**S**) (and it increases the probabilities that their education will be effective $<\mathbf{E}_{\mathbf{E}}>$) to have a constructive state of mind (**M**) (and a resultant attitude) which is willing to conduct appropriate practice with a newly acquired prescribed range of knowing ($\mathbf{K}_{\mathbf{2P}}$). We extend our level of knowing ($\mathbf{K}_{\mathbf{2L}}$) by practicing the knowing ($\mathbf{K}_{\mathbf{2}}$) until it becomes a habituated part of our range of knowing (conventional expert level $<\mathbf{K}_{\mathbf{2L3}}>$). Depending on the complexity of the range of knowing ($\mathbf{K}_{\mathbf{2KLF}}$) and the psychical and physical capabilities of the students (**S**), the practice may be for a short period of time, or the practice may be for months or even years.

For example, Margit is a young Norwegian woman, aged 22. She is an apprentice lock operator on the Telemark Canal in Norway. Under the guidance and supervision of the lock master, Arvid, Margit directs, scrutinizes, evaluates and corrects the way the lines from a canal boat are tied to the bollards along the sides of the lock. She operates the sluice gates to regulate the rate and direction of flow of water into each lock such that there is no damage done to the boat in the lock. When the lock is at an optimal depth, she opens the lock gates with the control levers to allow the progress of the boat in the canal. At each stage of progressing a boat through the lock, she describes what she is doing and why she is doing it to her supervisor, Arvid. She performs these procedures again and again until she masters, at the expert level, the tying of the boat to the bollards, the draining and filling of the locks and the opening and closing of the lock gates. Through appropriate practice, she progresses her knowing-how ($\mathbf{K}_{2K3}$) to operate the locks safely and efficiently from Level 1 ($\mathbf{K}_{2K3L1}$) to Level 2 ($\mathbf{K}_{2K3L2}$) to Level 3 ($\mathbf{K}_{2K3L3}$) in physical form ($\mathbf{K}_{2F5}$) and linguistic form ($\mathbf{K}_{2F1}$). To achieve her certificate as a lock operator requires her to serve an apprenticeship and to practice, under supervision, operation of the sluice gates and lock levers for a period of two years.

In another example, George is a year 9 (9th grade) student in a mathematics class, and his class is studying how to solve quadratic equations by factoring, taking the square root and completing the square. George practices solving quadratic equations every day for 50 minutes, Monday through Friday, for two weeks. By the end of the two weeks, George progresses his knowing-how ($\mathbf{K}_{2K3}$) to solve quadratic equations using the three methods from Level 1 ($\mathbf{K}_{2K3L1}$) to Level 2 ($\mathbf{K}_{2K3L2}$) to Level 3 ($\mathbf{K}_{2K3L3}$) in written linguistic form ($\mathbf{K}_{2F1}$).

In a third example, Lisa is a year 10 student in a high school Mandarin-as-a-second-language class. Her first language is English. She practices her spoken Mandarin every day, Monday through Friday, for 20 minutes, for each of the school terms over a three-year period. By the end of the third year, she progresses her knowing-how ($\mathbf{K}_{2K3}$) to speak idiomatic grammatical Mandarin from Level 1 ($\mathbf{K}_{2K3L1}$) to Level 2 ($\mathbf{K}_{2K3L2}$) in spoken linguistic form ($\mathbf{K}_{2F1}$) and physical form ($\mathbf{K}_{2F5}$).

Willingness to Use Knowing

It enhances the effectiveness of the persons playing the role of student (**S**) (and it increases the probabilities that their education will be effective $<\mathbf{E}_{E}>$) to have a constructive state of mind (**M**) (and a resultant attitude) which is willing to use some newly acquired prescribed range of knowing ($\mathbf{K}_{2P}$) to solve a range of problems, some familiar and some novel.

For example, Christina is a 13-year-old in the 8th grade. Each week, in her English class, her teacher gives her class a set of new words to learn to spell and to use in sentences. Christina loves adding new words to her vocabulary. She keeps a notebook for her vocabulary, and for every new word, she enters it into her notebook, along with a definition and two or three sentences which use the word. Outside of class, she makes up sentences in which to use the new words, and she plays word games with her classmates in which she uses the new words. She challenges her friends to make up sentences with the new words, and she competes with them to determine who has the largest vocabulary. Christina also makes a point of using her new vocabulary in her written assignments for her English class and also in her other classes (history, geography, science, etc.). Christina is willing to use her newly acquired prescribed range of knowing ($\mathbf{K}_{2P}$) of vocabulary to solve a range of problems.

Peter is a 14-year-old. At his school, he has just completed a unit of study about the benefits of eating fresh fruits and vegetables, and he decides that he would like to grow his own vegetables at home from seeds. He asks permission from his parents to turn part of the backyard of the home into a vegetable garden, and they agree. He wants to fertilize his garden with worm castings from compost. He conducts some inquiry about ways to compost kitchen and garden waste, and he makes a composting bin. He draws to scale several designs for a vegetable garden, and he chooses what he believes to be the best design. From his design, he uses a measuring tape to measure out the dimensions of the garden, the width of the rows, the distance between the holes for the seeds and the depth for sowing the seeds. He wants to water the garden with a drip irrigation system. He measures the length of the rows, and he counts the seed holes which will require watering. He makes some calculations to estimate the cost of seeds, tubing and fittings for the drip irrigation system and to determine whether he has enough money in his savings to cover the costs of creating the garden. Peter proceeds to buy seed and irrigation materials. He prepares the soil, plants his seeds and installs his irrigation system. With all of this work, Peter clearly demonstrates his willingness to use his newly acquired prescribed range of knowing (**K_{2P}**) about the benefits of fresh fruits and vegetables in his planning and establishing a vegetable garden of his own.

Willingness to Extend Knowing Through Inquiry

It enhances the effectiveness of the persons playing the role of student (**S**) (and it increases the probabilities that their education will be effective <**E_E**>) to have a constructive state of mind (**M**) (and a resultant attitude) that is willing to extend a newly acquired prescribed range of knowing (**K_{2P}**) through additional inquiry (**Q**).

An example of extending one's prescribed range of knowing (**K_{2P}**) through additional inquiry (**Q**) is that of Darren, an apprentice tire fitter. A leading hand at Darren's place of employment shows Darren how to use the basic tools (a tire iron, rubber hammer and air compressor) to remove a worn truck tire from a double wheel assembly and replace the old tire with a new one without removing the wheel from the truck. Darren is at first slow and clumsy in the use of the tire iron, rubber hammer and air compressor. He conducts inquiry (**Q**) about how to become more efficient by watching his work mates change tires. He practices replicating what his work mates do. As he improves his range of knowing (knowing-how <**K_{2K3}**>) in physical form (**K_{2F5}**), he conducts further inquiry (**Q**) by trying a number of variations in moves with the tire iron, hammer and compressor. From his trial and error (his inquiry <**Q**>) he gradually improves his efficiency in changing tires until he can do a complete change of a tire with the wheel still mounted to the truck within two minutes. Darren thereby progresses his knowing-how (**K_{2K3}**) from protocolic knowing-how (**K_{2K3A}**) at the conventional expert level (**K_{2L3}**) to adaptive knowing-how (**K_{2K3B}**) at the expert postconventional level (**K_{2L4}**) by means of trial-and-error inquiry (**Q**).

An example of a student who does not extend his prescribed range of knowing (**K_{2P}**) through additional inquiry (**Q**) is Dennis. Dennis is a first-year university student. He has completed a one-semester course in introductory macro-economics. He has found the course difficult, confusing and boring, and after the final exams, he whoops with joy as he throws his notes from the economics class out of the window of his dormitory. He sells his used textbook on economics to the student bookstore. He vows never to read another book or article about economics, and he is determined to keep his vow. Clearly, with his obstructive state of mind (**M**), and his resultant attitude, Dennis is never going to conduct additional inquiry (**Q**) about economics, and he is never going to advance his extant prescribed range of knowing ($\mathbf{K_{2P}}$) about economics.

Willingness to Emend Extant Knowing

It enhances the effectiveness of the persons playing the role of student (**S**) (and it increases the probabilities that their education will be effective $<\mathbf{E_E}>$) to have a constructive state of mind (**M**) (and a resultant attitude) which is willing to emend an extant range of knowing ($\mathbf{K_{2KLF}}$) to accommodate a newly acquired prescribed range of knowing ($\mathbf{K_{2P}}$).

Louis is a 15-year-old boy who has been raised in a devout fundamentalist Christian family. His parents have insisted throughout his childhood and early teenage years that he habitually reads the King James Version of the Christian Bible and that he accepts all the assertions in the Bible as absolutely true. He has read and memorized the account of creation in the book of Genesis, which states that the sun, the stars, the planets, the earth, the oceans, the forests and all living creatures, including humankind, were created by God in six days, and on the seventh day, God rested. Louis is 15 years of age, and he is in the 10th grade (year 10). He is studying a unit on the origin of species in his biology class. He studies the evidence for evolution, including homologous structures of different species, vestigial structures in the anatomy of animals and human beings, the chemical and fossil records of different species dating back millions (even billions) of years, the genetic structures of animals, plants and microbes, the embryological similarities of different species, the geological evidence of the eras in which different species have lived and the explanatory principles of genetic variation and natural selection working in concert, favoring new species and eliminating older species. Louis accepts the evidence for the appearance and disappearance of species on planet Earth over a period of some 3.7 billion years. He also accepts the reasonable explanation that species have appeared and disappeared as a result of genetic variation, changes in environment and natural selection. His new range of knowing about evolution and the origin of species contradicts his previous range of knowing of the origin of species from divine creation. He decides that the authors of the book of Genesis were not biologists and geologists, but rather, story tellers, who created a myth that is consistent with their premise that a single divine being, God, created the universe. He decides that the scientific explanation of the origin of species is based on experiential material evidence, whereas the creationist explanation of the origin of species is a nonscientific myth, created by story tellers wanting to make sense about the possible purpose of their lives and their place in the universe. Louis emends his extant range of knowing ($\mathbf{K}_{2KLF}$) about the origin of species. He rejects the divine creation explanation for the origin of species to accommodate his newly acquired prescribed range of knowing ($\mathbf{K}_{2P}$) about the origin of species as the result of fortuitous environmental circumstances, genetic variation and natural selection.

Kathleen has been raised by parents who are adamantly opposed to vaccines and vaccination. From her early childhood, they teach Kathleen that vaccines cause more harm than good and that pharmaceutical companies promote vaccination solely for the purpose of making a profit. They teach Kathleen that vaccines cause autism and introduce harmful chemicals into the body. Throughout her childhood and into her early teens, they have refused to allow Kathleen to receive any kind of vaccination. Kathleen is 14 years old. In her science class, she studies the work of Louis Pasteur and others who recognized and proved the causal link between disease and microbial infections. She studies some of the major developments made in microbiology and immunology. She studies how common lethal diseases (smallpox, pertussis, diphtheria, polio) have been brought under control and nearly (or entirely) eradicated by mass vaccination campaigns. On the examination for the science unit on microbiology and immunology, she achieves a high score of 95% correct answers to questions. Even with this new prescribed range of knowing-that ($\mathbf{K}_{2PK2}$) in linguistic form ($\mathbf{K}_{2F1}$), Kathleen maintains her strongly held belief that vaccinations do more harm than good and that pharmaceutical companies advocate widespread vaccination as a means to maximize profits (not to promote community health). Kathleen does not emend her extant range of knowing ($\mathbf{K}_{2KLF}$) about the harmful effects of vaccination, as learned unintentionally but with guidance ($\mathbf{L}_3$) from her parents, to accommodate the newly acquired prescribed range of knowing (**K_{2P}**) about microbiology and immunology, as learned intentionally with guidance (**L_1**) from her science teacher.

Willing to Integrate New Knowing with Extant Knowing

It enhances the effectiveness of the persons playing the role of student (**S**) (and it increases the probabilities that their education will be effective <**E_E**>) to have a constructive state of mind (**M**) (and a resultant attitude) which is willing to integrate a newly acquired prescribed range of knowing (**K_{2P}**) with an extant range of knowing (**K_{2KLF}**).

As an example, Donna studied art in university, and she learned$_1$ (**L_1**) that primary colors are red, blue and yellow. Kevin studied physics and engineering in university, and he learned$_1$ (**L_1**) that primary colors are red, blue and green. While enjoying a cup of coffee with each other, Donna and Kevin become engaged in a conversation which leads to a discussion of primary colors. Donna maintains that they are red, blue and yellow. Kevin is adamant that they are red, blue and green. Donna explains that in her painting classes, all other colors are achieved by some mixture of red, blue and yellow paints. Kevin argues that all other colors are achieved by projecting some combination of red, blue and green. They wonder who is correct? They do some further inquiry and find that when light is projected, the primary colors are red, blue and green. When light is reflected from painted or pigmented surfaces, the primary colors are red, blue and yellow. Both Donna and Kevin thereby extend their range of knowing (knowing-that <**K_{2K2}**>) about primary colors to include knowing-that (**K_{2K2}**) the colors which function as primary colors are dependent upon whether the light is projected (as for example in a television), or whether the light is reflected (as for example from a painting). Both Donna and Kevin are willing to integrate their newly acquired range of knowing (**K_{2KLF}**) with their extant range of knowing (**K_{2KLF}**) about primary colors.

A counter example is that of Ignaz Philipp Semmelweis (1818-1865), the Hungarian medical practitioner and scientist. During his work at the Vienna General Hospital in the 1840s, he decided to wash his hands before he examined the vaginas of women who had recently given birth. He found that washing his hands in a solution of chlorinated lime before examining postpartum women drastically reduced the rate of infection and consequential death from "childbed fever" (puerperal fever caused by bacterial infection of the vagina). He advocated that all medical practitioners wash their hands before examining postpartum women, and he published his recommendations in 1861 in his book, *Die Ätiologie, der Begriff und die Prophylaxis des Kindbettfiebers* (English title, *Etiology, Concept and Prophylaxis of Childbed Fever.* Semmelweis did not know of the connection between microbial infection and disease, and he did not provide an explanation of why handwashing reduced incidences of disease. He only knew from his experience that handwashing was strongly associated with reduced incidences of disease. He had developed a range of knowing-how ($\mathbf{K}_{2K3}$) to reduce disease, but not a range of knowing-that ($\mathbf{K}_{2K2}$) the hygienic practices removed infection-causing bacteria. His colleagues scoffed at his findings and refused to accept his recommendations. They were unwilling to integrate the newly acquired range of knowing-how ($\mathbf{K}_{2K3}$), which Semmelweis had established, with their extant range of knowing-how ($\mathbf{K}_{2KLF}$) to examine postpartum women. It was not until many years later, after the work of Louis Pasteur (1822-1895) and Joseph Lister (1827-1912), that medical practitioners accepted the practice of handwashing and sterilizing medical instruments before touching patients and/or providing therapeutic treatments such as surgery.

Constructive Attitudes for Teachers

Just as a constructive state of mind (**M**) (and the resultant attitude) held by students (**S**) contributes to effective education ($\mathbf{E}_E$), so too does a constructive state of mind (**M**) (and the resultant attitude) held by teachers (**T**). It enhances the effectiveness of the persons playing the role of teacher (**T**) (and it increases the probabilities that education will be effective <$\mathbf{E}_E$>) to have a constructive state of mind (M) (and a set of resultant attitudes) which includes the following.

(1) **Intended learning outcomes**. Teachers (**T**) enhance their effectiveness in their teaching ($\mathbf{T}_P$) when

- (a) they have a clear conception of their intended learning outcomes (**ILO**s) (prescribed, nominated and/or chosen by teachers, students, third parties and/or a combination of the three) for the students (**S**),
- (b) they (the teachers <**T**>) have a commitment to writing and keeping records of their intended learning outcomes (**ILO**s) and

(c) they keep their intended learning outcomes (**ILO**s) continually in mind (M) as guides to their activities in their teaching (**T**$_P$).

(2) **Warranted belief in the worth of intended learning outcomes.** Teachers (**T**) enhance their effectiveness in their teaching (**T**$_P$) when they have a warranted belief that their intended learning outcomes (**ILO**s) have value (merit, significance, worth).

(3) **Authentic desire for students' success.** Teachers (**T**) enhance their effectiveness in their teaching (**T**$_P$) when they have a genuine desire for their students (**S**) to achieve their intended learning outcomes (**ILO**s).

(4) **Desire for student appreciation of intended learning outcomes.** Teachers (**T**) enhance their effectiveness in their teaching (**T**$_P$) when they have a genuine desire for the students (**S**) to attach value to their intended learning outcomes (**ILO**s).

(5) **Warranted belief in the students' capability to learn.** Teachers (**T**) enhance their effectiveness in their teaching (**T**$_P$) when they have a warranted belief that the students (**S**) have the capability (psychical and physical) of achieving their intended learning outcomes (**ILO**s).

(6) **Belief in teachability of the students.** Teachers (**T**) enhance their effectiveness in their teaching (**T**$_P$) when they have a reasonable and warranted expectation that the students (**S**) will trust the guidance, help and judgment that are provided by the teacher (**T**).

(7) **Respect for students.** Teachers (**T**) enhance their effectiveness in their teaching (**T**$_P$) when they have a genuine respect and appreciation for the students' (**S**) current (extant) psychical and physical abilities, qualities, and rights and responsibilities in their role as students (**S**).

(8) **Desire to provide opportunities to study and learn.** Teachers (**T**) enhance their effectiveness in their teaching (**T**$_P$) when they have a genuine desire to provide students (**S**) with opportunities to study$_1$ (**S**$_{P1}$) that are appropriate, necessary and sufficient to achieve the intended learning outcomes (**ILO**s).

(9) **Desire for authentic engagement.** Teachers (**T**)

enhance their effectiveness in their teaching (**T_P**) when they have a genuine desire that their students (**S**) become authentically engaged with, and attribute value to, the study$_1$ activities (**S_{P1}**) and the content (**C**) offered to the students (**S**).

(10) **Commitment to purposeful activity**. Teachers (**T**) enhance their effectiveness in their teaching (**T_P**) when they have a genuine commitment to engaging students (**S**) in purposeful and worthwhile study$_1$ activities (**S_{P1}**) and avoiding time-filling activities or activities without extrinsic and/or intrinsic value.

(11) **Open minded and flexible**. Teachers (**T**) enhance their effectiveness in their teaching (**T_P**) when they are open to, and flexible in, changing derivative components of education ($<\mathbf{E_{DC}}>$– plans, methods, styles, resources, pace, etc.) to accommodate the needs of students (**S**) in their study$_1$ (**S_{P1}**).

(12) **Commitment to help**. Teachers (**T**) enhance their effectiveness in their teaching (**T_P**) when they have a genuine commitment to supervise, guide and help students (**S**) appropriately in their conduct and completion of their study$_1$ activities (**S_{P1}**).

(13) **Commitment to conscientiousness and thoroughness**. Teachers (**T**) enhance their effectiveness in their teaching (**T_P**) when they have a desire for their students (**S**) to complete their study$_1$ (**S_{P1}**) activities competently.

(14) **Appropriate practice**. Teachers (**T**) enhance their effectiveness in their teaching (**T_P**) when they have a desire for their students (**S**) to conduct appropriate practice with their newly acquired prescribed range of knowing (**K_{2P}**).

(15) **Problem solving**. Teachers (**T**) enhance their effectiveness in their teaching (**T_P**) when they have a desire for their students (**S**) to use their newly acquired prescribed range of knowing (**K_{2P}**) to solve a range of problems, some familiar and some novel, some simple and some complex.

(16) **Extending knowing**. Teachers (**T**) enhance their effectiveness in their teaching (**T_P**) when they have a desire for their students (**S**) to extend their newly acquired

prescribed range of knowing ($\mathbf{K_{2P}}$) through additional inquiry (**Q**) and provide their students (S) with opportunities to conduct inquiry (**Q**) which requires the use of their newly acquired prescribed range of knowing ($\mathbf{K_{2P}}$).

(17) **Emending knowing.** Teachers (**T**) enhance their effectiveness in their teaching ($\mathbf{T_P}$) when they have a desire for their students (**S**) to emend their extant range of knowing ($\mathbf{K_{2KLF}}$) to accommodate their newly acquired prescribed range of knowing ($\mathbf{K_{2P}}$) and provide them (their students) with opportunities to effect emendments.

(18) **Integrating knowing.** Teachers (**T**) enhance their effectiveness in their teaching ($\mathbf{T_P}$) when they have a desire for their students to integrate their newly acquired prescribed range of knowing ($\mathbf{K_{2P}}$) with their extant range of knowing ($\mathbf{K_{2KLF}}$) and provide them (their students) with opportunities to effect integration.

(19) **Enthusiasm.** Teachers (**T**) enhance their effectiveness in their teaching ($\mathbf{T_P}$) when they have a genuine enthusiasm for the endeavors and the psychical and physical achievements of their students (**S**) and when they (the teachers **<T>**) communicate their enthusiasm to their students (**S**).

(20) **Justice.** Teachers (**T**) enhance their effectiveness in their teaching ($\mathbf{T_P}$) when they have a commitment to treat the students fairly and justly and when they (the teachers **<T>**) deal with their students (**S**) fairly and justly.

(21) **Evaluation.** Teachers (**T**) enhance their effectiveness in their teaching ($\mathbf{T_P}$) when they have a desire (and when they have the competence and commitment) to evaluate the achievement of their students (**S**) fairly and justly and to use the evaluation results appropriately (preparatively, formatively, summatively).

(22) **Inquiry.** Teachers (**T**) enhance their effectiveness in their teaching ($\mathbf{T_P}$) when they are open to conducting continuous inquiry (**Q**) to extend their range of knowing ($\mathbf{K_{2KLF}}$) about education (**E**).

Clear Conception of Intended Learning Outcomes

It enhances the effectiveness of the persons playing the role of teacher

(**T**) (and it increases the probabilities that education will be effective $<\mathbf{E_E}>$) to have a constructive state of mind (and a resultant attitude) which has a clear conception of the intended learning outcomes (**ILO**) (prescribed, nominated and/or chosen) for the students (**S**). Part of effective teaching ($\mathbf{T_{PE}}$) is for it to be purposeful teaching, and purposeful teaching is providing opportunities to study$_1$ ($\mathbf{S_{P1}}$) with the intention to achieve a prescribed range of knowing ($\mathbf{K_{2P}}$). The prescribed range of knowing ($\mathbf{K_{2P}}$) is specified by the statement of intended learning outcomes (**ILO**s). The intended learning outcomes (**ILO**s) may be prescribed by the teacher, the student or students, the teacher and students in collaboration with each other, or by some third party such as a school board, a state department of education, a national educational authority, a legislative body, etc. Teachers (**T**) who know what prescribed range of knowing ($\mathbf{K_{2P}}$) they want their students (**S**) to learn$_1$ ($\mathbf{L_1}$) have a criterial basis for selecting derivative components of education ($<\mathbf{E_{DC}}>$– study$_1$ activities, study$_1$ resources, assessment activities, evaluation criteria and procedures, etc.) that are appropriate and relevant to guiding the students (**S**) to achievement of the prescribed range of knowing ($\mathbf{K_{2P}}$).

Warranted Belief in the Worth of Intended Learning Outcomes

It enhances the effectiveness of the persons playing the role of teacher (**T**) (and it increases the probabilities that education will be effective $<\mathbf{E_E}>$) to have a constructive state of mind (and a resultant attitude) which has a warranted belief that the intended learning outcomes (**ILO**s) for the students (**S**) have value (merit, significance, worth). Effective teachers attach value to the prescribed range of knowing ($\mathbf{K_{2P}}$) which they intend for their students (**S**) to achieve. They can provide warrants for their assertion about the value of their intended learning outcome (**ILO**s) by the articulating a sound justificatory argument. The argument includes value verification, validation and vindication and rational choice. The value which teachers justifiably attribute to the prescribed range of knowing ($\mathbf{K_{2P}}$) may be intrinsic or it may be extrinsic. The prescribed range of knowing ($\mathbf{K_{2P}}$) may be, for example, knowing-how ($\mathbf{K_{2K3}}$) to play the piano, and the value of this knowing-how ($\mathbf{K_{2K3}}$) may be the pleasure which it brings to the pianist to make music (an intrinsic worth), or it may be the opportunity which the knowing-how ($\mathbf{K_{2K3}}$) presents to make one's living as a professional pianist (an extrinsic worth).

Authentic Desire for Students' Success

It enhances the effectiveness of the persons playing the role of teacher (**T**) (and it increases the probabilities that education will be effective <$\mathbf{E_E}$>) to have a constructive state of mind (and a resultant attitude) which has a genuine desire for their students (**S**) to achieve the intended learning outcomes (**ILO**s). Effective teachers ($\mathbf{T_E}$) want their students to learn$_1$ ($\mathbf{L_1}$) the prescribed range of knowing ($\mathbf{K_{2P}}$) that is specified by the statement of intended learning outcomes (**ILO**s), and effective teachers ($\mathbf{T_E}$) take genuine pleasure in the cognitive success of their students (**S**).

For example, Mrs Larson is a teacher in a public school, and she has a first grade class (year 1, or average age of 6 years). She wants all students in her class, by the end of the school year, to have developed their range of knowing-how ($\mathbf{K_{2K3}}$) to write and read at the intermediate conventional level (Level 2 <$\mathbf{K_{2L2}}$>) of knowing ($\mathbf{K_2}$). From her educological studies and her teaching experience, she has a knowing-that ($\mathbf{K_{2K2}}$) children learn intentionally under guidance ($\mathbf{L_1}$) at different rates and that children learn intentionally under guidance ($\mathbf{L_1}$) from a variety of study$_1$ activities ($\mathbf{S_{P1}}$) and experiences. She is willing to vary the time allowed and the activities provided for each child, until each child achieves a knowing-how ($\mathbf{K_{2K3}}$) to write and read at the intermediate conventional level of knowing ($\mathbf{K_{2L2}}$). She also intends to conduct periodic assessments and evaluations and to use the results of the evaluations formatively to provide guidance, help and advice to students about what they can do to develop their range of knowing-how ($\mathbf{K_{2K3}}$) to write and read. Her aspiration is that all students (**S**) in her class will achieve her intended learning outcome (**ILO**) of knowing-how ($\mathbf{K_{2K3}}$) to write and read at the intermediate conventional level ($\mathbf{K_{2L2}}$) by the end of the school year (approximately 40 weeks of teaching and studying intentionally under guidance). In this example, Mrs Larson clearly has a desire for the cognitive success of all her students.

A counter example (or opposite case) is that of Mr Hauser, a university lecturer. His responsibility is to conduct an introductory statistics class. It is a compulsory class for all first-year students in the university. He intends to administer a mid-semester examination and an end-of-semester examination. He intends to give the mid-semester examination a weight of one-third and the final examination a weight of two-thirds towards the final grade in the course. He intends to conduct a statistical analysis to determine the mean score and the standard deviation for the scores of all the students. The university uses a grading system of <*A*, *B*, *C*, *D*, *F*>. Mr Hauser intends to allocate the grades to correspond with ranges of standard deviation. He intends to allocate the grade of <*C*> to all students whose scores are equal to or less than one standard deviation above or below the mean. He intends to allocate the grade of <*B*> to all students whose scores are more than one standard deviation and equal to or less than two standard deviations, above the mean. He intends to allocate the grade of <*D*> to all students whose scores are more than one standard deviation and equal to or less than two standard deviations, below the mean. He intends to allocate the grade of <*A*> to all students whose scores are more than 2 standard deviations above the mean, and he intends to allocate the grade of <*F*> to all students whose scores are more than 2 standard deviations below the mean. Mr Hauser does not want, does not expect and does not plan to make any provision for all students to experience cognitive success in their study of statistics. By the design of his assessment and evaluation system, Mr Hauser plans for 13.6% of his students to be assigned <*D*'s> and 2.2% of his students to be assigned <*F*'s>.

Desire for Student Appreciation of Intended Learning Outcomes

It enhances the effectiveness of the persons playing the role of teacher (**T**) (and it increases the probabilities that education will be effective <$\mathbf{E_E}$>) to have a constructive state of mind (and a resultant attitude) of having a genuine desire for their students (**S**) to attach value (merit, significance, worth) to their intended learning outcomes (**ILO**s). Effective teachers ($\mathbf{T_E}$) want their students to believe in the value of, for example, achieving a prescribed range of knowing ($\mathbf{K_{2P}}$) of mathematics, history, joinery, sculpting, or whatever content (**C**) the teacher is offering to the students (**S**) to study$_1$ ($\mathbf{S_{P1}}$).

Henry is an avid surfer, and he runs a private surfing school. He has a passion for surfing, and he wants those who study$_1$ ($\mathbf{S_{P1}}$) surfing with him to develop the passion for surfing that he has. He believes deeply that you only become good at surfing when you love surfing. Henry is an example of a teacher (**T**) who genuinely wants his students (**S**) to value the intended learning outcome (**ILO**) of knowing-how

($\mathbf{K}_{2K3}$) to surf at the conventional expert level ($\mathbf{K}_{2L3}$).

Another example is that of Ms Huston. She teaches English to high school students. She has a passion for English literature. She loves to read and analyze fiction, and she wants her students to develop a passion which equals hers for reading and appreciating English literature. Ms Huston is an example of a teacher (**T**) who genuinely wants her students (**S**) to value the intended learning outcome (**ILO**) of having a knowing-that-one ($\mathbf{K}_{2K1}$) and a knowing-that ($\mathbf{K}_{2K2}$) about English literature.

Warranted Belief in the Students' Capability to Learn

It enhances the effectiveness of the persons playing the role of teacher (**T**) (and it increases the probabilities that education will be effective $<E_E>$ to have a constructive state of mind (and a resultant attitude) which has a warranted belief that the students (**S**) have the capability (psychical and physical) of achieving their intended learning outcomes (**ILO**s). Effective teachers ($\mathbf{T}_{\mathbf{E}}$) believe justifiably that their students can learn$_1$ ($\mathbf{L}_1$) the prescribed range of knowing ($\mathbf{K}_{2P}$) that is specified by the statements of intended learning outcomes (**ILO**s). The justification for the teachers' belief is previous teaching experience with similar students (**S**) and/or study (guided and/or unguided) of the educology of students who have similar ages and social/cultural experiences.

Belief in the Teachability of Students

It enhances the effectiveness of the persons playing the role of teacher (**T**) (and it increases the probabilities that education will be effective $<\mathbf{E}_{\mathbf{E}}>$) to have a constructive state of mind (and a resultant attitude) which has a reasonable and warranted expectation that the students (**S**) will trust the guidance, help and judgment that are provided by the teacher (**T**). Effective teachers ($\mathbf{T}_{\mathbf{E}}$) have a belief that the students (**S**) are teachable, that they are open to receiving opportunities to study$_1$ ($\mathbf{S}_{P1}$), that they are open to guidance and help in their study$_1$ activities ($\mathbf{S}_{P1}$) and that they want to work in cooperation with their teacher (**T**) to develop the prescribed range of knowing ($\mathbf{K}_{2P}$) that is specified by the intended learning outcomes (**ILO**s).

Respect for Students

It enhances the effectiveness of the persons playing the role of teacher

(**T**) (and it increases the probabilities that education will be effective $<\mathbf{E}_{\mathbf{E}}>$) to have a constructive state of mind (and a resultant attitude) which has a genuine respect and appreciation for the students' (**S**) current (extant) psychical and physical abilities, qualities, and rights and responsibilities in their role as students (**S**). The state of mind (**M**) of the teachers (**T**) is the set of controlling conditions for what the teachers (**T**) say to and about the students (**S**) and otherwise do (saying is a kind of doing, a linguistic doing) in relation to the students (**S**).

A counter example (opposite case) of respect for, and appreciation of, students (**S**) is the scenario in which Mr Hanson, a high school teacher, sees his colleague, Mr Cole, walking along a corridor with his students and remarks loudly to Mr Cole, "You don't have the sharpest tools in the box there, do you, Mr Cole!" "No, Mr Hanson. Working with these students is like trying to teach pigs to sing. You just end up annoying the pigs and frustrating yourself." "True enough, Mr Cole. You can't build bridges without steel," is Mr Hanson's retort. This conversation takes place in front of the students, and it is easily heard by the students. What is the degree of respect for the students being expressed by these teachers in their repartee? How likely are the students to feel respected and appreciated by these teachers' remarks? How motivated are they likely to feel to follow the directions, guidance and help provided by these teachers? What state of mind do these teachers have which leads them to make these remarks? This scenario exemplifies teachers with a state of mind which holds students in contempt and disdain, clearly the opposite of genuine respect and appreciation for students.

A state of mind (**M**) which has genuine respect and appreciation for students (**S**) leads teachers (**T**) to speak in the way that Ms Dufresnoy addresses her students. She is a primary school teacher, and she is teaching a year 4 class (4th grade, average age 9 years). She has a frame of mind such that she always avoids sarcasm, name calling and shouting. She always uses civil language. She always listens carefully to her students' concerns and issues. She always expects students to do their best, and when they do not, she asks them what needs to happen for them to get back on track to do their best. When a conflict arises with her students, she seeks to resolve the conflict by finding out what is causing the conflict and what solutions will work to resolve the conflict. She does not seek to dominate or bully her students, but rather to provide opportunities, within a safe, fair and just environment, for them to achieve new understandings and to extend their current range of knowing. She always communicates with her students with courtesy and civility. Ms Dufresnoy maintains a state of mind (**M**) (and a resultant attitude) which has, and expresses, genuine respect and appreciation for her students (**S**).

Desire to Provide Opportunities to Study$_1$ (S_{P1}) and Learn$_1$ (L_1)

It enhances the effectiveness of the persons playing the role of teacher (**T**) (and it increases the probabilities that education will be effective <E_E>) to have a constructive state of mind (and a resultant attitude) which has a genuine desire to provide students (**S**) with opportunities to study$_1$ (S_{P1}) that are appropriate, necessary and sufficient to achieve the intended learning outcomes (**ILO**s).

As a counter example (opposite case), Frank is in his early 30s. He would like to learn how to play the card game of contract bridge. He approaches Cynthia, an acquaintance who has been playing contract bridge several times a week for many years. He asks whether she would be willing to teach him how to play contract bridge. She hands him two books, Charles Goren's *Goren's Bridge Complete* and Louis Watson's *The Play of the Hand at Bridge.* She tells Frank that all he needs to know about bridge is in these two volumes and that he should read them. Cynthia conducts no follow-up meetings with Frank and provides no further information or instruction. In her mind, she has no desire to provide Frank with any opportunities to study$_1$ (S_{P1}) bridge under her guidance or with her help. She has loaned him the reference books, and she has done all that she is willing to do. Frank is on his own with the task of developing his range of <u>knowing-how</u> (K_{2K3}) to play contract bridge.

An example of someone who has a constructive state of mind and a resultant attitude which has a genuine desire to provide students (**S**) with opportunities to study$_1$ (S_{P1}) is the case of Brian. Brian is a golf pro who is attached to a local golf club. He describes himself as a seasoned professional who has a genuine interest in helping beginners learn how to play the game and in helping more advanced players learn how to improve all aspects of their game, including grip, stance, swing, choice of iron and putting. He offers a range of golf lessons for beginners, intermediate level players and expert players. His repertoire of lessons includes individual lessons of one-half hour or one-hour sessions, lessons with up to four players in a group in five 30-minute sessions, a short game master class of 90 minutes with up to four players and a putting master class of 90 minutes with up to four players. From the instructional programs which Brian offers, and from his enthusiasm for the game, it is clear that Brian has a constructive state of mind which has a genuine desire to provide students (**S**) with opportunities to study₁ ($\mathbf{S_{P1}}$) and learn₁ ($\mathbf{L_1}$) a range of knowing-how ($\mathbf{K_{2K3}}$) to play golf from the Level 1 through Level 3 range of knowing ($\mathbf{K_{2L1}}$ to $\mathbf{K_{2L3}}$).

Desire for Authentic Engagement

It enhances the effectiveness of the persons playing the role of teacher (**T**) (and it increases the probabilities that education will be effective <$\mathbf{E_E}$>) to have a constructive state of mind (and a resultant attitude) which has a genuine desire that students (**S**) become authentically engaged with, and attribute value to, the study$_1$ activities ($\mathbf{S_{P1}}$), the content (**C**) and the prescribed range of knowing ($\mathbf{K_{2P}}$) that is specified by the intended learning outcomes (**ILO**s). Genuine student engagement includes the following.

(1) Students study$_1$ ($\mathbf{S_{P1}}$) in good faith.
(2) Students make serious attempts to learn$_1$ ($\mathbf{L_1}$) the prescribed range of knowing ($\mathbf{K_{2P}}$) which is specified by the intended learning outcomes (**ILO**s).
(3) value the range of knowing (K_{2KLF}) which they aspire to learn (L_1) and
(4) Students integrate their newly acquired prescribed range of knowing ($\mathbf{K_{2P}}$) with their extant range of knowing ($\mathbf{K_{2KLF}}$) such that the newly acquired prescribed range of knowing ($\mathbf{K_{2P}}$) becomes knowing ($\mathbf{K_2}$) which is retained and which is used in the long term.

A counter example of a teacher who does not have a desire for genuine student engagement is the case of Dr Bolger, an economics professor in a university His teaching assignment is introductory economics. The course is conducted as a set of two weekly lectures of one and one-half hour each and a tutorial. Graduate students in economics conduct the tutorials, and Dr Bolger delivers the lectures. Dr Bolger often remarks during his lectures that he has given these lectures so many times that he can recite them to the class while he thinks of what to add to his grocery shopping list. He openly states that he really does not care whether the students have any interest in economics or whether they pass or fail his class or whether they achieve any benefit from understanding economics. He says that it is not a concern of his. Dr Bolger asserts that the degree of understanding the students achieve and what use the students make of the fund of knowledge denoted by the term <*economics*> is entirely their affair. It has little to do with him.

An example of a teacher who does have a desire for genuine student engagement is the case of Mr Clewes. Mr Clewes works for an organization which provides educational services to high schools with students of ages 12 to 17 who are at risk of discontinuing their studies$_1$ ($\mathbf{S_{P1}}$) prematurely. Mr Clewes has a strong desire for his students to continue their studies$_1$ ($\mathbf{S_{P1}}$), to engage in their studies$_1$ ($\mathbf{S_{P1}}$) in good faith, to attach a high value to achieving the prescribed range of knowing ($\mathbf{K_{2P}}$) that is specified by the nominated intended learning outcomes (**ILO**s) and to integrate their newly acquired prescribed range of knowing ($\mathbf{K_{2P}}$) with their extant range of knowing ($\mathbf{K_{2KLF}}$). Mr Clewes works with each of his students individually as a one-on-one tutor, mentor and counselor. He is alert to different expressions of student disengagement. He recognizes students who are in a state of mind (**M**) (and a resultant attitude) of open opposition, passive opposition, acquiescence or conditional commitment to their studies$_1$ ($\mathbf{S_{P1}}$).

(1) Mr Clewes recognizes open opposition to study$_1$ ($\mathbf{S_{P1}}$) and learning$_1$ ($\mathbf{L_1}$) a prescribed range of knowing ($\mathbf{K_2}$) from the behavior of the students in that they never pay attention to instructions, never attempt study$_1$ <$\mathbf{S_{P1}}$> tasks, never achieve intended learning outcomes (**ILO**s) and persistently endeavor to disrupt fellow students who might be focusing on their study$_1$ ($\mathbf{S_{P1}}$) tasks).

(2) He recognizes passive opposition to study$_1$ ($\mathbf{S_{P1}}$) and learning$_1$ ($\mathbf{L_1}$) a prescribed range of knowing ($\mathbf{K_2}$) from the behavior of the student in that they never attempt study$_1$ ($\mathbf{S_{P1}}$) tasks, never achieve intended learning outcomes (**ILO**) and consistently endeavor to avoid drawing attention to themselves and to avoid confrontation.

(3) He recognizes acquiescence to minimal study$_1$ ($\mathbf{S_{P1}}$) and minimal knowing ($\mathbf{K_2}$) from the behavior of the students in that they attempt to complete the study$_1$ ($\mathbf{S_{P1}}$) tasks as quickly as possible with minimal effort and with a view to

achieving a minimally acceptable prescribed range of knowing ($\mathbf{K_{2P}}$).

(4) He recognizes conditional commitment to maximal study$_1$ ($\mathbf{S_{P1}}$) and to maximal learning$_1$ ($\mathbf{L_1}$) of a prescribed range of knowing ($\mathbf{K_2}$) from the behavior of the students in that they will complete study$_1$ ($\mathbf{S_{P1}}$) tasks and endeavor to achieve intended learning outcomes (**ILO**s) as long as there is some conditional or extrinsic reward such as grades or some other form of acknowledgement of achievement.

Mr Clewes' ideal for each of his students is that each has a state of mind (M) of unconditional commitment to maximal study$_1$ ($\mathbf{S_{P1}}$) and maximal learning$_1$ ($\mathbf{L_1}$) of a prescribed range of knowing ($\mathbf{K_{2P}}$). He wants his students to be motivated by an intrinsic love of studying$_1$ ($\mathbf{S_{P1}}$) and learning$_1$ ($\mathbf{L_1}$) of a prescribed range of knowing ($\mathbf{K_{2P}}$). His ideal is that his students become, at heart, philomaths. He wants his students to focus on study$_1$ ($\mathbf{S_{P1}}$) tasks, to embrace challenging and complex study$_1$ ($\mathbf{S_{P1}}$) tasks and to choose to study$_1$ ($\mathbf{S_{P1}}$) even when the result of their achievements (their prescribe range of knowing $<\mathbf{K_{2P}}>$) is not being evaluated and graded, or otherwise extrinsically rewarded. He aspires for his students to achieve long term retention of their newly acquired prescribed range of knowing ($\mathbf{K_{2P}}$) and to achieve a use of their newly acquired prescribed range of knowing ($\mathbf{K_{2P}}$) to conduct inquiry (**Q**), to solve problems and to pursue worthwhile purposes which are meaningful and important to them. Mr Clewes aspires to stimulate his students, arouse their curiosity, evoke their creativity and empower them with authentically chosen purpose to become érevnaphiles (passionate life-long inquirers and problem solvers).

To achieve his aspirations, Mr Clewes talks with, and conducts inquiry with, each of his students about conceiving, choosing and pursuing a major definite purpose in life, about what range of knowing ($\mathbf{K_{2KLF}}$) is requisite for serving that purpose and what studies$_1$ ($\mathbf{S_{P1}}$) of what content (**C**) need to be completed to learn$_1$ ($\mathbf{L_1}$) that requisite range of knowing ($\mathbf{K_{2KLF}}$). He talks with, and inquires with, each of his students (and listens genuinely, carefully and actively) about the obstacles that impede and/or block progress in achieving their major definite purpose and what things need to be done to remove and/or overcome those obstacles. Mr Clewes devises programs of intentional guided study$_1$ ($\mathbf{S_{P1}}$) of content (**C**) to learn$_1$ ($\mathbf{L_1}$) a prescribed range of knowing (**K_{2P}**) which are tailored to the special circumstances and state of mind (**M**), including set of attitudes and major definite purposes, of each of his students. He monitors carefully the progress of his students in their achievement of their nominated ranges of knowing (**K_{2KLF}**), he evaluates their progress frequently, and he uses the results of his evaluations formatively to give advice, make recommendations and provide help to students for them to progress towards achievement of their nominated, authentically chosen and genuinely desired intended learning outcomes (**ILO**s).

Commitment to Purposeful Activity

It enhances the effectiveness of the persons playing the role of teacher (**T**) (and it increases the probabilities that education will be effective <**E_E**>) to have a constructive state of mind (and a resultant attitude) which has a genuine commitment to engaging students (**S**) in purposeful and worthwhile study$_1$ activities (**S_{P1}**) and avoiding time-filling activities or avoiding activities without extrinsic and/or intrinsic value. Effective teachers provide students with study$_1$ (**S_{P1}**) activities of some content (**C**) to learn$_1$ (**L_1**) some prescribed range of knowing (**K_{2P}**). The learning$_1$ (**L_1**) of the prescribed range of knowing (**K_{2P}**) serves the purpose of achieving some worthwhile intended learning outcome (**ILO**).

A counter example of teaching with purpose is that of Ms Hamilton. She has a class of 9th graders (year 9 or average age of 14 years) in a general science class. She has been pressed for time with personal matters, and she has not prepared anything for her class for a 50-minute period of science. Just before her class, she hastily takes a book of word recognition puzzles from the shelf in her staff room and photocopies a set of puzzles for the students to complete. The puzzles present a set of letters arranged in a square of 12 letters across and 12 letters down (a total of 144 individual letters). The task for the students is to recognize as many words as they can in the puzzle and to circle the words. For example, when they locate the word <*oxygen*> in the puzzle, they are to circle the word. She hopes that the activity will keep them busy for 50 minutes. Ms Hamilton has a vague, unarticulated idea that the completion of the puzzles by the students will extend and/or reinforce their science vocabulary, but she does not have this written as an intended learning outcome (**ILO**) in her lesson plan, nor in her unit plan. Her main concern is to keep the students busy for 50 minutes.

An example of teaching with purpose is that of Ms Ellis. She is a music teacher, and she has a class of students with mixed instruments (trumpets, clarinets, saxophones, trombones, flutes, drums, etc). Her intended learning outcome (**ILO**), which she has written in her unit plan and her lesson plan, is that the students will be able to play the tune *Greensleeves* as a unified, well-coordinated, harmonic band. She intends for them to follow her conducting of the band, to read the musical notation relevant to the instrument being played, to play in tune, with the correct rhythm, at the correct tempo, at the correct level and balance of sound and with the correct crescendos and diminuendos. She initially has her students listen to a recording of the tune with the intention that they form the tune in their perception (perception$_2$ of imaginal objects <$\mathbf{P_2}$>). She directs each section of the band to play its part of the tune. Then she directs the entire band to play the tune together. Every study$_1$ ($\mathbf{S_{P1}}$) task which Ms Ellis asks the students to perform has the purpose of advancing the students towards achieving the intended learning outcome (**ILO**) of performing the tune *Greensleeves.*

Open Minded and Flexible

It enhances the effectiveness of the persons playing the role of teacher (**T**) (and it increases the probabilities that education will be effective <$\mathbf{E_E}$>) to have a constructive state of mind (and a resultant attitude) which is open to and flexible in changing content (**C**) and/or derivative components of education (<$\mathbf{E_{DC}}$> – designs, plans, methods, styles, resources, pace, etc.) to accommodate the needs and characteristics of students (**S**) in their study$_1$ ($\mathbf{S_{P1}}$). The effective teacher ($\mathbf{T_E}$) makes changes in content (**C**) and/or the derivative components of education ($\mathbf{E_{DC}}$) with the purpose in mind of enhancing the probabilities that students (**S**) will achieve the intended learning outcomes (**ILO**s).

An example of flexibility in teaching is that of Prof Mathias. He has the responsibility of teaching a university course about the early national period in US history (from the presidencies of George Washington to Andrew Jackson, 1789 to 1837). His class consists of 16 students, and the class meets in sessions of 50 minutes, three times a week, for 16 weeks. In the first week, Prof Mathias immediately notices that his students do not appear to have the capabilities, attitudes and habits which he expected. They struggle with the readings, and many do not do the readings in preparation for class.

Those who do read the assigned chapters and articles, do not prepare for class discussions in the way that Prof Mathias expects them to. They do not organize their ideas about the reading. They do not remember (or make a note of) the main points of the reading. They do not relate what they read to their already established range of knowing (**K**$_2$) about American history and politics. Some students gaze at their mobile phones (cell phones) in class. Others arrive late and disrupt the class when they enter the classroom. Some do not bring books, pens or paper to take notes. The students do not speak in a civil manner to each other. Prof Mathias decides that he must make some major adjustments to the way that he has planned to conduct the class. Otherwise, the classroom experience for both teacher and students is going to be most unpleasant, and the fail rate is going to be perhaps 80 or 90% of the class.

Prof Mathias first reminds all students of reasons for classroom etiquette, distributes a proposal about classroom etiquette and invites discussion about whether the proposal is a reasonable one to adopt or whether it needs to be amended. After discussion among the students, and after any amendments have been made, Prof Mathias invites the class to give their consent and their self-resolve to commit to the code of classroom etiquette.

Prof Mathias then distributes information which provides guidelines on how to prepare for classroom discussion by critical and analytical reading, outlining appropriately, summarizing accurately and making useful notes of points to be discussed in class. He provides instructions on how to outline the readings, how to summarize the readings and what questions students should consider so as to be prepared to participate intelligently, and in a well-informed way, in the classroom discussion. He provides guidance on how to express one's point of view with well-reasoned argument and with necessary and sufficient evidence, without name calling, epithets, expletives and ad hominem attacks.

He meets with each student in his office outside of class hours to establish a rapport with the student, to develop a knowing-that-one (**K**$_{2K1}$) about the unique qualities of each student, to address the issues and personal challenges which might be confronting each student, to determine what obstacles to effective study$_1$ (**S**$_{P1E}$) might be impeding each student and to explore what might be done to remove those obstacles or otherwise compensate for them.

From his consultations, he determines that his students need a great deal of guidance in how to study$_1$ effectively (**S_{P1E}**) and how to become érevnaphiles (independent, self-directed inquirers). He also recognizes that the students need a great deal of feedback (formative use of evaluation results) on their progress towards achieving the intended learning outcomes (**ILO**s) of the class, and they need a great deal of practice in writing outlines, summarizing, analyzing and comparing viewpoints in historical texts. Prof Mathias decides that he needs some help in providing the support which his students need to succeed in their studies, and he hires a graduate student in history to assist him with providing instruction, evaluation and feedback to the students. Prof Mathias also makes the judgment that the students need a great deal of help in developing their knowing-how (**K_{2K3}**) to write historical analyses and essays. He devises a system of instruction in which students are given the opportunity to practice writing historical essays and to receive evaluation of them and feedback on them prior to writing historical essays whose evaluation results will be used summatively. Prof Mathias is thus using an instructional design in which there are multiple opportunities to practice achieving the intended learning outcomes (**ILO**s) prior to submitting the final assessment for evaluation for summative reporting of the evaluation results. He intends to use a rating system (rather than a ranking system) to report the results of his evaluation.

The choices which Prof Mathias makes, in response to coming to know the characteristics of his students, to modify the content (**C**) and the derivative components of education (**$<E_{DC}>$** – design, plans, methods, styles, resources, pace, etc.) in his instructional program to accommodate the needs and characteristics of his students (**S**) are clearly the result of his flexibility of mind (**M**) (and his resultant attitude). His main concern is to provide a set of study$_1$ (**S_{P1}**) opportunities from which the students will learn$_1$ (**L_1**) the prescribed range of knowing (**K_{2P}**) that is specified by the intended learning outcomes (**ILO**s).

What perhaps makes the example of Prof Mathias remarkable (and maybe unique) is that at the university level, the teachers expect students to be accomplished and committed érevnaphiles (self-directed, self-disciplined and self-motivated inquirers) with a sufficient range of knowing (**K_{2KLF}**) to study$_1$ effectively (**S_{P1E}**) and conduct inquiry (**Q**) competently. Because of these expectations, the instruction provided at the university level is typically designed to be far less supportive of the students than the instruction provided in secondary schools, and the instruction provided in secondary schools is designed to be substantially less supportive of the students than the instruction provided in primary schools. If students arrive at university without having the state of mind (**M**) (and the resultant attitude) of being self-directed, self-disciplined and self-motivated, and if they arrive without having achieved the range of knowing ($\mathbf{K}_{2KLF}$) requisite to conducting effective study$_1$ ($\mathbf{S}_{P1E}$) and competent self-directed inquiry ($\mathbf{Q}_{E}$), they typically struggle to succeed in their university studies$_1$ ($\mathbf{S}_{P1}$).

Flexibility in effective teaching ($\mathbf{T}_{E}$) is a matter of having a state of mind (and resultant attitude) that is open to making changes to the content (**C**) and/or to the derivative components of education ($<\mathbf{E}_{DC}>$ – design, methods, styles, resources, organization, goal structures, assessment, evaluation, etc.) such that the probabilities are maximized that the students (**S**) will learn$_1$ ($\mathbf{L}_1$) the prescribed range of knowing ($\mathbf{K}_{2P}$) that is specified by the intended learning outcomes (**ILO**s) of an educational episode (e.g. lesson, unit, course).

Commitment to Help

It enhances the effectiveness of the persons playing the role of teacher (**T**) (and it increases the probabilities that education will be effective $<\mathbf{E}_{E}>$) to have a constructive state of mind (and a resultant attitude) which has a genuine commitment to supervise, guide and help students (**S**) appropriately in the conduct and completion of their study$_1$ activities ($\mathbf{S}_{P1}$). Effective teaching ($\mathbf{T}_{PE}$) is altruistic. The effective teacher has a genuine desire and self-resolve to provide adequate supervision, appropriate guidance and effective help to students (**S**) as they endeavor to learn$_1$ ($\mathbf{L}_1$), through undertaking their study$_1$ tasks ($\mathbf{S}_{P1}$), the prescribed range of knowing ($\mathbf{K}_{2P}$) that is specified by the intended learning outcomes (**ILO**s).

Having an attitude of wanting to provide appropriate help to students is not wanting to do for them what they could and should do for themselves in their study$_1$ ($\mathbf{S}_{P1}$) activities. Rather, helping appropriately is undertaking linguistic and physical action (and sometimes withholding action) which will advance the progress of the students in extending their prescribed range of knowing ($\mathbf{K}_{2P}$). Helping students appropriately may take the form of, for example, piquing their curiosity, presenting them with difficult, but achievable, challenges, engaging them in problem solving which has personal importance and significance for them, referring them to sources of information, asking them open-ended questions and providing them with feedback about how they can improve and extend their prescribed range of knowing ($\mathbf{K_{2P}}$).

Commitment to Conscientiousness and Thoroughness

It enhances the effectiveness of the persons playing the role of teacher (**T**) (and it increases the probabilities that education will be effective $<\mathbf{E_E}>$) to have a constructive state of mind (and a resultant attitude) which has a genuine desire for the students (**S**) to complete their study$_1$ ($\mathbf{S_{P1}}$) activities and their assessment tasks competently and in good faith. This attitude is one of conscientiousness and thoroughness. It is one of self-resolve to monitor the completion of study$_1$ tasks ($\mathbf{S_{P1}}$), the completion of assessment tasks and the progress of students (**S**) in the achievement of their prescribed range of knowing ($\mathbf{K_{2P}}$) that is specified by their intended learning outcomes (**ILO**s).

To test the conscientiousness and thoroughness of a teacher, more than one student has placed a bogus citation of a source in an essay, or written the words in the middle of a research paper, "If you read this, you are a better teacher than I think you are." Students have the right to expect their teachers to be thorough and conscientious, and teachers, in turn, have the obligation to be thorough and conscientious in monitoring, assessing and evaluating the study$_1$ ($\mathbf{S_{P1}}$) tasks, the assessment tasks and the products of the study$_1$ ($\mathbf{S_{P1}}$) and assessment tasks of their students and in advising their students how to improve their prescribed range of knowing ($\mathbf{K_{2P}}$).

Practicing Appropriately

It enhances the effectiveness of the persons playing the role of teacher (**T**) (and it increases the probabilities that education will be effective $<\mathbf{E_E}>$) to have a constructive state of mind (and a resultant attitude) which has a desire and a self-resolve to assure that students have the opportunity to conduct appropriate practice with their newly acquired prescribed range of knowing ($\mathbf{K_{2P}}$).

Appropriate practice by students (**S**) is any set of study$_1$ ($\mathbf{S_{P1}}$) tasks which extends, in kind, level and/or form, the students' prescribed range of knowing ($\mathbf{K_{2P}}$), and appropriate practice is also any set of study$_1$ ($\mathbf{S_{P1}}$) tasks which promotes the transformation of the students' prescribed range of knowing (**K_{2P}**) from short-term and temporary knowing (**K_{2KLF}**) to long-term and permanent knowing (**K_{2KLF}**). As well as being apposite to the prescribed range of knowing (**K_{2P}**) which the students are endeavoring to develop, appropriate practice by students (**S**) is appropriate because it is suitable for their age group, their capabilities (physical and psychical), their previously achieved range of knowing (**K_{2KLF}**), their curiosities and interests and the cultural and social context in which they are living.

An example of a teacher with an attitude of wanting to assure that students have opportunities for appropriate practice is that of Ms Foster. She teaches Italian as a second language in a high school. One of her classes is a year 11 class (11th grade or average age of 16 years), and she is guiding them in their development of conversational Italian within different social contexts. One of the contexts is that of ordering a meal in a restaurant. The intended learning outcomes (**ILO**s) include being able to understand the written options on a menu, to understand the spoken questions asked by a waiter or waitress and to say (fluently, in idiomatic, grammatically correct and understandable Italian) what is desired for food and beverages. Ms Foster provides the students with a view of a video of some Italian people in a restaurant in Rome ordering their meals. She provides them with a list of words which are commonly used in ordering meals. She provides them with a written and spoken dialogue of some people talking with a waiter and ordering food and beverage. She asks the students to memorize the dialogue in preparation for playing different roles in a scenario in which some friends go to a restaurant and order food and beverage. She organizes the students into groups so that each student can take turns playing each of the roles in the dialogue. She continues to have the students take turns practicing the different roles in the dialogue until they are all fluent. She then introduces the students to a new dialogue in a new context, for example, ordering some medicines from a pharmacy.

Solving Problems

It enhances the effectiveness of the persons playing the role of teacher (**T**) (and it increases the probabilities that education will be effective <**E_E**>) to have a constructive state of mind (and a resultant attitude) which has a desire and commitment to provide opportunities for the students to use their newly acquired prescribed range of knowing (**K_{2P}**)

to solve a range of problems, some familiar and some novel, some simple and some complex.

Problem solving is encountering a situation for which we do not have an adequate range of knowing to achieve what we want to achieve, and we conduct inquiry to develop the range of knowing that is sufficient to achieve what we want to achieve. Problems can be familiar or unfamiliar, and they can be simple or complex.

One example of a teacher wanting to present her students with problems to solve is that of Ms Bowen, a kindergarten teacher. She distributes three-dimensional puzzles to her students (average age of 5 years). The puzzles consist of matching slots and pieces of different shapes – hearts, triangles, squares, rectangles, birds, fish, etc. The children play with the puzzles and endeavor to place the matching pieces into the matching shapes in the puzzles.

A second example is that of Dr Layne. She is a university chemistry teacher. She gives each of her students a small sample of an unknown substance each week, and she instructs each student to conduct the appropriate tests to identify the elements in the substance and to submit a written report which describes the laboratory analytic procedures and the conclusions.

A third example is that of Prof Browne, a university professor of biology. He wants his graduate student, Andrew, to develop a mathematical model which simulates and predicts the way a set of proteins within genes interact with each other to control a specific cell function. Andrew completes a literature review about how single-stranded messenger RNA (mRNA) molecules are complementary to one of the DNA strands of a gene and how the mRNA leaves the cell nucleus, moves to the cytoplasm and establishes the controlling conditions for chemical reactions to form proteins. Andrew searches for algorithms to simulate the chemical interactions of the target proteins and writes a computer code in MATLAB to simulate the concentration changes of different mRNA and protein and dimer species over a specified period of time as thousands of reactions are fired per minute.

From an educological viewpoint, the benefits of student engagement in problem solving are several. Problem solving provides students with opportunities to use their newly acquired prescribed range of knowing ($\mathbf{K}_{2P}$) in a variety of circumstances to achieve a variety of goals. In doing so, the students have opportunities to transform their prescribed range of knowing ($\mathbf{K}_{2P}$) from temporary, short-term, inert, irrelevant, insignificant and fragmented knowing ($\mathbf{K}_{2KLF}$) into permanent, long-term, useful, relevant, significant and integrated knowing ($\mathbf{K}_{2KLF}$). Problem solving also provides opportunities for students to extend their level of knowing from Level 2 to Level 3 or Level 4 ($\mathbf{K}_{2L2}$ to $\mathbf{K}_{2L3}$ or $\mathbf{K}_{2L4}$), their kinds of knowing from knowing-that ($\mathbf{K}_{2K2}$) to knowing-that-one ($\mathbf{K}_{2K1}$), knowing-how ($\mathbf{K}_{2K3}$) and/or knowing-to ($\mathbf{K}_{2K4}$) and their forms of knowing ($\mathbf{K}_{2F}$) from linguistic knowing ($\mathbf{K}_{2F1}$) to emotional ($\mathbf{K}_{2F2}$), imaginal ($\mathbf{K}_{2F3}$), physiological ($\mathbf{K}_{2F4}$) and/or physical ($\mathbf{K}_{2F5}$) forms.

Extending Knowing

It enhances the effectiveness of the persons playing the role of teacher (**T**) (and it increases the probabilities that education **<E>** will be effective <$\mathbf{E}_E$>) to have a constructive state of mind (and a resultant attitude) which has a desire to provide opportunities for the students to extend their newly acquired prescribed range of knowing (K_{2P}) through additional intentional guided study$_1$ ($\mathbf{S}_{P1}$) and/or additional inquiry (**Q**). Extending a range of knowing ($\mathbf{K}_{2KLF}$) is increasing knowing ($\mathbf{K}_2$) to some additional kind ($\mathbf{K}_{2K}$), some higher level ($\mathbf{K}_{2L}$) and/or additional form ($\mathbf{K}_{2F}$). Extending a range of knowing ($\mathbf{K}_{2KLF}$) intentionally is achieved either through inquiry (**Q**), which, when successful, results in the process of intentional unguided learning$_2$ ($\mathbf{L}_2$) of some discovered range of knowing ($\mathbf{K}_{2D}$), or through education (**E**), which, when successful, results in the process of intentional guided learning$_1$ ($\mathbf{L}_1$) of some prescribed range of knowing ($\mathbf{K}_{2P}$). The product of either process of learning$_1$ ($\mathbf{L}_1$) or learning$_2$ ($\mathbf{L}_2$) is always the cognitive state of mind of some range of knowing ($\mathbf{K}_{2KLF}$). Learning$_1$ ($\mathbf{L}_1$) produces a prescribed range of knowing ($\mathbf{K}_{2P}$). Learning$_2$ ($\mathbf{L}_2$) produces a discovered range of knowing ($\mathbf{K}_{2D}$). The contribution which teachers (**T**) can make to the process of students extending their knowing, therefore, is either the provision of a set of study$_1$ ($\mathbf{S}_{P1}$) activities for students to complete under guidance to learn$_1$ ($\mathbf{L}_1$) a prescribed range of knowing ($\mathbf{K}_{2P}$) or the provision of a set of opportunities for students to undertake inquiry (**Q**) without guidance to learn$_2$ ($\mathbf{L}_2$) a discovered range of knowing ($\mathbf{K}_{2D}$).

An example of having commitment to providing opportunities for students to extend their newly acquired prescribed range of knowing ($\mathbf{K}_{2P}$) is that of Mr Alvarez, a driver education teacher. He has had his students (ages 16 to 17) read the state road rules for everyday driving, and he has had them answer questions about the rules. He has had his students watch a set of videos which demonstrates and explains principles of safe driving and answer questions about the principles of safe driving. He has had them spend sessions on computer simulators which have given them practice in virtual driving in different conditions. From these study$_1$ ($\mathbf{S_{P1}}$) activities, the students have achieved an initial prescribed range of knowing ($\mathbf{K_{2P}}$) in relation to driving a car. Mr Alvarez, with a view to providing students the opportunity to extend their prescribed range of knowing ($\mathbf{K_{2P}}$) in relation to driving, arranges for each student to drive in one-hour sessions for a minimum of 20 hours, under the supervision of a driving instructor, an actual car in a variety of weather conditions, in a range of traffic conditions, at different times of day (morning, midday, afternoon, evening, night), on different road surfaces (paved, gravel, unsurfaced) and on different types of roads (flat, curved, hilly; freeway, two way, one way, lane way).

A second example is that of Arn, a snow ski instructor. Arn has a beginner's skiing class of four adults who have never gone skiing. He demonstrates how to stand on the skis and how to hold the poles. He then examines each of the students, evaluates the stance of each student and advises each student how to improve his or her stance. He demonstrates to them how to stand up from a fall by using the poles as a prop. He has each of the students practice using their poles to pull themselves up from a fall. He demonstrates how to ski straight down a gentle slope and come to a stop by using the wedge maneuver to brake. He has each of the students ski down a gentle slope and use the wedge maneuver for braking. He then demonstrates how to turn, using the snowplow maneuver, while skiing down a slope, first turning left, then turning right, then left, etc. He has each of the students practice turning. He watches each student, encourages them and advises them how to improve. At this point, Arn's students have an initial range of knowing how to stand on their skis, how to pull themselves up from a fall, how to ski straight down a gentle slope, how to brake using the wedge maneuver and how to execute turns left and right using the snowplow maneuver while skiing down a slope. Before he progresses them to parallel skiing, he wants his students to extend their range of knowing and to develop their confidence by having them ski for the rest of the day on their own using the snowplow maneuver to turn and the wedge maneuver to stop. He intends, on the following day, to teach them how to parallel ski.

A third example is that of Mrs Greenland. She teaches a 6th grade class (year 6 or ages 11 to 12). All her students have a range of knowing sufficient to read out loud and silently with comprehension. She wants to give them the opportunity to extend their range of knowing in relation to reading. She assigns them the task of selecting six books to read. The choice of book is entirely a matter for each student. Each week, she wants them to read silently to themselves one of the six books, write a book report for each book, construct a list of new words found in each book, write the definition for each word and write a sentence which uses each of the new words. She monitors their progress weekly by collecting their book reports and their word lists, definitions and sentences for assessment and evaluation.

Emending Knowing

It enhances the effectiveness of the persons playing the role of teacher (**T**) (and it increases the probabilities that education <**E**> will be effective <$\mathbf{E}_{\mathbf{E}}$>) to have a constructive state of mind (and a resultant attitude) which has a desire for the students to emend their extant range of knowing ($\mathbf{K}_{\mathbf{2KLF}}$) to accommodate their newly acquired prescribed range of knowing ($\mathbf{K}_{\mathbf{2P}}$). Part of effective teaching ($\mathbf{T}_{\mathbf{PE}}$) is having an attitude which encourages students (**S**) to reflect upon what they knew (or believed that they knew) before having developed their most recent prescribed range of knowing and how their most recently acquired prescribed range of knowing relates to what they knew (or believed that they knew) and how they might have to change what they believed that they knew to accommodate their new prescribed range of knowing ($\mathbf{K}_{\mathbf{2P}}$).

An example of a teacher with an attitude of wanting his students to emend their previous range of knowing to accommodate their new prescribed range of knowing is that of Prof Richards. Prof Richards has a class of university students who are preparing to qualify as high school science teachers. They have all completed at least two semesters of courses in physics, including the study of mechanics. In his lecture, he has a bowling ball and a solid steel ball (the size of a baseball) suspended at a height of 5 meters. There is a mechanism rigged to release both balls simultaneously. There is a tank of water positioned below the balls to catch them. He asks his students to observe which ball strikes the surface of the water first. Ninety-eight percent of the 60 students in his class report that they observed the bowling ball striking the surface of the water first. He also has made a video recording of the falling balls. He shows the students the descent of the balls in slow motion. In the slow-motion video, it is clear to all that both balls strike the surface of the water simultaneously. Prof. Richards explains to his students that we, as human beings, have certain intuitive beliefs. One of them is that large objects fall towards the Earth faster than small objects, but in fact, all objects (when friction is not a significant factor) accelerate towards the Earth at the same rate, regardless of size or density. He further demonstrates this relationship between mass and acceleration by showing a video of a feather and a large ball bearing (diameter 3 centimeters) in a glass vacuum chamber. Both the feather and the ball bearing are released simultaneously, they fall a distance of 1.5 meters, and they strike the bottom of the vacuum chamber simultaneously. He invites his students to change their preconceptions such that their conceptions match the facts about the rate of acceleration of objects towards each other when friction is not a significant factor.

A second example of a teacher with an attitude of wanting the students to emend their previous range of knowing to accommodate their newly developed prescribed range of knowing is that of Ms Cunningham, a primary teacher. She has a 6th grade class (year 6 or average age of 11 years). She is teaching a unit on volume. The students already have a range of knowing which includes knowing how to measure distance and knowing how to calculate area by multiplication. She presents the class with three rectangular containers, and she has the students measure the height, width and depth of each container. The students determine that the dimensions of the containers are as follows. The first container has a width and depth of 10 centimeters and a height of 20 centimeters. The second container has a width and depth of 20 centimeters and a height of 10 centimeters. The third container has a width and depth of 40 centimeters and a height of 5 centimeters. She then asks her students to guess whether the second container will hold more, less or the same amount of water as the first container and to give their reasons. She also asks them to guess whether the third container will hold more, less or the same amount of water as the second container and to give their reasons. Most students guess that the second container will hold the same as the first container because it is twice as wide but only half as high, and they guess that the third container will hold the same as the second because it, too, is twice as wide but only half as high as the second container. Ms Cunningham then has the students fill the first container with water. She instructs the students to fill the second container with water from the first container, note how much water it takes to fill the second container and write their results. The students are surprised that the second container holds twice as much water as the first container even though it is one-half the height of the first container. She has them fill the third container with water from the first container. The students are even more surprised that the third container holds four times as much water as the first container even though it is one-fourth the height of the first container. "How can this be?" asks Ms. Cunningham. She tells them that when they estimated the volumes of the second and third containers, they were using the dimensions of height and width. They left out of their thinking the third dimension of depth. Calculations of volume, she explains, requires that they use all three dimensions, width, depth and height. Ms. Cunningham then assigns some problems for the students to calculate the volume of a number of three-dimensional rectangular and square objects using the dimensions of width, height and depth.

A third example is that of Prof Bowen. He teaches political science in a university, and he is currently teaching a class about different forms of government – democracy, theocracy, autocracy, plutocracy, etc. He poses a question to his class that if a democracy is defined as a system in which one person has one vote and in which the majority rules, does the US qualify as a democracy? The students respond unanimously that yes, of course, the US is a democracy. Prof Bowen gives them the challenge of proving the assertion that the US is a democracy by presenting evidence that there a system in which one person has one vote and that majority decisions prevail. He has 18 students in his class, and he organizes the class into nine teams of two students to conduct some relevant research and to report to the class at a later date. Each of the nine teams undertakes research about the conditions that were established in the US to qualify as a voter (or elector) in local, state and federal elections in eight different periods of US history:

(1) early national period of the republic (1788 – 1837),
(2) reform and expansionist period (1838 – 1861),

(3) the Civil War and reconstruction period (1861 – 1877),
(4) development of the industrial US (1870 – 1900),
(5) emergence of modern America (1900 – 1930,
(6) the Great Depression and World War II (1929 – 1945),
(7) postwar US (1945 – 1968),
(8) contemporary US (1968 to the present),
(9) strategies and tactics used to suppress voting and thwart majority rule.

The teams conduct their research over a period of a week. They write their reports, return to class, distribute copies of their reports and give oral presentations of 30 minutes each to the class about what they have found. The overall narrative which the students establish is that the issue of which groups of people should be enfranchised (and which groups should be disenfranchised) in the US has been a contentious question for the entire history of the US. The question of enfranchisement (and disenfranchisement) has been contested continually in legislative law and through case law in challenges in state and federal courts. The conclusion which the students make is that the US has never had a situation in which every person of legal age has been enfranchised regardless of gender, race, color, creed, religious affiliation, legal status, social standing, amount of schooling, location of residence or economic circumstances. At the conclusion of the presentations, Prof Bowen asks the students once again, that if a democracy is defined as a system in which one person has one vote and in which the majority rules, does the US qualify as a democracy? In light of the results of their research, the students emend their view that the US is unequivocally a democracy. They conclude that the US has aspired (and continues to aspire) to function as a democracy, but it has fallen short of its ideals because in every period of American history, special interest groups with power, resources and assets have opposed (and continue to oppose) extending the franchise to all US citizens, and the same special interest groups have used features of the US political system to thwart the majority will by restricting voter registration, purging voter rolls, rationing polling booths, requiring strict documentation of identity, gerrymandering, filibustering and other anti-democratic practices. The students thus emend their previous range of knowing to accommodate their newly developed range of knowing, through the guidance from their teacher.

Integrating Knowing

It enhances the effectiveness of the persons playing the role of teacher (**T**) (and it increases the probabilities that education <**E**> will be effective <$\mathbf{E_E}$>) to have a constructive state of mind (and a resultant attitude) which has a desire for the students to integrate their newly acquired prescribed range of knowing ($\mathbf{K_{2P}}$) with their extant range of knowing ($\mathbf{K_{2KLF}}$). Having an integrated range of knowing ($\mathbf{K_{2KLF}}$) is having a state of mind (where mind <**M**> is the mutual effects of volition <**V**>, perception <**P**> and cognition <**N**>, i.e. where mind <$\mathbf{M = V \rightleftarrows P \rightleftarrows N \rightleftarrows V}$>) which brings the knower's full range of knowing ($\mathbf{K_{2KLF}}$) to bear upon the problem-solving process, and especially in the conduct of independent unguided inquiry (**Q**) which deals with novel problems in circumstances never before encountered.

An example of a group of teachers with an attitude of wanting to provide students with opportunities to integrate their range of knowing is that of Templeton Community School (a fictitious school imagined for this example). Templeton is a small elementary school for kindergarten through 6th grade. The teachers arrange a Templeton bank which issues Templeton money. The students earn Templeton money by doing work around the school, mainly cleaning, picking up rubbish, washing windows, tending to the school grounds, caring for the compost, preparing the soil in the school garden, planting and cultivating the vegetables in the garden, fertilizing and watering the fruit trees, feeding the school chickens, cleaning the school chicken coop and collecting the eggs. The teachers organize a Templeton store, which the students take turns managing. The students sell their crafts and art works, the vegetables and fruits from the school garden and the eggs from the school chickens. The students take turns keeping and auditing the accounts for the store. They bank the earnings from the store with the Templeton bank, and the students collect their earnings from the sale of their crafts and art from the bank. In this example of Templeton Community School, the teachers provide students with the opportunity to integrate their prescribed range of knowing ($\mathbf{K_{2P}}$) through participating in the Templeton economic system with Templeton money.

A second example is that of Ms Kaplan. She is a 6th grade teacher (year 6 or average age of 11), and she is having her students do a unit of study on bridges and bridge designs. She organizes her class of 24 students into four groups of six students each. She tells the students in each team to find information about six different bridge designs and to negotiate among themselves to decide which member of the team will write a report about which one of the six designs. Each team member is to prepare and present one report about one bridge design. Thus, each team is to produce six reports about six different bridge designs. Each report is to include a diagram of the design, an explanation about how the design works, a comparison of the advantages and disadvantages of the design and a photograph and a description (including the location) of a bridge which has the design. Each team member is to give an oral presentation to the team and is to submit the report to the teacher. After the students have completed their research and presented their reports to their team, Ms. Kaplan reorganizes the class into six teams of four members each, and she tells each team that it has the task of constructing a bridge. She assigns each team one of the six bridge designs to use, and she provides them with the construction materials – popsicle sticks, glue, cotton thread and thin cardboard. She tells her students that they are to test the strength of their bridges with a 2.5 kilogram weight. In this educational episode, Ms. Kaplan exemplifies a teacher with an attitude of wanting to provide her students with opportunities to integrate their newly acquired prescribed range of knowing ($\mathbf{K_{2P}}$) with their extant range of knowing ($\mathbf{K_{2KLF}}$) through engaging in inquiry (**Q**) and problem solving.

Enthusiasm

It enhances the effectiveness of the persons playing the role of teacher (**T**) (and it increases the probabilities that education <**E**> will be effective <$\mathbf{E_E}$>) to have a constructive state of mind (and a resultant attitude) which has a genuine enthusiasm for the endeavors and the achievements (psychical and physical) of the students (**S**). Enthusiasm is infectious. Students enjoy and mirror the enthusiasm of their teachers for the subject matter (the content <**C**>), the $study_1$ activities ($\mathbf{S_{P1}}$), the intended learning outcomes (**ILO**s) and the prescribed range of knowing ($\mathbf{K_{2P}}$) specified by the intended learning outcomes (**ILO**s). Students (**S**) find the enthusiasm of their teachers (**T**) motivational, inspirational and affirmational.

Justice

It enhances the effectiveness of the persons playing the role of teacher (**T**) (and it increases the probabilities that education <**E**> will be effective <$\mathbf{E}_{E}$>) to have a constructive state of mind (and a resultant attitude) which has a commitment to treat the students fairly and justly. Students have a keen sense of fairness and justice. They may not be able to articulate clearly the forms of justice which they want and expect, but they are able to recognize when justice is being applied and not being applied. The kinds of justice which students want and expect include distributive, procedural, retributive and restorative justice (Michelle Maiese and Heidi Burgess, 2020). They want their fair share of resources (distributive justice). They want fair treatment (procedural justice). They want punishments to be commensurate with their wrongdoings (retributive justice). They want wrongs to be set right (restorative justice). Teachers (**T**) enhance the probabilities of their effectiveness as teachers (and increase the probabilities that education <**E**> will be effective <$\mathbf{E}_{E}$>) when they have an attitude of self-resolve (and of course have the competence) to treat their students with justice in all its forms.

Evaluation

It enhances the effectiveness of the person playing the role of teacher (T) (and it increases the probabilities that education <**E**> will be effective <$\mathbf{E}_{E}$>) to have a constructive state of mind (and a resultant attitude) which has a desire to evaluate the achievement of the students fairly and justly and to use the evaluation results appropriately (preparatively, formatively, summatively).

An example of a teacher with an attitude of being committed to conducting fair evaluations of her students and to making appropriate use of evaluation results is that of Mrs Grady. She is a piano teacher who gives private lessons. In her lessons, she follows the syllabus provided by the Australian Music Examinations Board (AMEB). The AMEB uses a rating scale of 9 categories to evaluate the range of knowing ($\mathbf{K}_{2KLF}$) of a pianist. When she accepts a new student, she first has the student play a variety of pieces and evaluates their proficiency at reading musical notation and playing with technical accuracy and artistic expression. In her evaluation, she uses the criteria established by the AMEB to make her judgment about what level of proficiency her student has achieved relative to the 9 categories of proficiency used by the AMEB. From her evaluation results, she decides what books to use with her student and what exercises to assign to her student. In making these judgments, she is using the results of her evaluation preparatively, i.e. she is making arrangements to assure that her instruction is appropriate for the range of knowing ($\mathbf{K}_{2KLF}$) already achieved and the prescribed range of knowing ($\mathbf{K}_{2P}$) to be achieved by her student.

Mrs Grady provides her music lessons for each student in sessions of one lesson per week for ten weeks. During each lesson, she conducts assessments and makes evaluations to determine the progress of her students, and she uses the results of her evaluation to give guidance, provide help and make recommendations to each student about how to improve her or his performance. She is using her evaluation results formatively, i.e. she is using her evaluation results to advise, guide and assist her students to develop their musical proficiency.

At the conclusion of each ten-week session of lessons, Mrs Grady consults with her students about whether the student feels that she or he is confident to sit the relevant AMEB music examination to be certified for the next grade level in the AMEB rating scale. Once agreement is reached between Mrs Grady and her student, arrangements are made for the student to enroll to sit the AMEB music examination. The student completes the exam, and the AMEB accredited examiners report their judgment as to whether the student's performance satisfies the criteria for the examination. If the criteria are matched, the examiners authorize the AMEB to issue a certificate of attainment to the student. The AMEB is using the evaluation results summatively, i.e. it is reporting and certifying that a student has achieved a prescribed range of knowing ($\mathbf{K}_{2P}$) in relation to playing the piano and reading musical notation.

Mrs Grady, upon receiving notification of the student's certification of having achieved a specified level of proficiency (a prescribed range of knowing <$\mathbf{K}_{2P}$>), is in a position to make plans for further instruction with the student. She is thus using the notification of certification (the evaluation report) preparatively.

Inquiry

It enhances the effectiveness of the persons playing the role of teacher (**T**) (and it increases the probabilities that education <**E**> will be effective <$\mathbf{E}_{E}$>) to have a constructive state of mind (and a resultant attitude) which is open to conducting continuous inquiry (**Q**) to extend their discovered range of knowing ($\mathbf{K}_{2D}$) about education (**E**). The range of knowing ($\mathbf{K}_{2KLF}$) about teaching ($\mathbf{T}_{P}$) and how to teach effectively ($\mathbf{T_{PE}}$) is not a protocolic knowing-how ($\mathbf{K_{2K3A}}$). The evidence of whether teaching ($\mathbf{T_{P}}$) has been effective ($\mathbf{T_{PE}}$) is not whether a teacher (**T**) has followed a set of invariant procedures (protocolic knowing-how $<\mathbf{K_{2K3A}}>$), but rather whether the students (**S**) have achieved the prescribed range of knowing ($\mathbf{K_{2P}}$) as specified by the intended learning outcomes (**ILO**s). Knowing-how ($\mathbf{K_{2K3}}$) to teach effectively ($\mathbf{T_{PE}}$) is an adaptive knowing-how ($\mathbf{K_{2K3B}}$) and creative knowing-how ($\mathbf{K_{2K3C}}$). Adaptive ($\mathbf{K_{2K3B}}$) and creative ($\mathbf{K_{2K3C}}$) knowing-how are ranges of knowing-how ($\mathbf{K_{2K3}}$) at the postconventional level of knowing ($\mathbf{K_{2L4}}$). Preconventional level of knowing ($\mathbf{K_{2L1}}$) and conventional levels of knowing (intermediate $<\mathbf{K_{2L2}}>$ and expert $<\mathbf{K_{2L3}}>$) can be taught. But postconventional level knowing ($\mathbf{K_{2L4}}$) can not be taught. It can only be achieved by inquiry (**Q**). Postconventional level knowing ($\mathbf{K_{2L4}}$) is discovered knowing ($\mathbf{K_{2D}}$). Thus, for teachers to improve their teaching, they must necessarily engage in inquiry (**Q**) about their teaching ($\mathbf{T_{P}}$), either by trial and error, or by reflection upon previous experience and adjustments to ways of dealing with future experience, or by systematic research. All three are forms of inquiry (**Q**). Persons playing the role of teacher (**T**) enhance the probabilities that they will succeed in improving their teaching (and increase the probabilities that education $<\mathbf{E}>$ will be effective $<\mathbf{E_{E}}>$) when they have an attitude of being committed to inquiring (**Q**) about their teaching ($\mathbf{T_{P}}$) with a view to improving the effectiveness of their teaching ($\mathbf{T_{P}}$). With teaching ($\mathbf{T_{P}}$), as with so many endeavors, there is always something new to learn (**L**), and there is always room for improvement (i.e. to extend a range of knowing in kind, level and form $<\mathbf{K_{2KLF}}>$).

Constructive Attitudes in Communities

Just as constructive states of mind (**M**) (and the resultant attitudes) held by students (**S**) and teachers (**T**) enhance the probabilities that education (**E**) will be effective education ($\mathbf{E_{E}}$), so too does constructive states of mind (**M**) (and the resultant attitudes) held by members of the community and wider society ($\mathbf{X_{S}}$) (in which teaching $<\mathbf{T_{P}}>$ and studying$_1$ $<\mathbf{S_{P1}}>$ take place) enhance the probabilities that education (**E**) will be effective education ($\mathbf{E_{E}}$).

The context (**X**) of education (**E**) is one of the four essential elements (**T, S, C, X**) of education (**E**). The context (**X**) is physical, social and cultural ($\mathbf{X = X_{P} \cup X_{S} \cup X_{C}}$). The physical context ($\mathbf{X_{P}}$) is the physical setting in which teachers (**T**) and students (**S**) transact with content (**C**) so that students learn$_1$ (**L$_1$**) some prescribed range of knowing (**K$_{2P}$**). Examples of physical setting (**X$_P$**) include classrooms, lecture halls, gymnasiums, laboratories, playing fields, swimming pools, etc. The social context (**X$_S$**) is the social setting in which teachers (**T**) and students (**S**) transact with content (**C**). A family, a church, a swimming club or a golf club is a social setting. A school, an academy, an institute, a college or a university is a social setting. A community, a village, a town or a city is a social setting. A wider society or a nation is a social setting. The cultural context (**X$_C$**) is the cultural setting in which teachers (**T**) and students (**S**) transact with content (**C**). Cultural settings include American culture, Australian culture, Vietnamese culture, French culture, etc. Each member of the community has a state of mind (**M**) (and a resultant attitude) toward what teachers (**T**) and students (**S**) do, toward the content (**C**) which they teach (**T$_P$**) and study (**S$_{P1}$**) and toward the prescribed range of knowing (**K$_{2P}$**) which the students aspire to learn$_1$ (**L$_1$**) and/or actually learn$_1$ (**L$_1$**). Collectively, the state of mind (**M**) (and resultant attitude) of each member of the community forms the range of states of mind (**M**) (and resultant attitudes) within the community toward teachers (**T**), students (**S**), content (**C**), prescribed ranges of knowing (**K$_{2P}$**) and the educational institution (school, academy, institute, college, etc.) where teachers and students do their work. Community attitudes towards education (**E**) can be united in support of what is happening with teachers (**T**), students (**S**), content (**C**) and prescribed ranges of knowing (**K$_{2P}$**). The community can be united in opposition to the way education (**E**) is being conducted. The community can be divided in its attitudes, with some members of the community being supportive of, others being opposed to, and others being indifferent to what is happening with teachers (**T**), students (**S**), content (**C**) and prescribed ranges of knowing (**K$_{2P}$**) in education (**E**).

The probabilities that education (**E**) will be effective education (**E$_E$**) are enhanced with supportive attitudes in the community, and it is the ideal situation that the community is supportive, even enthusiastically supportive of the way in which education (**E**) is being conducted within families, schools and other educational institutions (churches, synagogues, mosques, temples, sporting clubs, recreational clubs, service clubs, etc.) in the community.

An example of community attitudes which were in opposition to official education (**E$_O$**) was that of community attitudes towards the

MACOS curriculum. MACOS, or *Man: A Course of Study*, arose from the initiative of the American psychologist, Jerome Seymour Bruner (1915-2016), of Harvard University. In the early 1960s, he collaborated with a team of curriculum developers and secured funding from the US National Science Foundation (NSF) to develop a curriculum, the aim of which was to provide elementary (primary) school students (years 4 through 6) with opportunities to develop a prescribed range of knowing-how ($\mathbf{K}_{2PK3}$) to conduct careful, well-disciplined inquiry (**Q**) about the place of humankind within the physical and living environment. Course materials included teachers' guides, reading materials, film cassettes, visual aids and games. The curriculum presented students with three recurrent questions.

(1) "What is human about human beings?"
(2) "How did they get that way?"
(3) "How can they be made more so?"

The course provided students with recurrent opportunities ("the spiral curriculum") to conceive answers (and refine answers) for these questions by studying$_1$ ($\mathbf{S}_{P1}$) the challenges which living organisms face in deriving a living from, surviving in and reproducing within their natural environments. Students were given opportunities to examine the similarities between the way human beings, on the one hand, and different species of animals (salmon, herring gulls, baboons), on the other, deal with and derive their living from the physical and living environment. The students were provided with the opportunity to conclude their inquiry (**Q**) by studying$_1$ ($\mathbf{S}_{P1}$) a society and a culture very different from their own, the nomadic hunting culture of the Netsilik Inuit of early 20th century in northern Canada.

Bruner explained that with the three recurrent questions and the supporting MACOS curriculum materials,

> We seek exercises and materials through which our pupils can learn wherein man [humankind] is distinctive in his [its] adaptation to the world, and wherein there is discernible continuity between him and his animal forbears. For man represents that crucial point in evolution where adaptation is achieved by the vehicle of culture, and only in a minor way by further changes in his morphology. Yet there are chemical tides that run in his blood that are as ancient as the reptiles. We make every effort at the outset to tell the children where we hope to travel with them. Yet little of such recounting gets through. It is much more useful, we have found, to pose the three questions directly to the children so that their own views can

> be brought into the open and so that they can establish some points of view of their own (Jerome Bruner, 1965, p. 5).

Many schools and school systems in the USA, Great Britain and Australia used the MACOS curriculum in the early 1970s, but schools ultimately abandoned the curriculum in the late 1970s largely because of strident well-organized community opposition. Conservative fundamentalist Christians interpreted the curriculum as a program of indoctrination in Darwinism, evolution and moral and cultural relativism, and an attack on their Christian faith (as they interpreted it), their belief in divine creation and their conviction that morality is divinely prescribed, rather than constructed by communities in relation to their environmental needs and adaptations. Although a minority within communities, the conservative fundamentalist Christians garnered sufficient political support to convince school authorities to remove MACOS from the curriculum. (See the 2004 documentary film, *Through These Eyes*, directed by Charles Laird, which chronicles the development, implementation and objections to the MACOS curriculum.)

An example of community attitudes which supported reforms to official education ($\mathbf{E}_\mathrm{O}$) was that of community attitudes towards the university and school reforms of 1984 and 85 in Kenya. Under the presidency of Daniel arap Moi (1924-2020), the second President of Kenya, Kenyatta University College was upgraded to university status (Kenyatta University, 1985), a third university (Moi University) was established (1984) and the school system was reorganized (1985) from a 7-4-2-3 into an 8-4-4 system. Seven years of primary school was reorganized into 8 years of primary school. Four years of lower secondary school and two years of upper secondary school were reorganized into four years of secondary school. Three years of university for the bachelor's degree were reorganized into four years of university for the bachelor's degree. The creation of two new universities and the reorganization of schools were viewed in the wider community as a further break with the colonial past, a development of an education system with a genuine Kenyan identity and a broadening of opportunities for the children and youth of Kenya to improve their prospects for employment, for contribution to nation building and for further economic prosperity. Wide community approval prevailed.

An example of community attitudes which support reforms to unofficial education ($\mathbf{E}_\mathrm{U}$) is that of a community which wants to establish a skate park with open access and free admission to the youth of the town. The current situation is that skateboarding is very popular among the children and youth of the community. All skateboarding education (**E**) in the community is unofficial education ($\mathbf{E}_U$). There are no skateboarding schools. Skateboarding education (**E**) is achieved peer to peer. The skateboarders learn (**L**) from each other. Sometimes one skateboarder learns intentionally with guidance (learns$_1$ <$\mathbf{L}_1$>) by playing the role of student (**S**) while another plays the role of teacher (**T**). At other times, skateboarders learn intentionally without guidance (learn$_2$ <$\mathbf{L}_2$>) from inquiry (**Q**) by watching and imitating other skateboarders or by trying movements themselves. The skateboarders are always striving to achieve new movements and thereby develop their postconventional (Level 4 or $\mathbf{K}_{2L4}$) discovered range of knowing-how (<$\mathbf{K}_{2DK3L4}$> which is the the union of <U> knowing <$\mathbf{K}_2$> with discovered knowing <$\mathbf{K}_{2D}$>, knowing-how <$\mathbf{K}_{2K3}$> and level 4 postconventional knowing <$\mathbf{K}_{2L4}$>). Almost all skateboarders in the community watch YouTube videos of champion skateboarders. The community does not as yet have a skate park, and the children and youth of the community desperately want one. They form an association, which they call "The Skate Park Foundation," and they enlist sympathetic adults to help them petition the local city council to establish a free skate park. A majority of members of the council agree that having a skate park would enrich the recreation facilities of the community. The council agrees to work with the Skate Park Foundation to fund the land acquisition and construction of the park. The Skate Park Foundation conducts fund raisers. The council allocates some funds. The Foundation and the council collaborate in developing submissions for funding from state and national bodies which provide funds for sporting facilities. From the combined efforts of the Skate Park Foundation and the council, sufficient funds are secured to finance the construction of a skate park. The skate park becomes a community center where children and youths congregate to engage in unofficial education ($\mathbf{E}_U$) and inquiry (**Q**) to develop their prescribed ($\mathbf{K}_{2P}$) and discovered ($\mathbf{K}_{2D}$) range of knowing-how ($\mathbf{K}_{2K3}$) about skate boarding.

Supportive Relationships for Effective Education

Each of the elements of education (**E**) has a mutual effect on each of the other elements. The relationship of mutual effects among the four elements of education (**T**, **S**, **C**, **X**) can be expressed as follows.

<**T** → **S**> and <**S** → **T**> or <**T** ⇄ **S**>
<**T** → **C**> and <**C** → **T**> or <**T** ⇄ **C**>
<**T** → **X**> and <**X** → **T**> or <**T** ⇄ **X**>
<**S** → **C**> and <**C** → **S**> or <**S** ⇄ **C**>
<**S** → **X**> and <**X** → **S**> or <**S** ⇄ **X**>
<**X** → **C**> and <**C** → **X**> or <**X** ⇄ **C**>
<**T** → **S ∪ C ∪ X**> and <**S ∪ C ∪ X** → **T**> or <**T** ⇄ **S ∪ C ∪ X**>
<**S** → **T ∪ C ∪ X**> and <**T ∪ C ∪ X** → **S**> or <**S** ⇄ **T ∪ C ∪ X**>
<**C** → **T ∪ S ∪ X**> and <**T ∪ S ∪ X** → **C**> or <**C** ⇄ **T ∪ S ∪ X**>
<**X** → **T ∪ S ∪ C**> and <**T ∪ S ∪ C** → **X**> or <**X** ⇄ **T ∪ S ∪ C**>

Expressed in ordinary English,

(1) <**T** → **S**> reads that the teacher (**T**) has effects on (→) the student (**S**), <**S** → **T**> reads that the student (**S**) has effects on (→) the teacher (**T**), and <**T** ⇄ **S**> reads that the teacher (**T**) and the student (**S**) have mutual effects (⇄).

(2) <**T** → **C**> reads that the teacher (**T**) has effects on (→) content (**C**), <**C** → **T**> reads that content (**C**) has effects on (→) the teacher (**T**), and <**T** ⇄ **C**> reads that the teacher (**T**) and content (**C**) have mutual effects (⇄).

(3) <**T** → **X**> reads that the teacher (**T**) has effects on (→) the context (**X**), <**X** → **T**> reads that the context (**X**) has effects on (→) the teacher (**T**), and <**T** ⇄ **X**> reads that the teacher (**T**) and context (**X**) have mutual effects (⇄).

(4) <**S** → **C**> reads that the student (**S**) has effects on (→) the content (**C**), <**C** → **S**> reads that the content (**C**) has effects on (→) the student (**S**), and <**S** ⇄ **C**> reads that the student (**S**) and content (**C**) have mutual effects (⇄).

(5) <**S** → **X**> reads that the student (**S**) has effects on (→) the context (**X**), <**X** → **S**> reads that the context (**X**) has effects on (→) the student (**S**), and <**S** ⇄ **X**> reads that student (**S**) and the context (**X**) have mutual effects (⇄).

(6) <**X** → **C**> reads that the context (**X**) has effects on (→) the content (**C**), <**C** → **X**> reads that the content (**C**) has effects on (→) the context (**X**), and <**C** ⇄ **X**> reads that content (**C**) and the context (**X**) have mutual effects (⇄).

(7) <**T** → **S ∪ C ∪ X**> reads that the teacher (**T**) has effects on (→) the union of (∪) the student (**S**), the content (**C**)

and the context (**X**), <**S ∪ C ∪ X → T**> reads that the union of (∪) the student (**S**), the content (**C**) and the context (**X**) has effects on (→) the teacher (**T**), and <**T ⇄ S ∪ C ∪ X**> reads that the teacher (**T**) and the union of (∪) the student (**S**), the content (**C**) and the context (**X**) have mutual effects (⇄).

(8) <**S → T ∪ C ∪ X**> reads that the student (**S**) has effects on (→) the union of (∪) the teacher (**T**), the content (**C**) and the context (**X**), <**T ∪ C ∪ X → S**> reads that the union of (∪) the teacher (**T**), the content (**C**) and the context (**X**) has effects on (→) the student (**S**), and <**S ⇄ T ∪ C ∪ X**> reads that the student (**S**) and the union of (∪) the teacher (**T**), the content (**C**) and the context (**X**) have mutual effects (⇄).

(9) <**C → T ∪ S ∪ X**> reads that the content (**C**) has effects on (→) the union of (∪) the teacher (**T**), the student (**S**) and the context (**X**), <**T ∪ S ∪ X → C**> reads that the union of (∪) the teacher (**T**), the student (**S**) and the context (**X**) has effects on (→) the content (**C**), and <**C ⇄ T ∪ S ∪ X**> reads that the content (**C**) and the union of (∪) the teacher (**T**), the student (**S**) and the context (**X**) have mutual effects (⇄).

(10) <**X → T ∪ S ∪ C**> reads that the context (**X**) has effects on (→) the union of (∪) the teacher (**T**), the student (**S**) and the content (**C**), <**T ∪ S ∪ C → X**> reads that the union of (∪) the teacher (**T**), the student (**S**) and the content (**C**) has effects on (→) the context (**X**), and <**X ⇄ T ∪ S ∪ C**> reads that the context (**X**) and the union of (∪) the teacher (**T**), the student (**S**) and the content (**C**) have mutual effects (⇄).

These ten pairs of mutual effects are extant in both official ($\mathbf{E_O}$) and unofficial ($\mathbf{E_U}$) education. Education (<**E**> which includes <$\mathbf{E_O}$> and <$\mathbf{E_U}$>) is a system with the elements of teacher (**T**), student (**S**), content (**C**) and context (**X**).

The mutual effects of the elements of education (**E**) are the controlling conditions for the relationships among the elements of education (**E**). The relationships among the elements of education (**E**) are dynamic, always in flux. The relationships range on a continuum from supportive, to neutral (or acquiescent) to oppositional. The relationships among the elements of education (**E**) can be expressed as follows.

$$\mathbf{R = R_S \; v \; R_N \; v \; R_O}$$

$$\mathbf{R \rightarrow E_E \; v \; E_I}$$

In ordinary English, the statement <$\mathbf{R = R_S \; v \; R_N \; v \; R_O}$> reads that the relationships (**R**) among the elements of education (**E**) are supportive relationships ($\mathbf{R_S}$) or (denoted by <**v**>) neutral (acquiescent) relationships ($\mathbf{R_N}$) or (**v**) oppositional relationships ($\mathbf{R_O}$).

In ordinary English, the statement <$\mathbf{R \rightarrow E_E \; v \; E_I}$> reads that the set of relationships (**R**) among the elements of education (**E**) is the set of determining conditions (denoted by <$\rightarrow$>) for the resultant of effective education ($\mathbf{E_E}$) and/or (denoted by <**v**>) ineffective education ($\mathbf{E_I}$).

The probabilities that education (**E**) will be effective ($\mathbf{E_E}$) are maximized when the relationships among the elements of education (**E**) are supportive. The probabilities that education (**E**) will be effecttive ($\mathbf{E_E}$) diminish as the relationships among the elements transition from supportive to neutral (acquiescence). The probabilities that education (**E**) will be ineffective ($\mathbf{E_I}$) increase when the relationships among the elements of education (**E**) are oppositional. These relationships can be expressed as follows.

$$\mathbf{R_N \rightarrow E_E \; v \; E_I}$$

$$\mathbf{\uparrow R_S \rightarrow \uparrow P_{EE}}$$

$$\mathbf{\uparrow R_O \rightarrow \uparrow P_{EI}}$$

In ordinary English, the statement <$\mathbf{R_N \rightarrow E_E \; v \; E_I}$> reads that the set of neutral (acquiescent) relationships ($\mathbf{R_N}$) among the elements (**T, S, C, X**) of education (**E**) is the set of controlling conditions for ($\rightarrow$) the resultant of effective education ($\mathbf{E_E}$) and/or (**v**) the resultant of ineffective education ($\mathbf{E_I}$). In other words, neutral relationships among the elements of education can result in either effective education or ineffective education.

In ordinary English, the statement <$\mathbf{\uparrow R_S \rightarrow \uparrow P_{EE}}$> reads that as the amount and/or intensity of supportive relationships among the elements (**T, S, C, X**) of education (**E**) increases (denoted by <$\mathbf{\uparrow R_S}$>) the resultant is (denoted by <$\rightarrow$>) an increase in the probability of effective education (denoted by <$\mathbf{\uparrow P_{EE}}$>).

In ordinary English, the statement <$\mathbf{\uparrow R_O \rightarrow \uparrow P_{EI}}$> reads that as the amount and/or intensity of oppositional relationships among the elements (**T, S, C, X**) of education (**E**) increases (denoted by <$\mathbf{\uparrow R_O}$>), the resultant is (denoted by <→>) an increase in the probability of ineffective education (denoted by <$\uparrow \mathbf{P_{EI}}$>).

To maximize the probabilities that education (**E**) will be effective (**E**$_E$), the general praxiological educological principle to follow in education (**E**) is for all players (**T**, **S**, **X**) in education (**E**) to establish and maintain supportive or highly supportive relationships (**R**$_S$) among the elements (**T**, **S**, **C**, **X**) of education (**E**) and to transform neutral, oppositional and highly oppositional relationships (**R**$_O$) into supportive or highly supportive ones (**R**$_S$).

Productive Practices for Effective Education

In addition to constructive states of mind and supportive relationships, practices by students, teachers and third parties (i.e. parties who constitute the context of education) have effects on the effectiveness and/or ineffectiveness of education. There are practices by students, teachers and third parties that increase the probabilities that education will be effective, and there are practices which increase the probabilities that education will be ineffective.

Constructive Practices by Students

Actions which students (**S**) can take to increase the probabilities that education (**E**) will be effective (**E**$_E$) include

(1) identifying major definite purposes, aims, goals and/or objectives to pursue,

(2) identifying ranges of knowing required to achieve major definite purposes, aims, goals and/or objectives,

(3) selecting study$_1$ (**S**$_{P1}$) activities and/or courses of study$_1$ (**S**$_{P1}$) to learn$_1$ (**L**$_1$) the requisite (prescribed) ranges of knowing (**K**$_{2P}$),

(4) deliberately striving to achieve authentically chosen intended learning outcomes (**ILO**s) through the selected study$_1$ (**S**$_{P1}$) and/or courses of study$_1$ (**S**$_{P1}$),

(5) explicitly placing and demonstrating trust in the teacher's guidance, help and judgment,

(6) explicitly demonstrating respect for the teacher's abilities, qualities, achievements and rights in the role of teacher,

(7) explicitly accepting opportunities to study$_1$ (**S**$_{P1}$) the

relevant content (**C**) to $learn_1$ ($\mathbf{L_1}$) the prescribed range of knowing ($\mathbf{K_{2P}}$) that is specified by the authentically chosen intended learning outcomes (**ILO**s),

(8) willingly completing $study_1$ ($\mathbf{S_{P1}}$) activities that are relevant to $learn_1$ ($\mathbf{L_1}$) the prescribed range of knowing ($\mathbf{K_{2P}}$) that is specified by the authentically chosen intended learning outcomes (**ILO**s),

(9) willingly conducting appropriate practice with some newly acquired prescribed range of knowing ($\mathbf{K_{2P}}$),

(10) willingly using some newly acquired prescribed range of knowing ($\mathbf{K_{2P}}$) to solve a range of problems, some familiar and some novel, some simple and some complex,

(11) willingly extending some newly acquired prescribed range of knowing ($\mathbf{K_{2P}}$) through additional inquiry (**Q**),

(12) willingly emending an extant range of knowing ($\mathbf{K_{2KLF}}$) to accommodate the newly acquired prescribed range of knowing ($\mathbf{K_{2P}}$) and

(13) willingly integrating some newly acquired prescribed range of knowing ($\mathbf{K_{2P}}$) with the extant range of knowing ($\mathbf{K_{2KLF}}$).

Identifying Major Definite Purposes, Aims, Goals and/or Objectives to Pursue

Persons playing the role of student (**S**) increase the probability that their education (**E**) will be effective ($\mathbf{E_E}$) by identifying, clarifying and expressing to themselves (in spoken and/or written statements) the major definite purposes, aims, goals and/or objectives that they wish to pursue and/or achieve. The expression can be as simple, immediate and short-term as a child asking another child to show the first child how to play "Rock, Paper, Scissors." The major definite purposes of the first child are to have fun by playing a fast and exciting game, to have the enjoyment of competing with a peer and to share an experience with a friend. The major definite purpose may be more complex and long-term, such as wanting to qualify as a professional soccer player, work as a concert pianist or practice medicine as a dermatologist. Whatever the major definite purpose, it establishes the basis for conducting inquiry (**Q**) about some object of knowing ($\mathbf{O_{K2}}$) and/or intentional guided $study_1$ ($\mathbf{S_{P1}}$) of some content (**C**) to $learn_1$ ($\mathbf{L_1}$) some authentically chosen prescribed range of knowing ($\mathbf{K_{2P}}$). Intentional guided $study_1$ ($\mathbf{S_{P1}}$) which is driven by purpose, aims, goals and/or objectives increases the probability that the education (**E**) which the student undertakes will be effective education ($\mathbf{E_E}$).

Identifying Ranges of Knowing Required to Achieve Major Definite Purposes, Aims, Goals and/or Objectives

Persons playing the role of student (**S**) increase the probability that their education (**E**) will be effective ($\mathbf{E_E}$) by identifying, clarifying and expressing to themselves (in spoken and/or written statements) the ranges of knowing ($\mathbf{K_{2KLF}}$) that they need to achieve to attain their chosen major definite purpose, aim, goal and/or objective.

Marcus is a boy of age six. He is just starting 1st grade (year 1) of school. He wants to learn to count, add, subtract and multiply and do whatever else can be done with numbers. He wants to know how to do these things because he loves numbers. His major definite purpose is to feel the pleasure and satisfaction which he derives from doing things with numbers. He has made up his mind that mathematics is the subject for him, and he is keen to undertake $study_1$ activities ($\mathbf{S_{P1}}$) to learn ($\mathbf{L_1}$) mathematics.

There are as many major definite purposes as there are human beings. Each human being is unique, and the purposes which each human chooses to pursue is unique. Frank decides at a young age that he wants to play professional baseball. The range of knowing which he wants to develop is knowing how to play baseball at the level of professional players. Letitia wants to be a professional politician at the federal level of politics. The range of knowing which she wants to develop includes knowing about how government works, how to garner support for nominations, how to raise funds for election campaigns, how to conduct persuasive arguments, how to form alliances, how to negotiate to achieve mutually agreeable outcomes, how to follow and lead within a political party, how to form policies which will attract support, how to handle interrogations from the press, how to present an attractive public image, etc. Allen decides that he would like to work as a commercial airline pilot. He realizes that to achieve this goal, he needs to develop a range of knowing about how to operate and navigate aircraft. The range of knowing that she wants to learn is how to handle all the medical aspects of eye care, including treatment, surgery and the prescription of contact lenses and glasses as well as medicines for eye problems.

Selecting Courses of Study to Develop the Nominated Ranges of Knowing

The persons playing the role of student (**S**) increase the probability that their education (**E**) will be effective (**E_E**) by selecting courses of study$_1$ (**S_{P1}**) that allow them to develop the range of knowing which they have identified as relevant to helping them achieve their major definite purposes, aims, goals and/or objectives.

For example, Henry decides that he would like to work as a CAD (computer assisted design) drafter with an engineering, manufacturing and/or architectural firm. He conducts some inquiry about courses in how to use AutoCAD software. He finds that his local technical and further education college provides a series of courses in the use of AutoCAD. The courses include the study of the drafting capabilities of AutoCAD and the editing functions of AutoCAD, including drawing, modifying, layering, linetypes, lineweights, colors, blocks, attributes, hatching, text, dimensioning, title blocks, scaling, printing and plotting. Henry applies for enrolment in the course. He is successful in his application, and he proceeds with the introductory course in AutoCAD.

As a second example, Melanie, as a child, has always been interested in cooking and food preparation. As she approaches the completion of secondary school, she decides that she would like to pursue a career as a chef or perhaps running her own restaurant. She starts searching for courses which provide opportunities to develop the range of knowing that she requires to qualify as a chef and also to run her own restaurant. She finds a private college in a nearby city which advertises courses that combine practical cookery, internships in commercial kitchens and study of how to develop a business plan and run a restaurant or café business. She applies for admission to the college.

Deliberately Striving to Achieve Intended Learning Outcomes (ILOs)

Persons playing the role of student (**S**) increase the probability that their education (**E**) will be effective (**E_E**) by deliberately striving to achieve the intended learning outcomes (**ILO**s) which have been nominated (either by teachers, students, some third party or some combination of the three). Deliberately striving to achieve a nominated set of intended learning outcomes (**ILO**s) is not a matter of being passive, obedient and/or conforming. Rather it is the habituated practice of genuinely seeking to understand the implicative meaning of the nominated intended learning outcomes (**ILO**s), authentically endeavoring to achieve the prescribed range of knowing (**K_{2P}**) implied by the intended learning outcomes (**ILO**s), reflecting upon the progress being made in achieving the prescribed range of knowing (**K_{2P}**), seeking evaluation from the teacher about the degree to which progress is being made in achieving the intended learning outcomes (**ILO**s) and determining what else needs to be done to achieve the prescribed range of knowing (**K_{2P}**).

The opposite is also true. Persons playing the role of student (**S**) increase the probability that education (**E**) will be ineffective (**E_I**) by deliberately avoiding to strive to achieve the intended outcomes (**ILO**s). If, when we play the role of student (**S**), we choose to ignore and/or dismiss the intended learning outcomes (**ILO**s), to sit back and disengage and/or reject the opportunities to study$_1$ (**S_{P1}**) or to be reluctantly dragged along and cajoled and/or coerced into engaging in study$_1$ (**S_{P1}**) activities, or to disengage from study$_1$ (**S_{P1}**) activities as soon as supervision is not focused on us, we reduce the probabilities that our study$_1$ (**S_{P1}**) activities will be successful and that the education (**E**) in which we are engaging will be effective (**E_E**) for us, and we increase the probabilities that the education (**E**) in which we are engaging will be ineffective (**E_I**).

Explicitly Demonstrating Trust in the Teacher

In playing the role of student (**S**) we increase the probability that our education (**E**) will be effective (**E_E**) by explicitly demonstrating trust in our teacher's guidance, help and judgment. Once again, this is not a matter of passivity, obedience and conformity. Rather it is placing ourselves in the position of attending attentively, accepting willingly and using actively the guidance, help and judgment provided by our teacher (**T**) to undertake opportunities to study$_1$ (**S_{P1}**) and to extend our prescribed range of knowing (**K_{2P}**) in relation to our nominated intended learning outcomes (**ILO**s).

A trainee metal lathe operator places his (or her) trust in the leading hand who demonstrates how to operate the lathe to produce a machinist's hammer. A trainee surgeon places his (or her trust) in the senior surgeon who demonstrates how to replace an aortic value using the procedure of transcatheter aortic valve replacement (TAVR). A trainee pilot places his (or her) trust in the senior training pilot who demonstrates how to complete the checklist for take-off in a Beechcraft G36 Bonanza. A 9th grade (year 9) girl places her trust in her English teacher who provides instruction on how to write a Shakespearean sonnet with 14 iambic pentameter lines divided into three quatrains and a couplet.

In none of these examples do the students (**S**), in exercising their trust, have any commitment to passivity, obedience and/or conformity. Their focus is on trusting the guidance of their teachers and on mastering the prescribed range of knowing ($\mathbf{K}_{2P}$) that they have chosen to learn intentionally and under guidance (learn$_1$ <$\mathbf{L}_1$>).

Explicitly Demonstrating Respect for the Teacher

Persons playing the role of student (**S**) increase the probability that their education (**E**) will be effective ($\mathbf{E}_E$) by explicitly demonstrating respect for their teacher's abilities, qualities, achievements and rights in the role of teacher. Respectfulness is not a matter of being passive, conformist, obedient, obsequious, unctuous or sycophantic. Rather, respectfulness is genuine and authentic admiration, appreciation and caring. The admiration is an esteem (or approbation) for the teacher's abilities, qualities and achievements. The appreciation is a valuing of the teacher's abilities, qualities and achievements. The caring is having consideration and due regard for the rights and well-being of the teacher. Respectfulness expressed by students for teachers is not a relationship of underclass to overclass, or of submissives to dominants. Respectfulness, for example, is admiration, appreciation and caring shown by a junior surgeon to a senior surgeon in acknowledgement of the extensive range of knowing ($\mathbf{K}_{2KLF}$) of the senior surgeon, or the respect shown by an apprentice builder to a master builder, or of an apprentice seaman to a master seaman, or of a trainee pilot to a senior flight instructor. Expressions of respectfulness are expressions of genuine and authentic admiration, appreciation and caring by someone (a student <**S**>) with a lesser range of knowing ($\mathbf{K}_{2KLF}$) for someone (a teacher <**T**>) with a more extensive range of knowing ($\mathbf{K}_{2KLF}$) who is willing to provide opportunities, guidance and help in the process of extending the student's desired range of knowing ($\mathbf{K}_{2KLF}$).

Explicitly Accepting Opportunities to Study$_1$ (S_{P1})

Persons playing the role of student (**S**) increase the probability that their education (**E**) will be effective (E_E) by explicitly accepting opportunities to study$_1$ (S_{P1}). The opportunity to study$_1$ (S_{P1}) is not an obligation. Rather, it is an offering, an opening, an option or an avenue to engage in activities that can lead to achieving a new range of knowing (K_{2KLF}). When we, playing the role of student (**S**), embrace the opportunity to study intentionally under guidance (S_{P1}) and proceed willingly with the study$_1$ (S_{P1}) activities, we increase the probability that the education (**E**) in which we engage ourselves will be effective education (E_E). Likewise, when we reject the opportunity to study under guidance (S_{P1}), we are assuring that we will not achieve learning$_1$ (L_1) of the prescribed range of knowing (K_{2P}) that is specified by some set of intended learning outcomes (**ILO**s).

Willingly Completing Study (S_{P1}) Activities

Once having accepted the opportunities to study$_1$ (S_{P1}), persons playing the role of student (**S**) increase the probability that their education (**E**) will be effective (E_E) by proceeding to complete the study$_1$ (S_{P1}) activities on offer with genuine engagement and good faith. If the study$_1$ (S_{P1}) activities are not completed, the probabilities are greatly diminished (or even drop to nil) that intentional guided learning (L_1) will take place and that the resultant prescribed range of knowing (K_{2P}) as specified by the intended learning outcomes (**ILO**s) will be achieved.

Consider the example of Georgina. She likes mathematics, and she has ranked at the top of her classes in mathematics in middle school and high school. In her last year in secondary school, she investigates careers in which she might be able to use her mathematical talents. She finds some information about actuarial science, and the description of work done by actuaries in the insurance industry, pension funds and social welfare programs appeals to her. She conducts some inquiry and finds that a university near her home city provides a bachelor's degree program in actuarial science. She applies and gains admission to the program. The first course of the program is financial accounting. The topics for study$_1$ (S_{P1}) include measurement systems and their relationship with accounting, double-entry and accrual accounting, assets, liabilities, incomes, expenses, financial statements, types of business structures (sole trader, partnerships, companies, trusts). The study$_1$ ($\mathbf{S}_{P1}$) activities consist of weekly tasks of reading, summarizing and problem solving, sometimes working as an individual and sometimes working in teams with fellow students. Georgina likes the independence afforded in university life. She draws up a timetable for study$_1$ ($\mathbf{S}_{P1}$) outside of class to establish for herself a routine for study$_1$ ($\mathbf{S}_{P1}$) on a daily basis and follows the timetable. In doing so, she allocates sufficient time to complete all study$_1$ ($\mathbf{S}_{P1}$) tasks required for the course. Georgina exemplifies a student (**S**) who completes the study$_1$ ($\mathbf{S}_{P1}$) activities on offer with genuine engagement and good faith. In doing so, she increases the probability that her education (**E**) in actuarial science will be effective ($\mathbf{E}_{E}$) for her.

As a counter example, Bradley, like Georgina, is in the last year of secondary school. He has achieved high enough grades in his classes, and also sufficiently high scores on his SAT (Scholastic Aptitude Test), to gain admission to the university of his choice. Bradley has heard from his friends and family that a person can make a lot more money as a business owner than as an employee, and that appeals to him. He decides that he wants to establish his own business. After high school, he elects to enroll in a bachelor's degree program in business management. One of the first classes which he is required to study$_1$ ($\mathbf{S}_{P1}$) in the program is financial accounting. The topics for study$_1$ ($\mathbf{S}_{P1}$) include measurement systems and their relationship with accounting, double-entry and accrual accounting, assets, liabilities, incomes, expenses, financial statements, types of business structures (sole trader, partnerships, companies, trusts). The study$_1$ ($\mathbf{S}_{P1}$) activities consist of weekly tasks of reading, summarizing and problem solving, sometimes working as an individual and sometimes working in teams with fellow students. Bradley finds it all a big bore. He wants credit for the course, but he doesn't want to do the work that the course requires. He locates and hires someone who has completed the course and is willing to do Bradley's assignments for him for a substantial fee. There are no exams in the course. The grades assigned are based on a series of case studies, problem sets and research reports. Bradley's proxy completes all the case studies, problem sets and research reports, and Bradley submits them as his work. Bradley's subterfuge goes undetected, and he is awarded a satisfactory grade for the course. Bradley exemplifies a student (**S**) who refuses to complete the study$_1$ ($\mathbf{S}_{P1}$) activities on offer with genuine engagement and good faith. In doing so, he eliminates any probability that his education (**E**) in financial accounting will be effective (**E_E**) for him. He achieves his goal of certification (fraudulently), but he obviously does not have the prescribed range of knowing (**K_{2P}**) for which the certification is supposed to be a testament.

Willingly Conducting Appropriate Practice

Persons playing the role of student (**S**) increase the probability that their education (**E**) will be effective (**E_E**) by willingly conducting appropriate practice with some newly acquired prescribed range of knowing (**K_{2P}**) with a view to extending their range of knowing in kind, level and form (**K_{2KLF}**).

For example, Philippa, at age 6, sees a video of the American dancer, Eleanor Powell (1912-1982), perform a tap dance routine. Powell's performance inspires Philippa, and she tells her parents that she wants to learn to tap dance like Eleanor Powell. Her parents tell her that it is a wonderful aspiration, and they enroll her in a dance school. Over a series of elementary lessons, Philippa's teacher shows her the basic moves in tap dancing – ball dig, heel drop, ball-heel, brush forward, brush back, shuffle, ball-heel shuffle. Her teacher encourages her to practice the basic moves at home. Philippa is very keen, and she practices each move that is introduced in her lessons. She starts with the ball dig, going slowly at first, then gradually going faster and faster. She repeats her daily practice routine with each of the basic moves. She continues with her tap dance lessons for the next 8 years, until at age 14, she has achieved a high degree of proficiency in tap dancing (conventional expert level knowing <**K_{2L3}**>). Philippa's practice of tap dancing over those 8 years, from age 6 to age 14, exemplifies a student (S) who willingly conducts appropriate practice with some newly acquired prescribed range of knowing (**K_{2P}**) with a view to extending her range of knowing in kind, level and form (**K_{2KLF}**).

In a second example, Kevin is in 7th grade (year 7). His first language is English, and his school offers Mandarin as an elective $study_1$ (**S_{P1}**). Kevin decides that he would like to $learn_1$ (**L_1**) how to speak, listen to (and comprehend), read and write Mandarin. He chooses Mandarin as his elective language to $study_1$ (**S_{P1}**), and he completes all $study_1$ (**S_{P1}**) activities offered in his Mandarin course. In addition to the in-class $study_1$ (**S_{P1}**) activities, Kevin practices his Mandarin at home. He allocates time to speak Mandarin, to record his speech and to compare his pronunciation with recordings of people who speak Mandarin as their first language. At home, he also practices listening to recordings of Mandarin to develop his comprehension of spoken Mandarin. He reads articles and books written in Mandarin on a regular basis. He practices writing Chinese characters and composing sentences, short stories and essays written in Chinese. Kevin borrows DVD recordings of Mandarin language movies, watches the movies and uses the movies as a means of improving his comprehension of Mandarin. Kevin continues his study$_1$ ($\mathbf{S_{P1}}$) of Mandarin in school from 7th through 12th grade (years 7 through 12), and he continues to practice his Mandarin outside of school. By 12th grade (year 12), Kevin has developed his Mandarin speaking, listening comprehension, reading comprehension and written expression to a high degree of proficiency (conventional expert level knowing <$\mathbf{K_{2L3}}$>). Kevin's practice of Mandarin over those 6 years, from age 12 to age 18, exemplifies a student (**S**) who willingly conducts appropriate practice with some newly acquired prescribed range of knowing ($\mathbf{K_{2P}}$) with a view to extending his range of knowing in kind, level and form ($\mathbf{K_{2KLF}}$).

Willingly Using Some Newly Acquired Range of Knowing ($\mathbf{K_{2KLF}}$)

Persons playing the role of student (**S**) increase the probability that their education (**E**) will be effective ($\mathbf{E_E}$) by willingly using some newly acquired prescribed range of knowing ($\mathbf{K_{2P}}$) to solve a range of problems, some familiar and some novel, some simple and some complex.

For example, Rodrigo is a high school student (10th grade or year 10), and for one of his subjects, he is studying$_1$ ($\mathbf{S_{P1}}$) graphic technology. Rodrigo and his classmates have developed proficiency in using the basic functions of a 3D CAD (three-dimensional computer assisted design) system to produce technical drawings. Rodrigo's teacher presents his class with the task of using their 3D CAD system to create a technical drawing for a household object made from timber (a stool, a cabinet, a chair, etc.). The object is to have no metal fasteners (screws, nails, staples, etc.). The joints are to be secured by dowls and/or mortise and tendon, dovetail, half-lap and/or square joints. Rodrigo decides to design a shoeshine box for his father. He wants the box to be large enough to hold brushes, cans of shoe polish and polishing cloths, and he wants it to be high enough that his father, while he sits, can rest his foot on top of the box to polish his shoe, one shoe at a time. Rodrigo creates a design for a shoeshine box which resembles a miniature house with a gabled roof. The dimensions of the box are 25 cm in height, 30 cm in length and 24 cm in width. The box is held together with dovetail joints and dowls. Rodrigo specifies that the timber be camphor wood, 1 cm thick, except for the footrest, which is to be 2 cm thick. He specifies that the finish be a clear acrylic coating on the inside and outside. In creating the design for a shoeshine box, Rodrigo is clearly using his newly acquired prescribed range of knowing ($\mathbf{K}_{2P}$) how to use a 3D CAD system to solve the complex problem of designing a household object constructed from timber and joined without metal fasteners.

As another example, Sarah is age 12, and she has been studying$_1$ ($\mathbf{S}_{P1}$) rhythmic gymnastics since she was 8. She has specialized in the ribbon as her apparatus, and she has become proficient in the basic elements (or movements) with the ribbon, including holding the handle of the stick correctly (correct grip), making coils, snakes, small, medium and large circles, switching hands, stepping through circles and executing tosses. In addition, Sarah has been practicing floor poses and movements (arabesque, curtsey, demi-plié, cat steps, jump, leap, etc.). Her gymnastics teacher has now presented her with the problem to solve of how to synchronize a selection of music lasting 2¼ to 2½ minutes with a smooth and flowing combination of correctly executed elements of the ribbon, floor poses and movements that end exactly with the conclusion of the music. Sarah proceeds to search for suitable music. She listens to several pieces and selects her preferred music. She edits the music to a duration of 2 minutes and 22 seconds. She selects the sequence of elements that she wants to perform. She selects the floor poses and movements and makes plans for their sequence. She proceeds to practice her performance in 10 second segments. She eventually puts all the segments together into a smooth flowing, well-coordinated performance. She makes necessary adjustments to parts of her performance to assure that her performance is completed at the moment the music stops. She arranges for video recordings of her performance, and she studies the recordings with a view to improving her elements, poses and movements. She continues to practice and make adjustments to her routine until she achieves the standard of performance to which she aspires in synchronization of the ribbon elements, poses, floor movements and music. In this example, Sarah exemplifies a student (**S**) who willingly uses her newly acquired prescribed range of knowing ($\mathbf{K_{2P}}$) of the basic elements, poses and movements of rhythmic gymnastics to solve the complex problem of developing a smooth flowing rhythmic gymnastics performance with the ribbon, and in producing a solution to her problem, she extends her range of knowing ($\mathbf{K_{2KLF}}$) of rhythmic gymnastics.

Willingly Extending Some Newly Acquired Range of Knowing ($\mathbf{K_{2KLF}}$)

Persons playing the role of student (**S**) increase the probability that their education (**E**) will be effective ($\mathbf{E_E}$) by willingly extending some newly acquired prescribed range of knowing ($\mathbf{K_{2P}}$) through additional inquiry (**Q**).

For example, Fatima is a girl, age 9. She is in the 3rd grade (year 3). Her teacher, Mr Faisal, in preparation for his students to develop their prescribed range of knowing ($\mathbf{K_{2P}}$) of fractions, has presented some lessons on whole objects and partitioning whole objects into equal parts. With Mr Faisal's help, Fatima has achieved, in her prescribe range of knowing ($\mathbf{K_{2P}}$), an understanding that the term <*whole*> denotes an entire object such as a whole cake, a whole apple or a whole watermelon, that the term <*partition*> denotes a separating of a whole object into parts such as cutting a slice of a cake, cutting a slice of an apple or cutting a slice of a watermelon, and that the term <*part*> denotes the portion of a whole object that is partitioned such as the slice of a cake, a slice of an apple or a slice of a watermelon. Mr Faisal gives each of his students, Fatima included, a set of Cuisenaire rods, and he demonstrates with an orange rod (representing 10). He says,

> Let this orange rod be the whole object. Let's partition it into two equal parts with two yellow rods (representing 5). We can write, *The whole orange rod = 1, and the two yellow parts = 2/2.* We read the numerals *2/2* as *two parts of two*, and we read *2/2 = 1* as *two parts of two equal parts is the same as 1 whole.*

Mr Faisal says to the class,

> Now let's take the blue rod (representing 9), and let's call the blue rod the whole object. Let's partition it into three equal parts with the three light green rods (each representing 3). We can write <*The whole blue rod = 1*> and <*the three light green parts = 3/3.*>. We read the numerals <*3/3*> as <*three parts of three equal parts*>, and we read <*3/3 = 1*> as <*three parts of three equal parts are the same as one whole*>.

Mr Faisal continues,

> The value of the numeral <*1*> is one, so if <*2/2 = 1*>, and <*3/3*

= *1*>, then <*2/2* = *3/3*> because both groups of parts make one whole.

Mr Faisal then tells his class to take each of the rods, starting from the largest, see how many parts each of the rods can be partitioned into and write each group of parts they find as <*2/2*>, <*3/3*>, <*4/4*>, <*5/5*>, etc. Fatima, with her classmates, proceed to make partitions of each of the rods and record what they find. In making the partitions, Fatima is conducting inquiry (**Q**), using her understanding of the terms <*whole*>, <*partition*> and <*part*>, to extend her prescribed range of knowing ($\mathbf{K_{2P}}$) of the partitions that are possible with the numbers ranging from one to ten.

As a second example, the American chemist, Harry Wesley Coover Jr (1917-2011) earned a Bachelor of Science, a Master of Science and a PhD, specializing in chemistry. He used the range of knowing ($\mathbf{K_{2KLF}}$) which he developed from his university studies$_1$ ($\mathbf{S_{P1}}$) to pursue a career in chemical research. He was hired by the Eastman Kodak company to conduct research on a number of projects, and during the course of his inquiry (**Q**), he developed a cyanoacrylate compound (1942) in an effort to create a material suitable for use in clear plastic gunsights. The compound proved unsuitable for gunsights, but several years later (1958), Coover recognized the possible uses for cyanoacrylate compounds for a quick-drying, extremely strong bonding agent. The compound was eventually marketed as Super Glue. Thus, Coover, used a prescribed range of knowing ($\mathbf{K_{2P}}$) learned$_1$ ($\mathbf{L_1}$) from his university studies to conduct inquiry (**Q**) and thereby extend his range of knowing ($\mathbf{K_{2KLF}}$) about cyanoacrylate compounds.

As a third example, Hadley is a 13-year-old boy in the 8th grade (year 7). His class has just completed a unit of study$_1$ ($\mathbf{S_{P1}}$) about animals which organize themselves into societies, and one of the animal groups that he studied$_1$ ($\mathbf{S_{P1}}$) was ants. Hadley has found the unit very interesting. From his studies$_1$ ($\mathbf{S_{P1}}$), he has achieved the prescribed range of knowing ($\mathbf{K_{2P}}$) that ants form societies, they live in colonies, they divide into discrete physical forms (queens, workers, soldiers, drones), and they cannot survive alone as individuals. Hadley decides that he would like to develop further his range of knowing ($\mathbf{K_2}$) about ants and that he would like to establish and develop his own colony of ants at home. He conducts unguided inquiry (**Q**) about suitable habitats for ants, how to recognize, catch and care for a queen, how to provide an environment in which an ant colony will thrive, what foods ants prefer, how much food to provide a colony, what diseases ants might develop and how to prevent those diseases. After conducting his inquiry (**Q**), Hadley proceeds to build an ant habitat from a disused fish tank. He observes the types of ants in his neighborhood and their mating season. He searches for and captures a queen ant without harming it. He provides care for the queen ant in the initial stages when the queen lays its first eggs and attends to its larvae. He establishes conditions for the queen and her new workers to transfer themselves from their initial habitat to a new habitat. Hadley's example is a clear case of a student (**S**) who uses a newly acquired prescribed range of knowing ($\mathbf{K}_{2P}$) acquired from his initial guided studies$_1$ ($\mathbf{S}_{P1}$) to conduct unguided inquiry (**Q**) and thereby extend his range of knowing ($\mathbf{K}_{2KLF}$) to new kinds, levels and forms of knowing (discovered knowing <$\mathbf{K}_{2D}$>).

Willingly Emending an Extant Range of Knowing ($\mathbf{K}_{2KLF}$)

Persons playing the role of student (**S**) increase the probability that their education (**E**) will be effective ($\mathbf{E}_E$) by willingly emending an extant range of knowing ($\mathbf{K}_{2KLF}$) to accommodate some newly acquired prescribed range of knowing ($\mathbf{K}_{2P}$).

Lawrence is a young man (age 27), and he uses his computer on a regular basis. He uses his two index fingers to key in data (words and numbers) on his keyboard. He decides that he would like to become more efficient in the use of the keyboard, and he enrolls in a touch typing course in his local technical and further education college. He follows the guidance of his instructor and completes the study$_1$ ($\mathbf{S}_{P1}$) exercises. Over a ten-week course, he develops sufficient proficiency to be able to touch type at the rate of 20 words per minute with two mistakes. He decides that this rate is too slow, and he enrolls in a second ten-week touch typing course to develop his speed and accuracy. By the end of the second course, he improves his speed and accuracy to 45 words per minute with only two mistakes. He is satisfied with his progress. He abandons his two-finger typing (his previous range of knowing <$\mathbf{K}_{2KLF}$>) and replaces it with his newly developed touch typing skill (his newly acquired prescribed range of knowing <$\mathbf{K}_{2P}$>).

A second example is that of the Australian novelty performer, Shannen Jones (see interview with Kobi Facto, 2020). Shannen (b. 2000) started her study$_1$ ($\mathbf{S}_{P1}$) of ballet and gymnastics at the age of four.

As a young girl and teenager, she continued her study$_1$ (**S_{P1}**) of rhythmic gymnastics throughout primary and secondary school. As she approached the completion of high school, she had developed an extensive range of knowing (**K_{2KLF}**) of how to perform rhythmic gymnastic and contortionist poses and movements. She found that the performance side of gymnastics attracted her more than competitions. On a whim, she decided to try busking. Her initial street performances consisted of 5 to 10 minute routines of contortionist poses and movements. To attract audiences, she waved at people with her feet while doing handstands or manipulated a Rubik's Cube™ with her feet while performing handstands. She worked on her skills in establishing rapport with audiences and on extending her performances into 15, 20 and 30-minute routines. She extended her performances to include foot-archery while doing handstands. She also conducted inquiry (**Q**) to connect with other novelty performers, to find a mentor who could advise her how to improve her performances and to identify venues and events in which she could perform. The case of Shannen Jones is clearly an example of a person who has willingly emended her extant prescribed range of knowing (**K_{2P}**) about gymnastic and contortionist performances to accommodate newly acquired (through inquiry <**Q**>) ranges of knowing (**K_{2KLF}**) about routines, communities, mentors, venues and events for novelty performances.

A third example is that of Alistair. He started playing golf with his friends when he was 34. He has never taken any golf lessons, and what he knows about how to play golf has been learned$_2$ (**L_2**) by listening to and watching his friends play. At age 38, Alistair is at the stage in his game where he would like to improve significantly. He would like to lower his handicap. He would like to reduce or even eliminate his frequency of top hitting balls. He would like to reduce or eliminate the number of slices and hooks in his game. He would like to improve the distance and placement of his drives and the accuracy of his putts. He decides that he would probably benefit from some golf lessons. Alistair enrolls in some golf lessons with the golf pro of his local golf course. The pro provides instruction, guidance and advice on

(1) how to keep the mind focused (**F**) on the present while playing a game of golf,
(2) how to practice the fundamentals of golf (grip, posture, distance from the ball, alignment to the target, shape and

tempo of the swing),

(3) how to visualize (perceive$_2$ <**P**$_2$>) in the imagination the target and shot shape,

(4) how to imagine (perceive$_2$ <**P**$_2$>) the desired feel (perception$_3$ <**P**$_3$>) of the swing,

(5) how to establish and maintain the same productive routine to follow before, during and after each shot,

(6) how to develop and use emotional knowing (**K**$_{2F2}$) to achieve and maintain a perception (perception$_1$ <**P**$_1$>) of calmness and tranquility while playing,

(7) how to develop and maintain an emotional state of acceptance of and indifference to (perception$_1$ <**P**$_1$>) each shot, whether it be good or bad.

Alistair heeds the advice, help and guidance (the teaching <**T**$_P$>) of his golf pro. He practices (studies$_1$ <**S**$_{P1}$>) each of the seven components which his pro advises him to practice, and Alistair learns$_1$ (**L**$_1$) to make the components become part of his prescribe range of knowing (**K**$_{2P}$) about golf. He emends the range of knowing (**K**$_{2KLF}$) which he had developed before his golf lessons to accommodate his new prescribed range of knowing (**K**$_{2P}$) about golf, and over a period of six months, he consequently improves his game substantially in the ways that he aspired to improve.

Willingly Integrating a Newly Acquired Range of Knowing (K$_{2KLF}$) with an Extant Range of Knowing (K$_{2KLF}$)

Persons playing the role of student (**S**) increase the probability that their education (**E**) will be effective (**E**$_E$) by willingly integrating some newly acquired prescribed range of knowing (**K**$_{2P}$) with their extant range of knowing (**K**$_{2KLF}$).

Students are integrating their newly acquired prescribed range of knowing (**K**$_{2P}$) with their previously developed range of knowing (**K**$_{2KLF}$) when they are connecting, relating and/or unifying their newly acquired prescribed range of knowing (**K**$_{2P}$) with their prior range of knowing (**K**$_{2KLF}$). Students achieve integration of their range of knowing (**K**$_{2KLF}$) by

(1) adding their new prescribed range of knowing (**K**$_{2P}$) to their previously developed range of knowing (**K**$_{2KLF}$) and thereby

extending their total range of knowing (a) in quantity and/or (b) in kind (**K_{2K}**), level (**K_{2L}**) and/or form (**K_{2F}**),

(2) identifying and resolving contradictions between their newly acquired prescribed range of knowing (**K_{2P}**) with their previously developed range of knowing (**K_{2KLF}**) and thereby emending their total range of knowing (**K_{2KLF}**),

(3) using their newly emended range of knowing (**K_{2KLF}**) to solve problems which they were unable to solve with their prior range of knowing (**K_{2KLF}**).

An example of integrating a prior range of knowing (**K_{2KLF}**) with a newly acquired prescribed range of knowing (**K_{2P}**) that results in an increase in the quantity of knowing (**K_2**) is that of Marion. She is a student in high school, and she is studying intentionally under guidance (**S_{P1}**) trigonometry. Her prior range of knowing (**K_{2KLF}**) in mathematics includes her range of knowing (**K_{2KLF}**) of arithmetic, algebra and geometry. She uses her knowing-that (**K_{2K2}**) and knowing-how (**K_{2K3}**) of arithmetic, algebra and geometry in linguistic form (**K_{2F1}**) to develop her range of knowing (**K_{2KLF}**) of trigonometry. In the course of her intentional studies under guidance (**S_{P1}**), she conceives the logical connections and relations among arithmetic, algebra and geometry with trigonometry, and she thereby achieves an increase in quantity (and an integration) in her range of knowing (**K_{2KLF}**) of mathematics.

An example of integrating a prior range of knowing with a new range of knowing that results in an increase in kind, level and form of knowing is that of Roger. Roger is 19 years old, and he decides that he would like to learn to ice skate. He enrolls in an ice skating class. His first set of intentional guided study activities (**S_{P1}**) is to watch a video about the fundamentals of ice skating. He notes in his mind from the video that it is important to have properly fitted ice skates, that the skates have two edges (an inside and an outside edge), that the skater should keep the skates about a shoulder width apart, that the skater should keep the knees bent just over the toe caps of the skates, that the skater should keep the chest up, that the shoulders should be held parallel to the ice, that the skater should avoid leaning forward or backward while standing, that the skater should stand with the skates parallel and on the inside edge, that the first move in skating is to shift one's weight to the left skate while turning the right skate out and pushing off with the right skate on the inside edge, glide on the left skate, then shift weight to the right skate on the inside edge while turning the left skate out and pushing off with the left skate on the inside edge and glide on the right skate. Roger, from watching the video, adds to his range of knowing-that ($\mathbf{K}_{2K2}$) in linguistic ($\mathbf{K}_{2F1}$) and imaginal ($\mathbf{K}_{2F3}$) forms. The next set of intentional guided study activities ($\mathbf{S}_{P1}$) for Roger is to put on some skates, assure that they fit properly and practice the proper stance, push off and glides that were illustrated in the video. Roger completes the intentional guided study activities ($\mathbf{S}_{P1}$), and from them, he extends is range of knowing ($\mathbf{K}_{2KLF}$) from knowing-that ($\mathbf{K}_{2K2}$) to knowing-how ($\mathbf{K}_{2K3}$) and his forms of knowing from linguistic ($\mathbf{K}_{2F1}$) and imaginal ($\mathbf{K}_{2F3}$) to physical ($\mathbf{K}_{2K5}$) and physiological ($\mathbf{K}_{2K4}$) knowing. In this example, Roger integrates his prior range of knowing (knowing-that in linguistic and imaginal forms $<\mathbf{K}_{2K2F1}>$ and $<\mathbf{K}_{2K2F3}>$) with his new range of knowing (knowing-how in physical and physiological forms $<\mathbf{K}_{2K3F5}>$ and $<\mathbf{K}_{2K3F4}>$), and the cognitive resultant for Roger is an increase in kind, level and forms of knowing about ice skating ($\mathbf{K}_{2KLF}$).

An example of integrating a prior range of knowing with a new range of knowing by identifying and resolving contractions between the prior and the new range of knowing is that of Phyllis. Phyllis has enrolled in a first-year university course in biology. When she was in high school, she intentionally studied under guidance ($\mathbf{S}_{P1}$) biology, and one of the topics in her course of study$_1$ ($\mathbf{S}_{P1}$) was classification of living organisms. She was taught ($\mathbf{T}_{P}$), she studied$_1$ ($\mathbf{S}_{P1}$) and she learned ($\mathbf{L}_1$) that living organisms could be classified into five all-inclusive categories (or kingdoms) – monera, protista, fungi, plantae and animalia. She integrated these five categories into her range of knowing-that ($\mathbf{K}_{2K2}$) in linguistic form ($\mathbf{K}_{2F1}$) about living organisms. In her biology course in university, Phyllis is taught ($\mathbf{T}_{P}$), she studies ($\mathbf{S}_{P1}$) and she learns ($\mathbf{L}_1$) that there have been many classification systems for living organisms developed over the years, including the taxonomies of Carl Linnaeus (1735), Ernst Heinrich Philipp August Haeckel (1866), Edouard Chatton (1925), Herbert Faulkner Copeland (1938) Robert Harding Whittaker (1969), Carl Richard Woese et al. (1990), Thomas Cavalier-Smith (1998 and 2015). Phyllis studies ($\mathbf{S}_{P1}$) and learns ($\mathbf{L}_1$) that each classification system was conceived in the light of new knowledge (neo $<\mathbf{K}_1>$) about the structures, functions and evolutionary origins of living organisms. Phyllis reflects upon the classification system which she studied ($\mathbf{S}_{P1}$) and learned ($\mathbf{L}_1$) in high school, and she recognizes it as the system developed by Robert Harding Whittaker

(1969). She notes that the existence of multiple classification systems contradicts her earlier conception that there was one, and only one, definitive classification system. She resolves the contradiction with her new range of knowing (<u>knowing-that</u> $<\mathbf{K}_{2K2}>$) in linguistic form ($\mathbf{K}_{2F1}$) that classification systems are based on the question of what should constitute the distinguishing characteristics of a living organism, that classification systems are always subject to review and inquiry, and that new classification systems are conceived and proposed to account for new knowledge (neo $<\mathbf{K}_{1}>$) about the genetic composition of contemporary living organisms and about the evolutionary connections of current genetic compositions with the genetic compositions of living organisms of the distant past. Thus Phyllis achieves integration of her range of knowing ($\mathbf{K}_{2KLF}$) about biology by identifying and resolving contractions between her prior and her new range of knowing ($\mathbf{K}_{2KLF}$).

An example of integrating a prior range of knowing with a new prescribed range of knowing ($\mathbf{K}_{2P}$) by solving a new problem is that of four children, all aged 10, playing the spelling game, Scrabble™, with each other. Each player brings to the game his or her range of knowing ($\mathbf{K}_{2KLF}$) of arithmetic, vocabulary, word meanings, word spellings, game rules, game ethics, game strategies and sportsmanship. Each player uses his or her prior range of knowing ($\mathbf{K}_{2KLF}$) in an integrated way to play the game. Playing the game requires the solution of a set of problems, viz. from seven randomly drawn letters, how to form correctly spelled words which are recognized as ones in common usage (cited in dictionaries) and how to maximize one's score. Playing the game requires, not only an integration of a range of knowing ($\mathbf{K}_{2}$) about words, their meaning and their spelling, but also the use of arithmetic to keep score and to maximize scores. In addition, the game requires that the players use their <u>knowing-to</u> ($\mathbf{K}_{2K4}$) to play the game fairly and with good humor.

Constructive Practices by Teachers

Actions which teachers (**T**) can take to increase the probabilities that education (**E**) will be effective ($\mathbf{E}_{E}$) include

(1) creating circumstances and providing activities which guide and assist students to identify and state in writing their major definite purposes, aims, goals and/or objectives which they authentically value and choose to pursue,

(2) creating circumstances and providing activities which guide

and assist students to identify and state in writing the ranges of knowing which they need to have to achieve their major definite purposes, aims, goals and/or objectives,

(3) creating circumstances and providing activities which guide and assist students to select $study_1$ (**S_{P1}**) activities and/or courses of $study_1$ (**S_{P1}**) to develop the prescribed ranges of knowing (**K_{2P}**) which the students have authentically chosen,

(4) preparing appropriately and comprehensively for providing an educational episode or set of episodes (lessons, units, courses),

(5) organizing records, resources and plans with a filing and retrieval system,

(6) habitually following a system of time management,

(7) maintaining a vigilance and awareness of the dynamics (and the implications of the dynamics) of the educational episodes in which students are engaged,

(8) maintaining flexibility in guiding, assisting and directing students in their $study_1$ (**S_{P1}**) activities,

(9) establishing and maintaining a set of reasonable and effective classroom routines,

(10) creating and maintaining constructive relationships,

(11) communicating appropriately and clearly,

(12) assuring that all $study_1$ (**S_{P1}**) opportunities and activities are purpose driven,

(13) assuring that students (**S**) become engaged and stay engaged (keeping students on task) with their $study_1$ (**S_{P1}**) activities,

(14) presenting students with content (**C**), $study_1$ (**S_{P1}**) tasks and intended learning outcomes (**ILO**s) which are at an optimal level of difficulty,

(15) matching teaching (**T_P**) and intentional guided study (**S_{P1}**) resources, methods and styles with the volition (**V**), perception (**P**) and cognition (**N**) of the students (**S**),

(16) providing circumstances such that students experience ($perceive_1$ <**P_1**>) positive emotions as they undertake $studying_1$ (**S_{P1}**) activities and make progress in their $learning_1$ (**L_1**) of the prescribed range of knowing (**K_{2P}**) that is specified by the selected intended learning

outcomes (**ILO**s),

(17) devising and using appropriate instructional designs (**D**) which suit the purpose of the educational episode, the students (**S**), the study$_1$ (**S_{P1}**) tasks, the intended learning outcomes (**ILO**s), the assessment tasks, the evaluation procedures and the use of the evaluation results,

(18) providing circumstances and/or opportunities for students (**S**) to emend their extant range of knowing (**K_{2KLF}**) to accommodate their newly acquired prescribed range of knowing (**K_{2P}**),

(19) providing circumstances and/or opportunities for students (**S**) to integrate their newly acquired prescribed range of knowing (**K_{2P}**) with their extant range of knowing (**K_{2KLF}**).

Major Definite Purpose

Persons playing the role of teacher (**T**) increase the probabilities that the educational episodes (**E**) which they provide will be effective education (**E_E**) by creating circumstances and providing activities which guide and assist students (**S**) to identify and state (in writing and in speech) their major definite purpose or purposes. Students (**S**) who have chosen, genuinely and authentically, some major definite purpose (or purposes) have aims, goals and/or objectives for which to strive. Their set of purposes provides a basis for choosing some range of knowing (**K_{2KLF}**) to learn (**L_1**) and for completing some set of relevant intentionally guided study (**S_{P1}**) to achieve their prescribed range of knowing (**K_{2P}**).

A Nominated Range of Knowing (K_{2KLF})

Persons playing the role of teacher (**T**) increase the probabilities that the educational episodes (**E**) which they provide will be effective education (**E_E**) by creating circumstances and providing activities which guide and assist students (**S**) to identify and state (in writing and in speech) the ranges of knowing (**K_{2KLF}**) which they need, want and/or desire to have to achieve their major definite purposes (and related aims, goals and/or objectives). The probabilities are increased that students (**S**) will achieve a range of knowing (**K_{2KLF}**) when students have freely, willingly and authentically chosen the range of knowing (**K_{2KLF}**) to learn (**L_1**). Contrast the student, Robert, who says, "Do I have to $learn_1$ (L_1) this?" with the student, Larissa, who says, "I really want to $learn_1$ (L_1) this!" Larissa declares her enthusiasm for $studying_1$ (S_{P1}) and $learning_1$ (L_1) because the range of knowing (K_{2KLF}) to which she is referring meets her needs, wants and/or desires. She has some major definite purpose (and related set of aims, goals and/or objectives) in mind. In contrast, either Robert has not yet clarified and stated to himself his set of major definite purposes, or the range of knowing (K_{2KLF}) being offered to Robert does not match his set of major definite purposes. Robert either needs assistance in clarifying his set of major definite purposes, or he needs to be allowed to make some authentic choices about the ranges of knowing (K_{2KLF}) which he needs, wants and/or desires to $study_1$ (S_{P1}) and $learn_1$ (L_1). Teachers (**T**) can enhance the probabilities that education (**E**) will be effective (E_E) by assisting students (**S**) to clarify their major definite purposes and to identify the ranges of knowing (K_{2KLF}) which will serve them (**S**) in the pursuit of their purposes.

Choice of Subjects, Courses and/or Educational Episodes

Persons playing the role of teacher (**T**) increase the probabilities that the educational episodes (**E**) which they provide will be effective education (E_E) by creating circumstances and providing activities which guide and assist students (**S**) to select $study_1$ (S_{P1}) activities and/or courses (or subjects) of $study_1$ (S_{P1}) which are appropriate for the development of the ranges of knowing (K_{2KLF}) which the students (**S**) have freely, willingly and authentically chosen to learn (L_1).

Students who want to $study_1$ (S_{P1}) and $learn_1$ (L_1) some range of knowing (K_{2KLF}) are more likely to succeed in achieving their desired range of knowing (K_{2KLF}) – and thereby make their educational experience effective education (E_E) – than students who are reluctant (or do not want or are explicitly opposed) to $study_1$ (S_{P1}) and $learn_1$ (L_1) some range of knowing (K_{2KLF}). It is a sound teaching practice to provide circumstances and activities which afford students with opportunities to discover what they want to $study_1$ (S_{P1}) and learn (L_1) and to choose courses of $study_1$ (S_{P1}) and/or educational episodes which move them along the path towards their aim, goals and/or objectives.

It is a misconception of education (**E**) to think of it as a system in which some authority decides what range of knowing (K_{2KLF}) some population should know (K_2) and then the agents of the authority compel the population to undertake coerced study ($\mathbf{S_{PC}}$) with a view to learning$_3$ (coerced learning <$\mathbf{L_3}$>) the mandated range of knowing (coerced knowing <$\mathbf{K_{2C}}$>). Coerced learning$_1$ ($\mathbf{L_3}$) is the resultant of socialization, enculturation, indoctrination or some other means of compulsion, not of education ($\mathbf{E}$). School systems may be commonly denoted by the term <*education systems*>, but if school programs are compelling students to study (denoted not by <$\mathbf{S_{P1}}$>, intentional guided study, but rather, denoted by <$\mathbf{S_{PC}}$>, compelled or forced study) to achieve coerced learning ($\mathbf{L_3}$), then the school systems are not providing education ($\mathbf{E}$). They are providing programs of compelled study activities ($\mathbf{S_{PC}}$), which at times result in coerced learning ($\mathbf{L_3}$) of some compelled range of knowing ($\mathbf{K_{2C}}$), and at times result in little or no learning ($\neg\mathbf{L}$) of some compelled range of knowing ($\mathbf{K_{2C}}$). In schools with only compelled study activities ($\mathbf{S_{PC}}$), and therefore without education ($\mathbf{E}$), there is, of course, no possibility of effective education ($\mathbf{E_E}$). There is only the possibility of coerced learning ($\mathbf{L_3}$) of some compelled range of knowing ($\mathbf{K_{2C}}$), and in the experiential material world, the possibility is sometimes realized and sometimes not.

Conduced learning ($\mathbf{L_1}$) of some prescribed range of knowing ($\mathbf{K_{2P}}$), not coerced learning ($\mathbf{L_3}$), of some compelled range of knowing ($\mathbf{K_{2C}}$), is the resultant of effective education ($\mathbf{E_E}$). Students ($\mathbf{S}$) in education ($\mathbf{E}$) undertake intentionally, freely and willingly study$_1$ ($\mathbf{S_{P1}}$) activities with a view to achieving conduced learning ($\mathbf{L_1}$) of some authentically chosen prescribed range of knowing ($\mathbf{K_{2P}}$). The probabilities that education ($\mathbf{E}$) will be effective education ($\mathbf{E_E}$) are greatly enhanced by the teacher ($\mathbf{T}$) engaging students ($\mathbf{S}$) in making authentic, well considered choices. The choices begin with the students ($\mathbf{S}$) clarifying and selecting some set of major definite purposes. By implication, the set of major definite purposes chosen by the students ($\mathbf{S}$) indicate some set of aims, goals and/or objectives. The aims, goals and/or objectives chosen by the students require some range of knowing ($\mathbf{K_{2KLF}}$) for their pursuit and/or achievement. Some range of knowing ($\mathbf{K_{2KLF}}$) nominated by the students ($\mathbf{S}$) necessitates the selection by the students ($\mathbf{S}$) of some relevant course of studies ($\mathbf{S_{P1}}$) or some set of educational episodes for intentional guided study ($\mathbf{S_{P1}}$) to learn$_1$ (conduced learning <$\mathbf{L_1}$>) the student-nominated prescribed range of knowing ($\mathbf{K_{2P}}$).

Preparation for Teaching

Persons playing the role of teacher (**T**) increase the probabilities that the educational episodes (**E**) which they provide will be effective education ($\mathbf{E_E}$) for their students (**S**) by preparing appropriately and comprehensively for providing an educational episode or set of episodes (courses, units, lessons) which are appropriate, suitable and relevant to a set of students (**S**) engaged in study$_1$ ($\mathbf{S_{P1}}$) activities to learn$_1$ ($\mathbf{L_1}$) a prescribed range of knowing ($\mathbf{K_{2P}}$) as specified by some nominated set of intended learning outcomes (**ILO**s).

Appropriate and comprehensive preparation for teaching ($\mathbf{T_P}$) includes

(1) reading, scrutinizing, comprehending and inferring the implicative meaning of relevant curriculum documents and syllabi,

(2) writing plans (course plans, subject plans, unit plans and lesson plans) which logically cohere with curriculum and syllabus documents,

(3) including in written plans (course plans, subject plans, unit plans and lesson plans) statements of

- (a) intended learning outcomes (**ILO**s),
- (b) assessment requirements and procedures,
- (c) criteria for evaluation of student achievement of intended learning outcomes (**ILO**s),
- (d) forms and frequencies of evaluation reports (ratings or rankings),
- (e) uses of evaluation reports (preparative, formative, summative),
- (f) instructional design or designs ($\mathbf{D_1}$, $\mathbf{D_2}$, etc.),
- (g) time allocation for study activities ($\mathbf{S_{P1}}$),
- (h) required teaching ($\mathbf{T_P}$) and studying ($\mathbf{S_{P1}}$) resources,
- (i) set of study$_1$ ($\mathbf{S_{P1}}$) activities and sequence of study$_1$ ($\mathbf{S_{P1}}$) activities and
- (j) content ($<\mathbf{C_1}>$ and/or $<\mathbf{C_2}>$) to be taught ($\mathbf{T_P}$) and studied$_1$ ($\mathbf{S_{P1}}$).

(4) assuring that written lesson plans derive from the implicative meaning of written unit plans, that written unit plans derive from the implicative meaning of written course plans (or subject plans), that written course plans or subject plans derive from the implicative meaning of a

syllabus and that a syllabus derives from the implicative meaning of related curriculum documents,

(5) assuring that required resources are available and that all resources are in place for purpose-driven lessons or educational episodes to proceed.

As with all practices by participants in education (**E**), appropriate and comprehensive preparation for teaching ($\mathbf{T_P}$) by the persons playing the role of teacher (**T**) does not guarantee that education (**E**) will be effective education ($\mathbf{E_E}$). All that appropriate and comprehensive preparation for teaching ($\mathbf{T_P}$) can achieve is to increase the probabilities that education (**E**) will be effective education ($\mathbf{E_E}$).

Organization

Persons playing the role of teacher (**T**) increase the probabilities that the educational episodes (**E**) which they provide will be effective education ($\mathbf{E_E}$) for their students (**S**) by establishing and maintaining sound organization. Sound organization is achieved by habitually finding a place for everything, keeping everything in its place after use and keeping records of the location of everything for easy retrieval. Resources, lesson plans, unit plans, syllabi, curriculum documents, roll records, grade records, files for ongoing and/or completed student work, books, journals, reference materials, tests, examinations, worksheets, questions sets, project assignments, games, puzzles, videos and any other resources are allocated their locations, their locations are recorded in a searchable file system, and the file system makes them readily locatable and retrievable.

Time Management

Persons playing the role of teacher (**T**) increase the probabilities that the educational episodes (**E**) which they provide will be effective education ($\mathbf{E_E}$) by habitually following a system of time management. An adequate time management system has a number of essential components. Values, major definite purposes, short-term, intermediate and long-term goals are specified, expressed in writing, regularly reviewed and continually revised as circumstances change. A written list of tasks to be completed is developed, maintained, revised and updated. Tasks are evaluated in terms of values and goals, and the evaluated tasks are subsequently given written ratings (<1, 2, 3> or <A, B, C>) by priority. Accurate time estimates (without overestimating or underestimating the time required) are made for completion of tasks. Dates and times are allocated for action on tasks, and an action diary is maintained. Realistic and realizable deadlines are set for completion of tasks and for production of deliverables. Records are kept of the progress achieved on completion of tasks. Time is allocated on a daily basis for planning. Time is set aside for emergencies, rest and relaxation. Overbooking is avoided. Procrastination is eliminated by adhering to the action diary.

Vigilance and Awareness

Awareness (**W**) is consciousness of some state of affairs, and vigilance is direction for awareness (**W**), which is given by focus of attention (**F**). Focus of attention (**F**) coordinates our conation (**V**), perception (**P**) and cognition (**N**) such that, in relation to some state of affairs, we have perceptions (**P**) of the state of affairs, develop cognition (**N**) about it and take it into account in making decisions (**V**). Our awareness (**W**), or mindfulness (**M**), is extended through extending our range of knowing ($\mathbf{K_{2KLF}}$) through educological $study_1$ ($\mathbf{S_{P1}}$) of education (**E**), through educological inquiry (**Q**) about education (**E**) and through experience playing the roles of teacher (**T**) and student (**S**) in education (**E**).

Persons playing the role of teacher (**T**) increase the probabilities that the educational episodes (**E**) which they provide will be effective education ($\mathbf{E_E}$) by maintaining vigilance (focusing their volition <**V**>, perception <**P**> and cognition <**N**> on), and thus maintaining their volitional, perceptive and cognitive awareness (**W**) of, important and significant aspects of education (**E**), including

(1) whether what they (**T**) and their students (**S**) are experiencing constitutes an educational episode or does not constitute an educational episode, and, if necessary, what they need to do to transform the state of affairs into an educational episode,

(2) whether their preparation for their teaching ($\mathbf{T_P}$) has been adequate for the educational episode which they intend to provide, and if not, what they need to do to make it adequate,

(3) whether they have established the necessary conditions for effective education ($\mathbf{E_E}$), i.e.

(a) whether the resources ($\mathbf{E_{DC2}}$) are adequate, and if not, what needs to be done to make them adequate,

(b) whether the content (<**C**> including <$\mathbf{C}_1$> and/or <$\mathbf{C}_2$>) is at an optimal level of difficulty, and if not, what needs to be done to make it optimal,

(c) whether the intended learning outcomes (**ILO**s) are clearly specified and achievable, and if not, in what ways do they need to be modified to make them clearly specified and achievable,

(d) whether the students (**S**) want to achieve the intended learning outcomes (**ILO**s), and if not, what needs to be done to make the intended learning outcomes (**ILO**s) more appealing to them, or what alternative intended learning outcomes (**ILO**s) appeal to them,

(e) whether the study$_1$ ($\mathbf{S}_{P1}$) activities for the students (**S**) are appropriate, and if not, what needs to be done to make them appropriate,

(f) whether the students have a sufficient prior range of knowing (K_{2KLF}) and the capability (physical and/or psychical) to achieve the ILOs, and if not, what needs to be modified to place the ILOs within their capabilities,

(g) whether sufficient time has been allocated for the students (**S**) to complete the study$_1$ ($\mathbf{S}_{P1}$) activities and to achieve the prescribed range of knowing ($\mathbf{K}_{2P}$),

(h) whether the study$_1$ ($\mathbf{S}_{P1}$) activities provided for the students (**S**) are appropriate and relevant to the achievement of the prescribed range of knowing ($\mathbf{K}_{2P}$),

(i) whether the physical, social and cultural setting (**X**) is supportive and constructive of the teachers (**T**), the students (**S**), the content (**C**), the study$_1$ ($\mathbf{S}_{P1}$) activities and the intended learning outcomes (**ILO**s), and if not, what needs to be done to attain and maintain approval and support for them,

(4) what evidence there is of progress in learning$_1$ ($\mathbf{L}_1$) of a prescribed range of knowing ($\mathbf{K}_{2P}$) by the students, whether the students believe and feel satisfaction that they are making progress in their learning$_1$ ($\mathbf{L}_1$) and what needs to be done to guide the students in their progression,

(5) what evidence there is of impediments which are

obstructing $learning_1$ (**L_1**) of a prescribed range of knowing (**K_{2P}**) by the students and what ways and means there are available to remove or reduce the impediments and smooth the path to $learning_1$ (**L_1**),

(6) what evidence there is of constructive relationships between teachers (**T**) and students (**S**) and what needs to be done to create and/or maintain the constructive relationships,

(7) what evidence there is of constructive relationships among students (student to student relationships) and what needs to be done to create and/or maintain the constructive relationships,

(8) what evidence there is of constructive relationships with and among fellow teachers (**T**) and what needs to be done to create and/or maintain the constructive relationships,

(9) what evidence there is of constructive relationships with interested third parties (supervisors, administrators, parents, etc.) and what needs to be done to create and/or maintain the constructive relationships,

Flexibility

Persons playing the role of teacher (**T**) increase the probabilities that the educational episodes (**E**) which they provide will be effective education (**E_E**) by maintaining flexibility in guiding, assisting and directing students in their $study_1$ (**S_{P1}**) activities. It is sound teaching practice (**T_P**) always to have plans in place for teaching (**T_P**) and for intentionally studying under guidance (**S_{P1}**) with a view in mind that students (**S**) will achieve some nominated set of intended learning outcomes (**ILO**s). But plans can always be altered or set aside when occasions arise which present better alternatives to the specified plans for intentional guided studying (**S_{P1}**) and $learning_1$ (**L_1**) some prescribed range of knowing (**K_{2P}**).

Suppose that, in a year 7 or 7th grade class (age 12 years), the students are $studying_1$ (**S_{P1}**) the harmful effects of pollution, and one of the students (**S**) suggests that they go to the nearby beach and investigate how much and what kind of pollution is on or near the beach. This activity was not written in the lesson plan, but it is something that the students would like to do, and it is a $study_1$ (**S_{P1}**) activity which is consistent with the set of intended learning outcomes (**ILO**s) for the lesson plan and the unit plan. The teacher (**T**) wisely says that the suggestion is a great idea, provides students (**S**) with materials to complete the activity and arranges for the class to walk to the beach, collect discarded plastic and other pollutants, weigh the collection and calculate the weight of pollution per square meter of beach.

In a second scenario, suppose that a year 3 or 3rd grade (age 8 years) brings some tadpoles to school to share with the class. The class becomes excited to learn more about where they come from and how they change over time. The teacher recognizes the genuine interest, curiosity and engagement of the students, sets aside the written lesson plans and organizes the class to conduct inquiry about tadpoles and report the results of their inquiry, using the media of drawings, photos, videos and posters.

Classroom Routines

Persons playing the role of teacher (**T**) increase the probabilities that the educational episodes (**E**) which they provide will be effective education ($\mathbf{E_E}$) by establishing and maintaining a set of reasonable and effective classroom routines.

Routines establish order in the classroom and reduce undesired and disruptive behaviors of students. Routines provide certainty for the students and a basis for cooperation with each other. Routines make for more efficient use of time in the classroom because the teachers do not have to repeat instructions for routine matters. Routines help students form habits of self-directed studying$_2$ ($\mathbf{S_{P2}}$) and self-directed learning$_2$ ($\mathbf{L_2}$) of discovered ranges of knowing ($\mathbf{K_{2D}}$). Routines have a calming effect on students, and they provide opportunities for students to develop responsibility and accountability. Routines provide students with a rhythm for the day (or the class) and a pattern of activities which they can anticipate. With routines, once students have completed one activity, they know the next set of activities they should undertake.

Which particular set of routines is the appropriate set to establish depends on the institution (school, college, institute, academy, etc.) and the age of the students – kindergarten, lower primary, upper primary, middle school, junior high school, senior high school, further and tertiary education, adult education. Most schools, colleges, universities, etc. have routines and policies in place for teachers to use. Thus, any particular set of routines which the teachers establish are typically created within the context of a larger, more inclusive and comprehensive set of institutional routines and policies.

It is best practice to establish routines which are reasonable and effective. It is wise to provide explanations to students for the routines and classroom policies such that the students can understand the justifications for, and the importance of, the routines. The routines and policies should make sense to the students, and the routines and policies should be applied consistently and fairly. Routines and policies should also be reviewed periodically to evaluate them and to decide what might be done to improve them.

Constructive Relationships

Persons playing the role of teacher (**T**) increase the probabilities that the educational episodes (**E**) which they provide will be effective education ($\mathbf{E_E}$) by creating and maintaining constructive relationships between (1) the teacher and students, (2) students and their fellow students, (3) the teacher and other (or fellow) teachers, (3) the teacher and interested third parties – supervisors, administrators, parents, community leaders, etc. All four categories of relationships share some common properties. All parties, when in a constructive relationship, have mutual respect, esteem and trust for each other. They have genuine care for the well being of each other. They assist each other in the pursuit of their goals. They act in good faith in communicating openly and honestly with each other. When conflicts occur among themselves, they maintain respect for each other, and they seek to resolve the conflicts by finding mutual ground for agreement and by formulating solutions which all parties are willing to accept, implement and support. They act in good faith and seek consensus. They refuse to resort to anger, insults, sarcasm, attack, violence, threat, menace, intimidation, coercion, avoidance, evasion and/or deception.

Constructive relationships between teachers and students are ones in which teachers care for the well being of their students, provide them with guidance in their studies and genuinely want their students to succeed in achieving the nominated intended learning outcomes. With respect to the students, in a constructive relationship, they willingly accept the guidance provided by their teacher, study in good faith and genuinely endeavor to achieve the nominated set of intended learning outcomes. There is mutual respect, esteem and trust between the teacher and students. When conflicts arise, resolution of conflict, depending on the age of the student and the student's ability to engage in good faith using well-informed reasoning and negotiation, is sought, by both teacher and student. They seek to find common ground and mutually agreeable solutions. They eschew resorting to insults, sarcasm, anger, attack, violence, coercion, threat, menace, intimidation, denigration, disrespect, manipulation, mocking, exploitation, avoidance, evasion and/or deception.

Of course, there are students who do not accept opportunities to intentionally study under guidance (**S_{P1}**) and intentionally learn under guidance (**L_1**), who choose not to cooperate, who decide to behave disruptively, who do not do their homework, who waste their time in class, who play pranks and annoy their fellow students, who deliberately attempt to annoy their teachers, who reject the guidance of their teachers and rebel against the rules and policies of their educational institution (their school, academy, institute, college, etc.). When they do so, there obviously is no constructive relationship between teacher and student. There is no effective teaching and intentional guided studying. In fact, there is no education (**E**) taking place at all because the individual who is being asked to play the role of student has rejected playing the role of student. In such circumstances, resolving conflict through engaging in good faith and seeking mutually agreeable solutions may not be an appropriate course of action. The person who refuses to play the role of student has chosen not to act in good faith. The best course of action, in such a case, is that the persons who choose to misbehave are presented with the unpleasant consequences of their choices – some admonition, rebuke, penalty or deprivation. In addition, they need to be engaged in counselling about what major definite purposes they have (or might have) chosen for themselves, what goals they wish to pursue, what plans they can put into place to achieve those goals. They need to be engaged in discourse and thought about how they can reduce impulsiveness and how they can develop anticipation and evaluation of the consequences of their choices.

Without constructive relationships among teachers, students and interested third parties, who make up the social and cultural context in which teaching and intentional guided studying take place, effective teaching and effective intentional guided studying (and by implication, effective education) cannot take place. Thus, it is an imperative for us, if we aspire to effective teaching, to develop the range of knowing necessary for creating and maintaining constructive relationships, for forestalling destructive relationships and for transforming extant destructive relationships into constructive ones.

Communication

Persons playing the role of teacher (**T**) increase the probabilities that the educational episodes (**E**) which they provide will be effective education ($\mathbf{E_E}$) by communicating appropriately and clearly. An appropriate communication is one in which the form and delivery of the message are well suited to the cognitive, social and cultural characteristics of the audience. A clear communication is one in which the message is not easily misinterpreted. It is one without ambiguity, conflation, vagueness, equivocation, contradiction or obscurity. It is one in which the sender of the message gives the same interpretation to the message as the receiver of the message.

The theory of signs developed by the American scientist and philosopher, Charles Sanders Peirce (1839-1914) is instructive in developing a clear conception of what the term *communication* denotes. Peirce maintained that communication is achieved by messages formed from signs. A sign, he wrote,

> … is something, *A*, which brings something, *B*, its *interpretant* sign determined or created by it, into the same sort of correspondence with something, *C*, its *object*, as that in which itself stands to *C*. (C.S. Peirce, 1902, *The New Elements of Mathematics*, Vol. 4, pp. 20-21).

Over his lifetime, as he evaluated and refined his thinking about communication, Peirce developed several systems for classification of signs. In one of his classification systems, he distinguished among three categories of signs – physical, iconic and symbolic.

We hear laughter in the next room. The laughter is a physical sign <*A*>. We, the interpretants <*B*>, interpret the laughter as a sign of the presence of people in a joyful mood. The people in an emotional state of joyfulness in the next room are the objects <*C*>, for which the physical sign of laughter <*A*> stands in correspondence. They are also the determinants of the sign, for they are the ones who created the laughter. We see a photograph of our grandparents. The photograph is an iconic sign <*A*>. We, the interpretants <*B*>, interpret the photograph as an iconic sign of our grandparents. Our grandparents are the object <*C*> for which the iconic sign of the photograph <*A*> stands in correspondence. The determinant of the photograph is the group of persons who created the photograph – the person who wanted the photograph taken, the photographer and the technician who developed the film and made a print of the film. We read the words <*No parking*> on a road sign located along the roadside. The set of words <*No parking*> is a set of symbolic signs <*A*>. We, the interpretants <*B*>, interpret the words <*No parking*> as a command to avoid parking in that area. The designated no parking zone along the roadside is the object <*C*> for which the symbolic sign <*No parking*> stands in correspondence. The determinants of the <*No parking*> sign were the set of people who authorized, purchased, made and installed the sign.

Within education (**E**), appropriate and clear communication consists of a set of signs (physical, iconic or symbolic signs, created by some determinant – teacher, student, content, third parties) that forms an unambiguous message (a set of signs that, without ambiguity, conflation, vagueness, equivocation, contradiction or obscurity, denotes or corresponds with an entity or state of affairs) which is delivered by some means to an interpretant (teacher, student or third party) who has the relevant perception (**P**), cognition (**N**) and volition (**V**) to perceive (perceive$_6$ <$\mathbf{P}_6$>) the message, to conceive (**O**) the meaning of the message and to choose (**V**) to accept the message and/or respond to the message appropriately.

It is patent that in education (**E**), communication takes place from

(1) one teacher to another teacher <$\mathbf{T}_1 \rightarrow \mathbf{T}_2$> and vice versa <$\mathbf{T}_2 \rightarrow \mathbf{T}_1$>, or teacher to teacher mutually <$\mathbf{T}_1 \rightleftarrows \mathbf{T}_2$>,

(2) a teacher to a student or set of students <$\mathbf{T} \rightarrow \mathbf{S}$> and vice versa <$\mathbf{S} \rightarrow \mathbf{T}$>, or teacher to student mutually <$\mathbf{T} \rightleftarrows \mathbf{S}$>,

(3) one student to another student <$\mathbf{S}_1 \rightarrow \mathbf{S}_2$> and vice versa <$\mathbf{S}_2 \rightarrow \mathbf{S}_1$>, or student to student mutually <$\mathbf{S}_1 \rightleftarrows \mathbf{S}_2$>,

(4) student to third parties <$\mathbf{S} \rightarrow \mathbf{X}$> and third parties to students <$\mathbf{X} \rightarrow \mathbf{S}$>, or student to third party mutually <$\mathbf{S} \rightleftarrows \mathbf{X}$>,

(5) teachers to third parties <$\mathbf{T} \rightarrow \mathbf{X}$> and third parties to teachers <$\mathbf{X} \rightarrow \mathbf{T}$>, or teacher to third party mutually <$\mathbf{T} \rightleftarrows \mathbf{X}$>,

(6) one third party to another third party <$\mathbf{X}_1 \rightarrow \mathbf{X}_2$> and vice versa <$\mathbf{X}_2 \rightarrow \mathbf{X}_1$>, or third party to third party mutually <$\mathbf{X}_1 \rightleftarrows \mathbf{X}_2$>,

(7) teacher to student to third party, and vice versa, in a three-way communication pattern <$\mathbf{T} \rightleftarrows \mathbf{S} \rightleftarrows \mathbf{X} \rightleftarrows \mathbf{T}$>.

The ideal state of affairs to which persons who play the role of teacher ($\mathbf{T}_1$) can aspire in their communications is that their interpretation of the messages which they provide for their colleagues (other teachers <$\mathbf{T}_2$>), students (**S**) and third parties (**X**) matches the interpretation given by the recipients of their messages, and that the interpretation by teachers ($\mathbf{T}_1$) of the messages which they receive from their colleagues ($\mathbf{T}_2$), students (**S**) and third parties (**X**) matches the interpretation given by the senders (creators, determinants) of the messages – their colleagues ($\mathbf{T}_2$), students (**S**) and third parties (**X**).

To form messages, teachers have available to them the three categories of signs – physical signs, iconic signs and symbolic signs – which they can use one at a time or in combinations.

A physical sign is any entity or phenomenon <*A*> which can be perceived$_6$ ($\mathbf{P}_6$) by an interpretant <*B*> using extrospection, and which stands in an existential relationship of correspondence with another entity or state of affairs, <*C*>. Messages formed from physical signs can be perceived$_6$ ($\mathbf{P}_6$) as sounds, sights, smells, tastes and touches (hot, cold, rough, smooth, liquid, solid, gas, etc.). Physical signs include, for example, prints of deer hooves in mud (giving the message that a deer has been in the vicinity recently), the call of a dove (giving the message that a dove is nearby), the croak of a frog (giving the message that a frog is looking for a mate), a smiling facial expression (giving the message of friendship, safety, approval and/or encouragement), a gesture of crossed arms (giving a message of defensiveness and/or exclusion), a wink (giving the message of a special understanding and/or inclusion), a pat on the back (giving a message of approval and/or comfort), a physical model of the terrain and deployment of soldiers at the Battle of Gettysburg (giving the message of who was involved and what occurred at Gettysburg, Pennsylvania, 1-3 July, 1863), two pieces of steel welded into a tee joint (giving the message of the properties of a well-executed tee joint weld of two pieces of steel), execution of a three turn on ice skates (giving the message of the properties of a well-executed three turn), the swing of a baseball bat (giving the message of the properties of a well-executed swing), the warmth of a kettle on a stove (giving the message that the kettle has been used recently), etc.

An iconic sign is any image <*A*> which can be perceived$_6$ ($\mathbf{P}_6$) by an interpretant <*B*> using extrospection, and which stands in a pictorial representational relationship of correspondence with some entity, action, process or state of affairs <*C*>. Messages formed from iconic signs can be paintings, diagrams, maps, still photographs, motion pictures, videos, etc., which represent some entity or state of affairs. Iconic signs include, for example, a street map of Los Angeles, giving the message of where streets, buildings, parks and other features of the city are located, a painting of the American president, Abraham Lincoln (1809-1865), giving the message of the distinguishing features of Lincoln's physical appearance and the manner of dress and grooming of a prominent man in 19th century America, a photograph of the American abolitionist and advocate for women's rights, Sojourner Truth (1797-1883), giving the message of the distinguishing features of Truth's physical appearance and of the manner of dress and grooming of a prominent African American woman in 19th century America, photographs of rock art in the Kimberley region of Western Australia, giving messages about Australian First Nation people's religious beliefs, creation stories, mythical creatures and real animals extant some 40,000 years ago, a figure wearing a dress painted on a door, giving the message that the door is the entry to a women's toilet, a silent motion picture taken in 1916 of British troops leaping from a trench to engage in battle during the Battle of the Somme, 1 July to 13 November, 1916, giving the message of how war was conducted in Europe in 1916, etc.

A symbolic sign is any linguistic object <*A*> which can be conceived (**O**) by an interpretant <*B*> and which stands in a semantic representational relationship of correspondence with some entity, phenomenon or state of affairs <*C*> and/or which stands in a conceptual relationship of coherence with another set of linguistic objects <A_1>. Messages formed from symbolic signs include words and sentences, either spoken, written (using some symbol system such as the Roman alphabet, Chinese characters, Arabic script, Braille, etc.) and/or signed (as in AUSLAN or ASL). They can also be numerals, equations and formulae. Examples of symbolic signs are

(1) the sound that corresponds with <*homme*> in French, denoting man, the sound that corresponds with <*voegel*> in German, denoting bird and the sound that corresponds with <طائر> in Arabic, denoting airplane,

(2) the English phonetic symbols <*eɪ*>, <*əʊ*>, <*ʊə*>, the Greek alphabetic letters, <Σ>, <Δ>, <Ψ> and the Thai abugida symbols <ฆ ระฆัง>,

(3) the spoken and written English words <*tree*>, <*bird*> and <*rain*>,

(4) the sentences <*An elm is a species of tree*>, <*A cow is a mammal*> and <*Sir Edmund Barton was the first Prime Minister of Australia*>,

(5) the numerals <*1, 2, 3*>, the equations <$y = ax^2 + bx + c$> and <$e = mc^2$> and the formulae <H_2O> and <C_2H_4>.

Symbolic signs can have either connotative meaning, denotative meaning or both connotative and denotative meaning. Connotative meaning is the set of symbols which have the same meaning as a symbol. For example, the term <*mammal*> has the same meaning as the set of terms <*warm blooded animal which has hair, gives live birth and provides milk to its young*>. The two sets of terms have a relationship of coherence with each other. Denotative meaning is the experiential entity, phenomenon, process or state of affairs to which a symbol refers. For example, the term <*mammal*> denotes animals such as cows, horses, cats and dogs. The term <*mammal*> has a relationship of correspondence with the perceivable$_6$ (**P**$_6$) objects that are cows, horses, cats and dogs.

Some symbolic signs have only connotative meaning, for example, the numerals <*1, 2, 3*> or <*I, II, III*> and the words <*if, but, and*>. These examples of numerals and words do not denote any experiential entity, phenomenon, process or state of affairs. Nothing in the experiential material world has a relationship of correspondence with them. Some symbolic signs have only denotative meaning. For example, the names <*Franklin Delano Roosevelt*>, <*Winston Churchill*> and <*John Fitzgerald Kennedy*> denote specific unique people, but the names do not connote any other set of terms which has the same meaning. No other set of terms has a relationship of coherence with them.

In addition to messages requiring a sign (or a set of signs) of some kind (physical, iconic, symbolic) to form them, they require some means to deliver them. To deliver (or convey) messages, teachers have available to them (1) in-person, face-to-face communication and (2) delivery by some means other than face-to-face, e.g. hand delivery, post, radio, audio-video recordings, telephone, television and/or Internet.

Delivery of messages by face-to-face is any communication which a teacher presents in the physical presence of the students. The messages can be ones consisting of physical signs such as body posture, gestures, facial expressions, properties of voice (pitch, timbre, loudness), rate of speech (rapid or slow), actual objects (animals, plants, minerals, samples of chemicals, physical models, etc.), sounds (musical tunes, whale songs, jet engine roars, train whistles, etc.). The messages can be ones of iconic signs (representational images) such as diagrams, drawings, motion pictures, paintings, photographs, videos (animated and/or live figures). The messages can be ones of symbolic signs (language) such as spoken and/or printed words and sentences, spoken and/or printed numerals and mathematic operations, signed language (e.g. AUSLAN, ASL), language recorded by means other than printed script (e.g. Braille). Messages consisting of symbolic signs can also be audio recordings and audio-visual recordings.

Delivery of messages by other than face-to-face is any communication which a teacher presents without being physically present in the same room or environs (same physical space) of the students. Correspondence studies$_1$ (**S$_{P1}$**), achieved by means of letters and parcels in the post, were historically the first means of delivery of other than face-to-face communications between teachers and students. With the development of two-way radio, remote intentional guided studies (**S$_{P1}$**) were conducted by two-way radio communication between teachers and students (e.g. the School of the Air program operated from Alice Springs, Northern Territory, Australia). With the development of the Internet, communication between teachers and students has evolved into communication via electronic messaging systems, online recorded instructional materials on webpages and live electronic meetings between teachers and students.

Delivery of communication in education (**E**) by electronic means via the Internet is becoming more and more commonplace, important and even necessary. Electronic learning management systems (LMS) are becoming invaluable tools for communicating about intentional guided study (**S$_{P1}$**) tasks, content (**C**), assessment tasks, intended learning outcomes (**ILO**s), study$_1$ (**S$_{P1}$**) resources, criteria for evaluation of assessment tasks, information about variations to schedules, information about excursions, etc. Examples of LMS include Blackboard Learn™, Moodle, Synap™, SAP Litmos™, LearnUpon LMS™, Absord LMS™, Intuto™, Google Classroom™, Microsoft Classroom™ and Zoom™, and entrepreneurs are continuously developing new renditions of LMS with improved functionality. An LMS can be used for online tutoring and online student-to-student conversations and discussions. It can be used for online examinations. It can be used for online submission of assignments and assessment tasks. The possibilities for uses of LMS continue to multiply as the experiences of teachers and students with LMS proceed and mature. Typically most educational institutions (school, academy, institute, college, university, etc.) have their own LMS in place, and it is the professional obligation of the effective teacher to master the use of the adopted LMS, either under the tutelage (study$_1$ $<\mathbf{S}_{P1}>$) of a supervisor or colleague, or through self-directed inquiry and self-guided study (study$_2$ $<\mathbf{S}_{P2}>$ or autodidactism).

Persons playing the role of teacher (**T**) increase the probabilities that the educational episodes (**E**) which they provide will be effective education ($\mathbf{E}_E$) by not only sending clear and unambiguous messages by means of some appropriate sign system (physical, iconic, symbolic) and some appropriate means of delivery (in person or remotely), but also by listening to messages (from fellow teachers, from students and from third parties) and carefully and accurately interpreting them. While actively listening, the effective communicator gives clear indications of paying attention to the message and correctly interpreting the message from the sender. Active listening is an important range of knowing ($\mathbf{K}_{2KLF}$) for teachers to master. It is just as important that teachers understand what messages their students, fellow teachers and interested third parties are sending as it is for the students, fellow teachers and interested third parties to understand what messages a teacher (or group of teachers) is wanting to communicate.

When language (a set of symbolic signs used in accordance with a set of rules) is the means by which communication is being achieved, persons playing the role of teacher (**T**) increase the probabilities that the educational episodes (**E**) which they provide will be effective education ($\mathbf{E}_E$) by using language which is appropriate for the age level of the student and the previous language experiences of the student. Appropriate language includes using sentence structure, terms, expressions and idioms familiar to the students and linking new terms, expressions and idioms with ones which the students are already using. Appropriate language also includes presenting new terms with both denotative meanings (pointing to the referents of the terms) and connotative meanings (giving words and expressions which mean nearly the same as, or have very similar meanings as, the new terms).

With communication, as with other aspects of education (**E**), the avoidance of miscommunication is never guaranteed. Clear communication is always a matter of probabilities, because misinterpretation of messages is always possible.

Purpose Driven Activities

Persons playing the role of teacher (**T**) increase the probabilities that the educational episodes (**E**) which they provide will be effective education (**E_E**) by assuring that all study$_1$ (**S_{P1}**) opportunities and activities are purpose driven by clearly stated, unambiguous intended learning outcomes (**ILO**s).

Purpose driven intentional guided study$_1$ (**S_{P1}**) activities are not ones which are provided to fill in some spare time. Rather, they are provided to develop a prescribed range of knowing (**K_{2P}**) which contributes to the achievement by the students (**S**) of some nominated set of intended learning outcomes (**ILO**s). That which gives purpose to intentional guided study$_1$ (**S_{P1}**) activities is the implicative meaning of the set of intended learning outcomes (**ILO**s). Study$_1$ (**S_{P1}**) activities are purposeful when they are part of the implicative meaning of the intended learning outcomes (**ILO**s) and/or when they are causally (materially) connected to the achievement of the intended learning outcomes (**ILO**s). Statements of intended learning outcomes (**ILO**s) can be generated by teachers (**T**), by students (**S**), by teachers and students in cooperation with each other and/or by third parties (**X**) (school authorities, legislative authorities, curriculum authorities, etc.). The appropriate locations for statements of intended learning outcomes (**ILO**s) are in lesson plans, unit plans, syllabi and curriculum documents. Statements of intended learning outcomes (**ILO**s) provide the conceptual basis for descriptions of the study$_1$ (**S_{P1}**) activities, the expressions of the worth of the opportunities to study$_1$ (**S_{P1}**), the relevance of the study$_1$ (**S_{P1}**) activities, the efficacy of the study$_1$ (**S_{P1}**) activities and the justification for the study$_1$ (**S_{P1}**) activities.

Study$_1$ (**S_{P1}**) tasks, driven by purpose, of course, can (and should) include activities which incorporate play, games, spontaneity and fun. Purposeful activity and pleasurable activity are entirely compatible. Furthermore, it is not always necessary that the students understand the purpose of the study$_1$ (**S_{P1}**) activities in the way that the teachers (**T**) understand them. Students (**S**) will typically join in and play games because they are fun, not because the games serve to achieve some intended learning outcome (**ILO**), even though the teacher (**T**) knows that student participation in the game does assist the students in achieving a nominated intended learning outcome (**ILO**). Students may follow their teacher's instructions without fully understanding the worth, the reasons and the justifications for the study$_1$ (**S**$_{P1}$) activities. But should the questions ever arise as to why the study$_1$ (**S**$_{P1}$) activities are being undertaken, what is the value of the activities and what justification there might be for the activities, ready answers for these questions should be available in the statements of the intended learning outcomes (**ILO**s) in the lesson plans, unit plans, syllabi and curriculum documents.

In most (if not all) official (**E**$_O$) educational settings (schools, academics, institutes, colleges, universities, etc.), it is an administrative requirement that teachers communicate to their students (and to their supervisors) in spoken word and written statements the intended learning outcomes (<**ILO**s> – the educational aims, goal and objectives) of the lessons, units and/or courses which are being taught (**T**$_P$) and studied$_1$ (**S**$_{P1}$). It is often a further requirement that there be written statements, provided in a syllabus, which specify the attendance requirements, the class behavior protocols, relevant deadlines, the assessment tasks, the criteria for evaluation, the form of evaluation report, the study$_1$ (**S**$_{P1}$) resources available and/or required, the homework requirements and the daily, weekly and term and/or semester study$_1$ (**S**$_{P1}$) tasks. If these requirements are part of an official educational setting (**E**$_O$), then fulfillment of these requirements is a professional responsibility as well as an effective teaching practice.

Student Engagement

Persons playing the role of teacher (**T**) increase the probabilities that the educational episodes (**E**) which they provide will be effective education (**E**$_E$) by judiciously arranging the physical, social and cultural environment such that it maximizes the probabilities that the students will genuinely, authentically and in good faith become engaged and remain engaged with the study$_1$ (**S**$_{P1}$) activities provided for them until they complete the activities.

Student engagement is a state of mind (**M**). Students are genuinely and authentically engaged in good faith in their studies$_1$ (**S**$_{P1}$) when the focus (**F**) of their mind (**M**) is coordinating their volition (**V**), perception (**P**) and cognition (**N**) to attend to the study$_1$ (**S**$_{P1}$) activities on offer. The focus (**F**) of their mind (**M**) gives direction for their volition, perception and cognition (their <**VPN**> or <**V** ⇄ **P** ⇄ **N** ⇄ **V**>) such that they recognize, accept, participate in, contribute to, have a concern for and complete, in good faith, the study$_1$ (**S**$_{P1}$) activities provided to them. These conditions for engagement are true for all age levels of students whether they be infants, young children, children in middle childhood, teenagers, young adults, mature adults or seniors.

Having a relevant and sufficient range of educological knowing (**K**$_{2KLF}$) improves the probabilities that persons playing the role of teacher (**T**) will discern and recognize when students (**S**) are (or are not) engaged with their studies$_1$ (**S**$_{P1}$), understand (**U**) why they are (or are not) engaged with their studies$_1$ (**S**$_{P1}$) and know (have a knowing-how <**K**$_{2K3}$>) what to do (and what not to do) to conduce students to become engaged (and remain engaged) with their studies$_1$ (**S**$_{P1}$).

Educological knowing-that-one (**K**$_{2K1}$) gives teachers (**T**) the cognitive ability to recognize, be well acquainted with and appreciate the moods, interests, patterns of behavior and swings in focus of attention of each of their students.

Educological knowing-that (**K**$_{2K2}$) (1) informs teachers (**T**) that the focus of attention (**F**) of their students (**S**) is fleeting, (2) enables teachers (**T**) to anticipate, discern, describe, explain and predict the transience of the focus of attention (**F**) of their students (**S**) and (3) empowers teachers (**T**) with the ability to predict the likely effects of change and variation in study$_1$ (**S**$_{P1}$) activities upon the focus of attention (**F**) of their students (**S**).

Educological knowing-how (**K**$_{2K3}$) equips teachers (**T**) with the skill set to undertake effective action which creates circumstances and relationships to attract the focus of attention (**F**) of their students through deliberately and purposively presenting their students (**S**) with continuous variety in the

(1) initiation of study$_1$ (**S**$_{P1}$) activities (initiation by teachers, by students or by third parties),
(2) pace (from slow, to medium, to fast) of their study$_1$ (**S**$_{P1}$) activities,
(3) duration of their study$_1$ (**S**$_{P1}$) activities (from 5 to 10 to 20, 30, 40 or 50 minutes duration, with transitional moments between activities),
(4) goal structures (individual, cooperative, competitive) for their study$_1$ (**S**$_{P1}$) activities,

(5) grouping (individual, small group, whole group, teams),
(6) kinds of study$_1$ ($\mathbf{S}_{P1}$) activities (listening, speaking, reading, writing, drawing, observing, making models, conducting experiments, performing, presenting, etc.),
(7) choice of content ($<\mathbf{C}_1>$ and/or $<\mathbf{C}_2>$) and problems for inquiry (**Q**),
(8) resources used in study$_1$ ($\mathbf{S}_{P1}$) activities,
(9) design of educational episodes (Design 1, Design 2, etc.).

Organizing for variation in the combinations of these derivative components ($\mathbf{E}_{DC}$) of education (**E**) maximizes the probability of student (**S**) engagement in study$_1$ ($\mathbf{S}_{P1}$) activities, but does not guarantee student engagement. The relationship of teaching ($\mathbf{T}_P$) and studying$_1$ ($\mathbf{S}_{P1}$) is transactive, not reactive. The teaching ($\mathbf{T}_P$) can be competent, professional and exemplary of best practice, and the person (child, adolescent, adult) playing the role of student (**S**) can choose not to accept guidance and not to undertake the study$_1$ ($\mathbf{S}_{P1}$) activities on offer, at which point, education (**E**) ceases to function.

Optimal Level of Difficulty

Persons playing the role of teacher (**T**) increase the probabilities that the educational episodes (**E**) which they provide will be effective education ($\mathbf{E}_E$) by presenting students (**S**) with content (**C**), study$_1$ ($\mathbf{S}_{P1}$) tasks and intended learning outcomes (**ILO**s) which are at an optimal level of difficulty.

Content (**C**), study$_1$ ($\mathbf{S}_{P1}$) tasks and intended learning outcomes (**ILO**s) which are too simple present no challenge to the students (**S**). They quickly become bored with the study$_1$ ($\mathbf{S}_{P1}$) tasks, or they simply refuse to complete them because the tasks are too easy. Study$_1$ ($\mathbf{S}_{P1}$) tasks which are too difficult for the students (**S**) frustrate them, and they will typically give up in defeat. Effective teaching ($\mathbf{T}_{PE}$) presents students (**S**) with content (**C**) and study$_1$ ($\mathbf{S}_{P1}$) tasks which are challenging, but, at the same time, are ones which are within the students' (**S**) psychical and physical capabilities to complete successfully.

Persons playing the role of teacher (**T**) increase the probabilities that the educational episodes (**E**) which they provide will be effective education ($\mathbf{E}_E$) by presenting students (**S**) with study$_1$ ($\mathbf{S}_{P1}$) activities which are sequenced in their degree of difficulty. Appropriate sequencing requires consideration of what the students already know

(**K**$_{2KLF}$), the complexity of the study$_1$ (**S**$_{P1}$) tasks relative to the students' psychical and physical capabilities, the difficulty of the intended learning outcomes (**ILO**s) and the simpler intermediate ranges of knowing (**K**$_{2KLF}$) to be achieved en route to developing the more complex total prescribed range of knowing (**K**$_{2P}$) implied by the intended learning outcomes (**ILO**s).

Matching Teaching and Studying$_1$ (S$_{P1}$) Resources, Methods and Styles

Persons playing the role of teacher (**T**) increase the probabilities that the educational episodes (**E**) which they provide will be effective education (**E**$_E$) by achieving an optimal fit between

(1) resources (**E**$_{DC2}$) which teachers (**T**) make available to students (**S**) to study$_1$ (**S**$_{P1}$) and resources (**E**$_{DC2}$) from which students (**S**) learn$_1$ (**L**$_1$) a prescribed range of knowing (**K**$_{2P}$),
(2) teaching (**T**$_P$) methods and studying$_1$ (**S**$_{P1}$) methods,
(3) teaching (**T**$_P$) styles and studying$_1$ (**S**$_{P1}$) styles.

Resources

Resources for teaching (**E**$_{DC2T}$) are the physical materials which teachers (**T**) use in their guidance and management of students undertaking study$_1$ (**S**$_{P1}$) tasks. Resources for teaching (**E**$_{DC2T}$) include lesson plans, unit plans, notes, textbooks, worksheets, maps, diagrams, posters, videos, computers, etc. Resources (**E**$_{DC2S}$) for studying$_1$ (**S**$_{P1}$) are the physical materials which students (**S**) use in undertaking and completing their study$_1$ (**S**$_{P1}$) tasks. Resources (**E**$_{DC2S}$) for studying$_1$ (**S**$_{P1}$) include books, computers, computer applications (spreadsheet, data base, etc.), videos, worksheets, diagrams, photos, charts, games, problem sets, libraries, playing fields, swimming pools, saws, drills, balls, etc.

Resources (**E**$_{DC2S}$) for studying$_1$ (**S**$_{P1}$) may be non-linguistic or linguistic. Non-linguistic resources (**E**$_{DC2S}$) for studying$_1$ (**S**$_{P1}$) have no language in them as a component of the resource. Examples include things like rocks, water, sand, fire, hand tools, photographs, paintings, jigsaw puzzles, chess pieces and board, playing fields, swimming pools, microscopes, magnets, test tubes, Bunsen burners, beakers, graduated cylinders, musical instruments, welding equipment, brushes, paints, sheep, goats, cattle, chickens, eggs, etc. Linguistic resources (**E**$_{DC2S}$) for studying$_1$ (**S**$_{P1}$) have language as a component of them. Examples include things like books, computer applications, worksheets, periodic tables, charts, graphs, labeled diagrams, maps, videos with narration, pictures with explanatory and/or expository language, games with language, etc.

It maximizes the probabilities that an educational episode (**E**) will be effective education (**E_E**) by providing (or providing guidance about where to find) resources (**E_{DC2S}**) for studying$_1$ (**S_{P1}**) which are appropriate for the abilities and interests of the students (**S**) and which are relevant to assisting the students (**S**) to learn$_1$ (**L_1**) the prescribed range of knowing (**K_{2P}**) specified by the nominated intended learning outcomes (**ILO**s).

Methods

Methods of teaching (**E_{DC3T}**) are procedures which teachers (**T**) follow in providing guidance and management of their students' study$_1$ (**S_{P1}**) activities. Methods of studying intentionally under guidance (**E_{DC3S}**) are procedures which students (**S**) follow in undertaking to learn$_1$ (**L_1**) some prescribed range of knowing (**K_{2P}**) under the guidance and management of a teacher (**T**). Examples of methods of teaching (**E_{DC2T}**) include answering questions, arranging resources, asking questions, assigning activities, defining terms, demonstrating procedures, etc. Methods of intentionally studying under guidance (**E_{DC3S}**) include conducting experiments, drawing diagrams, finding resources, playing games, playing roles, practicing procedures, solving problems, etc. It maximizes the probabilities that an educational episode (**E**) will be effective education (**E_E**) when there is a match between teaching methods (**E_{DC3T}**) and studying$_1$ (**S_{P1}**) methods (**E_{DC3S}**). The matching of teaching methods (**E_{DC3T}**) with studying$_1$ (**S_{P1}**) methods (**E_{DC3S}**) is a synchronization between what the teacher (**T**) does and what the students (**S**) do such that the guidance provided by the teacher (**T**) assists the students (**S**) in making progress with their studying$_1$ (**S_{P1}**) some content (**C**) to learn$_1$ (**L_1**) a prescribed range of knowing (**K_{2P}**) specified by a nominated set of intended learning outcomes (**ILO**s).

Styles

It maximizes the probabilities that an educational episode (**E**) will be effective education (**E_E**) when the style of teaching (**E_{DC4T}**) complements the style of intentional guided studying (**E_{DC4S}**). When teaching styles (**E_{DC4T}**) and intentional guided studying styles (**E_{DC4S}**) complement each other, the social interaction between teachers (**T**) and students (**S**) is positive, constructive and supportive of the students (**S**) successfully completing their $study_1$ ($\mathbf{S_{P1}}$) tasks and consequently $learning_1$ ($\mathbf{L_1}$) the prescribed range of knowing ($\mathbf{K_{2P}}$) specified by a nominated set of intended learning outcomes (**ILO**s).

Style of teaching ($\mathbf{E_{DC4T}}$) is the pattern of social interaction which teachers (**T**) follow while implementing their teaching methods. Terms which characterize style include <*supportive* vs. *unsupportive, personable* vs. *impersonal, friendly* vs. *aloof, humorous* v. *humorless, kind* vs. *menacing, calm* vs. *animated, jaded* vs. *enthusiastic, positive* vs. *negative, confident* vs. *diffident, dogmatic* vs. *inquiring, open* vs. *closed*>. Style of intentional guided studying ($\mathbf{E_{DC4S}}$) is the pattern of social interaction which students follow while they implement their intentional guided studying methods. The same terms which characterize teaching style ($\mathbf{E_{DC4T}}$) also characterize intentional guided studying style ($\mathbf{E_{DC4S}}$).

We, as human beings, typically develop our patterns of social interaction without being self-conscious of them and, also, without being aware that other people have different patterns from our own patterns. Our intention guided study ($study_1$ <$\mathbf{S_{P1}}$>) and our intentional unguided study ($study_3$ or inquiry <$\mathbf{S_{P3}}$>) of patterns of social interaction (our own and others) enable us to become self-aware of our own patterns of social interaction and the consequences of following those patterns. Through our intentional guided study ($study_1$ <$\mathbf{S_{P1}}$>) and our independent research ($study_3$ <$\mathbf{S_{P3}}$>) of patterns of social interaction, we can develop our knowing-that-one ($\mathbf{K_{2K1}}$), knowing-that ($\mathbf{K_{2K2}}$), knowing-how ($\mathbf{K_{2K3}}$) and knowing-to ($\mathbf{K_{2K4}}$) about our own patterns of social interaction and the patterns of others.

Our knowing-that-one ($\mathbf{K_{2K1}}$) gives us sensitivity to recognize, become acquainted with and appreciate our own unique patterns of social interactions and the unique patterns of those whom we encounter. Our knowing-that ($\mathbf{K_{2K2}}$) gives us theoretical adequacy to classify, explain and predict patterns of social interaction and the relations (the mutual effects) among patterns of social interaction. Our knowing-how ($\mathbf{K_{2K3}}$) gives us the skills to engage in social interaction positively and constructively and to avoid and/or eliminate negative and destructive social interaction. Our knowing-to ($\mathbf{K_{2F4}}$) gives us the ability to make rational choices about the social interactions we wish to encourage, discourage and/or eliminate.

Persons playing the role of teacher (**T**), with a sufficient range of knowing ($\mathbf{K_{2KLF}}$), in all four kinds of knowing ($\mathbf{K_{2K1}}$, $\mathbf{K_{2K2}}$, $\mathbf{K_{2K3}}$, $\mathbf{K_{2K4}}$), about their own patterns of social interactions and the patterns of others, can adjust their patterns of social interaction to complement the patterns of their students. Teachers (**T**) can thereby optimize the social environment for their students (**S**) for the purpose of maximizing the probabilities that an educational episode (**E**) will be effective education ($\mathbf{E}_{E}$), i.e. that students (**S**) will be effective in their intentional guided study (study$_1$ $<\mathbf{S}_{P1}>$) and will learn intentionally under guidance (learn$_1$ $<\mathbf{L}_{1}>$) the prescribed range of knowing ($\mathbf{K}_{2P}$) that is specified by a set of nominated intended learning outcomes (**ILO**s).

Positive Emotional Experience

Persons playing the role of teacher (**T**) increase the probabilities that the educational episodes (**E**) which they provide will be effective education ($\mathbf{E}_{E}$) by providing circumstances such that students (**S**) experience (perceive$_1$ $<\mathbf{P}_{1}>$) positive emotions as they undertake intentional guided study (study$_1$ $<\mathbf{S}_{P1}>$) activities and make progress in their intentional guided learning (learning$_1$ $<\mathbf{L}_{1}>$) of a prescribed range of knowing ($\mathbf{K}_{2P}$) that is specified by a set of intended learning outcomes (**ILO**s). Their emotional experience is positive when they feel interested and challenged by their study$_1$ ($\mathbf{S}_{P1}$) activities, they feel pleased and satisfied with the progress they make in their studying$_1$ ($\mathbf{S}_{P1}$), and their learning$_1$ ($\mathbf{L}_{1}$) of a prescribed range of knowing ($\mathbf{K}_{2P}$) is cause for fun, excitement, celebration and feelings of fulfilment.

A judicious mix of various derivative components of education ($\mathbf{E}_{DC}$) maximizes the probabilities that students (S) will experience (perceive$_1$ $<\mathbf{P}_{1}>$) positive emotions in association with their study$_1$ ($\mathbf{S}_{P1}$) activities. The judicious mix of derivative components of education ($\mathbf{E}_{DC}$) includes

(1) manifesting a style of teaching ($\mathbf{E}_{DC4T}$) of genuine, sincere and authentic enthusiasm for being with the students (**S**), for the content (**C**) being taught and studied$_1$ ($\mathbf{S}_{P1}$), for the guided study$_1$ ($\mathbf{S}_{P1}$) activities and for the intended learning outcomes (**ILO**s),

(2) manifesting a style of teaching ($\mathbf{E}_{DC4T}$) of genuine, sincere and authentic compassion, empathy and care for the well being of the students (**S**), for the effort which they put into their study$_1$ ($\mathbf{S}_{P1}$) activities, for the success of the students (**S**) in their studies$_1$ ($\mathbf{S}_{P1}$) and for their achievement of the nominated set of intended learning outcomes (**ILO**s),

(3) manifesting a style of teaching ($\mathbf{E}_{DC4T}$) of positive, light hearted, good spirited and inclusive humor, which everyone can enjoy, from which no one ever feels offended, hurt or victimized and which is never biting, insulting, cutting, cruel, teasing, humiliating or demeaning of anyone,

(4) using the teaching method ($\mathbf{E}_{DC3T}$) of reward, which provides private and public recognition, praise and reward for the effort which students (**S**) put into their studies$_1$ ($\mathbf{S}_{P1}$) and the success which they achieve in attaining intended learning outcomes (**ILO**s), including rewards which are age appropriate, rewards for the students (**S**) who achieve the best, rewards for those who improve the most, rewards for those who try the hardest, rewards for those who complete their assigned study$_1$ ($\mathbf{S}_{P1}$) activities consistently, rewards for those with the best attitudes and/or rewards for those who set the best examples for other students (**S**) and recognition and rewards for achievement by students (**S**) for all kinds of knowing ($\mathbf{K}_{2K}$) – <u>knowing-that-one</u> ($\mathbf{K}_{2K1}$), <u>knowing-that</u> ($\mathbf{K}_{2K2}$), <u>knowing-how</u> ($\mathbf{K}_{2K3}$) and <u>knowing-to</u> ($\mathbf{K}_{2K4}$), expressed in linguistic ($\mathbf{K}_{2F1}$) and physical ($\mathbf{K}_{2F5}$) forms,

(5) using the teaching method ($\mathbf{E}_{DC3T}$) of student choice, which provides students (**S**) with choices as to what content (**C**) to study$_1$ ($\mathbf{S}_{P1}$), what resources ($\mathbf{E}_{DC2}$) to use, what study$_1$ ($\mathbf{S}_{P1}$) activities to undertake, what intended learning outcomes (**ILO**s) to nominate, what problems to investigate, what phenomena to observe, describe & analyze, what organization of students to arrange for study$_1$ ($\mathbf{S}_{P1}$) activities (as independent individuals, small groups and/or teams, whole group), what assessment tasks to complete, what criteria to use in evaluating assessment tasks, what uses to make of the evaluation reports, etc.,

(6) using the teaching method ($\mathbf{E}_{DC3T}$) of linking one prescribed range of knowing ($\mathbf{K}_{2P}$) to another prescribed range of knowing ($\mathbf{K}_{2P}$) to guide students (**S**) in the development of their understanding (**U**) of the connections between a prescribed range of knowing ($\mathbf{K}_{2P}$) that they have previously learned$_1$ ($\mathbf{L}_1$) and the a prescribed range of knowing ($\mathbf{K}_{2P}$) they are currently endeavoring to learn$_1$ ($\mathbf{L}_1$),

(7) using the teaching method ($\mathbf{E}_{DC3T}$) of games and play to

provide students (**S**) with a variety of games (including electronic and/or computer generated games, non-electronic games, solo games, pairs, groups and team games), which, when played, contribute to developing the prescribed range of knowing (K_{2P}) specified by some nominated set of intended learning outcomes (**ILO**s),

(8) using the teaching method ($\mathbf{E_{DC3T}}$) of active participation to elicit the active participation by students (**S**) in educational episodes (**E**) such that the students (**S**) habitually practice active listening and contribute with exemplifications and applications of the prescribed range of knowing ($\mathbf{K_{2P}}$) about the content (**C**) that is specified by the intended learning outcomes (**ILO**s),

(9) providing appropriate and well-timed variations in the goal structures ($<\mathbf{E_{DC11}}>$ – individualized, cooperative, competitive) for study$_1$ ($\mathbf{S_{P1}}$) activities and for the nominated intended learning outcomes (**ILO**s),

(10) providing and/or advising where and how to find a wide range of study$_1$ ($\mathbf{S_{P1}}$) resources ($\mathbf{E_{DC2}}$), both non-linguistic and linguistic, including charts, diagrams, pictures, audio recordings, audio-video recordings, cameras, books, short articles, supplemental readings, worksheets, computers, computer applications, games, tools, equipment, etc.,

(11) providing appropriate and judicious variations in the pace ($<\mathbf{E_{DC7}}>$ – slow, medium, fast) of study$_1$ ($\mathbf{S_{P1}}$) activities for the whole class, for groups and for individuals,

(12) providing appropriate and judicious variations in the organization ($\mathbf{E_{DC12}}$) of study$_1$ ($\mathbf{S_{P1}}$) activities for the students, as individuals working independently, as small groups or teams working cooperatively and as one whole, undivided group,

(13) providing variations in the intended focus ($\mathbf{E_{DC5}}$) of attention of the students, moving their focus ($\mathbf{E_{DC5}}$) back and forth among (1) what the teacher is doing, (2) what other students are doing, (3) what the self as student is doing, (4) the resources provided for studying$_1$ ($\mathbf{S_{P1}}$) and/or (5) situations in which study$_1$ ($\mathbf{S_{P1}}$) activities take place (a court room, a cheese factory, a dairy farm, a water purification plant, a wool combing plant, a field full of

different species of flowers, a forest with different species of animals, a body of water with microbes in the water, a sale yard with cattle, a cliff with exposed strata of rock, a sky with different types of clouds, a beach with wave patterns in the surf, a beach strewn with plastic objects, a coral reef, etc.),

(14) introducing new content (**C**) continuously for students (**S**) to study$_1$ (**S**$_{P1}$) and use to build upon and extend previously learned$_1$ (**L**$_1$) prescribed ranges of knowing (**K**$_{2P}$), all the while avoiding requiring students (**S**) unnecessarily to repeat studying$_1$ (**S**$_{P1}$) previously studied$_1$ (**S**$_{P1}$) content (**C**) from which they have already learned$_1$ (**L**$_1$) some previously prescribed range of knowing (**K**$_{2P}$).

So, by providing circumstances (through the judicious mix of derivative components of education <**E**$_{DC}$>), which increase the probabilities that students (**S**) will experience (perceive$_1$ <**P**$_1$>) positive emotions as they undertake their study$_1$ (**S**$_{P1}$) activities, persons playing the role of teacher (**T**) increase the probabilities that the educational episodes (**E**) which they provide will be effective education (**E**$_E$) for their students.

Appropriate Instructional Designs

Persons playing the role of teacher (**T**) increase the probabilities that the educational episodes (**E**) which they provide will be effective education (**E**$_E$) by devising and using appropriate instructional designs (**E**$_{DC19}$) which suit the purpose of the educational episode, the students (**S**), the study$_1$ (**S**$_{P1}$) tasks, the intended learning outcomes (**ILO**s), the assessment tasks, the evaluation procedures and the use of the evaluation results. The possibilities of designs include Design 1 (**D**$_1$), Design 2 (**D**$_2$), Design 3 (**D**$_3$), Design 4 (**D**$_4$), Design 5 (**D**$_5$), Design 6 (**D**$_6$) or some other design. It may well be the case that the educational institution in which the teacher works (school, academy, institute, college, university, military unit, etc.) determines and/or prescribes a single instructional design, or designates a range of prescribed, permitted and/or proscribed designs. But whether prescribed by the institution or devised by the teacher, use of an appropriate instructional design is part of effective education (**E**$_E$). The appropriateness of a design is determined by the degree to which the design matches the purpose of the educational episode (lesson, unit, course, curriculum), the intended learning outcomes (**ILO**s), the available resources, the amount of time allocated for teaching (**T_P**) and studying$_1$ (**S_{P1}**), the assessment and evaluation of student achievement of the intended learning outcomes (**ILO**s) and the uses to be made of the evaluation results (preparative, formative and/or summative).

Provision of Opportunities for Emendment of Extant Knowing

Persons playing the role of teacher (**T**) increase the probabilities that the educational episodes (**E**) which they provide will be effective education (**E_E**) by creating circumstances and/or prescribing study$_1$ (**S_{P1}**) tasks which provide opportunities, encouragement and guidance for students (**S**) to emend their extant range of knowing (**K_{2KLF}**) to accommodate their newly acquired prescribed range of knowing (**K_{2P}**). An emendment of a range of knowing (**K_{2KLF}**) is an improvement to a range of knowing (**K_{2KLF}**) through an extension of that range and/or a correction to that range.

Provision of Opportunities for Integration of Extant Knowing with New Knowing

Persons playing the role of teacher (**T**) increase the probabilities that the educational episodes (**E**) which they provide will be effective education (**E_E**) by creating circumstances and/or prescribing study$_1$ (**S_{P1}**) tasks which provide opportunities, encouragement and guidance for students (**S**) to integrate their newly acquired prescribed range of knowing (**K_{2P}**) with their extant range of knowing (**K_{2KLF}**). Integration of a new range of knowing (**K_{2KLF}**) with an extant range of knowing (**K_{2KLF}**) includes creating circumstances in which students (**S**) have the opportunity and/or the challenge of

(1) identifying the mutual effects of their new range of knowing and their prior range of knowing,
(2) identifying the conflicts between their new range of knowing and their prior range of knowing,
(3) identifying the explanatory power of their prior range of knowing for their new range of knowing and vice versa,
(4) extending their range of knowing beyond the new information provided in their study$_1$ (**S_{P1}**) activities,
(5) generalizing from instances to classes of phenomena, or from members of categories denoted by concepts to

categories denoted by concepts,
(6) resolving conflicts between new ranges of knowing and prior ranges of knowing
(7) reacting to new ranges of knowing,
(8) seeking additional information to extend new ranges of knowing,
(9) exploring the significance of new ranges of knowing,
(10) investigating the uses of new ranges of knowing.

Constructive Practices by Third Parties

Education (**E**) functions within a social system in which teachers (**T**) provide opportunities for students (**S**) to study$_1$ (**S$_{P1}$**) and the students voluntarily accept study$_1$ (**S$_{P1}$**) opportunities in good faith and make genuine efforts to complete the study$_1$ (**S$_{P1}$**) tasks on offer with a view to learning$_1$ (**L$_1$**) a prescribed range of knowing (**K$_{2P}$**) specified by some nominated set of intended learning outcomes (**ILO**s). It is challenging, if not impossible, for the activities of teaching (**T$_P$**) and studying$_1$ (**S$_{P1}$**) of some content (**C**) to function properly without support from the physical, social and cultural context (**X**) in which the teaching (**T$_P$**) and studying$_1$ (**S$_{P1}$**) take place. Actions which third parties (i.e. members of the physical, social and cultural context – school administrators, parents, community leaders, local municipalities, boards of governors, etc.) can perform to increase the probabilities that education (**E**) will be effective education (**E$_E$**) include

(1) assuring student safety,
(2) expressing affection for and among students,
(3) providing inclusion of students,
(4) assuring fairness for students,
(5) expressing positive attitudes towards and among students.

Safety

The probabilities are increased that education (**E**) will be effective education (**E$_E$**) when the context (**X**) for the teachers (**T**) and the students (**S**) is a safe one. A safe context (**X**) for education (**E**) includes physical, social and emotional safety.

Physical safety is a state of affairs in which teachers and students are provided with adequate protection from actions, events, circumstances and surroundings which might cause physical injury and/or illness. Adequate physical safety includes clean, structurally sound accommodation which provides protection from the weather, insects, rodents and other pests. It includes sufficient space, indoors and outdoors, for the activities of teaching and intentional guided studying. It includes sanitation (sanitary rubbish disposal and pure water in ample supply for drinking, hand washing, toilet flushing, equipment washing etc.). Adequate physical safety includes measures to protect teachers and students from physical assault, sexual abuse, illness from communicable diseases and injuries from hazardous equipment, surrounds, toxic substances and/or unsafe practices while at work, play or during travel to and from school. The set of events at Sandy Hook Elementary School (Newtown, Connecticut, 14 December 2012) in which 20-year-old Adam Lanza shot and killed six adults and 20 children is an example of an obviously egregious failure to provide a physically safe environment for the teachers and students at that school. Other examples of failures to provide a physically safe environment are the kidnapping of 276 female students by members of Boko Haram from the secondary school in the town of Chibok, Borno State, Nigeria (14-15 April 2014) and the shooting of Malala Yousafzai on her way home from school in Swat, Pakistan (9 October 2012). Being shot or stabbed en route to and/or from school, or at school, being kicked, punched, spat upon or having rocks, furniture, bottles and other objects hurled at one's self (in the role of teacher or student) or being sexually assaulted are all too common in schools and universities in Australia, the United States and elsewhere, and they are obviously all intolerable breaches of the basic conditions for physical safety within a school environment. Another important part of physical safety for schools are programs to minimize the spread of infectious diseases. Measures that are important to achieve this include careful hygiene, mass inoculation against communicable diseases and quarantine regimens to avoid infectious diseases, when necessary. Physical safety is a vital state of affairs for education (**E**), and it is an imperative for effective education ($\mathbf{E_E}$) that those with influence and those who are in leadership positions in the context (**X**) of education (**E**) assure that the threat of physical harm and incidences of actual bodily harm, accidental injury and infectious diseases are prevented and/or eliminated.

Social safety is a state of affairs in which teachers and students are at liberty to express their thoughts, disclose their feelings and undertake teaching ($\mathbf{T_P}$) and studying$_1$ ($\mathbf{S_{P1}}$) without fear of intimidation, ridicule, reprisal, bullying, punishment, threat, ostracism or abuse (verbal and nonverbal). Social safety includes protection of teachers (**T**), students (**S**) and third parties (<**X**> – school administrators, counselors, etc.) regardless of their physical appearance, linguistic accents, intellectual abilities or disabilities, ethnic origins, religious affiliations, sexual orientation, gender identity and/or social class or caste. Like physical safety, social safety is a vital state of affairs for education (**E**), and it is an imperative for effective education ($\mathbf{E}_{\mathbf{E}}$) that those with influence and those who are in leadership positions in the context (**X**) of education (**E**) assure that social safety be established and maintained through sound policies and conscientious execution of those policies.

Emotional safety in education (**E**) is a state of affairs in which the participants in education (**E**) – teachers (**T**), students (**S**) and third parties (**X**) – are protected from emotional abuse. Emotional abuse is mistreatment of someone with the view in mind of manipulating, controlling and/or exploiting the one being abused. Emotional abuse is achieved by communication (using physical, iconic and symbolic signs) between the abuser and the abused. In education (**E**), the abuser can be teachers (**T**), students (**S**) and/or third parties (**X**), and the abused can be teachers, students and/or third parties. Indications of emotional abuse include

(1) the abused party shuns activities and people because the abused feels that the abuser disapproves and/or opposes the activities and the associations of the abused,
(2) the abused party feels a loss of confidence and/or self-esteem in his or her value, intelligence and/or judgment because the abuser belittles, demeans, insults and/or dismisses the views, values, intelligence, range of knowing ($\mathbf{K}_{\mathbf{2KLF}}$) and opinions of the abused,
(3) the abused party feels obliged to ask permission from the abuser to conduct ordinary activities (to go shopping or to associate with friends and family), and the abused party also feels obliged to report his or her whereabouts frequently to the abuser,
(4) the abused party feels stupid and/or worthless because the abuser often interrupts the abuser in conversations and/or discussions, or says something like, "You aren't going to talk about that, are you?" or "You're not still harping on about that, are you?" or "Everything you say

is so stupid," or the abuser changes the subject abruptly or accuses the abused to have committed some fabricated transgression,

(5) the abused party feels stupid and/or worthless because the abuser often uses sarcasm, ridicule and insults to demean the abused, then accuses the abused of being overly sensitive and unable to take a joke,

(6) the abused party often apologizes for actions and/or situations for which the abused party has no responsibility because the abuser has demanded an apology,

(7) the abused party feels guilt for actions and/or situations for which the abused party has no responsibility because the abuser has insisted that the abused party must bear the guilt,

(8) the abused party often finds himself or herself being silenced and demeaned while the abuser speaks on behalf of the abused or attributes to the abused statements which the abused party has never uttered,

(9) the abused party often finds himself or herself in the role of the anxious dependent appeaser because the abuser engages in wild mood swings from anger to affection and from adamant rejection to professions of profound love,

(10) the abused party suffers from doubt about his or her accuracy of memory and/or sanity because the abuser denies that past events ever happened and tells the abused that he or she did not see and/or hear what he or she actually saw and heard,

(11) the abused party harbors deep-seated doubts about his or her accomplishments and abilities because the abuser habitually belittles and demeans the accomplishments and talents of the abused party,

(12) the abused party feels he or she is in a state of deprivation and of fear of loss because the abuser regularly administers punishments by withholding affection, permission and/or money,

(13) the abused party feels guilt and pity for the abuser because the abuser habitually communicates disappointment in the way that the abused party does not satisfy the expectations, the standards and/or the needs,

wants and desires of the abuser,

(14) the abused party feels (and is) isolated because the abuser takes away the possessions of the abused, ridicules the abused party's relatives and friends, refuses permission for the abused to visit his or her relatives and friends, blocks communication between the abused and his or her relatives and friends and dictates what the abused party must say and/or do in relation to his or her relatives and friends,

(15) the abused party is filled with self-doubt, indecision and hesitancy because the abuser rejects the viewpoint, thoughts and/or wishes of the abused.

An emotionally safe environment for participants in education (**E**) – teachers (**T**), students (**S**) and third parties (**X**) – is one in which emotional abuse is absent (prevented and/or eliminated) and in which the sense of self-worth (and self-confidence) of each person is encouraged, authentic efforts at improvement are praised and genuine achievements are recognized, celebrated and rewarded.

Emotional safety for participants (**T, S, X**) in education (**E**) is a vital state of affairs for education (**E**), and it is an imperative for effective education ($\mathbf{E_E}$) that (1) participants (**T, S, X**) in education (**E**), (2) those with influence in the context (**X**) of education (**E**) and (3) those who are in leadership positions in the context (**X**) of education (**E**) assure that (1) the threat of emotional abuse and incidences of actual emotional abuse are prevented and/or eliminated and (2) policies are formulated and executed faithfully and effectively for assuring the emotional safety of all participants in education (**E**).

Affection

The probabilities are increased that education (**E**) will be effective education ($\mathbf{E_E}$) when the context (**X**) for education (**E**) is one in which it is made clear (through all means of communication – physical signs, iconic signs and linguistic signs) to the students (**S**) by teachers (**T**) and interested third parties (administrators, supervisors, counselors, advisors, the wider community, etc.) who make up the social context (**X**) of education (**E**) that the students (**S**) are welcome, they are liked, they are respected and there is genuine care and concern for their well being and their physical and psychical (volitional <**V**>, perceptual <**P**> and cognitive <**N**>) development.

Inclusion

The probabilities are increased that education (**E**) will be effective education ($\mathbf{E_E}$) when the context (**X**) for education (**E**) is one which builds a sense of classroom and school community among the students (**S**) such that each student feels that he or she is a valued member of the group, class and/or year, is respected and is appreciated. In an inclusive context (**X**), there are no inner groups and outer groups, or those who belong and those who do not belong, or those who have special privileges and those who do not, or those who are unjustly praised and those who are unjustly denigrated.

Fairness

The probabilities are increased that education (**E**) will be effective education ($\mathbf{E_E}$) when the context (**X**) for education (**E**) is one in which there is fairness and justness for all. The same rules of conduct for students (**S**) apply to all students (**S**), without fear or favor. There is no one exempt from the rules of conduct or from the criteria for achievement of intended learning outcomes (**ILO**s), and there are no scapegoats nor victims. There is no arbitrariness. The rules and standards of conduct are clear (easily understandable), reasonable and soundly justified. The rules and standards are applied consistently, firmly and fairly, with understanding and humaneness.

Attitude

The probabilities are increased that education (**E**) will be effective education ($\mathbf{E_E}$) when the context (**X**) for education (**E**) is one which encourages and engenders positive attitudes among students (**S**) towards studying intentionally under guidance ($\mathbf{S_{P1}}$) and learning intentionally under guidance ($\mathbf{L_1}$) prescribed ranges of knowing ($\mathbf{K_{2P}}$) specified by some set of intended learning outcomes (**ILO**s). The context (**X**) of education (**E**) includes all third parties who are not playing the roles of teacher and/or student. The third parties include personnel within school systems and people outside of school systems. Inside school systems, there are counselors, assistant principals, principals, headmasters, superintendents, school boards, boards of governors, county education officials, state, provincial or regional education officials and federal or national school officials. Outside of education systems, there are parents, community members, community leaders, special interest groups, groups with religious affiliations, legislative bodies, funding bodies (private and government), etc. Positive attitudes towards education (**E**) from the context (**X**) of education include third parties who encourage the following. They encourage students (**S**) to be ambitious to know and understand as much as they can. They encourage students (**S**) to want to learn (intentionally and under guidance <$\mathbf{L_1}$>) the range of knowing ($\mathbf{K_2}$) that is prescribed by the intended learning outcomes (**ILO**s) which are offered to them. They encourage students (**S**) to make genuine efforts to complete $study_1$ ($\mathbf{S_{P1}}$) tasks and to develop the ranges of knowing ($\mathbf{K_{2KLF}}$) specified by the intended learning outcomes (**ILO**s). They encourage students to value the prescribed ranges of knowing ($\mathbf{K_{2P}}$) that are available to learn ($\mathbf{L_1}$) in schools. They encourage students (**S**) to become emotionally involved with their $study_1$ ($\mathbf{S_{P1}}$) tasks and to attach merit, significance and worth to their cognitive achievements.

Community Support

The probabilities are increased that education (**E**) will be effective education ($\mathbf{E_E}$) when the context (**X**) for education (**E**) is one in which the wider community in which the teaching ($\mathbf{T_P}$) and intentional guided studying ($\mathbf{S_{P1}}$) take place is supportive of the teaching ($\mathbf{T_P}$) and the intentional guided studying ($\mathbf{S_{P1}}$). Conditions for effective education ($\mathbf{E_E}$) are favorable when the community approves of the

(1) administrators and/or school leaders who are employed to supervise and coordinate the operation of the schools,
(2) teachers who are employed in the schools,
(3) students who are enrolled in the schools,
(4) teaching methods ($\mathbf{E_{DC3T}}$) being used,
(5) intentional guided study ($\mathbf{S_{P1}}$) methods ($\mathbf{E_{DC3S}}$) being used,
(6) content (**C**) being taught and studied,
(7) teaching and intentional guided studying resources ($\mathbf{E_{DC2}}$) being used,
(8) prescribed ranges of knowing ($\mathbf{K_{2P}}$) that are specified by the intended learning outcomes (**ILO**s),
(9) systems of assessment and evaluation and the uses of the evaluation reports.

Without positive community support, it becomes an extremely challenging social and cultural context (**X**) for teaching ($\mathbf{T_P}$) and intentional guided studying ($\mathbf{S_{P1}}$) to function effectively, and the probabilities are that the teaching ($\mathbf{T_P}$) and intentional guided studying ($\mathbf{S_{P1}}$) will function ineffectively or simply cease to function.

Summary

Explanatory educological theory consists of scientific educological theory and praxiological educological theory.

Scientific educological theory uses the well-defined terms from descriptive educological theory to conduct empirical inquiry about education (**E**), verify facts about education (**E**) and accurately, adequately and justifiably describe, explain and predict extant phenomena, processes and states of affairs in education (**E**).

Praxiological educological theory uses the well-defined terms from descriptive educological theory to conduct empirical inquiry about education (**E**), verify facts about education (**E**) and accurately, adequately and justifiably describe, explain, predict and prescribe practices and relationships which are effective for achieving desired states of affairs in education (**E**) and desired outcomes from education (**E**).

From scientific educological theory, we are informed that

(1) $<\mathbf{E} = \mathbf{T} \cup \mathbf{S} \cup \mathbf{C} \cup \mathbf{X}>$ which states that education (**E**) is (=) a system whose essential properties consist of the union ($\cup$) of the essential properties of teacher (**T**), student (**S**), content (**C**) and context ($<\mathbf{X}>$ – physical, social and cultural setting) all standing in relation to each other,

(2) $<\mathbf{E_O} \vee \mathbf{E_U}>$ which states that education (**E**) can be official education ($\mathbf{E_O}$) or ($\vee$) it can be unofficial education ($\mathbf{E_U}$),

(3) $<\mathbf{E_E} \vee \mathbf{E_I}>$ which states that education (**E**) can be effective education ($\mathbf{E_E}$) or ($\vee$) ineffective education ($\mathbf{E_I}$),

(4) $<\mathbf{E_G} \vee \mathbf{E_B}>$ which states that education (**E**) can be good education ($\mathbf{E_G}$) or ($\vee$) bad education ($\mathbf{E_B}$)

(5) $<\mathbf{E_E} \rightarrow \mathbf{L_1} \rightarrow \mathbf{K_{2P}}>$ which states that effective education ($\mathbf{E_E}$) is the set of controlling conditions ($\rightarrow$) for the resultant of the process of conduced learning ($\mathbf{L_1}$), and the process of conduced learning ($\mathbf{L_1}$) is the set of controlling conditions ($\rightarrow$) for the cognitive state of having a prescribed range of knowing ($\mathbf{K_{2P}}$),

(6) $<\mathbf{E_I} \rightarrow \neg\mathbf{L_1} \rightarrow \neg\mathbf{K_{2P}}>$ which states that ineffective education ($\mathbf{E_I}$) is the set of controlling conditions ($\rightarrow$) for the resultant of no conduced learning ($\neg\mathbf{L_1}$), and no

conduced learning ($\neg \mathbf{L_1}$) is the set of controlling conditions ($\rightarrow$) for the resultant the cognitive state of having no prescribed range of knowing ($\neg \mathbf{K_{2P}}$),

(7) $<\mathbf{K_2} \in \mathbf{N}>$ which states that a range of knowing ($\mathbf{K_2}$) is one of the elements of ($\in$) cognition ($\mathbf{N}$),

(8) $<\mathbf{M} = \mathbf{V} \cup \mathbf{P} \cup \mathbf{N}>$ which states that mind or mindfulness ($\mathbf{M}$) consists of ($=$) the union of ($\cup$) volition ($\mathbf{V}$), perception ($\mathbf{P}$) and cognition ($\mathbf{N}$).

From praxiological educological theory, we are informed that

(1) $<\mathbf{M} \rightleftarrows \mathbf{E}>$ which states that mind or mindfulness ($\mathbf{M}$) and education ($\mathbf{E}$) have mutual effects ($\rightleftarrows$),

(2) $<\mathbf{M} \rightleftarrows \mathbf{E_E} \vee \mathbf{E_I}>$ which states that mind, mindfulness or mindset ($\mathbf{M}$), depending on whether it is supportive of, acquiescent to or in opposition to, education ($\mathbf{E}$), is the set of controlling conditions ($\rightarrow$) for the resultant of effective education ($\mathbf{E_E}$) and/or ($\vee$) ineffective education ($\mathbf{E_I}$), and vice versa, effective education ($\mathbf{E_E}$) and/or ($\vee$) ineffective education ($\mathbf{E_I}$) is the set of controlling conditions ($\rightarrow$) for mind, mindfulness or mindset ($\mathbf{M}$),

(3) $<\{\mathbf{T_{PE}} \cup \mathbf{S_{P1E}} \cup \mathbf{C_O} \cup \mathbf{X_O}\} \rightarrow \mathbf{E_E} \rightarrow \mathbf{L_1} \rightarrow \{\mathbf{K_{2P}} \subset \mathbf{ILO}\}>$ which states that the union ($\cup$) (or combination) of effective teaching ($\mathbf{T_{PE}}$) and effective intentional guided studying ($\mathbf{S_{P1E}}$) with optimal content ($\mathbf{C_O}$) and with optimal context ($\mathbf{X_O}$) is the set of controlling conditions ($\rightarrow$) for effective education ($\mathbf{E_E}$), that effective education ($\mathbf{E_E}$) is the set of controlling conditions ($\rightarrow$) for the process of conduced learning ($\mathbf{L_1}$), that conduced learning ($\mathbf{L_1}$) is the set of controlling conditions ($\rightarrow$) for the resultant of a prescribed range of knowing ($\mathbf{K_{2P}}$), and that a prescribed range of knowing ($\mathbf{K_{2P}}$) is part of ($\subset$) an intended learning outcome (**ILO**) that has been specified for students (**S**) to achieve from an educational episode (**E**),

(4) $<(\mathbf{A_C} \cup \mathbf{R_S} \cup \mathbf{A_P}) \rightarrow \mathbf{S_{P1E}}>$ which reads that the union of ($\cup$) the constructive attitudes ($\mathbf{A_C}$) which persons playing the role of student (**S**) hold, supportive relationships ($\mathbf{R_S}$) which they establish and maintain and the productive activities ($\mathbf{A_P}$) which they perform is ($=$) the set of controlling conditions for ($\rightarrow$) effective intentional guided studying ($\mathbf{S_{P1E}}$), which is the set of activities by

students (**S**) that result in their conduced learning (**L_1**) of some prescribed range of knowing (**K_{2P}**) as specified by some set of intended learning outcomes (**ILO**s),

(5) <**$(A_C \cup R_S \cup A_P) \rightarrow T_{PE}$**> which reads that the union of ($\cup$) the constructive attitudes which persons playing the role of teacher (**T**) hold, supportive relationships (**R_S**) which they establish and maintain and the productive activities which they perform (**A_P**) is (=) the set of controlling conditions for ($\rightarrow$) effective teaching (**T_{PE}**), which is the set of activities by teachers (**T**) that result in the conduced learning (**L_1**) by their students (**S**) of some prescribed range of knowing (**K_{2P}**) specified by some set of intended learning outcomes (**ILO**s),

(6) <**$C_O = C_{1O} \vee C_{2O}$**> which reads that optimal content (**C_O**) for effective education (**E_E**) is (=) an optimal fund of knowledge (**C_{1O}**) and/or ($\vee$) an optimal range of knowing (**C_{2O}**) which is

(a) organized for the purposes of teaching (**T_P**) and intentional guided studying (**S_{P1}**),
(b) appealing to the interests, motivations and aspirations of the students (**S**),
(c) appropriate to the age of the students (**S**),
(d) appropriate to the previous experiences and extant range of knowing (**K_{2KLF}**) of the students (**S**),
(e) sequenced appropriately for the students (**S**),
(f) presented at the optimal level of difficulty (not to easy, not too difficult) for the students (**S**),

(7) <**$X_O = X_{PO} \cup X_{SO} \cup X_{CO}$**> which reads that optimal context (**X_O**) for effective education (**E_E**) is (=) the union of ($\cup$) an optimal physical setting (**X_{PO}**), an optimal social setting (**X_{SO}**) and an optimal cultural setting (**X_{CO}**). An optimal context (**X_O**) for effective education (**E_E**) is a state of affairs in which

(a) the physical setting (**X_P**) is appropriate to and supportive of the teaching activities (**T_P**) of the teachers (**T**) and the study$_1$ (**S_{P1}**) activities of the students (**S**),
(b) the social setting (**X_S**) consists of people who have a supportive attitude towards (and act in supportive

ways for) the activities of the teachers (**T**) and students (**S**), the content (**C**) being taught and studied$_1$ ($\mathbf{S}_{P1}$) and the prescribed range of knowing ($\mathbf{K}_{2P}$) that is specified by the intended learning outcomes (**ILO**s),

(c) the cultural setting ($\mathbf{X}_C$) consists of norms, customs, traditions and a way of life (**WoL**) which are supportive of the activities of the teachers (**T**) and students (**S**), the content (**C**) being taught and studied$_1$ ($\mathbf{S}_{P1}$) and the prescribed range of knowing ($\mathbf{K}_{2P}$) that is specified by the intended learning outcomes (**ILO**s).

3 NORMATIVE EDUCOLOGICAL THEORY

Descriptive educological theory provides us with well-defined terms and well-explicated definitions of terms that we can use to discern, describe and analyze education (**E**). It provides us with the linguistic means to engage in clear, unambiguous and careful discourse about education (**E**). It guides our perceptions (perception$_6$ $<\mathbf{P}_6>$) of education (**E**). It enables us to discern and recognize instances of education (**E**). It gives us the means to distinguish between phenomena which are and phenomena which are not instances of education (**E**). It gives us the words and terms to form statements about education (**E**) which have clear denotative and connotative meaning and which can be verified by well-disciplined inquiry (**Q**) that uses the relevant principle of verification (necessity reasoning, observation, normative reasoning) to adduce the necessary and sufficient evidence to affirm or disaffirm the truth of the statement about education (**E**). Questions addressed by descriptive educological theory are ones about the meanings of terms that can be used in disciplined discourse about education (**E**).

Explanatory educological theory uses descriptive educological theory to discern phenomena, activities, processes and states of affairs in education, to describe what happens in education, to explain why it happens and to predict what will happen, given a particular set of controlling conditions. Explanatory educological theory includes scientific educological theory and praxiological educological theory.

Scientific educological theory describes relations among the elements of education (**E**). It describes, explains and predicts what happens (and what will happen, given a specified set of circumstances) in education (**E**). Scientific educological theory informs us about how education (**E**) works, what variables facilitate the function of education (**E**) and what variables impede the function of education (**E**). Questions addressed by scientific educological theory are about the elements, structure and function of education (**E**).

Praxiological educological theory describes effective relations and practices in education (**E**). It describes, explains, predicts and prescribes relations and practices that will work (and not work) in education (**E**) to achieve some desired state of affairs in education (**E**) and/or to achieve some desired set of intended learning outcomes from education (**E**). Praxiological educological theory informs us about actions to take (and actions to avoid) and about relations to establish (and relations to avoid) that are efficacious and/or efficient in the achievement of some desired effect in and/or with education (**E**). Questions addressed by praxiological educological theory are about the effectiveness and efficiency of actions and relations in education (**E**).

Normative educological theory provides evaluations of activities, processes, relationships and/or states of affairs in education (**E**), and it provides prescriptions for correct, right, moral and/or ethical actions to take in and/or for education (**E**). Normative educological theory also provides justifications for educological evaluations and prescriptions. Evaluations express value judgments about whether some entity, activity, relationship and/or state of affairs in education (**E**) is good or bad (or better or worse). Prescriptions express recommendations about what action is best (or is better than alternative actions) to take within and/or for education (**E**). Questions addressed by normative educological theory are about the ethicality, morality and value of education (**E**).

It has already been noted that education (**E**) can be official or unofficial ($\mathbf{E_O} \vee \mathbf{E_U}$), effective or ineffective ($\mathbf{E_E} \vee \mathbf{E_I}$) and good or bad ($\mathbf{E_G} \vee \mathbf{E_B}$). The question, "What is good education ($\mathbf{E_G}$)?" requires disambiguation. The term <*good*> in the question denotes both extrinsic value and intrinsic value. Something which has extrinsic value is something which is judged good to the extent that it is instrumental in achieving some desirable outcome. Education (**E**) may be valuable, for example, in that it us enables to learn$_1$ (**L$_1$**) a prescribed range of knowing (**K$_{2P}$**) that is necessary for us to have achieved to perform our civic duties as a responsible citizen, to function competently as a parent, to manage our personal finances, investments and expenditures, or to perform our job expertly as a ship's pilot, a welder, a carpenter, a radiographer, an electrician, a plumber, a truck driver, a lawyer, a musician, a translator, an editor, an ophthalmologist, etc.

Anything which has intrinsic value is judged good in and of itself. Happiness, for example, has intrinsic value. Rationality has intrinsic value. Integrity has intrinsic value. Health and well-being have intrinsic value. When the question, "What is good education (**E$_G$**)?" is posed in the sense of "What is intrinsically good education (**E$_G$**)?" the question can be restated as "What characteristics of education (**E**) are good in and of themselves?"

The question of "What is intrinsically good education (**E$_G$**)?" is neither an analytic one nor an empirical one. It does not require well-formed definitions and sound deductive argument nor careful observations to form warranted answers to it. Rather, the question is a normative one. Normative questions require normative answers. Normative answers are produced by the conduct of normative inquiry (**Q**). Normative inquiry (**Q**), when successful, produces normative knowledge (**K$_1$**). Normative knowledge (**K$_1$**) is any verified normative statement. Normative statements are verifiable by the principle of normative reasoning. The principle of normative reasoning is the principle of verify-cation that is used to establish the coherency relationship between normative statements and the conceivable evidence of logical objects (words and sentences) and the adherency relationship between normative statements and the evidence of acts as objects (actions emanating from volition, choice, self-resolve).

Statements (declarative sentences) which are verified by normative reasoning and which are recorded in some medium are normative knowledge (**K$_1$**). Normative knowledge is normative philosophy, and normative knowledge (**K$_1$**) about education (**E**) is normative philosophical educology. Normative reasoning includes evaluative reasoning, prescriptive reasoning and justificatory reasoning. Evaluative reasoning is the rational process of coming to a judgment about the value (merit, significance, worth) of something in relation to some set of criteria (either rules or standards) and reporting that value as a rating or a ranking. Prescriptive reasoning is the rational process of coming to a judgment about what course of action is the right action or the best action or the better action to take in relation to some criteria (either rules or standards). Justificatory reasoning is the rational process of proving that evaluations and prescriptions are sound. The process includes value verification, value validation, value vindication and rational choice of a way of life (Paul Taylor, 1961).

The term <*intrinsically good education*> requires disambiguation. The term denotes both ethical education and worthwhile education. Ethical education (**E**) is education (**E**) in which there is correct, right and proper conduct by the persons playing the role of teacher (**T**), the role of student (**S**) and the role of interested third parties in the social and cultural setting (**X**) for education (**E**). Worthwhile education (**E**) is education (**E**) in which there is teaching ($\mathbf{T_P}$) and studying$_1$ ($\mathbf{S_{P1}}$) of some selection of valuable content (**C**) with valuable purposes, goals and intentions (valuable intended learning outcomes <**ILO**s>) in mind (in the minds of the teachers <**T**>, students <**S**> and/or members of the context <**X**>) for the students (**S**) to achieve.

Ethical Education

With the question, "What is ethical education (**E**)?" a productive approach to developing an adequate answer to the question is to imagine incorrect, wrong and improper conduct of people playing the role of teachers (**T**), students (**S**) and interested third parties (**X**). Our focus is upon official education ($\mathbf{E_O}$) in secular, government funded and administered schools, and thus it is fruitful to ask ourselves a set of questions.

(1) What it is that we don't want to happen in our schools?
(2) In what ways do we not want our children to be treated by their teachers?
(3) In what ways do we not want our teachers to be treated by our children?
(4) In what ways do we not want interested third parties (school administrators, school boards or governing groups, parents, community members) to be treating our teachers and children, and vice versa?

For example, do we want our children to be mocked by their teachers because their skin is a different color, or their hair is a different texture, or their accent is different from the majority of their classmates? Do we want the teachers to assign lower grades to our children because of their gender, race, creed, ethnic origins, social class, financial status or skin color? Do we want them to be ridiculed by their teachers because they are slower at achieving the intended learning outcomes than the majority of their classmates? Do we want them to be insulted by their teachers because their religion is different from the majority of their classmates or because they profess no religion? Do we want them to be told that their gender identity or that their sexual orientation is abnormal or is twisted and sick? Do we want them to be told that trying to teach them is a waste of time and resources because they are so slow and stupid? Do we want them to be ridiculed because their names are different from the names of the majority of their classmates? Do we want them to be told that, because they are immigrants or refugees, they are an economic and social burden and do not rightfully belong in the school and the community? Do we want them to be forced to have sex with their teachers, or to be fondled and sexually abused by them? Do we want their teachers to lie to them, or intimidate them, or bully them, or treat them as scapegoats?

Do we want our children to mock their teachers? Do we want them to use abusive language with their teachers or to refuse to cooperate with their teachers? Do we want them to cheat on their tests and assignments? Do we want our children to bully their teachers on social media or to vandalize their property? Do we want our teachers to be insulted by their students because their religion is different from the prevailing religion of the community or because they profess no religion? Do we want our teachers to be told by their students that their gender identity or that their sexual orientation is abnormal or is twisted and sick? Do we want our teachers to be ridiculed by their students because their names are different from the names that are common in the community? Do we want them to be told that, because they are immigrants or refugees, they are an economic and social burden and do not rightfully deserve to be teachers and do not belong in the school and the community? Do we want them to be forced to have sex with their students, or to be fondled and sexually abused by them? Do we want their students to lie to them, or intimidate them, or bully them, or treat them as scapegoats?

Do we want school administrators, counselors, members of school boards, parents and/or members of the community harassing, intimidating or bullying teachers and/or students? Do we want parents mounting an online campaign of hate and invective toward teachers and/or students for their race, ethnic origins, religious convictions or sexual orientation?

If our answer to all these questions is "No," then we are in a good position to engage in value verification of standards for the ethical conduct of teachers (**T**), students (**S**) and interested third parties (**X**). We know what we do not want the teachers (**T**) of our children to do. We know what we do not want our children in the role of students (**S**) to do. We know what we do not want third parties (**X**) interested in official education ($\mathbf{E_O}$) to do. By implication, we can easily infer the things that we do want teachers (**T**), students (**S**) and third parties (**X**) to do. We can readily undertake value verification by specifying the correct, right and proper standards of conduct for teachers (**T**), students (**S**) and third parties (**X**). The opposite to the above examples of bad conduct would be examples of good conduct. They would be examples of teachers (**T**), students (**S**) and third parties (**X**) assuring that their conduct is respectful, authentic, truthful, impartial, fair, just, equitable, inclusive, kind, caring, rational, accountable and responsible. In our specification of these standards, we are verifying the values which we want teachers (**T**), students (**S**) and third parties (**X**) to uphold while dealing with and/or engaging in official education ($\mathbf{E_O}$) in public schools.

Not surprisingly, this set of standards for ethical official education ($\mathbf{E_O}$) is found in secular liberal democracies consisting of culturally diverse societies made up of recent immigrants and descendants of immigrants. The standards are implied by the core values and norms of liberal democratic societies. Within English-speaking secular liberal democracies such as Australia, Canada, Great Britain, New Zealand and the USA, codes of ethical conduct for teachers (**T**), students (**S**) and third parties (**X**) have been comprehensively developed, published and widely circulated for many years.

Some examples of codes of ethics for teachers (**T**), school administrators and governing bodies (members of the context <**X**> of official education < $\mathbf{E_O}$ >) include the following.

- **Australia. Queensland College of Teachers (N.D.):** *Code of Ethics for Teachers in Queensland.* Retrieved 13 April 2020. https://www.qct.edu.au/standards-and-conduct/code-of-ethics
- **Australia. Victorian Institute of Teaching (N.D.):** *The*

Victorian Teaching Profession Code of Conduct. Retrieved 13 April 2020. https://www.vit.vic.edu.au/__data/assets/pdf_file/0018/35604/Code-of-Conduct-2016.pdf

- **Canada. British Columbia. (N.D.):** *Code of Ethics of the British Columbia Teachers' Federation.* Retrieved 13 April 2020. http://teachercodes.iiep.unesco.org/teachercodes/codes/America/Canada/Canada_British_Columbia.pdf
- **New Zealand. Teaching Council (N.D.):** *Code of Ethics for Registered Teachers.* Retrieved 13 April 2020. https://teachingcouncil.nz/required/ethics/coe-poster-english.pdf
- **United Kingdom. Department of Education (2011):** *Teachers' Standards. Guidance for School Leaders, School Staff and Governing Bodies.* Retrieved 13 April 2020. https://assets.publishing.service.gov.uk/government/uploads/system/uploads/attachment_data/file/665520/Teachers__Standards.pdf
- **USA. National Education Association (1975):** *Code of Ethics.* Retrieved 13 April 2020. http://www.nea.org/home/30442.htm

Some examples of codes of ethical conduct for students (**S**) and parents (members of the context <**X**> of official education <$\mathbf{E_O}$>) include the following.

- **Queensland. Department of Education (23 June 2020)**: *Student Code of Conduct.* Retrieved 26 January 2021. https://behaviour.education.qld.gov.au/procedures-guidelines-and-forms/student-code-of-conduct
- **Canada. University of Alberta (2021)**: *Code of Student Behaviour* [sic]. Retrieved 26 January 2021. https://www.ualberta.ca/governance/resources/policies-standards-and-codes-of-conduct/code-of-student-behaviour.html
- **South Australia. Westbourne Park Primary School (2016)**: *Behaviour* [sic] *Code.* Retrieved 26 January 2021. https://www.wbourneps.sa.edu.au/wp-content/uploads/2016/05/Behaviour-Code-2016.pdf

Codes of ethics for teachers (**T**), students (**S**) and third parties (**X**) are always under review and emendation. Each generation within a society has ideas about how to improve the society, including how to improve standards of conduct for teachers (**T**), students (**S**) and third parties (**X**) in official education ($\mathbf{E_O}$). People within the same generation and the same society and culture have alternative views of ways to improve the society and culture, and they engage in competition with each other over those alternative views. People who belong to different societies and cultures within the same territory, state or country compete with each other over alternative views of how to improve the ethical conduct of professional teachers (**T**), students (**S**) and third parties (**X**) in government funded and government administered schools. These competitions, while emanating from conflicts of values, are typically played out as political advocacy.

From the educological perspective, the proper way to settle the question of what is ethical education (official education $<\mathbf{E_O}>$) is not by taking political action to gain acceptance or coerce compliance, but by conducting careful, disciplined normative educological inquiry. The inquiry, if successful, produces normative educological theory of ethical education (official education $<\mathbf{E_O}>$). The theory consists of statements, verified by necessary and sufficient evidence, which describe the distinguishing characteristics of ethical education (official education $<\mathbf{E_O}>$) and which justify the claim that the nominated distinguishing characteristics are the right and proper ones to use in distinguishing ethical education (official education $<\mathbf{E_O}>$).

The first step in the educological normative inquiry (the step of value verification) has been completed. The question addressed in the inquiry was, "What is ethical education (official education $<\mathbf{E_O}>$)?" The question was identified as an educological normative question which called for specification of a set of criteria that distinguishes ethical education from unethical education. The set of criteria nominated included the following.

(1) Truthfulness
(2) Authenticity
(3) Respectfulness
(4) Impartiality
(5) Fairness
(6) Equitability
(7) Inclusiveness
(8) Kindness
(9) Caring
(10) Rationality
(11) Responsibility

(12) Accountability

The second step in the inquiry (the step of value validation) is achieved by asking and answering (adequately) the question, "Why are these criteria for ethical education (official education <$\mathbf{E}_O$>) correct, right or proper?" This second question is also a normative question, and the way we can answer it adequately is to show that these criteria are implied by a set of higher-order of norms.

Truthfulness and authenticity are appropriate standards of conduct for participants in ethical education (official education <$\mathbf{E}_O$>) because they are implied by the high-order norms of honesty and integrity. It is the duty of teachers (**T**), students (**S**) and third parties (**X**) in education (<**E**> both unofficial <$\mathbf{E}_U$> and official <$\mathbf{E}_O$>) to be honest, to be open and to maintain integrity in their dealings with each other. The very point of teaching ($\mathbf{T}_P$) and studying$_1$ ($\mathbf{S}_{P1}$) some content (**C**) is that students (**S**) extend their prescribed range of knowing ($\mathbf{K}_{2P}$) about the objects of knowing ($\mathbf{O}_{K2}$) in their environment (physical, biological and hominological) such that they can deal with their environment rationally and intelligently through using their range of knowing ($\mathbf{K}_{2KLF}$) to conduct inquiry (**Q**), solve problems, resolve issues and achieve goals. To make education (**E**) functional, the actions of the participants (teachers <**T**>, students <**S**> and third parties <**X**>) in education (**E**) must be characterized by honesty and integrity.

Impartiality, fairness, equitability and inclusiveness are appropriate standards of conduct for participants in ethical education (official education <$\mathbf{E}_O$>) because they are implied by the higher-order norm of justice. It is a basic tenet of justice that we should be treated as we deserve to be treated. The distribution of benefits and burdens among a community or society should be fair and equitable. It is the ethical obligation of relevant third parties (<**X**> – school administrators, school boards, state departments of education, etc.) and teachers (**T**) to provide the same resources, time and guidance to all students (**S**) who are alike in relevant ways. This is distributive justice. Sanctions and punishments should be fair and equitable. It is the ethical obligation of teachers (**T**) and school administrators (**X**) to mete out admonitions, sanctions and punishments fairly and equitably, without fear or favor. This is retributive justice. Special allowances and compensations should be made for those who suffer loss, injury or disadvantage. It is the ethical obligation of relevant third parties (**X**) and teachers (**T**) to make allowances for students (**S**) who suffer blindness, deafness, cerebral palsy, developmental delays or any other relevant disadvantage. This is compensatory justice (Velasquez et al., 1990, 2014). Distributive, retributive and compensatory justice are appropriate standards of conduct for all parties in education (teachers (**T**), students (**S**) and members of the context (**X**) of education) to practice and to enjoy.

Kindness and caring are appropriate standards of conduct for participants in ethical education (official education <$\mathbf{E}_O$>) because they are implied by the higher-order norms of compassion and altru-ism. Official education ($\mathbf{E}_O$) is a system in which interested third parties (**X**) and teachers (**T**) act in ways that are intended to guide, to assist and to otherwise help someone (the persons playing the role of student <**S**>) intentionally improve his or her prescribed range of knowing ($\mathbf{K}_{2P}$). In education (<**E**>, unofficial(<$\mathbf{E}_U$> and official <$\mathbf{E}_O$>), teach-ing ($\mathbf{T}_P$) is an inherently altruistic act of giving, and the intention of the giving is that the recipient (the student <**S**>) enjoy a benefit from the gift. Studying$_1$ ($\mathbf{S}_{P1}$) is an inherently appreciative act of accepting the gift and doing something with it to derive a cognitive benefit (an extension in a prescribed range of knowing <$\mathbf{K}_{2P}$>).

Rationality, responsibility and accountability are appropriate standards of conduct for participants in ethical education (official education <$\mathbf{E}_O$>) because they are implied by the higher-order norms of individual and community well being. We, as human beings, never live alone. Our well being depends upon living in and contributing to our families, communities and societies. Communities and societies rely upon individuals to play their roles rationally, responsibly and accountably. Rationality is a state of mind (**M**) and a way of life (**WoL**) of

(1) knowing (knowing-that-one <$\mathbf{K}_{2K1}$>) what values and what way of life (**WoL**) one has chosen,
(2) having sound reasons (knowing-that <$\mathbf{K}_{2K2}$>) for choosing and continuing to hold those values and to follow that way of life (**WoL**),
(3) having a knowing-how ($\mathbf{K}_{2K3}$) to reason soundly and how to adhere to one's values and way of life (**WoL**) and
(4) having consistent and persistent self-resolve (knowing-to <$\mathbf{K}_{2K4}$>) to reason soundly (deduce, reduce, induce, etc.) and to conduct one's self in ways that are consistent with

one's values and way of life (**WoL**).

Responsibility is the obligation of duty, and the obligation of duty is the imperative to perform a set of prescribed tasks consistently, adequately and in a timely way. It is among the duties (the responsibilities) of participants (teachers <**T**>, students <**S**>, third parties <**X**>) in ethical education (official education <$\mathbf{E_O}$>) for

(1) teachers (**T**), students (**S**) and/or relevant third parties (**X**) to prepare adequately for educational episodes,
(2) teachers (**T**) and/or relevant third parties (**X**) to provide appropriate study$_1$ ($\mathbf{S_{P1}}$) opportunities and for students (**S**) to accept appropriate study$_1$ ($\mathbf{S_{P1}}$) opportunities and complete appropriate study$_1$ ($\mathbf{S_{P1}}$) activities,
(3) teachers (**T**) and/or relevant third parties (**X**) to provide helpful evaluations and evaluation reports and for students (**S**) to accept, attend to and heed helpful evaluations and evaluation reports and
(4) teachers (**T**) and/or relevant third parties (**X**) to assure the well being and safety of students (**S**) and for students (**S**), to the extent that their maturation permits, to assure the well being and safety of themselves and their fellow students (**S**).

Accountability is the obligation of liability, and the obligation of liability is to stand answerable for the consequences of performing a set of prescribed tasks consistently, adequately and in a timely way. The test of accountability is when the prescribed tasks are either not performed, or performed inconsistently, inadequately and/or in an untimely way. Accountability then becomes culpability, and culpability requires some remedy or redress from the culpable party. It is among the liabilities of participants (**T, S, X**) in ethical education (official education <$\mathbf{E_O}$> to stand answerable for the consequences of

(1) having prepared as teachers (**T**), students (**S**) and/or third parties (**X**) (adequately or inadequately) for educational episodes,
(2) having provided as teachers (**T**), and/or third parties (**X**) (appropriate or inappropriate) study$_1$ ($\mathbf{S_{P1}}$) opportunities and study$_1$ ($\mathbf{S_{P1}}$) activities and having accepted and completed as students (**S**) study$_1$ ($\mathbf{S_{P1}}$) activities (appropriately or inappropriately) that have been provided,
(3) having provided as teachers (**T**) and/or third parties (**X**)

(helpful or unhelpful) evaluations and evaluation reports and having attended to and heeded (appropriately or inappropriately) as students (**S**) evaluations and evaluation reports and

(4) having assured as teachers (**T**) and/or third parties (**X**) (adequately or not adequately) the well being and safety of students (**S**) and having heeded (adequately or inadequately) as students (**S**) provisions for student well being and safety.

For any set of standards and/or rules for ethical conduct in education (official education $<\mathbf{E_o}>$), the question can always be asked, "What makes this set of standards and/or rules appropriate ones for ethical education?" In particular, "What makes the norms of honesty, integrity, justice, compassion, altruism and well-being (individual and community) appropriate norms for ethical education (official education $<\mathbf{E_o}>$)?" The task of addressing this question requires value vindication. Value vindication is the task of justifying a set of norms with a higher set of norms. The norms of honesty, integrity, justice, compassion, altruism and well being (individual and community) are justifiable because they are the necessary implication of a higher set of norms. Those higher set of norms is the set of norms which is fundamental to the way of life (**WoL**) as practiced in secular liberal democracies consisting of culturally diverse societies made up of recent immigrants and descendants of immigrants.

In secular liberal democracies, there is a social contract between the government and the members of the society. It is understood in the social contract that government rules with the consent of and for the benefit of all members of the society. The social contract between the society and the government is specified and articulated either in a written and ratified constitution or in well established, widely accepted historical conventions and precedents.

Secular liberal democracies assure freedom of religion and worship, but they give no special status nor preferential treatment for any particular religious organization. Moreover, there is no compulsion to accept and/or embrace any religious convictions, lifestyles and/or affiliations. Public office is open for nomination by any member of society, and selection to public office is by self-nomination and open, fair, free and competitive election. Eligibility for participation as a voter is determined by a minimum age limit and citizenship status.

Liberal democracies maintain a separation of power among the divisions of government (judiciary, legislative, executive). Authority over the military is maintained by the civilian government, and the military submits to the civilian government. Secular liberal democracies guarantee and protect human rights and civil liberties. Besides freedom of religion and worship, those rights and liberties include the right to life, free expression, free association, free assembly, peaceful protest, free movement and travel, due process of law, speedy, fair and public trial, the presumption of innocence until proven guilty, protection from arbitrary arrest and indefinite detention, participation in elections, nomination for public office, ownership of private property, protection from harm (domestic and foreign), personal privacy, access to truthful and accurate information and access to education.

Secular liberal democracies may be constitutional monarchies (e.g. Australia, Belgium, Canada), or they may be republics (e.g. France, Germany, Italy). Of the constitutional monarchies, the most prevalent system of government is a parliamentary system (e.g. Denmark, Sweden, New Zealand). Of the republics, the most typical system of government is a presidential system (e.g. Brazil, Mexico, the United States of America). From the end of the second world war, the form of government to have been most widely adopted has been secular liberal democracy.

A form of government, of course, is not the entirety of a way of life (**WoL**). It is one of many features of a way of life (**WoL**). One of the great virtues of a secular liberal democracy, as a form of government, is that it can accommodate many different ways of life (**WoL**) in the form of many different ethnic groups, religious groups and nonreligious groups. In schools, the accommodation of different cultural groups includes the ethical treatment of members of all groups by teachers with rationality, responsibility, accountability, truthfulness, authenticity, respectfulness, impartiality, fairness, equitability, inclusiveness, kindness and caring. The essential values which need to be honored to make a secular liberal democracy work are those of acceptance, understanding, appreciation and celebration of different ways of life (**WoL**) and a commitment to the resolution of conflict by peaceful means, i.e. by negotiation to achieve mutually acceptable solutions and by open, free and fair elections to achieve peaceful transfer of power and to enact laws, amendments to laws and repeals of laws in response to new challenges and changing circumstances.

The fourth step in normative educological inquiry about ethical education (official education <**E**$_o$>) is rational choice of a way of life (**WoL**). The norms of the way of life (**WoL**) in secular liberal democracies were partly explicated through the step of value vindication. After value vindication comes rational choice. The question which needs to be addressed at this stage (the stage of rational choice) is "What makes life in a secular liberal democracy better than alternative ways of life (**WoL**)?" The justification for choosing life in a secular liberal democracy is that it is the way of life (**WoL**) that, in an ideal world, any rational person would choose from a set of well known and well considered alternatives, provided that the person was free from bias, prejudice, intimidation, threat or coercion, and provided that the person was sufficiently well informed by serious, well-disciplined inquiry and by extensive life experience.

Alternative ways of life (**WoL**) include life in an aristocracy, an autocracy, an ergatocracy, a geniocracy, a kraterocracy, a kritarchy, a meritocracy, a nepotocracy, a noocracy, an oligarchy, a plutocracy, a particracy, a stratocracy, a technocracy, a theocracy and a timocracy. Other ways of life include a master-slave society, a feudal society, a tribal society, a hereditary hierarchical society, a patriarchal society and a matriarchal society. An important part of the task of making a rational choice of the best way of life (**WoL**) among these many options is to develop an understanding of them, evaluate them and rank them from most desirable to least desirable.

We are inevitably products of our socialization and enculturation. From our childhood and teenage experiences, we develop the belief that our society and culture are normal, and all other ways of life are abnormal. Thus, the conditions for making a rational choice (free from bias, prejudice, intimidation, threat or coercion, and sufficiently well informed by serious, well-disciplined inquiry and by extensive life experience) may be impossible. It may well be the case that we can only aspire to rational choice. Nevertheless, the logic of justification remains unchanged. The final stage of a justificatory argument is rational choice of a way of life. After rational choice, there is no more justification to offer.

Developing a sound justificatory argument is part of normative reasoning, and it goes far beyond quoting people, constitutions, government department documents, laws or regulations or religious literature. It requires ultimately that we identify and explicate the way of life (**WoL**) which we can authentically and genuinely recommend on the basis of rational choice. This requires that we set aside our prejudices, personally engage in the reasoning process and not rely upon what someone else or some set of documents tells us to value. In these matters, our own reason and rationality must be our guide. It is a task of independent, well informed, rational thinking.

While the justification for the essential properties of ethical education has been completed, there is always the possibility that there can be improvement. There is the possibility that we might emend, add and/or delete some of the elements which we have previously judged appropriate as part of ethical teaching. There is the possibility that we can improve upon our conception of secular liberal democracy or that we can conceive of a better way of life than that lived in the context of a secular liberal democracy. The question always remains open as to whether we can create a society and culture better than the one in which we are currently living.

Worthwhile Education

As noted previously, the term <*intrinsically good education*> functions ambiguously. It denotes both ethical education and worthwhile education. Let us turn our attention to the question, "What is worthwhile education?" Think of the character of Fagin in the Charles Dickens novel, *Oliver Twist* (1838). He regularly picks up street urchins. He provides them with shelter and food and teaches them how to pick pockets on the streets of London. The boys practice their pick pocket skills until they become highly proficient. Fagin is effective in his teaching the art of thievery to the boys under his control, and the boys are effective in their study of thievery under Fagin's tutelage. The education (**E**) in which Fagin and his boys participate is an example of education (**E**) that is effective ($\mathbf{E_E}$), but is bad ($\mathbf{E_B}$) – effective bad education ($\mathbf{E_{EB}}$).

What makes the education (**E**) that goes on in Fagin's school for street urchin thieves bad ($\mathbf{E_B}$)? Fagin's intention to profit from the crimes of his gang of young thieves is bad. The content (<$\mathbf{C_2}$> the range of knowing how to pick pockets organized for the purposes of teaching and studying intentionally under guidance) that Fagan teaches ($\mathbf{T_P}$) and the boys study ($\mathbf{S_{P1}}$) is bad. The intended learning outcome (**ILO**) which Fagan wants his gang of boys to achieve (a knowing-how <$\mathbf{K_{2K3}}$> to pick pockets) is bad. What can we infer from the example of the education (**E**) that takes place in Fagin's school for thieves about what makes education good ($\mathbf{E_G}$)? In contrast to the bad education ($\mathbf{E_B}$) going on in Fagan's school, in good education ($\mathbf{E_G}$), teaching ($\mathbf{T_P}$) is an act of giving, and studying$_1$ ($\mathbf{S_{P1}}$) is an act of valuing and making use of the gift of teaching ($\mathbf{T_P}$) to develop and improve (through studying$_1$ <$\mathbf{S_{P1}}$>) the student's mind (**M**). One of the distinguishing characteristics of good education ($\mathbf{E_G}$) is the set of intentions (by teachers <**T**>, students <**S**> and third parties <**X**>) for the improvement of the cognition (**N**), perception (**P**) and volition (**V**) of students (**S**).

In good education ($\mathbf{E_G}$), teaching ($\mathbf{T_P}$) is an act of altruism, not an act of acquisition. Teachers of history and methods of historical inquiry (**Q**) do so, not because they will earn income from their students (**S**) who extend their range of knowing ($\mathbf{K_2}$) of history and historical inquiry, but rather for the purpose that their students (**S**) will have extended their range of knowing ($\mathbf{K_2}$) of history and historical inquiry. The same is true of teachers of music, art, literature, sociology, psychology, medical practice, metal working, mathematics, dance, etc. In good education ($\mathbf{E_G}$), teaching ($\mathbf{T_P}$) is performed for the purpose of extending the range of knowing ($\mathbf{K_2}$) and the mindfulness (**M**) of students. In good education ($\mathbf{E_G}$), teaching ($\mathbf{T_P}$) is not done for the profit of the teacher (**T**), the person doing the teaching ($\mathbf{T_P}$). Rather, it is done for the sake of the persons who engage in the role of student (**S**), the people who study$_1$ ($\mathbf{S_{P1}}$) with the aim to learn$_1$ ($\mathbf{L_1}$) some prescribed range of knowing ($\mathbf{K_{2P}}$). The gift of teaching ($\mathbf{T_P}$) is the extension in the range of knowing ($\mathbf{K_2}$) and mindfulness (**M**) which the students (**S**) achieve from the teaching ($\mathbf{T_P}$) and from their studying$_1$ ($\mathbf{S_{P1}}$) some content (**C**).

In good education ($\mathbf{E_G}$), teachers (**T**), students (**S**) and interested third parties (**X**) share the intention and expectation that there will be improvement in the minds ($\mathbf{M = V \cup P \cup N}$) of students (**S**) as a result of their having completed a set of study$_1$ ($\mathbf{S_{P1}}$) activities under the guidance of their teachers (**T**). There is the moral concern (in the minds of teachers and interested third parties) to improve the students' worthwhile range of knowing ($\mathbf{K_2}$) and to improve the students' worthwhile mindfulness (**M**). Among the distinguishing characteristics of good education ($\mathbf{E_G}$) is the value attributed to the intended learning outcomes (**ILO**s) specified (by teachers <**T**>, students <**S**> and/or third parties <**X**>) for the students (**S**). Knowing how to read is worthwhile. Knowing how to pick pockets is not. Knowing how to conduct disciplined fruitful inquiry is worthwhile. Knowing how to smoke meth (N-methylamphetamine) is not. Knowing how to resolve conflict peacefully and calmly is worthwhile. Knowing how to steal cars is not. Knowing how to eat sensibly and exercise adequately to maintain good health and well being is worthwhile. Knowing how to defraud a grandmother out of her life savings is not. The intended improvement from good education (**E_G**) is the achievement by the student (**S**) of some worthwhile range of knowing (**K_2**) and some valuable mindfulness (**M**).

Participants (**T, S, X**) in good education (**E_G**) are engaging in acts of custodianship. Participants (**T, S, X**) in good education (**E_G**) care for, sustain and perpetuate the best and the most treasured of the funds of knowledge (**K_1**) and ranges of knowing (**K_2**) of a society and culture. For teaching (**T_P**) and studying$_1$ (**S_{P1}**) to take place, some content (**C**) must be selected. In good education (**E_G**), the participants (**T, S, X**) select, not just any content (**C**), but the best content (**C**) from the funds of knowledge (**K_1**) and the ranges of knowing (**K_2**) available to the society and culture in which the teaching (**T_P**) and studying$_1$ (**S_{P1}**) take place. Good education (**E_G**) of English literature includes, for example, selection of not just any publications in English, but some of the best publications in English. Good education (**E_G**) of saddlery includes selection of, not just any technique of saddle making, but the best techniques of saddle making. Good education (**E_G**) of handling sail boats includes selection of, not just any technique of sailing a boat, but the best techniques of boat sailing. Good education (**E_G**) of history includes selection of, not just any historical writing, but the best written histories of a period. The acts of custodianship by participants (**T, S, X**) in good education (**E_G**) are achieved by providing opportunities to study$_1$ (**S_{P1}**) the best content (**C**) and learn (**L_1**) the best prescribed ranges of knowing (**K_{2P}**) related to that content (**C**) and thereby establishing and sustaining the best standards for the cognitive development of the community which the system of education (**E**) serves.

Good education (**E_G**) has good purposes. An example of an intrinsically good purpose for good education (**E_G**) is philomathic education (**E**). Philomathic education (**E**) is teaching (**T_P**) and studying$_1$ (**S_{P1}**) some content (**C**) for the purpose of satisfying the students' curiosities, interests and ambitions to have a prescribed range of knowing (**K_2**) about some object of knowing (**O_{K2}**). In philomathic education (**E**), teachers (**T**) are teaching (**T_P**) because they want students (**S**) to have a prescribed range of knowing ($\mathbf{K_{2P}}$) and understanding (**U**) of some content (**C**), and the students (**S**) are studying$_1$ ($\mathbf{S_{P1}}$) because they want to have a prescribed range of knowing ($\mathbf{K_{2P}}$) and understanding (**U**) of some content (**C**). Philomathic education (**E**) occurs because of the love of teaching ($\mathbf{T_P}$) by teachers (**T**) and the love by students (**S**) of studying$_1$ ($\mathbf{S_{P1}}$) and learning ($\mathbf{L_1}$) some prescribed range of knowing ($\mathbf{K_{2P}}$).

The following are some examples of philomathic education (**E**). Sarah takes violin lessons because she loves playing the violin. Richard takes courses in history because he loves history and historical inquiry. Jane takes courses in pottery because she loves creating pottery. Jason loves attending first grade (year one) of school because he loves learning to read. Dennis takes flying lessons because he loves flying aircraft. Harrison takes courses each year in a new language because he loves knowing ($\mathbf{K_2}$) different languages, including having a knowing-how ($\mathbf{K_{2K3}}$) to speak, read and write them and comprehend the spoken form of different languages. Philippa takes courses in philosophy because she loves philosophical discourse and inquiry. Alvin takes courses in joinery because he loves to make cabinets and furniture from timber. Christopher studies astronomy in university because he loves knowing ($\mathbf{K_2}$) about the elements and the relationship among the elements of the cosmos.

Students (**S**) who engage in philomathic education (**E**) ideally (and often do) progress to becoming self-directed inquirers and problem solvers. They not only develop the range of knowing ($\mathbf{K_2}$) that enables them to conduct well-disciplined, fruitful inquiry (**Q**), but they also develop the disposition to want to conduct inquiry (**Q**) and solve problems. They progress from learning$_1$ ($\mathbf{L_1}$) prescribed ranges of knowing ($\mathbf{K_{2P}}$) from education (**E**) to learning$_2$ ($\mathbf{L_2}$) discovered ranges of knowing ($\mathbf{K_{2D}}$) from careful disciplined inquiry (**Q**) without the guidance of a teacher (**T**). A notable historical example of this is the Australian virologist, Frank Fenner (1914-2010). Fenner, as a student (**S**), initially engaged in philomathic education (**E**) to learn$_1$ ($\mathbf{L_1}$) prescribed ranges of knowing ($\mathbf{K_{2P}}$) about viruses (his object of knowing $<\mathbf{O_{K2}}>$). He later became a self-directed inquirer (researcher), and he conducted innovative research (**Q**) to learn$_2$ ($\mathbf{L_2}$) discovered ranges of knowing ($\mathbf{K_{2D}}$) about viruses. He focused is research on devising ways to eliminate diseases caused by viruses and ways to use viruses to control and/or eradicate pests. He was instrumental in the eradication of smallpox from Australia in the 20th century and in the control of the rabbit plague in Australia (1940s and early1950s) through the use of the Myxoma virus, which, after its introduction in 1950, killed more than 99% of the rabbit population in Australia in the early 1950s.1950s.

As already mentioned, as well as intrinsically good purposes, good education (**E_G**) has extrinsically good purposes. An example of an extrinsically good purpose for good education (**E_G**) is occupational education. Occupational education (**E**) is teaching (**T_P**) and $studying_1$ (**S_{P1}**) some content (**C**) for the purpose of developing some prescribed range of knowing (**K_{2P}**) that is sufficient and relevant to gain access to, to participate in and to contribute to the production and distribution of goods and services in an economic system. Occupational education (**E**) provides benefits to individuals by helping them to become employable, and it provides benefits to an economic system by assuring that an adequate number of skilled labor, competent technicians and qualified professionals are available for the production and supply of necessary goods and services for the proper function of an economic system. Occupational education includes teaching (**T_P**) and $studying_1$ (**S_{P1}**) some content (**C**) to $learn_1$ (**L_1**) a prescribed range of knowing (**K_{2P}**) which is appropriate for tasks such as laying bricks, wiring buildings for electricity, performing heart surgery, administering anesthetics, presenting cases in courts of law, teaching primary school, interpreting X-rays, designing aircraft, cultivating vineyards, brewing beer, managing the water flow through a dam, etc. Occupational education (**E**) has strong community and government support, and one of the major motivations for governments to fund educational institutions is to produce a literate and skilled workforce.

A second example of an extrinsically good purpose for good education (**E_G**) is liberal education. Liberal education (**E**) is teaching (**T_P**) and $studying_1$ (**S_{P1}**) some content (**C**) for the purpose of $learning_1$ (**L_1**) by the students (**S**) a prescribed range of knowing (**K_{2P}**) that is sufficeent and relevant for living the life of free, well-informed, mindful, responsible and effective citizens within the context of a secular liberal democratic society. Liberal education (**E**), within the context of a liberal democracy, is the means for achieving and maintaining participation in and access to the economic, political and cultural resources of the society. It is the set of activities of teaching (**T_P**) and $studying_1$ (**S_{P1}**) some content (**C**) which leads to $learning_1$ (**L_1**) a prescribed range of knowing ($\mathbf{K_{2P}}$) about how to

(1) locate information (reliable facts, valid theories, sound justifications) and to make authentic choices from a well-informed and well-reasoned point of view,
(2) establish a sound, authentically chosen identity of self,
(3) articulate, clarify, evaluate, verify, validate and vindicate sound values in relation to a rationally chosen way of life,
(4) evaluate the accuracy and veracity of messages provided by the media (printed, TV, electronic), which are often manipulative in nature and deliberately deceptive, violent, aggressive and sensationalist,
(5) communicate clearly through speech and writing,
(6) engage constructively in the civic, economic and social life of one's community,
(7) engage in disciplined inquiry, sound reasoning and appropriate rational action in relation to the inquiry and reasoning,
(8) keep well-informed about politics, social issues, matters of justice, community health and any other matters affecting the well being of one's community.

Liberal education (**E**) empowers the students (**S**) who engage in it (and learn$_1$ <$\mathbf{L_1}$> the prescribed ranges of knowing <$\mathbf{K_{2P}}$> available from it) to celebrate their liberty through participating in the democratic process, through gaining access to the fruits of their society and through contributing to the richness of their society and culture.

A third example of an extrinsically good purpose for good education ($\mathbf{E_G}$) is health education. Health education (**E**) is teaching ($\mathbf{T_P}$) and studying$_1$ ($\mathbf{S_{P1}}$) some content (**C**) for the purpose of learning$_1$ ($\mathbf{L_1}$) by the students (**S**) of a prescribed range of knowing ($\mathbf{K_{2P}}$) that is appropriate and sufficient to use to achieve, maintain and/or improve good mental and physical health and well being. Health education (**E**) benefits the individual and the community in which the individual lives. Indeed, the health of the community establishes the controlling conditions for the health of individuals within the community. Good mental and physical health and well being are the bases for all other human activity and endeavors, as individuals and as communities. An understanding (**U**) of what constitutes good health and what needs to be done to establish, maintain and improve good health, for the individual and for the wider community, is vital to the well being of individuals, their society and their culture. A continuous supply of safe drinking water, adequate control, treatment and disposal of sewage and rubbish, access to well-balanced nutrition in optimal amounts and free of pathogens, habitual and conscientious hygiene and cleanliness, protection from pests, parasites and infectious diseases, opportunities for appropriate and adequate exercise and adequate accommodation are minimal requirements for individuals, communities and societies to function properly – economically, politically and culturally. The activities of teaching ($\mathbf{T_P}$) and studying$_1$ ($\mathbf{S_{P1}}$) (by individuals and/or by communities) the optimal content ($\mathbf{C_{1O}}$ and $\mathbf{C_{2O}}$) about the reasons and the ways to achieve, maintain and/or improve mental and physical health is good education ($\mathbf{E_G}$) because health education ($\mathbf{E}$) is a vital part of developing a sufficient range of knowing (<$\mathbf{K_2}$> including knowing-that-one <$\mathbf{K_{2K1}}$>, knowing-that <$\mathbf{K_{2K2}}$>, knowing-how <$\mathbf{K_{2K3}}$> and knowing-to <$\mathbf{K_{2K4}}$>) within a community for it to understand, appreciate and follow best practices to achieve, maintain and improve good mental and physical health and well being.

Disambiguation of the question, "What is good education ($\mathbf{E_G}$)?" reveals that the question implies at least three questions.

(1) What is ethical education?
(2) What is instrinsically worthwhile education?
(3) What is extrinsically worthwhile education?

This set of three questions presents a perennial challenge to each of us, as individuals, and all of us, as members of a generation of some society, community and culture within some frame of time. The challenge is for us, individually and collectively, to answer the set of questions with the best reasoned answers and with as much relevant and appropriate evidence as we can muster. Plausible warranted answers to these questions will always be dependent upon the social and cultural context in which the questions are posed. As social, cultural, economic, political and environmental circumstances change, so shall our answers change in relation to those circumstances.

Graduation ceremonies in high schools, colleges, institutes and universities are named <*commencement*> ceremonies for a very good reason. They are celebrations of the beginning of learning ($\mathbf{L}$), not the end of learning ($\mathbf{L}$) ranges of knowing ($\mathbf{K_2}$). The completion of the requirements for a diploma, certificate, degree, etc. may well be the end of our official studying$_1$ ($\mathbf{S_{P1}}$) and learning$_1$ ($\mathbf{L_1}$) of a prescribed range of knowing ($\mathbf{K_{2P}}$), at least for those of us who do not continue with official postsecondary education ($\mathbf{E}_O$). But it is by no means the end of our learning ($\mathbf{L}$) new ranges of knowing ($\mathbf{K}_2$) in all variations, whether it be

(1) conduced learning$_1$ ($\mathbf{L}_1$) of prescribed ranges of knowing ($\mathbf{K}_{2P}$) from unofficial education ($\mathbf{E}_U$),
(2) discovery learning$_2$ ($\mathbf{L}_2$) of discovered ranges of knowing ($\mathbf{K}_{2D}$) from inquiry ($\mathbf{Q}$),
(3) coerced learning$_3$ ($\mathbf{L}_3$) of compelled ranges of knowing ($\mathbf{K}_{2C}$) from socialization, enculturation and/or indoctrination or
(4) accidental learning$_4$ ($\mathbf{L}_4$) of accidental ranges of knowing ($\mathbf{K}_{2A}$) from misadventure and/or serendipity.

The process of learning ($\mathbf{L}$) extends our range of knowing ($\mathbf{K}_2$), and the process continues throughout our life, even to our last breath. Good education ($\mathbf{E}_G$), i.e. good official education ($\mathbf{E}_{OG}$), functions at its best when it is providing students ($\mathbf{S}$) with opportunities, encouragement and affirmations to develop two states of mind ($\mathbf{M}$), a cognitive one ($\mathbf{N}$) and a volitional one ($\mathbf{V}$). The cognitive state is the range of knowing ($\mathbf{K}_2$) requisite to conducting well-disciplined and fruitful inquiry ($\mathbf{Q}$) to verify answers to questions and to solve problems. The volitional state ($\mathbf{V}$) is the habit of choosing to answer questions and solve problems rationally by conducting well-disciplined and fruitful inquiry ($\mathbf{Q}$).

Within official education ($\mathbf{E}_O$), we have the opportunity as students ($\mathbf{S}$) to extend our prescribed range of knowing ($\mathbf{K}_{2P}$) at the conventional level ($\mathbf{K}_{2L2}$ and $\mathbf{K}_{2L3}$). Outside of official education ($\mathbf{E}_O$) or after completion of official education ($\mathbf{E}_O$), we have the challenge of extending our range of knowing ($\mathbf{K}_2$) beyond the conventional to the postconventional level of knowing ($\mathbf{K}_{2L4}$). Life experiences give us the opportunity to extend our postconventional knowing ($\mathbf{K}_{2L4}$) rationally and deliberately. Through reflection upon, and inquiry about, our life experiences, we have the opportunity to learn$_2$ (<$\mathbf{L}_2$> intentionally and without guidance), to innovate, to create and to achieve a range of knowing ($\mathbf{K}_2$) rationally and deliberately at the postconventional level of knowing ($\mathbf{K}_{2L4}$). Official education ($\mathbf{E}_O$), the teaching ($\mathbf{T}_P$) and studying$_1$ ($\mathbf{S}_{P1}$) some content ($\mathbf{C}$) within the social context ($\mathbf{X}_S$) of a school, college, institute, university, etc. can only lead us as students ($\mathbf{S}$) to achieving a prescribed range of knowing ($\mathbf{K}_{2P}$) at the conventional level ($\mathbf{K}_{2L2}$ and $\mathbf{K}_{2L3}$). The conventional level of knowing ($\mathbf{K}_{2L2}$ and $\mathbf{K}_{2L3}$) which we achieve from official education ($\mathbf{E}_O$) is the initial foundation for continuing the habit of lifelong discovery learning$_2$ (**L_2**), which extends our discovered range of knowing (**K_{2D}**) intentionally and without guidance, through inquiry (**Q**).

BIBLIOGRAPHY

Alkin, Marvin C. (Ed.), and American Educational Research Association (1992): *Encyclopedia of Educational Research.* 6th ed. New York; New York: Macmillan.

Allen, Dwight W. and Seifman, Eli (Eds.) (1971): *The Teacher's Handbook.* Glenview, Illinois: Scott, Foresman and Company.

BBC News (3 October 2005): *Nobel for Stomach Ulcer Discovery.* http://news.bbc.co.uk/2hi/43p04290.stm Accessed 16 Nov 2018.

Becker, Wesley C. and Engelmann, Siegfried (Winter, 1995-6): "Sponsor Findings from Project Follow Through," *Effective School Practices,* Vol. 15, No. 1. Eugene, Oregon: Association for Direct Instruction (ADI).

Becker, Wesley C.; Engelmann, Siegfried; and Thomas, Don R. (1971): *Teaching: A Course in Applied Psychology.* Chicago, Illinois: Science Research Associates.

Becker, Wesley C.; Engelmann, Siegfried; and Thomas, Don R. (1975a): *Teaching Vol. 1: A Modular Revision of Teaching.* Chicago, Illinois: Science Research Associates.

Becker, Wesley C.; Engelmann, Siegfried; and Thomas, Don R. (1975b): *Teaching Vol. 2: Cognitive Learning and Instruction.* Chicago: Science Research Associates.

Bergeron, Pierre-Jérôme (2017): "How to Engage in Pseudoscience with Real Data: A Criticism of John Hattie's Arguments in *Visible Learning* from the Perspective of a Statistician," *McGill Journal of Education,* Vol. 52, No. 1 https://mje.mcgill.ca/article/view/9475/7229 (Retrieved 14 March 2020).

Bertalanffy, Ludwig von (1968): *General Systems Theory: Foundations,*

Development, Applications. New York: George Braziller.

Bloom, Benjamin S., Ed. (1956): *Taxonomy of Educational Objectives, The Classification of Educational Goals, Handbook I: Cognitive Domain.* New York: Longman.

Bloom, Benjamin S. (1968): "Learning for Mastery," *Evaluation Comment,* Vol. 1, No. 2, p. 112.

Bloom, Benjamin S. (1974): "An Introduction to Mastery Learning Theory," in J.H. Block (Ed.), *Schools, Society, and Mastery Learning.* New York: Holt, Rinehart & Winston.

Bloom, B.S.; Hastings, J.T.; and Madaus, G. (1971): *Handbook on Formative and Summative Evaluation of Student Learning.* New York: McGraw-Hill.

Bode, Boyd H. (1921): *Fundamentals of Education.* New York: The Macmillan Company.

Bode, Boyd H. (1927): *Modern Educational Theories.* New York: The Macmillan Company.

Bode, Boyd H. (1938): *Progressive Education at the Crossroads.* New York: Newson & Company.

Boydston, Jo Ann, Ed. (1988): *John Dewey. The Later Works, 1925-1953. Volume 13: 1938-1939.* Carbondale, Illinois: Southern Illinois University Press.

Brezinka, Wolfgang (1981): "Chapter 1: Meta-Theory of Education: European Contributions from an Empirical-Analytic Point of View," in J.E. Christensen (Ed.), *Perspectives on Education as Educology.* Washington, D.C.: University Press of America, pp. 7-26.

Brezinka, Wolfgang (Translated by James Stuart Brice) (1992): *Philosophy of Educational Knowledge: An Introduction to the Foundations of Science of Education, Philosophy of Education and Practical Pedagogics.* Dordrecht: Kluwer Academic Publishers.

Brezinka, Wolfgang (Translated by James Stuart Brice) (1994): *Basic Concepts of Educational Science: Analysis, Critique, Proposals.* New York: University Press of America.

Brezinka, Wolfgang (Translated by James Stuart Brice) (1997): *Educational Aims, Educational Means, Educational Success: Contributions to a System of Science of Education.* Aldershot: Avebury.

Bruner, Jerome S. (1960): *The Process of Education.* Cambridge, Massachusetts: Harvard University Press.

Bruner, Jerome S. (June, 1965): *Man: A Course of Study.* Occasional Paper No. 3. The Social Studies Curriculum Program. Cambridge, Massachusetts: Educational Services Incorporated. Washington, DC: National Science Foundation, sponsoring agency.

Bruner, Jerome S. (1971): *The Relevance of Education.* New York, N.Y.: W.W. Norton & Company.

Bruner, Jerome S. (1997): *The Culture of Education.* Cambridge, Massachusetts: Harvard University Press.

Cantor, Jeffrey A. (1992): *Delivering Instruction to Adult Learners.* Toronto: Wall & Emerson.

Carnine, Douglas W.; Silbert, Jerry; Kame'enui, Edward J.; and Tarver, Sarah G. (2009): *Direct Instruction Reading* (5th Edition). Upper Saddle River, New Jersey: Pearson.

Cazden, C.B. (1986): "Classroom Discourse," in M.C. Wittrock (Ed.), *Handbook of Research on Teaching,* Third Edition. New York: Macmillan Publishing Company.

Ceri, Dean B., Ross Hubbell, Elizabeth, Pitler, Howard and Stone, Bj (2012): *Classroom Instruction That Works. Research Based Strategies for Increasing Student Achievement.* 2nd Edition. Alexandria, Virginia: ASCD (Association for Supervision and Curriculum Development).

Christenbury, Leila (2010, December, 2011, January): "The Flexible Teacher." *Educational Leadership* , Volume 68, Number 4, pp. 46-50. Alexandria, Virginia: Association for Supervision and Curriculum Development (ASCD). Retrieved 12 August 2020. http://www.ascd.org/publications/educational-leadership/dec10/vol68/num04/The-Flexible-Teacher.aspx

Christensen, James E. (1975): "Educational Research as Educology," *Australian Educational Researcher* (Australian Association for Research in Education), Vol. 2, No. 4, pp. 18-20.

Christensen, James E. (1977): "A Conversation about Education as Educology, Guest Editorial," *Educational Studies: A Journal of the American Educational Studies Association.* Vol 8, No. 1, pp. v-xii.

Christensen, James E. (1981): *Curriculum, Education, and Educology.* Sydney: Educology Research Associates.

Christensen, James E. (1981): *Education and Human Development: A Study in Educology.* Sydney: Educology Research Associates.

Christensen, James E. (1981): "Chapter 6: Educology and Some Related Concepts," in J.E. Christensen (Ed.), *Perspectives on Education as Educology.* Washington, D.C.: University Press of America, pp. 121-158.

Christensen, James E. (Ed.) (1981, 2018): *Perspectives on Education as Educology.* Amazon Kindle Edition, an e-book available at https://www.amazon.com/gp/product/B07DGYFX1S/ref=dbs_a_def_rwt_hsch_vamf_taft_p1_i0

Christensen, James E. (March, 1982): "The Educology of Curriculum." *Collected Original Resources in Education* (Taylor and Francis Group).

Christensen, James E. (23-27 November, 1983): "Cognition, Knowing, and Understanding: Levels, Forms, and Range." *Proceedings of the National Conference of the Australian Association for Research in Education.* Canberra, ACT: AARE.

Christensen, James E. (June, 1986): "Comparative Educology: A Bridging Concept for Comparative Educational Inquiry," A paper presented to the Fifth World Congress of Comparative Education, Paris, 2-6 Jul, 1984, *Resources in Education* (ERIC: Education Resources Information Center): Accession Numbers ED 266542, EA 018220.

Christensen, James E. (March, 1986): "Educational Research with an Educological Perspective," A paper presented to the Annual Conference of the American Educational Research Association, Chicago, Mar 31-Apr 4, 1985," *Resources in Education* (ERIC: Education Resources Information Center): Accession Numbers ED 263197, TM 850688.

Christensen, James E. (Ed.) (1986): *Educology 86: Proceedings of a Conference on Educational Research, Inquiry and Development with an Educological Perspective, Canberra, July 10-12, 1986.* Sydney: Educology Research Associates.

Christensen, James E. (1987): "Education, Educology and Educological Discourse: Theory and Structure for Education and Constructive Action in Education," *International Journal of Educology*, Vol. 1, No. 1, pp. 1-32, Sydney: Educology Research Associates.

Christensen, James E. (1992): "Education for Freedom: A Philosophical Educology," *International Journal of Educology*, Vol. 6, No. 2, pp. 97-131. Sydney: Educology Research Associates.

Christensen, James E. (2013): *Education, Knowledge and Educology.* Amazon Kindle Edition, an e-book available at https://www.amazon.com/gp/product/B0796NRNC5/ref=dbs_a_def_rwt_hsch_vamf_taft_p1_i5

Christensen, James E. (2014): *Education, Curriculum and Educology.* Amazon Kindle Edition, an e-book available at https://www.amazon.com/gp/product/B0797JBMRY/ref=dbs_a_def_rwt_hsch_vapi_taft_p1_i4

Christensen, James E. (2015): *Education, Universities and Educology.* Amazon Kindle Edition, an e-book available at https://www.amazon.com/gp/product/B088NW957H/ref=dbs_a_def_rwt_bibl_vppi_i0

Christensen, James E. (2016): *Education, Research and Educology.* Amazon Kindle Edition, an e-book available at https://www.amazon.com/gp/product/B0798C78ZF/ref=dbs_a_def_rwt_hsch_vapi_taft_p1_i3

Christensen, James E. (2017): *Education, Mindfulness and Educology.* Amazon Kindle Edition, an e-book available at https://www.amazon.com/gp/product/B07968L4ZP/ref=dbs_a_def_rwt_hsch_vamf_taft_p1_i6

Christensen, James E. (2018): *Education, Educology and Meta-Educology: A*

Conversation. Amazon Kindle Edition, an e-book available at https://www.amazon.com/gp/product/B07MB5GRFR/ref=dbs_a_def_rwt_hsch_vapi_tkin_p1_i2

Christensen, James E. (2020): *Educology of Teaching.* Amazon Kindle Edition, an e-book available at https://www.amazon.com/gp/product/B088DQ7RG2/ref=dbs_a_def_rwt_hsch_vapi_tkin_p1_i1

Christensen, James E. and Fisher, James E (1978): "An Organizational Theory for Schools of Teacher Education and Faculties of Education," *Australian Journal of Education*, Vol. 22, No. 1, pp. 52-71, Australian Council for Educational Research.

Christensen, James E. and Fisher, James E. (1979): *Analytic Philosophy of Education as a Sub-Discipline of Educology: An Introduction to its Techniques and Application.* Washington, D.C.: University Press of America.

Christensen, James E. and Fisher, James E (1981): "Chapter 12: Educology as an Organizational Concept for Schools of Teacher Education, College of Education, and Faculties of Education," in J.E. Christensen (Ed.), *Perspectives on Education as Educology.* Washington, DC: University Press of America, pp. 263-300.

Christensen, James E. and Fisher, James E (1983): *Organization and Colleges of Education: An Educological Perspective.* Sydney: Educology Research Associates.

Christensen, James E. and Fisher, James E. (1988): "The Need for Educological Research in the Areas of Secondary School Retention Rates, Educational Pathways and Recurrent Education," *International Journal of Educology*, Vol. 2, No. 2, pp. ix-xii. Sydney: Educology Research Associates.

Christensen, James E. and Fisher, James E. (1989): "Educology and the Educological Perspective," *International Journal of Educology*, Vol. 3, No. 1, pp. ix-xv. Sydney: Educology Research Associates.

Christensen, James E. and Fisher, James E. (1990). "Three Critical Distinctions for Advancing Educology," *International Journal of Educology*, Vol. 4, No. 1, pp. vi-viii. Sydney: Educology Research Associates.

Christensen, James E. and Fisher, James E. (1990): "Educology for Initial Teacher Education and for Professional Development of Practising Teachers - Changing Needs, Changing Demands," *International Journal of Educology*, Vol. 4, No. 2, pp. vi-xvii. Sydney: Educology Research Associates.

Christensen, James E. and Fisher, James E. (1991a): "A Challenge for Educologists of Curriculum," *International Journal of Educology*, Vol. 5, No. 1, pp. vi-ix. Sydney: Educology Research Associates.

Christensen, James E. and Fisher, James E. (1991b): "An Educology of Values, Goals and Action Plans," *International Journal of Educology*, Vol. 5, No. 2, pp. vi-ix. Sydney: Educology Research Associates.

Christensen, James E. and Fisher, James E. (1992): "The Educology of the Work Place," *International Journal of Educology*, Vol. 6, No. 1, pp. vi-xi. Sydney: Educology Research Associates.

Dewey, John (1910): *How We Think*. New York: D.C. Heath & Co, Publishers.

Dewey, John (1916): *Democracy and Education.* New York: The Macmillan Company.

Dewey, John (1938a): *Experience and Education.* New York: The Macmillan Company.

Dewey, John (1938b): *Logic: The Theory of Inquiry*. New York: Henry Holt and Company, Inc.

Discovery Channel (25 Apr 2008): "Spontaneous Savant, Orlando Serrell on Discovery Channel," https://www.youtube.com/watch?v=3fg75qRdzwo Retrieved 22 Sep 2017.

Dunkin, Michael J. and Biddle, Bruce J. (1974): *The Study of Teaching.* New York: Holt, Rinehart and Winston, Inc.

Eco, Umberto (1976): *A Theory of Semiotics*. Bloomington, Indiana: Indiana University Press.

Educology. *Everipedia*. https://everipedia.org/wiki/lang_en/Educology Retrieved 6 Aug 2020.

Educology. *Wikivisually*. https://wikivisually.com/wiki/Educology Retrieved 2 Feb 2021.

Educology: Knowledge of Education (N.D.): Indiana University. https://educology.indiana.edu/ Retrieved 2 Feb 2021.

Elder, Rachel (1971): "Three Educologies." (Mimeographed). A paper written for the Far West laboratory for Educational Research and Development. San Francisco, California.

Ennis, Robert T. (1969): *Logic in Teaching.* Englewood Cliffs, New Jersey: Prentice-Hall, Inc.

Eryaman, Mustafa Yunus and Riedler, Martina (2010): "Teacher-Proof Curriculum." *Encyclopedia of Curriculum Studies.* Edited by Craig Kridel. Thousand Oaks, California: Sage Publications. Retrieved 2 Sep 2020. https://sk.sagepub.com/reference/curriculumstudies/n457.xml

Facto, Kobi (October 2020): "Shannen Jones: How a Passion for Gymnastics Turned into a Career of Contortion and Foot-Archery." *We Are Goldcoast: The Official City Guide for Everything Gold Coast.* Gold Coast, Queensland. Retrieved 5 Nov 2020. https://wearegc.com.au/articles/artist-shannen-jones/?fbclid=IwAR0g_JgoDHRQPIUOE16znpZBKjB0LOz5xm1CSZ_jTCjqkSveycQiLNXMrBE

Fenstermacher, Gary D. and Soltis, Jonas F., with contributions from Matthew N. Sanger (2009): *Approaches to Teaching.* Fifth Edition.

Thinking about Education Series. New York: Teachers College Press.

Finkel, Michael (1 Mar 2011): "The Man Who Taught Himself To See," *Men's Journal* in *Cover Stories, Features* *https://my.vanderbilt.edu/course/files/2012/05/The-Blind-Man-Who-Taught-Himself-To-See.pdf* Accessed 15 Jul 2017.

Fisher, James E. (1981): "Chapter 13: The Concept of Educology and the Classification System used in *Educational Studies,*" in J.E. Christensen (Ed.), *Perspectives on Education as Educology*. Washington, DC: University Press of America, pp. 301–327.

Fisher, James E. (1986): "Chapter 4: Toward a Theory of Language for Educology and Education," in J.E. Christensen (Ed.), *Educology 86: Proceedings of a Conference on Educational Research, Inquiry and Development with an Educological Perspective, Canberra, July 10-12, 1986*. Sydney: Educology Research Associates, pp. 51–72.

Fisher, James E. (1991): "The Territory of Educology," *International Journal of Educology*, Vol. 5, No. 1, pp. 18-45. Sydney: Educology Research Associates.

Fisher, James E. (1992a): "Mapping Observations about Education in the Home: An Educology of Home," *International Journal of Educology*, Vol. 6, No. 1, pp. 53-93. Sydney: Educology Research Associates.

Fisher, James E. (1992b): "An Introduction to Home Educology and Home Education in the USA, Part I," *International Journal of Educology*, Vol. 6, No. 2, pp. 170-207. Sydney: Educology Research Associates.

Fisher, James E. (1993): "An Introduction to Home Educology and Home Education in the USA, Part II," *International Journal of Educology*, Vol. 7, No. 2, pp. 139-196. Sydney: Educology Research Associates.

Fisher, James E. (1996): "The Domain of Educology," *International Journal of Educology*, Vol. 10, No. 1, pp. 66-143. Sydney: Educology Research Associates.

Fisher, James E. (1998-2001): "An Outlined Introduction to the Universal and Unifying Experiential Research Methodology in the Domain of Educology: The Discipline of Educology Introduced to Graduate Students in Educology," *International Journal of Educology*, Vol. 12-15, pp. 59-76. Sydney: Educology Research Associates.

Fisher, James E. (1998-2001): "Educology Contributing to the Development of the New Democracy in Lithuania," *International Journal of Educology*, Vol. 12-15, pp. 77-79. Sydney: Educology Research Associates.

Fisher, James E. (2001): "Contributing Paper 1.1 in History and Philosophy of Educology, Part I (A paper used as the basis for a series of seven lectures to faculty and doctoral students in educology at Vytautas Magnus University (VMU) in December, 2001)," *Pedagogika*. Kaunus, Lithuania: Vytauto Didziojo universiteto leidykla.

Fisher, James E. (2003): "A General Sketch of a Semiotically Understood and Oriented Organic Experiential Philosophy of Educology for Developing Democracies in the World," *International Journal of Educology*, Vol. 17, No. 1&2, pp. 1-40. Sydney: Educology Research Associates.

Fisher, James E. and Reinhart, Marian (1981): "Chapter 14: Educology and the Teaching of Mathematics," in James E. Christensen (Ed.), *Perspectives on Education as Educology*. Washington, DC: University Press of America. pp. 328–340.

Ford, Henry (In collaboration with Samuel Crowther) (1924): *My Life and Work*. London: William Heinemann.

Forster, Daniella J. (2012): "Codes of Ethics in Australian Education: Towards a National Perspective." *Australian Journal of Teacher Education*, 37(9). http://dx.doi.org/10.14221/ajte.2012v37n9.4

Frick, Theodore W. (2012): *The Theory of Totally Integrated Education: TIE. A Monograph in Four Parts.* Bloomington: Department of Instructional Systems Technology, School of Education, Indiana University. http://educology.indiana.edu/Frick/TIEtheory.pdf

Gagné, R.M. (1977): *The Conditions of Learning.* Third Edition. New York: Holt, Rinehart and Winston.

Gagné, R.M.; Briggs, L.; & Wager, W. (1992). *Principles of Instructional Design.* Fourth Edition. Fort Worth, Texas: HBJ College Publishers.

Gardner, Howard (2006): *The Development and Education of the Mind: The Selected Works of Howard Gardner.* London: Routledge.

Gardner, Howard (2011): *Frames of Mind: The Theory of Multiple Intelligences.* New York: Basic Books.

Gee, David (Nov 21, 2018): "Christian Missionary Killed by Isolated Tribe When He Tried to Convert Them," *Patheos.* https://www.patheos.com/blogs/nosacredcows/2018/11/christian-missionary-killed-by-isolated-tribe-when-he-tried-to-convert-them/?fbclid=IwAR1l8AaGlpOkeQn5dwyfGWYEjyo3NixAdhIho4REOmfSLSLXLeG9REwhAcU Retrieved November 26, 2018.

Giudici, Claudia; Rinaldi, Carlina; Krechevsky, Mara; Barchi, Paola; Gardner, Howard (2001): *Making Learning Visible: Children as Individuals and Group Learners.* Project Zero, Cambridge, Massachusetts: Harvard Graduate School of Education; Reggio Emilia, Italy: Reggio Children, International Center for the Defense and Promotion of the Rights and Potential of All Children.

Gorovitz, Samuel and Williams, Ron G. (1969): *Philosophical Analysis.* 2nd Edition. New York: Random House.

Green, Thomas F. (1971): *The Activities of Teaching.* New York: McGraw-Hill.

Gronlund, N.E. (1991): *How to Write and Use Instructional Objectives.* Fourth Edition. New York, NY: Macmillan.

Hall, E.T. (1959): *The Silent Language.* Garden City, N.J.: Doubleday and Co.

Harding, L.W. (Ed.) (1951): *Anthology in Educology.* Dubuque, Iowa: Wm. C. Brown, Co

Harding, L.W. (Ed.) (1956): *Essays in Educology.* Dubuque, Iowa: Wm. C. Brown, Co

Harding, L.W. (Ed.) (1964): *More Essays in Educology.* Columbus, Ohio: Association for the Study of Educology.

Harding, L.W. (Ed.) (1965): *Educology: The Fourth Collection.* Columbus, Ohio: Association for the Study of Educology.

Harel, Idit and Papert, Seymour (Ed.) (1991): *Constructionism.* Norwood, New Jersey: Ablex Publishing.

Hattie, John (2008): *Visible Learning. A Synthesis of over 800 Meta-Analyses Relating to Achievement.* London: Routledge. Taylor & Francis Group.

Hattie, John (2012): *Visible Learning for Teachers. Maximizing Impact on Learning.* London: Routledge. Taylor & Francis Group.

Heath, Marilyn (retrieved 5 Dec 2019): "Madeline Cheek Hunter (1916-1994)." *Education Encyclopedia* – StateUniversity.com https://education.stateuniversity.com/pages/2074/Hunter-Madeline-Cheek-1916-1994.html

Hunter, Madeline (1967, 1994): *Teach More – Faster!* Los Angeles: Hunter Enterprises.

Hunter, Madeline (1969): *Improved Instruction.* Los Angeles: Hunter Enterprises.

Hunter, Madeline (1969): *Motivation Theory for Teachers.* Los Angeles: Hunter Enterprises.

Hunter, Madeline (1969): *Retention Theory for Teachers.* Los Angeles: Hunter Enterprises.

Hunter, Madeline (1982, 1994): *Mastery Teaching. Increasing Instructional Effectiveness in Elementary and Secondary Schools, Colleges, and Universities.* Los Angeles, California: Hunter Enterprises.

Hunter, Madeline (1994): *Discipline That Develops Self-Discipline.* Los Angeles: Hunter Enterprises

Hunter, Madeline (1995): *Teach for Transfer.* Los Angeles, California: Hunter Enterprises.

Jackson, Philip W. (1968): *Life in Classrooms.* New York: Teachers College Press.

Johnson, David W. and Johnson, Roger T. (1975): *Learning Together and Alone: Cooperation, Competition, and Individualization.* Englewood Cliffs, New Jersey: Prentice Hall.

Johnson, David W.; Johnson, Roger T.; and Holubec, Edythe (2008): *Cooperation in the Classroom*, Eighth Edition. Edina, Minnesota: Interaction Book Company.

Johnson, Richard (12 Feb 2005): "A Genius Explains," *The Guardian, Life and Style*, https://www.theguardian.com/theguardian/2005/feb/12/weekend7.weekend2 Retrieved 23 Sep 2017.

Joyce, Bruce and Weil, Marsha (2011): *Models of Teaching.* Eighth Edition. Upper Saddle River, New Jersey: Pearson Publishing.

Katziskji, Katarina L. (2009): *Educology: Una pedagogia curative per una nuova umanità.* Roma: Freebook.

Keller, Helen; Sullivan, Annie (1903, 1954): *The Story of My Life.* Garden City, NY: Doubleday & Co

Kilpatrick, William Heard (1918): *The Project Method: The Use of the Purposeful Act in the Educative Process.* New York: Teachers College, Columbia University.

Kilpatrick, William Heard (1949): *Modern Education: Its Proper Work.* New York: John Dewey Society.

Kilpatrick, William Heard (1951): *Philosophy of Education.* New York: Macmillan.

Kneller, George F. (1964): *Introduction to the Philosophy of Education.* New York: John Wiley & Sons.

Kneller, George F. (1966): *Logic and Language of Education.* New York: John Wiley & Sons.

Kotarbiński, Tadeusz (Translated from the Polish by Olgierd Wojtasiewicz) (1965): *Praxiology; An Introduction to the Sciences of Efficient Action.* London: Pergamon Press.

Krathwohl, D.R., et al. (1956): *Taxonomy of Educational Objectives: The Classification of Educational Goals: Handbook II: Affective Domain.* New York: David McKay Company, Inc.

Laird, Charles, Director (2004): *Through These Eyes.* Documentry Film. Canada. National Film Board. http://www.nfb.ca/film/through_these_eyes/

Lash, Joseph P. (1980): *Helen and Teacher: The Story of Helen Keller and Anne Sullivan Macy.* New York: Delacoret Press.

Lehrer, K. and Paxon, Jr., T. (April, 1968): "Knowledge: Undefeated Justified True Belief," *Journal of Philosophy*, Vol LXVI, No. 8.

Maccia, George (1967): "Science and Science of Education," in George F. Kneller (Ed.), *Foundations of Education, Second Edition.* New York: John Wiley & Sons.

Maccia, George (September, 1973a): "Contributions of Epistemology Toward a Science of Education." A paper presented to the International Congress of the International Association for the Advancement of Educational Research. Paris: The University of Paris.

Maccia, George (September, 1973b): "Epistemological Considerations of Educational Objectives." A paper presented to the Philosophy of

Education Section of the XVth World Congress of Philosophy. Varna, Bulgaria.

Maccia, George (November, 1973c): "Educological Epistemology." A paper presented to the 1973 annual meeting of the Ohio Valley Philosophy of Education Society. Cincinnati, Ohio.

Maccia, George (21-22 October, 1977): "Education for Humanity." A paper presented to a Symposium on Philosophy of Education, the Philosophical Society. Fredonia, New York: State University of New York.

Maccia, George (1981): "Chapter 2: The Genesis of Educology," in James E. Christensen (Ed.), *Perspectives on Education as Educology*. Washington, DC: University Press of America, pp. 27–50.

Maccia, George (1991): "A Philosophical Educology: Education and Dialectics of Person," *International Journal of Educology*, Vol. 5, No. 1, pp. 71-84. Sydney: Educology Research Associates.

Maccia, George (1992): "Education for Humanity: A Philosophical Educology," *International Journal of Educology*, Vol. 6, No. 1, pp. 1-10. Sydney: Educology Research Associates.

Maccia [Steiner], E. S., and Maccia, G. S., (1966): *Development of Educational Theory Derived from Three Educational Theory Models*. Project Number 5-0638, Office of Education, U.S. Department of Health, Education, and Welfare. Columbus, Ohio: The Ohio State University, Research Foundation.

Magee, John B. (1971): *Philosophical Analysis in Education*. New York: Harper & Row, Publishers.

Mager, Robert (1990): *Preparing Instructional Objectives*. London: Kogan Page Ltd.

Maiese, Michelle and Burgess, Heidi (2020): "Types of Justice." *Beyond Intractability. Knowledge Base & Conflict Fundamentals*. (Originally written by Michelle Maiese and published July 2003; updated by Heidi Burgess in June 2013, and again in July 2020) Retrieved 31 Aug 2020. https://www.beyondintractability.org/essay/types_of_justice#:~:text=This%20article%20points%20out%20that,All%20four%20of%20these%20are.

Margaret, K.T. (1999): *The Open Classroom: A Journey through Education*. Hyderabad, India: Orient Longman Private Limited.

Marzano, Robert J. (1992): *A Different Kind of Classroom. Teaching with Dimensions of Learning*. Alexandria, Virginia: ASCD (Association for Supervision and Curriculum Development).

Marzano, Robert J. (2003): *Classroom Management That Works: Research-Based Strategies for Every Teacher*. Alexandria, Virginia: ASCD (Association for Supervision and Curriculum Development).

Marzano, Robert J. (2007): *The Art and Science of Teaching. A Comprehensive Framework for Effective Instruction (Professional Development)*. Alexandria,

Virginia: ASCD (Association for Supervision and Curriculum Development).

Marzano, Robert J. (2017): *The New Art and Science of Teaching.* Bloomington, Indiana: Solution Tree Press.

Marzano, Robert J. and Brandt, Ronald S., Hughes, Carolyn Sue, Jones, Beau Fly, Presselsen, Barbara Z., Rankin, Stuart C. and Suhor, Charles (1988): *Dimensions of Thinking: A Framework for Curriculum and Instruction.* Alexandria, Virginia: ASCD (Association for Supervison and Curriculum.

Marzano, Robert J. and Pickering, Debra J. with Daisy E. Aredondo, Guy J. Blackburn, Ronald S. Brandt, Cerylle A. Moffett, Diane E. Paynter, Jane E. Pollock and Jo Sue Whisler (1997): *Dimensions of Learning: Teacher's Manual.* Second Edition. Alexandria, Virginia: Association for Supervision and Curriculum Development (ASCD) and Aurora, Colorado: Mid-continent Regional Educational Laboratory (McREL).

Marzano, Robert J. and Pickering, Debra J. with Daisy E. Aredondo, Guy J. Blackburn, Ronald S. Brandt, Cerylle A. Moffett, Diane E. Paynter, Jane E. Pollock and Jo Sue Whisler (1997): *Dimensions of Learning: Trainer's Manual.* Second Edition. Alexandria, Virginia: Association for Supervision and Curriculum Development (ASCD) and Aurora, Colorado: Mid-continent Regional Educational Laboratory (McREL).

Marzano, Robert J., Pickering, Robert J. and Pollock, Jane E. (2001): *Classroom Instruction That Works. Research Based Strategies for Increasing Student Achievement.* Alexandria, Virginia: ASCD (Association for Supervision and Curriculum Development).

Monshouwer, Anton (1981): "Chapter 3: The Formal Structure of an Emerging Science of Education, Part I: Some Opinions about the Scientific Status of a Science of Education," in James E. Christensen (Ed.), *Perspectives on Education as Educology*. Washington, DC: University Press of America, pp. 51–86.

Monshouwer, Anton (1981): "Chapter 7: The Formal Structure of an Emerging Science of Education, Part II: The Concept of Science," in James E. Christensen (Ed.), *Perspectives on Education as Educology.* Washington, DC: University Press of America, pp. 159–196.

Montessori, Maria (1947a, 1989) *Education for a New World.* The Clio Montessori Series. Santa Barbara, California: ABC CLIO.

Montessori, Maria (1947b, 1989) *To Educate the Human Potential.* The Clio Montessori Series. Santa Barbara, California: ABC CLIO.

Montessori, Maria (1949): *The Absorbent Mind.* Adyar, India: The Theosophical Publishing House.

Murray, Kenneth D. (May 1995): "Learning as Knowledge Integration."

PhD Dissertation. Austin, Texas: University of Texas.

Papert, Seymour (2001): *Project-Based Learning.* Edutopia Staff. http://www.edutopia.org/seymour-papert-project-based-learning

Peirce, Charles Sanders (1896): notes from "History of Science" (not published) in *Collected Papers of Charles Sanders Peirce, Principles of Philosophy*, Hartshorne, C. and Weiss, P. (Eds.). Cambridge, Massachusetts: The Belknap Press of Harvard University Press, 1960.

Peirce, Charles Sanders, Eisele, Carolyn, Ed. (1902, 1976): *The New Elements of Mathematics*, Vol. 4, The Hague, Netherlands, Mouton Publishers.

Perry, James F (1981): "Chapter 9: Praxiology of Education as a Branch of Educology," in James E. Christensen (Ed.), *Perspectives on Education as Educology*, pp. 213–222.Washington, DC: University Press of America.

Perry, James F (1986): "Chapter 11: What Works for What, and Why: Praxiology of Education," in James E. Christensen (Ed.), *Educology 86: Proceedings of a Conference on Educational Research, Inquiry and Development with an Educological Perspective, Canberra, July 10-12, 1986.* Sydney: Educology Research Associates, pp. 163–182.

Piaget, Jean (1926): *The Language and Thought of the Child.* London: Routledge & Kegan.

Piaget, Jean (1948): *The Moral Judgment of the Child.* New York: Free Press.

Piaget, Jean (1953): *The Origin of Intelligence in the Child.* New Fetter Lane, New York: Routledge & Kegan Paul.

Piaget, Jean (1971): "The Theory of Stages in Cognitive Development," in D. Green, M. Ford and G. Flamer (Eds.), *Measurement and Piaget.* New York: McGraw-Hill, pp. 1-11.

Pukelis, Kestutis and Savickiene, Izabela (2005): "The Challenge of Establishing a Common Set of Terms for Discourse, Inquiry, and Research in Educational Science: An Analytically Oriented Philosophy of Educology," *International Journal of Educology.* Educology Research Associates. Lithuanian Special Issue: pp.14–27.

Queensland. Department of Education (2001): *The Queensland School Reform Longitudinal Study, Volume 1.* Brisbane: State of Queensland, Department of Education.

Queensland. Department of Education (2002): *A Guide to Productive Pedagogies. Classroom Reflection Manual.* Brisbane: State of Queensland, Department of Education.

Raup, R. Bruce; Axtelle, George; Benne, Kenneth D; and Smith, B. Othanel (1950): *The Improvement of Practical Intelligence: The Central Task of Education.* New York: Harper and Brothers. Originally published as the 28th yearbook of the National Society of College Teachers of Education under the title, *The Discipline of Practical Judgment in a Democratic Society*, 1943.

Robinson, Francis Pleasant (1978): *Effective Study* (Sixth edition). New York: Harper Row.

Robertson, Richard (1954): *Definition.* Oxford: Oxford University Press.

Rogers, Carl (1969): *Freedom to Learn: A View of What Education Might Become.* First Edition. Columbus, Ohio: Charles Merrill.

Rosenshine, Barak and Stevens, Robert (1986): "Chapter 13: Teaching Functions," in Merlin C. Wittrock (Ed.), *Handbook of Research on Teaching* (Third Edition): A Project of the American Educational Research Association. New York, N.Y.: Macmillan Publishing Company, pp. 376-391.

Russell, Bertrand (1912, 1997 edition): *The Problems of Philosophy.* London: Oxford University Press.

Ryle, Gilbert (1949): *The Concept of Mind.* New York: Barnes and Noble.

Saina, E.K & Kipsat, Mary J. & Nyangweso, P. M. & Sulo, T. & Korir, M.K. (2012): "The Contribution of Agricultural Education in Secondary Schools to Rural Agricultural Productivity: The Case of Small Scale Farmers in Uasin Gishu County, Kenya," 2012 Eighth AFMA Congress, November 25-29, 2012, Nairobi, Kenya 159389, African Farm Management Association (AFMA). Retrieved 17 Jun 2020.

Saul, Wendy in collaboration with Dow, Peter (2009): *(Hu)mans: A Course of Study.* Education Development Center (EDC). https://www.macosonline.org/

Saxon, Wolfgang (Feb 3, 1994): "Madeline C. Hunter, Teaching Innovator and an Author, 78." *The New York Times*, Section B, Page 7.

Scheffler, Israel (1960): *The Language of Education.* Springfield, Illinois: Charles C. Thomas, Co.

Schlechty, Phillip C. (2002): *Working on the Work. An Action Plan for Teachers, Principals, and Superintendents.* Hoboken, New Hersey: John Wiley & Sons, Inc.

Schlechty, Phillip C. (2011): *Engaging Students: The Next Level of Working on the Work.* Hoboken, New Jersey: John Wiley & Sons, Inc.

Scriven, Michael (1967): "The Methodology of Evaluation," in R.W. Tyler, R.M. Gagné & M. Scriven (Eds.), *Perspectives of Curriculum Evaluation*, pp. 39-83. American Educational Research Association (AERA) Monograph Series on Curriculum Evaluation, No. 1. Chicago: Rand-McNally.

Scriven, Michael (1991): *Evaluation Thesaurus.* Fourth Edition. Thousand Oaks, California: Sage Publications, Inc.

Sheahan, Matthew (4 June 2019): "Could the Wonderfully Weird Inflated Wing Sail Make Sailing Easier?" *Yachting World.* Retrieved 30 May 2020. https://www.yachtingworld.com/extraordinary-boats/inflated-wing-sail-121282

Slaven, R.E. (2018): *John Hattie is Wrong.* Robert Slavin's Blog. The Laura and John Arnold Foundation. https://robertslavinsblog.wordpress.com/2018/06/21/john-hattie-is-wrong/ Retrieved 14 March 2020.

Slavin, R.E.; Madden, N.A.; Dolan, L.J.; Wasik, B.A.; Ross, S.; Smith, L.; and Dianda, M. (1996): "Success for All: A Summary of Research," *Journal of Education for Students Placed at Risk*, Vol. 1, No. 1, pp. 41-76.

Smith, B. Othanel and Robert H. Ennis (1961): *Language and Concepts in Education.* Chicago: Rand McNally and Co.

Smith, B. Othanel and Meux, Milton O. (1960): *A Study of the Logic of Teaching.* Urbana, Illinois: Bureau of Educational Research, College of Education, University of Illinois.

Smith, B. Othanel; Shores, J. Harlan; and Stanley, William O. (1951): *Fundamentals of Curriculum Development.* New York: World Book Company.

Smith, B. Othanel; Stanley, William O.; and Shores, J. Harlan (1950): *Social Diagnosis for Education.* New York: World Book Company.

Smith, Mortimer B. (1954): *The Diminished Mind.* Chicago, Illinois: The Henry Regnery Company.

Steiner Maccia, Elizabeth (1964): "Logic of Education and Educatology: Dimensions of Philosophy of Education," *Proceedings of the Philosophy of Education Society.* Lawrence, Kansas: Philosophy of Education Society.

Steiner Maccia, Elizabeth (Sep 1970): "Towards Educational Theorizing without Mistake," *Studies in Philosophy and Education*, Vol. 7, No. 2, pp. 154-157.

Steiner [Maccia], Elizabeth (1972): "The Non-Identity of Philosophy and Theory of Education," in John Martin Rich (Ed.), *Readings in the Philosophy of Education, Second Edition.* Belmont, California: Wadsworth Publishing Company.

Steiner [Maccia], Elizabeth (1977): "Educology: Its Origins and Future," A paper presented to the Annual Meeting of the American Educational Research Association, New York, N.Y., Apr 3-8, 1977. *Resources in Education* (ERIC: Education Resources Information Center): Accession Numbers ED 141201.

Steiner [Maccia], Elizabeth (1978): *Logical and Conceptual Analytic Techniques for Educational Researchers.* Washington, DC: University Press of America.

Steiner [Maccia], Elizabeth (1981): *Educology of the Free.* New York: Philosophical Library.

Steiner [Maccia], Elizabeth (1981): "Chapter 4: Logic of Education and of Educatology: Dimensions of Philosophy of Education," in James. E. Christensen (Ed.), *Perspectives on Education as Educology.* Washington, DC:

University Press of America. pp. 87–100.

Steiner [Maccia], Elizabeth (1981): "Chapter 5: Educology: Thirteen Years Later," in James E. Christensen (Ed.), *Perspectives on Education as Educology*. Washington, DC: University Press of America. pp. 101–120.

Steiner [Maccia], Elizabeth (1986): "Chapter 13: Crisis in Educology," in James E. Christensen (Ed.), *Educology 86: Proceedings of a Conference on Educational Research, Inquiry and Development with an Educological Perspective, Canberra, July 10-12, 1986*. Sydney: Educology Research Associates, pp. 221–228.

Steiner [Maccia], Elizabeth (1988): *Methodology of Theory Building*. Sydney: Educology Research Associates.

Taba, Hilda (1962): *Curriculum Development; Theory and Practice*. New York: Harcourt, Brace & World.

Taba, Hilda (1966): *Teaching Strategies and Cognitive Functioning in Elementary School Children*. Cooperative Research Project 2404. San Francisco, California: San Francisco State College.

Taylor, Paul W. (1961): *Normative Discourse*. Englewood Cliffs, N.J.: Prentice-Hall.

Thompson, Kenneth R. (2005, June): "Axiomatic Theories of Intentional Systems: Methodology of Theory Construction," *Scientific Inquiry*, Vol. 7, No. 1, pp. 13 – 24.

Thompson, Kenneth R. (2006, June 1): "*General System* Defined for Predictive Technologies of A-GSBT (Axiomatic-General Systems Behavioral Theory)," *Scientific Inquiry*, 7:1, 1 – 11 IIGSS Academic Publisher.

Thompson, Kenneth R. (1996-2015): *ATIS Theory Development: Logics, Models & Theories – Types of Systems – Research Methodologies*. Columbus, Ohio: System-Predictive Technologies.

Tripp, David (1994): "Creating Waves: Towards an Educological Paradigm of Teacher Education." *Australian Journal of Teacher Education* , Vol 19, Issue 2. http://dx.doi.org/10.14221/ajte.1994v19n2.10

Velasquez, Manuel; Andre, Claire; Shanks, S.J., Thomas; Meyer, Michael J. (2014): *Justice and Fairness*. Markkula Center for Applied Ethics, Santa Clara University, California. Originally published in *Ethics*, Vol. 3, No. 2, 1990. Retrieved 15 April 2020. https://www.scu.edu/ethics/ethics-resources/ethical-decision-making/justice-and-fairness/

Vygotsky, Lev S. (Edited by Alex Kozulin) (1934, 1986): *Thought and Language*. Revised Edition. Cambridge, Massachusetts: Massachusetts Institute of Technology.

Walker, Jamie (3 May 2008): "Tribute to Vaccine's Forgotten Man," *The* Australian http://www.theaustralian.com.au/archive/news/tribute-to-vaccines-forgotten-man/news-story/d9a9c9f41d2c3668048cc8e61a57c9b8?sv=d7c627794c783bdd73c496beac0a542c Retrieved 1 Aug 2017.

Weber, B. (26 Dec 2009): "Kim Peek, Inspiration for 'Rain Man,' Dies at 58," *New York Times*, p. A30, http://www.nytimes.com/2009/12/27/us/27peek.html?_r=1 Retrieved 21 Sep 2017.

Wilson, John (1969): *Language and the Pursuit of Truth.* Cambridge: Cambridge University Press.

Wilson, John (1971): *Thinking with Concepts.* Cambridge: Cambridge University Press.

Wortham, Stanton (1995): "An Educology of Classroom Discourse: A Triangular View of Classroom Discourse Which Illustrates How Classroom Relationships and Content Can Transform Each Other," *International Journal of Educology*, Vol. 9, No. 2, pp. 146-179.

Ye Lan (Translated by Li Lijuan) (2020): Life-Practice Educology: A Contemporary Chinese Theory of Education (Brill's Series On Chinese Education; Volume 4).

ABOUT THE AUTHOR

James E. Christensen is known as Jim to his family and friends. He was born in Missouri in 1941. He grew up in the American Midwest, Southwest and West Coast regions. He completed high school in California in 1959, and he earned his BA in history at the University of California, Berkeley, in 1963. He subsequently completed his California Secondary Teaching Credential and taught secondary school in Kenya from 1964 to 1966 as part of the United States Agency for International Development (USAID) Teachers for East Africa (TEA) Project. He returned to the USA and taught at Fountain Valley High School in the Huntington Beach High School District in California from 1966 to 1969. During that time, he also completed his MA in history at California State College (now California State University), Long Beach. In 1972, he completed his PhD in education (what he now calls educology) at the University of California, Los Angeles, and took up his first university teaching appointment as an Assistant Professor at Southern Illinois University, Carbondale, where he taught philosophy of education (philosophical educology) and comparative education (educology of societies and cultures). In 1974, he emigrated from the USA to Australia. From 1974 to 1989, he taught the educology of curriculum, the educology of instructional methods and the educology of assessment & evaluation at Riverina College of Advanced Education (now part of Charles Sturt University) in Wagga Wagga, NSW, in the School of Education. While on study leave from CSU in 1979, he taught at Colgate University, Hamilton, New York (in comparative educology), and in 1991, he taught at Newcastle University, Australia (in the educology of society). In 1987, he founded the *International Journal of Educology*, and from 1987 to 2003, he served as co-editor (with James E. Fisher) of the *IJE*. In 1992, he left university teaching to work in private enterprise. His lifelong research interests have focused on the questions of whether knowledge about education is possible, if so, what kinds of knowledge are possible, how can that knowledge be formed and how can it be organized in ways which are useful and fruitful for those who want to understand education and take constructive action in improving education.

Connect with James E. Christensen online at:

E-mail: educologist@gmail.com
Webpage: http://www.jamesechristensen.com

Other Publications by the Author

Most Recent Publications

***Education, Knowledge and Educology* (2013):** Amazon Kindle Edition.

This book addresses the questions of:

(1) What is education?
(2) What is knowledge about education?
(3) How can knowledge about education be organized in ways so that it can be used fruitfully to take rational action in the educational process to pursue and achieve worthwhile intentions and purposes?

The book is available as a paperback and an e-book at
https://www.amazon.com/gp/product/B0796NRNC5/ref=dbs_a_def_rwt_hsch_vamf_taft_p1_i5

***Education, Curriculum and Educology* (2014):** Amazon Kindle Edition.

This is book addresses the questions of:

(1) What is curriculum?
(2) How does curriculum relate to education?
(3) What are the essential components of a soundly designed curriculum?
(4) What are some established perspectives about what should be included in a curriculum?

The book is available as a paperback and an e-book at
https://www.amazon.com/gp/product/B0797JBMRY/ref=dbs_a_def_rwt_hsch_vapi_taft_p1_i4

***Education, Universities and Educology* (2015):** Amazon Kindle Edition.

This book addresses the questions of:

(1) What is knowledge about education?

(2) Why is it desirable to use the term <*educology*> to denote knowledge about education?
(3) What is the origin of the term <*educology*>?
(4) What kinds of knowledge about education are possible?
(5) What disciplines are required to produce knowledge about education?
(6) What are some different ways of organizing knowledge about education?
(7) How do discipline, study and fund of knowledge differ?
(8) How are the tasks of creating knowledge about education, teaching knowledge about education and using knowledge about education connected with each other and how do they differ?
(9) What constitutes education?
(10) What are the basic components of education?
(11) What are the basic processes of education?
(12) What are derivative features of education?
(13) Where does curriculum fit into education?
(14) How do official and unofficial education resemble and yet differ from each other?
(15) What is the proper domain for educological research?
(16) How are the tasks of creating knowledge about education, teaching knowledge about education and using knowledge about education connected with each other and how do they differ?
(17) What uses can be made of educology in naming of organizations whose purpose it is to conduct research about education, teach about education and disseminate knowledge about education?
(18) What uses can be made of the structure of educology in organizing faculties, curricula and research programs in universities?
The book is available as a paperback and an e-book at https://www.amazon.com/gp/product/B088NW957H/ref=dbs_a_def_rwt_hsch_vapi_tkin_p1_i0

Education, Research and Educology **(2016):** Amazon Kindle Edition. This book addresses the questions of:
(1) What constitutes educological research?
(2) What is the field of phenomena about which educological research inquires?
(3) What kinds of educological research are possible?
(4) What principles of verification are used in educological research?
(5) What techniques can be used in educological research to collect relevant, necessary and sufficient evidence?
(6) What procedures can be used in educological research to analyze evidence?
(7) What are the products of successful educological research?

(8) What intellectual perspectives can be used in the conduct of educological research?
(9) How can educological research be used to produce educological theory?
(10) How can educological theory be used to guide educological research?
(11) How can educological research be used to test educological theory?
(12) What uses can be made of the products of educological research?

The book is available as a paperback and an e-book at https://www.amazon.com/gp/product/B0798C78ZF/ref=dbs_a_def_rwt_hsch_vapi_taft_p1_i3

***Education, Mindfulness and Educology* (2017):** Amazon Kindle Edition. This book addresses the questions of:

(1) What constitutes education?
(2) What constitutes mindfulness?
(3) What relationships are there between education and mindfulness?

The book is available as a paperback and an e-book at https://www.amazon.com/gp/product/B07968L4ZP/ref=dbs_a_def_rwt_hsch_vamf_taft_p1_i6

***Education, Educology and Meta-Educology: A Conversation* (2018):** Amazon Kindle Edition. This is book addresses the questions of:

(1) What levels of language can be distinguished in discourse about education?
(2) How does discourse about education differ from participation in education?
(3) What needs to be done to make discourse about education clear and unambiguous?
(4) What rules of sentence formation, transformation and verification need to be used to convert discourse about education in knowledge about education?
(5) How does knowledge about education differ from knowing about education?
(6) How are descriptive, explanatory and normative theory devised and used to organize and extend knowledge about education?

The book is available as a paperback and an e-book at https://authorcentral.amazon.com/gp/books/book-detail-page?ie=UTF8&bookASIN=B07MB5GRFR&index=default&parentASIN=1792983670&tabName=

Perspectives on Education as Educology (1981, 2018): Amazon Kindle Edition. This book was first published in 1981 and republished as an Amazon Kindle Edition in 2018. Perspectives provides a discussion, from many points of view, of the justification for the use of the term *<educology>* to name knowledge about education and of the

distinguishing characteristics, applications and utility of educology. Questions addressed include
(1) What is education?
(2) What is knowledge about education:
(3) What is an appropriate name for knowledge about education?
(4) What kinds of knowledge about education can be distinguished?
(5) How is knowledge about education produced?
(6) What uses can be made of knowledge about education?
(7) How can knowledge about education be used to extend professional and vocational education?
(8) How can knowledge about education be used to extend liberal education?
The book is available as a paperback and an e-book at https://www.amazon.com/gp/product/B07DGYFX1S/ref=dbs_a_def_rwt_bibl_vppi_i3

***Educology of Teaching* (2020):** Amazon Kindle Edition. This is book addresses the questions of:
(1) What is teaching?
(2) What do teachers do?
(3) What is effective teaching?
(4) What is good teaching?
The book is available as a paperback and an e-book at https://www.amazon.com/gp/product/B088DQ7RG2/ref=dbs_a_def_rwt_hsch_vapi_tkin_p1_i1

Other Books

Christensen, James E. (1981): *Curriculum, Education, and Educology.* Sydney: Educology Research Associates. ISBN 094978401X

Christensen, James E. (1981): *Education and Human Development: A Study in Educology.* Sydney: Educology Research Associates. ISBN 0949784001

Christensen, James E. (Ed.) (1981, 2018): *Perspectives on Education as Educology.* Washington, D.C.: University Press of America. ISBN 0819113934. Now available as an Amazon Kindle Edition at https://www.amazon.com/gp/product/B07DGYFX1S/ref=dbs_a_def_rwt_hsch_vamf_taft_p1_i0

Christensen, James E. (Ed.) (1986): *Educology 86: Proceedings of a Conference on Educational Research, Inquiry and Development with an Educological Perspective, Canberra, July 10-12, 1986.* Sydney: Educology Research Associates. ISBN 0949784052

Christensen, James E. and Fisher, James E. (1979): *Analytic Philosophy of Education as a Sub-Discipline of Educology: An Introduction to its Techniques and Application.* Washington, D.C.: University Press of America. ISBN

0819108022

Christensen, James E. and Fisher, James E (1983): *Organization and Colleges of Education: An Educological Perspective.* Sydney: Educology Research Associates. ISBN 0949784028

Lane, David and Christensen, James E. (1985): *The School Librarian's Guide to Curriculum Development.* Sydney: Educology Research Associates. ISBN 0949784036

Articles

Christensen, James E. (1975): "Educational Research as Educology," *Australian Educational Researcher* (Australian Association for Research in Education), Vol. 2, No. 4, pp. 18-20. ISSN 03116999

Christensen, James E. (1977): "A Conversation about Education as Educology, Guest Editorial," *Educational Studies: A Journal of the American Educational Studies Association.* Vol. 8, No. 1, pp. v-xii. ISSN 0031946

Christensen, James E. (1981): "Chapter 6: Educology and Some Related Concepts," in J.E. Christensen (Ed.), *Perspectives on Education as Educology*, pp. 121-158. Washington, D.C.: University Press of America. ISBN 0819113934

Christensen, James E. (March, 1982): "The Educology of Curriculum". *Collected Original Resources in Education* (Taylor and Francis Group). ISSN 03086909

Christensen, James E. (23-27 November, 1983): "Cognition, Knowing, and Understanding: Levels, Forms, and Range." *Proceedings of the National Conference of the Australian Association for Research in Education.* Canberra, ACT: AARE.

Christensen, James E. (June, 1986): "Comparative Educology: A Bridging Concept for Comparative Educational Inquiry," A paper presented to the Fifth World Congress of Comparative Education, Paris, 2-6 Jul, 1984, *Resources in Education* (ERIC: Education Resources Information Center): Accession Numbers ED 266542, EA 018220

Christensen, James E. (March, 1986): "Educational Research with an Educological Perspective," A paper presented to the Annual Conference of the American Educational Research Association, Chicago, 31 Mar-4 Apr, 1985," *Resources in Education* (ERIC: Education Resources Information Center): Accession Numbers ED 263197, TM 850688

Christensen, James E. (1987): "Education, Educology and Educological Discourse: Theory and Structure for Education and Constructive Action in Education," *International Journal of Educology*, Vol. 1, No. 1, pp. 1-32, Sydney: Educology Research Associates. ISSN 08180563

Christensen, James E. (1992): "Education for Freedom: A Philosophical

Educology," *International Journal of Educology*, Vol. 6, No. 2, pp. 97-131. Sydney: Educology Research Associates. ISSN 08180563

Christensen, James E. and Fisher, James E (1978): "An Organizational Theory for Schools of Teacher Education and Faculties of Education," *Australian Journal of Education*, Vol. 22, No. 1, pp. 52-71, Australian Council for Educational Research. ISSN 00049441

Christensen, James E. and Fisher, James E (1981): "Chapter 12: Educology as an Organizational Concept for Schools of Teacher Education, College of Education, and Faculties of Education," in J.E. Christensen (Ed.), *Perspectives on Education as Educology*, pp. 263-300. Washington, DC: University Press of America. ISBN 0819113934

Christensen, James E. and Fisher, James E. (1988): "The Need for Educological Research in the Areas of Secondary School Retention Rates, Educational Pathways and Recurrent Education," *International Journal of Educology*, Vol. 2, No. 2, pp. ix-xii. Sydney: Educology Research Associates. ISSN 0818 0563

Christensen, James E. and Fisher, James E. (1989): "Educology and the Educological Perspective," *International Journal of Educology*, Vol. 3, No. 1, pp. ix-xv. Sydney: Educology Research Associates. ISSN 0818 0563

Christensen, James E. and Fisher, James E. (1990): "Three Critical Distinctions for Advancing Educology," *International Journal of Educology*, Vol. 4, No. 1, pp. vi-viii. Sydney: Educology Research Associates. ISSN 0818 0563

Christensen, James E. and Fisher, James E. (1990): "Educology for Initial Teacher Education and for Professional Development of Practising Teachers – Changing Needs, Changing Demands," *International Journal of Educology*, Vol. 4, No. 2, pp. vi-xvii. Sydney: Educology Research Associates. ISSN 0818 0563

Christensen, James E. and Fisher, James E. (1991): "A Challenge for Educologists of Curriculum," *International Journal of Educology*, Vol. 5, No. 1, pp. vi-ix. Sydney: Educology Research Associates. ISSN 0818 0563

Christensen, James E. and Fisher, James E. (1991): "An Educology of Values, Goals and Action Plans," *International Journal of Educology*, Vol. 5, No. 2, pp. vi-ix. Sydney: Educology Research Associates. ISSN 0818 0563

Christensen, James E. and Fisher, James E. (1992): "The Educology of the Work Place," *International Journal of Educology*, Vol. 6, No. 1, pp. vi-xi. Sydney: Educology Research Associates. ISSN 0818 0563

END

Printed in Great Britain
by Amazon

25045857R00205